Debates on the German Revolution of 1918–19

Manchester University Press

ISSUES IN HISTORIOGRAPHY

General editor
R. C. RICHARDSON
University of Winchester

Already published

The Debate on the Norman Conquest   Marjorie Chibnall
The Debate on the French Revolution   Peter Davies
Debates on Stalinism   Mark Edele
Debates on the Holocaust   Tom Lawson
The Debate on the American Revolution   Gwenda Morgan
The Debate on the English Reformation: New edition   Rosemary O'Day
The Debate on the Decline of Spain   Helen Rawlings
The Debate on the English Revolution, 3rd edn   R. C. Richardson
The Debate on the American Civil War Era   H. A. Tulloch
The Debate on the Crusades   Christopher Tyerman
The Debate on Black Civil Rights in America   Kevern Verney
The Debate on the Rise of the British Empire   Anthony Webster

Debates on the German Revolution of 1918–19

Matthew Stibbe

MANCHESTER UNIVERSITY PRESS

Copyright © Matthew Stibbe 2023

The right of Matthew Stibbe to be identified as the author of this work has been asserted by him in accordance with the Copyright, Designs and Patents Act 1988.

Published by Manchester University Press
Oxford Road, Manchester M13 9PL

www.manchesteruniversitypress.co.uk

British Library Cataloguing-in-Publication Data
A catalogue record for this book is available from the British Library

ISBN 978 1 5261 5748 5 hardback
ISBN 978 1 5261 5749 2 paperback

First published 2023

The publisher has no responsibility for the persistence or accuracy of URLs for any external or third-party internet websites referred to in this book, and does not guarantee that any content on such websites is, or will remain, accurate or appropriate.

Typeset by Newgen Publishing UK

Contents

List of figures	*page* vii
General editor's foreword	viii
Acknowledgements	xi
Timeline	xii
Glossary	xvii
List of abbreviations	xix
Introduction	1

Part I: The thirty years war: The Revolution as contemporary history, 1919–48

1 The German Revolution in the Weimar Republic	23
2 Alternatives to fascism: The 1918–19 Revolution and efforts to construct a unified left, 1933–48	52

Part II: Divided Europe and the politics of history: '1918' in the two Germanys

3 Revolution betrayed or democracy saved? West German debates, 1949–79	81
4 Who were the Spartacists? East Germany's '1918'	109
5 1989 and all that: The German Revolution of 1918–19 and the passing of the GDR	134

Part III: Forgotten or rediscovered? Debates on the German Revolution since the 1990s

6 The experience of revolution: Soldiers, sailors, civilians, young people	163

7 Urban space and the political imaginary of the Revolution 193
8 The German Revolution in European and global
   context: International and transnational perspectives   223

Conclusion   255

Further reading   269
Index   275

Figures

0.1 'Ebert and Noske in der Sommerfrische', front cover of the *Berliner Illustrirte Zeitung*, 24 August 1919. Getty Images. *page* 12
6.1 'So wird gewählt', front page of *Das Illustrierte Blatt*, 14 January 1919. Wikimedia Commons. 166
7.1 Recruitment poster for the pro-Government security force, Bremen, February 1919. Wikimedia Commons. 201
7.2 Recruitment poster for the Anti-Bolshevik League, Berlin, early 1919. Alamy. 202
7.3 Recruitment poster for the KPD, Berlin, early 1919. Alamy. 203
7.4 Architect Ludwig Mies van der Rohe's *Monument to the Revolution*, 1926. Wikimedia Commons. 217
7.5 Ceremony at the Memorial of Socialists, Berlin-Friedrichsfelde, to mark the centenary of the murders of Karl Liebknecht and Rosa Luxemburg. Getty Images. 217
8.1 Commemorative plaque on the house at Kuglerstraße 44, Berlin-Prenzlauer Berg, where Cameroon-born Martin Dibobe lived in 1918. Wikimedia Commons. 230
8.2 Front page of the second extra edition of *Vorwärts*, 9 November 1918. Archiv der sozialen Demokratie der Friedrich-Ebert-Stiftung, Bonn 238
8.3 Poster for the film *Different from the Rest*, Berlin, May 1919. Alamy. 248
9.1 Soldiers join striking workers on Unter den Linden, Berlin, 9 November 1918. Alamy. 263

General editor's foreword

History without historiography is not only oversimplified and impoverished but is a contradiction in terms. The study of the past cannot be divorced from a linked awareness and investigation of its practitioners and intermediaries. No historian writes in isolation from the work of his or her predecessors, nor can the commentator – however clinically objective or professional – stand aloof from the insistent pressures, priorities and demands of the ever-changing present, and they are sometimes deliberately prevented from doing so. In truth, there are no self-contained, impregnable 'academic towers'. Historians are responsive, porous beings. Their writings are an extension of who they are, where they are placed, and whom they speak for. Though historians address the past as their subject, they always do so in ways that are shaped – consciously or unconsciously as the case may be – by the society, politics and systems, cultural ethos, and pressing needs of their own day, and they communicate their findings in ways that are specifically intelligible and relevant to a present-minded reading public consisting initially of their own contemporaries. For these reasons the study of history is concerned most fundamentally not with dead facts and sterile, permanent verdicts, but with highly charged dialogues, disagreements, controversies and shifting centres of interest among its presenters, with the changing methodologies and discourse of the subject over time, and with audience reception. Issues in Historiography is a well-established, well-stocked series designed to explore such subject matter by means of case studies of key moments in world history and the interpretations, reinterpretations, challenges, debates and contests they have engendered.

General editor's foreword

The Revolution of 1918–19 stands out as one of the most controversial episodes in German history and, in the words of one commentator (Martin Sabrow), has been variously 'hated, honoured and forgotten'. Leading scholar Matthew Stibbe, in this well-structured, accessibly written book, presents an irresistible case for taking the Revolution seriously and according it a landmark status. With chapters arranged in three main chronological sections, it brings out very clearly the different ways over time that the Revolution has been defined, depicted, and 'owned' and 'disowned' in successive phases of German history – Weimar, Nazi, postwar divided Germany and Cold War, and then reunified Germany. It also examines how at times the 1918–19 Revolution has been crowded out of the national picture or rendered less clear by alternative and more insistent historical preoccupations with the First World War and with the Holocaust, and by changing historical emphases associated, for example, with the new cultural history. There is a helpful discussion in these pages of the gendering of the historiography of the Revolution and of its spatial turn. The transnational dimensions of the subject are never lost sight of, and useful bridges are constructed between the historiography of this revolution and those of other revolutions – English, French, German (1848) and Russian. Indeed, in one case at least, there is overlap between the actual cast list of Stibbe's German study and that of the mid-seventeenth-century English Revolution in the person of Eduard Bernstein, a participant in the German Revolution and also a commentator on Oliver Cromwell and the proto-Communists of the earlier period. Detailed, perceptive appraisals are offered of the contributions of differently positioned individual historians to the fraught historiography of this subject. The book ends with some thoughtful reflections on possible future trajectories of research: an understandable wariness of cultural determinism and its effects, a greater emphasis on the construction of revolutionary subjectivities, and a return to questions relating to sovereignty and the political history of the Revolution.

In these respects, as in others, Stibbe's volume will do much to guide student readers through an abundant and contentious literature, enabling them to make sense of the various items listed in its dense bibliography and the relationships among them.

The inclusion of graphic contemporary images provides another helpful dimension taking us beyond the written text itself. As such, *Debates on the German Revolution of 1918–19* makes a very welcome and provocative addition to the Issues in Historiography series. And to include reference to today's ongoing Russo-Ukrainian struggles certainly proclaims a self-conscious anchoring in the 'now' as well as the 'then' – the quintessence of historiography.

R. C. Richardson

Acknowledgements

Several friends and scholars read early drafts of all or parts of this book, allowed me to read their own work in progress, or gave expert advice on various aspects of the history and historiography of the German Revolution. In particular I would like to thank Robbie Aitken, Chris Dillon, Andy Donson, Martin H. Geyer, Veronika Helfert, André Keil, Corinne Painter, Nadine Rossol, Ingrid Sharp, Daniel Siemens, Kim Wünschmann and Benjamin Ziemann. Roger Richardson, the series editor, and Emma Brennan, editorial director at Manchester University Press, have been wonderfully supportive of and enthusiastic for the project, and I am greatly indebted to both. All errors are of course mine and mine alone.

Much love to Sam, Nick, Hannah, Mollie, Charlie, Harry and Bella, who encouraged me and distracted me during the COVID-19 lockdown, and without whom this book would not have been possible.

I dedicate this book to the late Hazel Mary Stibbe, née Rawlinson (1934–2022), with enormous thanks and huge respect for a life lived well and in service to others.

Timeline

Events before the Revolution

31 July 1914	State of siege declared; Germany enters First World War on following day.
2 December 1914	Karl Liebknecht becomes first Reichstag deputy to vote against extension of war credits.
1 May 1916	Liebknecht arrested at May Day demonstration on Potsdamer Platz, Berlin; Rosa Luxemburg and other leftists already in military detention.
March 1917	First Russian Revolution: provisional Government formed in Petrograd.
April 1917	First mass wartime strike wave in Germany; formation of anti-war USPD as breakaway from main Social Democratic Party (SPD).
19 July 1917	Reichstag passes non-binding Peace Resolution by 212 to 126 votes calling on Imperial Government to negotiate end to war.
November 1917	Second revolution in Russia: Bolsheviks come to power.
January–February 1918	Second mass strike wave in Germany.
October 1918	Attempt to transform Germany into parliamentary monarchy ahead of armistice negotiations with Allies.

Events during the Revolution

3–4 November 1918	Large-scale naval mutinies in Kiel and Wilhelmshaven.
4–7 November 1918	Revolution spreads across Germany.
8 November 1918	Revolution in Bavaria; USPD leader Kurt Eisner becomes Minister-President.
9 November 1918	Revolution in Berlin; abdication of Kaiser.
11 November 1918	Armistice on western front ends First World War.
12 November 1918	Council of People's Deputies lifts wartime state of siege, removes restrictions on freedom of speech and assembly, and grants female suffrage, among other executive measures.
15 November 1918	Stinnes–Legien Agreement between employers and trade unions, with former conceding eight-hour day and other workers' rights in exchange for *de facto* recognition of private ownership of industry.
20 November 1918	Rally at Tempelhofer Feld in Berlin and procession to Friedrichshain cemetery in honour of revolutionaries killed on 9 November.
16–20 December 1918	First Reich Congress of Soldiers' and Workers' Councils approves staging of parliamentary elections, but also calls for lifting of Stinnes–Legien Agreement and immediate nationalisation measures.
24–25 December 1918	Skirmishes around city palace in Berlin between armed left-wing units, including members of the People's Naval Division, and Government troops.
29 December 1918	USPD leaders Haase, Barth and Dittmann resign from Council of People's Deputies. SPD nominees Gustav Noske and Rudolf Wissell replace them.

30 December 1918–1 January 1919	Founding congress of the Communist Party of Germany (KPD) in Berlin.
5–12 January 1919	Spartacist Uprising in Berlin.
9 January 1919	Essen workers' and soldiers' council proclaims, but fails to secure, nationalisation of Ruhr mining industry.
10 January 1919	Councils Republic declared in Bremen.
15 January 1919	Arrest and murder of KPD leaders Liebknecht and Luxemburg by members of the Rifle Division of the Cavalry Guards of the Freikorps (Garde-Kavallerie-Schützendivision), commanded by Captain Waldemar Pabst. The latter had lines of contact with Reichswehr Minister Noske.
19 January 1919	Elections take place to Constituent National Assembly.
25 January 1919	Burial at Friedrichsfelde cemetery in Berlin of thirty-two revolutionaries killed during Spartacist Uprising, including Liebknecht and Luxemburg (the latter represented by an empty coffin as her body was not found until 31 May 1919).
4 February 1919	Government troops enter Bremen to overthrow Councils Republic.
6 February 1919	Constituent National Assembly meets for first time in Weimar.
10 February 1919	Law on the Provisional Authority of the Reich ends exclusive executive and law-making functions wielded since 9 November by Council of People's Deputies and establishes a legally sanctioned separation of governmental powers among a Reich President, a Reich Cabinet and individual German states.
11 February 1919	Ebert elected by Constituent National Assembly as provisional Reich President.

Timeline

13 February 1919	Ebert appoints Philipp Scheidemann as Reich Chancellor. Latter forms cabinet made up of members of the SPD, the Catholic Centre Party and the liberal German Democratic Party (DDP).
21 February 1919	Assassination of Bavarian Minister-President Eisner in Munich.
3–13 March 1919	'March Battles' between leftists and Government troops in Berlin.
6 April 1919	Declaration of Councils Republic in Munich.
7–14 April 1919	Second Reich Congress of Soldiers' and Workers' Councils meets in Berlin.
13–15 April 1919	Government troops and Freikorps units, acting for Noske and the Reich Government, enter State of Braunschweig to end general strike there.
23 April 1919	States of siege declared in Saxony and Bremen, followed by Hamburg, Altona and Wandsbek (30 June).
1–3 May 1919	Government troops, supported by Freikorps units, enter Munich to crush councils regime there – again on the instructions of Ebert and Noske.
11 May 1919	Short-lived military occupation of Leipzig allows Reich ministers to forestall general strike there, at request of Saxon Government in Dresden.
28 May 1919	World's first openly gay film, *Different from the Rest*, premiers in Berlin.
20 June 1919	Scheidemann Government resigns rather than sign Treaty of Versailles.
27 June 1919	Eighteen Africans living in Germany sign petition demanding equal rights for colonial subjects in wake of revolution.
28 June 1919	New SPD-led coalition Government headed by Gustav Bauer signs Treaty of Versailles.

6 July 1919	Institute for Sexual Research, run by gay rights activist Magnus Hirschfeld, opens in Berlin.
12 July 1919	Western Allies formally lift wartime economic blockade of Germany.
11 August 1919	Weimar Constitution comes into force.
21 August 1919	Ebert sworn in as first President of Weimar Republic.

Events after the Revolution

13–18 March 1920	Kapp–Lüttwitz Putsch, failed monarchist coup in Berlin.
13 March–April 1920	Ruhr Uprising, leading to large-scale Reichswehr intervention and military state of emergency in that part of Germany lasting until June.
4 October 1920	Gay rights activist Hirschfeld beaten almost to death by right-wing extremists in Munich.
12–17 October 1920	USPD delegates vote by two-thirds majority at Halle party convention to merge with KPD.
1920–21	National and international 'Black Shame' protests over use of French colonial troops in Allied occupation army in Rhineland; hostility also directed towards Germany's own small Black community.
17–29 March 1921	Communist uprising in central Germany crushed by armed detachments of the Prussian police, backed by small number of Reichswehr units.

Glossary

Bundestag	(West) German Parliament, founded Bonn, 1949, moved to Berlin, 2000.
Comintern	Communist International, founded Moscow, March 1919.
Constituent National Assembly	German Parliament elected on 19 January 1919 and charged with development of new constitution; between February and August 1919 it met in Weimar, and thereafter in the Reichstag in Berlin.
Council of People's Deputies	Transitional body that governed Germany from November 1918 to February 1919.
Freikorps	Irregular right-wing military units active in Germany in 1919.
Kaiserreich	The German empire, 1871–1918.
Kapp–Lüttwitz Putsch	Attempted monarchist coup against Weimar Republic, March 1920.
March Battles (*Märzkämpfe*)	Period of violent street battles between Government troops and leftists in working-class districts of Berlin, 3–13 March 1919.
Marinearchiv	Naval archive, founded 1921 to hold records of former Reich Naval Office and its War History department.
Munich Councils Republic	Short-lived anarchist and pro-Bolshevik republic in Munich, April–May 1919.
Neues Deutschland	SED daily newspaper, founded April 1946.

Reichsarchiv	Central archive for all records relating to the Reich, including records of Prussian army and its War History department, founded Potsdam, September 1919.
Reichsmarine	Imperial German navy.
Reichstag	German Parliament.
Reichswehr	New name for German armed forces from January 1919.
Revolutions of 1848	Series of popular uprisings across continental Europe, beginning in Paris in February and spreading to German states by March; revolutionary national and democratic forces were already in retreat in summer 1848 and were completely crushed by 1849.
Rote Fahne, Die	KPD daily newspaper, founded November 1918.
Ruhr Uprising	Workers' uprising against Kapp–Lüttwitz Putsch, leading to violent clashes between the 'Red Army of the Ruhr' and Government troops, March–April 1920.
Vierteljahrshefte für Zeitgeschichte	House journal of Institute for Contemporary History, founded Munich, 1953.
Volksmarine-division	People's Naval Division. Sailors' organisation, founded November 1918 to promote aims of revolution and combat counterrevolution. Sided with left-wing forces in Berlin from December 1918, dissolved March 1919.
Vorwärts	SPD daily newspaper, founded 1876.
Zeitschrift für Geschichtswis-senschaft	East Germany's leading academic journal for history, founded Berlin, 1953.

Abbreviations

APO	Extra-Parliamentary Opposition (West Germany, 1966–68)
CPGB	Communist Party of Great Britain, founded 1920
CPSU	Communist Party of the Soviet Union, founded 1918
DDP	German Democratic Party, founded December 1918
DHG	(East) German Historians' Society, founded March 1958
DKP	German Communist Party, founded West Germany, 1968
DNVP	German National People's Party, founded December 1918
FDP	Free Democratic Party, founded December 1948
FES	Friedrich-Ebert-Stiftung, SPD research foundation, established 1925, refounded Bonn, 1954
FRG	Federal Republic of Germany, founded May 1949
FSJ	Free Socialist Youth, founded October 1918
GDR	German Democratic Republic, founded October 1949
IfZ	Institute for Contemporary History, founded Munich, May 1949
IKD	International Communists of Germany, founded November 1918
IML	Institute for Marxism-Leninism, East German body responsible for preserving party archives of the KPD and SED, founded Berlin, 1949
KPD	German Communist Party, founded December 1918
KPD-O	Communist Party-Opposition, founded October 1928
LAI	League against Imperialism, founded February 1927

NATO	North Atlantic Treaty Organization
PDS	Party of Democratic Socialism, founded December 1989 as successor to SED
RFB	Red Front Fighters' League, founded July 1924.
SAPD	Socialist Workers Party of Germany, founded October 1931
SAPMO-BArch	Foundation for the Archive of the Parties and Mass Organisation of the Former GDR, housed in German federal archives, Berlin-Lichterfelde
SED	Socialist Unity Party of Germany, founded April 1946
SPD	Majority Social Democratic Party of Germany, founded 1875
TNA	The National Archives, Kew, London
USPD	Independent German Social Democratic Party, founded April 1917, merged with KPD October–December 1920
VHD	German Historians' Association, founded 1895, refounded 1948

Introduction

In a pamphlet published in 1979, the West German historian Heinrich August Winkler argued that 'to this very day, few events in recent German history have remained as controversial as the 1918–19 Revolution'.[1] Six decades after the overthrow of the German empire and the declaration of a German republic, opinions appeared to be as divided as ever. True, from 1919 onwards, the German left was united in opposing the anti-republican myth that the Revolution had been a 'stab-in-the-back' against the German army still fighting in the field, but it was otherwise completely split over who or what had caused the Revolution, and why it ended as it did – with a parliamentary democracy and not a socialist republic. Conservative opponents of both left- and right-wing extremism in the interwar years had seen it as one of many examples of the demagogic manipulation of the masses by unscrupulous agitators in Europe's new age of unrestrained democracy, and compared it with the Bolshevik Revolution in Russia in 1917, Benito Mussolini's Fascist takeover in Italy in 1922, and the Nazi seizure of power in Berlin in 1933. With the fall of the Prussian Hohenzollern monarchy in 1918, wrote the military historian Gerhard Ritter, 'a new era began, in which the relationship between army and state, and between statecraft and military calling, was fundamentally transformed'.[2] Meanwhile, since 1949, rival interpretations of the Revolution had helped to legitimise the respective ideological positions taken in the Cold War by the pro-western German Federal Republic (FRG) and its Communist rival in the East, the German Democratic Republic (GDR). Winkler himself pulled no punches in these Cold War era debates, describing the work of Marxist East German historians on the Revolution, and of non-academic leftist writers in West Germany such as the journalist

Sebastian Haffner, as 'polemical literature' that was 'not worthy of [serious] academic discussion'.³

Yet after the late 1970s, something changed. The 1918–19 Revolution was gradually marginalised from discussions of the recent German past, and instead of its meaning being fought over as part of the historical profession's intellectual contribution to the Cold War, it became the 'forgotten revolution'.⁴ Worse still, it was lambasted as a 'beginning that was [also] an end', a particularly damning verdict because of the utter sense of 'nowhere else to go' that this designation communicated.⁵ In other words, the Revolution was recast as a short interlude on the nation's path to Weimar and the Third Reich without much to offer in didactic or story-telling terms. Historians were now drawn to alternative explanatory models that sidestepped the Revolution, and sometimes ignored it altogether. In particular they took to exploring and deconstructing what West German scholar Detlev J. K. Peukert referred to in 1987 as the burgeoning 'crisis of classical modernity' in the years 1890–1930.⁶ For if the November revolutionaries had failed to sweep away the entirety of the old imperial order and its outmoded structures in 1918–19 – a criticism often laid against them in studies before the 1980s – they now faced the new and somewhat different charge of not being able to keep pace politically with the unprecedented rate of technological, demographic and intellectual change that Germany encountered as it entered the age of late industrial and commercial capitalism in the last decade of the nineteenth century and first three decades of the twentieth.⁷

Definitions 1   The new cultural history

There were a number of specific reasons for this abrupt shift in attitudes towards the German Revolution of 1918–19 after 1978–79, some of which will be discussed in more detail in Chapter 5 of this book. Yet there is also a more general cause: the emergence in the 1980s and beyond of the new cultural history, which impacted on the writing of other revolutions too, including the English Revolution of 1640, the French Revolution of 1789, and the Russian Revolutions of 1905 and 1917.⁸ As Ronald Hutton, one of the world's foremost experts on the English Civil War of

1641–49, has noted, the key scholarly development at the end of the twentieth century and the beginning of the twenty-first 'was a recognition that ideas have an independent life of their own, and that human beliefs, decisions and reactions are often, in objective terms, irrational'. In particular, the apparent death of Marxism-Leninism – 'an ideology which seemed to be expanding all over the world in the middle of the century' but which largely failed to recover from the collapse of the Soviet bloc in 1989–91 – and the simultaneous rise of Islamist extremism, beginning with the Iranian Revolution of 1979 and reaching its apex with the 9/11 attacks in Manhattan in 2001, also ended previous certainties among liberal and leftist historians about the 'primacy of economic forces' in shaping political events and, more generally, about the possibility of clearly separating 'true' explanations and timeframes for historical developments from 'untrue' ones.[9]

The Swiss historian Philipp Sarasin has labelled 1977 as the turning point when, in the West, mid-century concerns with collective 'modernist' projects for the liberation of all of humankind gave way to an interest in cultural diversity, esoteric narratives and niche lifestyles.[10] German scholar Frank Bösch, taking a less western-centred approach, prefers 1979 as the moment 'when the world of today began',[11] whereas the Yale professor of jurisprudence Samuel Moyn identifies the 1970s as a whole as a time when the world briefly turned to what was to be its 'last utopia', human rights.[12] This was before the arrival of a new moral and philosophical relativism in the early 1980s and beyond, during which deference to '"high" Westernized culture' as the epitome of universal human achievement gave way to what Sir Ian Kershaw describes as a 'pervasive sense of scepticism ... uncertainty and fragmentation'.[13] Certainly, by the time that the conservative American political scientist Samuel P. Huntington published his controversial book *The Clash of Civilizations and the Remaking of World Order* in 1996, his notion that 'people use politics not just to advance their interests but also to define their identity' had already entered mainstream academic conversation in the western world.[14] On the post-Communist left, too, history was increasingly seen through the lens of cultural theory and in particular through the critical re-evaluation of categories of knowledge, power, surveillance and resistance offered in the works of French philosopher Michel Foucault.[15]

The outcome was a switch from 'objective' questions about structural causes and consequences of revolutions to the subjective realms of discourse, memory, cultural belief and (hidden or unhidden) desires. The notion of a 'grand historical design' or of epic battles fought amidst the shifting sands of class relations and technological inventions was no longer central; instead greater emphasis was placed on the language and scripts of revolutionary movements; on the role of 'contingencies' and 'unforeseen consequences', on emotions, sensibilities and intimate spaces rather than formal institutions and material 'interests'; and above all on chronicling the use of rhetorical and actual acts of violence as (non-rational) ends in themselves, not just as 'an unfortunate by-product of [rational revolutionary] politics'.[16] When writing his major work on the French Revolution in the late 1980s, British historian Simon Schama identified himself as a passionate advocate of the 'cultural turn', celebrating the return of a close reading of texts, pictures and individual biography to the practice of history. Since the late nineteenth century, he argued, and not least during the Cold War, scholars had 'been overconfident about the wisdom to be gained by distance, believing it somehow confers objectivity, one of those unattainable values in which they have placed so much faith. Perhaps there is something to be said for proximity.' Now was the time for a change, he suggested, for a focus on the 'poetic' rather than the 'scientific', the 'impassioned' rather than the 'impersonal'.[17]

Just over a quarter of a century after Schama wrote these words, Keith Michael Baker and Dan Edelstein published an influential essay collection – based on a 2011 conference held at Stanford University, California – arguing that the way to identify the historically distinct character of any given revolution was to establish the scripts that had guided it and the scripts that it in turn created. All revolutions are culturally unique, they contended, taking place in contexts determined by the historical specificities of time and place and giving rise to their own received traditions and historiographies. However, all have one influential aspect in common, namely the 'self-conscious awareness with which revolutionaries model their actions on those of revolutions past'.[18]

> Revolutions do not occur ex nihilo. Revolutionaries are ... often highly knowledgeable about ... how previous revolutions unfolded. These revolutionary scripts offer frameworks for political action.

Whether they serve as models or counterexamples, they provide the outlines on which revolutionary actors can improvise. And revolutionaries, in turn, can transform the scripts they inherit.[19]

The point, they continued, was not to 'deploy the concept of a revolutionary script in exactly the same fashion' in every case, but rather to use it as a 'historically grounded method for the comparative study of revolutions'.[20] Among other things, this was a critique of Karl Marx's notion, in his essay 'The Eighteenth Brumaire of Louis Bonaparte' (1852), that major political events in the modern world took on one of two forms: those able to transcend the weight 'of dead generations' to achieve universal, if tragic, historical significance, and those farcical episodes such as the Second French Republic from 1848 to 1852, which 'knew no better than to parody' the resurrected happenings of 1789, 1793–95 or 1799.[21] Marx, they argued, had overlooked the ability of scripts to shape culturally distinct and context-specific revolutionary subjectivities beyond the aloof categories of 'tragedy', 'comedy' or 'farce'. His mocking portrayal of the Second Republic in 'The Eighteenth Brumaire' may have been an appropriate response to Louis Napoleon's *coup d'état* on 2 December 1851, but in its detached haughtiness it failed to capture the basic point that *all* revolutions are scripted. The social and political sciences, in other words – and here Baker and Edelstein agreed with Schama – had run out of road, and cultural history methodologies were the future.[22]

Overview and key arguments

Whatever the benefits of the 'cultural turn' might have been for our understanding of the English, French, Russian, Chinese or Iranian Revolutions, a key argument of this book is that the German Revolution of 1918–19 was initially a major loser in this paradigm shift, and remained so, at least until the 2010s. Indeed, when it came to writing histories of emotions and experience in particular, the First World War, and the Weimar Republic from August 1919 onwards, proved to be far more attractive areas for research. Here were rediscovered subjectivities to interpret, performances to unravel and symbols to decode – particularly in the spheres of gender, sexuality, family, reproduction and bio-politics, and in real and imagined sites of mourning, memory and cultural de- or remobilisation.[23] Even when it came to new investigations of the 'problem of revolution in Germany', it seemed, the study of 'the ideas of 1914' and of popular mobilisation for war had more to offer than 'the ideas of 1918/19'.[24] For much of the 1990s and 2000s, the fluid events of November 1918 and the months that followed somehow managed to fall between the two increasingly solid – and ever more frequently studied – socio-cultural stools of 1914–18 and 1919–33. The Revolution itself was demoted to a non-story, or worse still, reduced to a 'terrifying landscape of violence' that somehow foreshadowed the rise of fascism.[25] Many scholars were indeed still taken with sociologist Klaus Theweleit's two-volume study of the *Freikorps*, published in German as *Männerphantasien* in 1977–78 and in English as *Male Fantasies* in 1987–89, which for a while completely stole the show as far as writing on paramilitary cultures in the early Weimar period was concerned.[26]

A further contention of this book will be that the 'cultural turn' also initially failed to benefit scholarship on the German Revolution of 1918–19 because before the 1980s the leading protagonists in debates about that Revolution, for all their talk of economic interests, social structures and 'objective' causes, were themselves suffering from a seemingly unbreakable *Distanzverlust*, or inability to distance themselves, both from the period they were writing about and from the hard-won subjective positions established by their forebears. According to the Israeli historian and public intellectual Yuval Noah Harari, 'Nations are ultimately built on stories'.[27] This was certainly the case for German scholars who wrote about the revolution in the years 1945–2009, many of whom had witnessed or even taken part in the events of November 1918–August 1919, or knew people who had, whether as supporters or ardent opponents of the radical left. They had a passionate story they wanted to tell, and although it was still largely imagined as a national story, it was nonetheless an intensely political one, with implications for understandings of Europe and the world as a whole before, during and after the Cold War.

That said, a third major contention of this book is that, in a belated manner, beginning from around 2010, academic understanding of the German Revolution has begun to benefit in substantial ways from approaches drawn from the new cultural history. The starting point here was the publication of a collection of essays on the ninetieth anniversary of the Revolution, edited by Alexander Gallus, which charted new territory by focusing on hitherto almost entirely neglected areas, such as notions of 'democracy' in debates in the Constituent National Assembly in 1919; the intersections between the granting of female suffrage and new ideas about citizenship; the transnational dimensions of the German 'November'; and the 'historicisation' of the Revolution as an event in Germany's past.[28] This was followed by the appearance of a number of highly specialist works on various aspects of the cultural experience and memory of the Revolution, such as Julian Aulke's urban-spatial history of the years 1918–20, focused on the city landscapes of Berlin and Munich and the Ruhr valley; Mark Jones's study *Founding Weimar: Violence and the German Revolution of 1918–19*; Nadine Rossol's investigation of a set of essays written by male trainee-teachers in a college in Essen, *Kartoffeln, Frost und Spartakus* (*Potatoes, Frost and Spartacus*); and Michael Brenner's account of Jewish experiences in post-1918 Munich, *Der lange Schatten der Revolution* (*The Long Shadow of the Revolution*).[29] In 2015 another important collection of essays, edited by Klaus Weinhauer, Anthony McElligott and Kirsten Heinsohn, was published: *Germany 1916–1923: A Revolution in Context* – with contributions on crowds, policing, gender, revolutionary subjectivities and intellectuals, among other themes.[30] Papers from an international conference held in London in 2018 under the title 'Living the German Revolution 1918–19: Expectations, Experiences, Responses' are due to be published soon in an even larger volume edited by Christopher Dillon and Kim Wünschmann.[31] The Amsterdam-based German historian Moritz Föllmer also wrote a ground-breaking journal article on masculinities in the Revolution, which came out in 2018.[32] So far, though, little of this new research seems to have been incorporated into mainstream histories of the Revolution written for non-specialist audiences – as seen in many of the narrative accounts published in Germany in the run-up to the centenary in 2018–19.[33]

The final contention of this book is one that looks more to the future. Cultural history approaches have greatly enriched academic understanding of the 1918–19 Revolution, it will be argued, and deserve to be integrated more fully into conventional political history narratives. However, this integration must come in the form of a dialogue rather than a takeover. Cultural historians, in other words, also have a great deal to learn from earlier political history perspectives; both approaches stand to benefit from a process of mutual recognition and enhancement. This is the only way to avoid a further fragmentation on the left, and with it, the danger of a renationalisation of historical memory coming from the newly resurgent right.

Definitions 2 The German Revolution of 1918–19

What, then, was the German Revolution of 1918–19? This book understands it as a unique episode in German history made up of four distinct yet entangled elements, and shows how difficulties in establishing where one of the elements begins and the others end have often been at the root of scholarly disagreements on the Revolution and its historical significance.

The four elements are as follows:

(1) *A movement of liberal political change from above.* On 9 November 1918 the Prussian King and German Kaiser, Wilhelm II, was forced to abdicate, ending the era of the Kaiserreich, or German empire, as founded by Otto von Bismarck in 1871. It was replaced by a Council of People's Deputies, made up of the two main left-wing parties, the Majority Social Democratic Party (SPD) led by Friedrich Ebert and Philipp Scheidemann, and the more radical Independent German Social Democratic Party (USPD). This body ruled Germany until the newly elected parliament, the Constituent National Assembly, met in Weimar in February 1919. From the beginning there were differences between the SPD and USPD, and within the USPD itself, about the future political form that the new republic should take. Following the resignation of the USPD leaders from the Council of People's Deputies on 29 December 1918, the defeat of an attempted Communist coup, the Spartacist Uprising, and the overwhelming victory of moderate, pro-parliamentary parties in the National Assembly elections on 19 January 1919, the new State was purged of all radical left elements and foundations were laid for a new liberal-democratic constitution, formally approved in August 1919.

(2) *A moment of mass social protest at the First World War and the sacrifices it had demanded from ordinary people.* Unlike the Bolshevik Revolution of 1917, the German Revolution of 1918–19 was not a full-scale social revolution. Indeed, as Eric Hobsbawm suggests, in the economically 'advanced' countries of western Europe, the notion that liberal political revolution might be accompanied by a 'general social revolution' – in other words a major change in property relations – died in 1848, or at the latest in 1871, in both cases in Paris (the 'June days' of 1848 and the crushing of the Commune by French Government troops in May 1871). Henceforth, liberal 'challenge[s] to the forces of tradition' and involvement of the masses in the political and communicative realms were only allowed if such forces could be controlled by the guardians of order and property.[34] However, this does not mean that there was no grass-roots democratic protest in Germany in 1918–19. On the contrary, the Revolution was preceded, accompanied and followed by large-scale political and industrial unrest, caused by the privations brought on by more than four years of war, and by the failure of successive governments – representing the old regime and the new – to solve the crisis in living standards. Food riots; strikes; street demonstrations calling for peace; and the naval mutinies in the port cities of Kiel and Wilhelmshaven, which actually sparked the Revolution, are all part of this picture. While the Spartacist Uprising of 5–12 January 1919 involved only small numbers of determined revolutionaries, support for further rounds of left-wing insurrection – such as the strikes in the Ruhr coalfield and the councils regime in Bremen in January–February 1919, the 'March Battles' (*Märzkämpfe*) in Berlin (3–13 March 1919), and the far left republics in Munich (6 April–3 May 1919) and Braunschweig (9–15 April) – was sufficiently large to bracket these events under the heading of 'social protest' as well.

(3) *A spur to new political imaginaries and cultural mindsets.* Ordinary Germans were not only acted upon by events and processes during the period 1918–19, but also developed their own individual political subjectivities and shared ambitions, which they communicated to others through external symbols and performances. Political imaginaries can be identified and analysed when 'utopian visions' and 'collective goals' take on 'representational concreteness' in the form of posters, works

of art, songs, revolutionary pamphlets, street demonstrations, silent films, picture postcards and even dance crazes.³⁵ The political imaginaries being represented through such means at the time of the German Revolution might include the future of citizenship, a particularly important theme in relation to gender.³⁶ Women were given the vote on equal terms with men by decree of the Council of People's Deputies on 12 November 1918, but were still not accepted as equal partners with men in the realm of organised parties, pressure groups, trade unions and so on. Masculinities were reimagined too, sometimes leaning in the direction of republicanism and civic nationalism, and sometimes in the direction of violent opposition to the new political order. Political imaginaries associated with 1918–19 might also include new ways of claiming ownership, real or symbolic, over urban space; of expressing private feelings and sexual desires; of imagining Germany and its place in the world beyond its existing geopolitical borders; and of performing everyday rituals and speech codes associated with class, gender or youth, and specific occupational, regional or national identities. Even the spectacle of voting in national elections under conditions of universal suffrage had to be seen and visualised before it could be worked through in terms of what it said about the chances of preserving, transforming or revolutionising the social body as it existed before 1918. This is illustrated perfectly by the image from *Das Illustrierte Blatt* on 14 January 1919, some five days before the elections to the Constituent National Assembly, which is reproduced in Chapter 6 of this book (Figure 6.1).

(4) *A transnational as well as national phenomenon.* The German Revolution had significant impacts on ways of *imagining revolution* in other parts of Europe and the wider world. In particular it proved a spur to visions of social democracy in Austria, Switzerland, the Netherlands, and neighbouring countries in western and central Europe. It cemented the international divisions on the left between those who advocated liberal or parliamentary roads to socialism, and those who believed, as Marx and Engels once had, in a self-empowering 'dictatorship of the proletariat'. It was hailed by members of the radical feminist campaign group the Women's International League for Peace and Freedom, some of whose German members had been keen supporters of Bavaria's revolutionary socialist-pacifist Minister-President Kurt Eisner before his assassination in February 1919.³⁷ And it influenced and gave hope to a number

of cross-border emancipatory movements, ranging from decolonisation and black liberation initiatives through anti-violence and anti-militarist campaigns to support for equal rights for LGBTQ+ communities.

It is certainly the case that until the end of the Cold War, historians were largely concerned with interpreting the Revolution in national rather than transnational terms, in other words as something that either failed to change political and social structures in Germany, or created a new range of economic 'winners' and 'losers' at national level. Few were interested explicitly in the impact of 1918–19 on cultural mindsets at home or abroad, except perhaps when it came to thinking about unworldy conservative intellectuals who rejected the Revolution outright.[38] However, Schama's contention that pre-1980s scholarship was all about identifying abstract 'forces' rather than chronicling contemporaries' perceptions of what actually happened is wide of the mark. In fact, from the 1920s, historians of this period were often acutely aware of what Schama calls the 'spontaneous brutality of events'.[39] They also frequently offered 'animated description[s]' of individual decision-makers and their direct media presentation.[40] Questions of 'public eloquence' and sartorial dignity or their opposites – as the much discussed photograph of Reich President Friedrich Ebert and Reichswehr (Armed Forces) Minister Gustav Noske standing in the sea in their swimming trunks, published on the front cover of the *Berliner Illustrirte Zeitung* on 24 August 1919 (Figure 0.1), demonstrates – have long been incorporated into interpretations of the 'speech [and mood-music] of [the] revolution'.[41]

Emotive ideas such as 'liberty', 'democracy', 'nation' and 'citizenship', and the rhetoric that surrounded them in 1918–19, have also consistently been understood as having a subjective and performative as well as 'objective' and 'scientific' dimension, even by scholars heavily influenced by social science or labour history methodologies such as Marxism. Empathic understanding and awareness of past sensibilities – albeit of the more sober rather than the elevated kind – have been cast as being as much an attribute of good history writing as sense and scholarly judgement. In his posthumously published memoirs, Joachim Petzold, one of the leading East German experts on the First World War and Weimar eras, outlined how he and his colleagues in the GDR's

Figure 0.1 'Ebert and Noske in der Sommerfrische' ['Ebert and Noske in the Fresh Summer Air'], front cover of the *Berliner Illustrirte Zeitung*, 24 August 1919, three days after Ebert was officially sworn in as Reich President. Getty Images.

Academy of Sciences understood their task as historians from the late 1950s onwards:

> We did not see why the determination of doubtful historical laws would be a more profitable exercise than the conclusive demonstration of unused possibilities and thus the establishment of responsibilities. In our opinion it was part of the ABC of Marxism that humans shape their own destiny and are not powerless instruments [of wider social forces].[42]

What Petzold refers to as 'unused possibilities' and 'responsibilities' (or perhaps we might say here the human capacity to feel pity; identify romance, tragedy or comedy; or find straightforward hope and inspiration in the vast range of cultural meanings given to any given historical situation) have also always been connected in narratives of 1918–19 with unique political events and singular decisions made by groups or individuals – and never exclusively with anonymous structures or forces. Well before the late 1970s and early 1980s, deciding *what* happened and *how* contemporaries felt about it when it did happen has been given as much weight by historians of the German Revolution as explaining *why* it happened. As this will be important to our understanding of debates about the Revolution more generally, it seems right to end this introduction by discussing how the author sees the study of historiography and its role in generating knowledge about what took place in Germany and why during the period 1918–19.

Definitions 3   Historiography and the German Revolution of 1918–19

In line with other contributions to the Manchester University Press series Issues in Historiography, this book understands historiography as a socially constructed scientific and political undertaking, ventured by professional historians whose methodological approaches and interpretative standpoints 'are entangled with personality, biography and the environment [they] move in'.[43] In other words, it does not look to provide a balanced or non-partisan survey of the current state of knowledge, measuring different works against 'objective' or timeless standards of what academic scholarship is supposed to look like. Rather, it investigates the history of historiography on the German Revolution in order to uncover the changing relationship between previous and current debates. It regards this aspect of historiography as an object worthy of study in its own right, helping us to make sense of how the field has developed over time and to challenge lazy assumptions that certain lines of interpretation – for instance, Marxist ones – are no longer relevant. Understanding historians as real persons who lived in times and places not of their own choosing but who also sought to shape the political world around them enables us to avoid making value judgements as to whether today's interpretations are any more 'real' or realistic than those developed in the different imaginative, institutional, social and personal life circumstances of the early, mid- and late twentieth century.[44]

Alongside examining the historiography of the German Revolution over the past 100 years, this book takes a two-pronged approach to the question of periodisation of the Revolution itself. On the one hand, it will focus primarily on debates over what happened and why in the period November 1918 to August 1919, i.e. from the naval uprising in Kiel on 3 November 1918 to the formal approval of the new constitution by the Weimar National Assembly on 11 August 1919 and the swearing in of Ebert as Reich President on 21 August. However, it will also stray beyond these chronological confines where this is necessary in order to shed further light on how particular controversies about the legacies and meaning of the Revolution have developed over time. The decision to locate the endpoint of the Revolution in August 1919 is one that reflects how the majority of historians have come to frame their understanding of the founding of Weimar. Strictly speaking, however, there is an equally strong case for arguing that, as the events of April–August 1919 did not necessitate any further substantial legal readjustments, Weimar was already effectively 'founded' in February–March 1919. The key turning point came on 10 February when the National Assembly, during its first week in session, voted through a law on the Provisional Authority of the Reich that was later enshrined into Article 48 of the Weimar Constitution. This provisional law, as Achim Kurz rightly argues, ended the Revolution by removing the executive and law-making functions wielded since 9 November by the Council of People's Deputies and establishing in its place a legally sanctioned separation of Government powers among a Reich President, a Reich Cabinet and the individual German states.[45] By defining the provisional responsibilities of the President and Reich Government in a way that – for political rather than juridical reasons – ultimately differentiated the 'business of the Reich' from the practice adopted in November 1918 of enforcing executive measures by revolutionary decree, council declaration or appeals to 'the German people', the 10 February 1919 law also established what 'normal', *postrevolutionary* government was supposed to look like.[46] In essence, political order, existing property relations and the State's domestic and external reputation for economic competence would ultimately be backed up by the exceptional instrument of military force to protect public security in case of large-scale strikes and other forms of social unrest, or attempted coups against the Reich in individual provinces or states. Under Article 9 of the 10 February law, the Reich President needed the countersignature of a Reich Minister – until the end of March 1920 usually Gustav Noske – for any military action or executive order in the civil sphere, meaning in effect that the President and the Reich Government were now regarded by those State officials responsible for upholding domestic security (police, army, and the system of ordinary and extraordinary courts or courts martial) as legal successors to the Council of People's Deputies *and* the Kaiser.[47] From March to April 1919, the newly created Reich Ministry of Finance was also entrusted with pushing through extraordinary interim and supplementary budgets (*vorläufige-* and *Nachtragshaushalte*) to help meet the Allies' initial demands under the 11 November 1918 armistice agreement and to cover other necessary taxation measures and expenditure during the transition period from war to peace. These latter financial powers in fact went significantly beyond the prerogative rights enjoyed by the Kaiser under the 1871 constitution and, *de facto*, by the extra-constitutional decision-makers represented in the Council of People's Deputies.[48]

That said, for the purpose of examining a century's-worth of historical debate as opposed to the more narrow, constitutional issue of 'states of exception' and 'states of normality', this book will bow to the convention of defining the German Revolution of 1918–19 as beginning on 9 November 1918 and ending with Ebert's formal presidential inauguration on 21 August 1919.[49] The book itself is divided into three parts. Part I examines historical debates on the

1918–19 Revolution in the first three decades after it happened, with one chapter on the pre-Nazi period and a second chapter on the years 1933 to the violent end and immediate aftermath of the Third Reich. Part II covers scholarship on the Revolution during the Cold War era. Here two chapters will look at debates in West Germany and East Germany down to the late 1970s, while a third chapter will devote attention to how the Revolution was understood at the time of German reunification in the 1980s and early 1990s. Finally, Part III investigates four areas of debate that have emerged since the late 1990s and in the run-up to the Revolution's centenary year in 2018–19. Arguments about revolutionary actors – sailors, soldiers and civilians – will be analysed alongside discussions of the 'gender' of the Revolution, the conquest and relinquishment of revolutionary 'space' in the period 1918–19, and transnational and international aspects of the Revolution. A short conclusion will consider the future of historical scholarship on the Revolution in the centenary's aftermath, and argue for a coming together of political and cultural history approaches.

Notes

1 Heinrich August Winkler, *Die Sozialdemokratie und die Revolution von 1918/19: Ein Rückblick nach sechzig Jahren* (Bonn, 1979), 5.
2 Gerhard Ritter, *Staatskunst und Kriegshandwerk: Das Problem des 'Militarismus' in Deutschland*, Vol. IV, *Die Herrschaft des deutschen Militarismus und die Katastrophe von 1918 (1917–1918)* (Munich, 1968), 470.
3 Winkler, *Die Sozialdemokratie*, 72 n. 64. See Sebastian Haffner, *Failure of a Revolution: Germany, 1918–19*, trans. Georg Rapp (London, 1973; German original, 1969).
4 Alexander Gallus (ed.), *Die vergessene Revolution von 1918/19* (Göttingen, 2010). See also Gallus's review of Robert Gerwarth's *November 1918: The German Revolution* (Oxford, 2020), in *Bulletin of the German Historical Institute London*, 43.1 (2021), 143–9 (143).
5 Ralf Höller, *Der Anfang, der ein Ende war: Die Revolution in Bayern 1918/19* (Berlin, 1999).
6 Detlev J. K. Peukert, *The Weimar Republic: The Crisis of Classical Modernity*, trans. Richard Deveson (London, 1991; German original, 1987).

7 On German modernities see also Geoff Eley (ed.), *Society, Culture, and the State in Germany, 1870–1930* (Ann Arbor, MI, 1996); and Geoff Eley, Jennifer L. Jenkins and Tracie Matysik (eds), *German Modernities from Wilhelm to Weimar: A Contest of Futures* (London, 2016).
8 For a broader overview of the new cultural history see Lynn Hunt, 'Introduction: History, Culture, and Text', in Lynn Hunt (ed.), *The New Cultural History* (Berkeley, CA, 1989), 1–22.
9 Ronald Hutton, *Britain, 1485–1660: The Tudor and Stuart Dynasties* (London, 2010), 259.
10 Philipp Sarasin, *1977: Eine kurze Geschichte der Gegenwart* (Berlin, 2021).
11 Frank Bösch, *Zeitenwende 1979: Als die Welt von heute begann* (Munich, 2019).
12 Samuel Moyn, *The Last Utopia: Human Rights in History* (Cambridge, MA, 2010).
13 Ian Kershaw, *Roller-Coaster: Europe, 1950–2017* (London, 2018), 340–1.
14 Samuel P. Huntington, *The Clash of Civilizations and the Remaking of World Order* (London, 1996), 21.
15 Simon Gunn, *History and Cultural Theory* (Harlow, 2006), 89–96.
16 Simon Schama, *Citizens: A Chronicle of the French Revolution* (London, 1989), xiv–xv. See also Keith Michael Baker and Dan Edelstein (eds), *Scripting Revolution: A Historical Approach to the Comparative Study of Revolutions* (Stanford, CA, 2015); and Benjamin Ziemann, 'The Missing Comedy and the Problem of Emplotment: New Perspectives on the German Revolution of 1918–19', in Christopher Dillon and Kim Wünschmann (eds), *Living the German Revolution 1918–19: Expectations, Experiences, Responses*, forthcoming.
17 Schama, *Citizens*, xiii.
18 Keith Michael Baker and Dan Edelstein, 'Introduction', in Baker and Edelstein, *Scripting Revolution*, 1–21 (4).
19 *Ibid.*, 2.
20 *Ibid.*, 21.
21 Karl Marx, 'The Eighteenth Brumaire of Louis Bonaparte' (1852), reproduced in Karl Marx, *Surveys from Exile*, ed. David Fernbach, trans. Ben Fowkes (London, 2010; first published in 1973), 143–249 (146–7).
22 Baker and Edelstein, 'Introduction', 5–8.
23 The two landmark books in this respect, both published in the first half of the 1990s, were George L. Mosse, *Fallen Soldiers: Reshaping the Memory of the World Wars* (Oxford, 1990); and Jay Winter, *Sites*

of Memory, Sites of Mourning: The Great War in European Cultural History (Cambridge, 1995).
24 Wolfgang Kruse, 'The First World War: The "True German Revolution"?', in Reinhard Rürup (ed.), The Problem of Revolution in Germany, 1789–1989 (Oxford, 2000), 67–92 (84). See also Wolfgang J. Mommsen, 'The "Spirit of 1914" and the Ideology of a German "Sonderweg"', in Wolfgang J. Mommsen, Imperial Germany, 1867–1918: Politics, Culture and Society in an Authoritarian State, trans. Richard Deveson (London, 1995; German original, 1990), 205–16; and Jeffrey R. Smith, A People's War: Germany's Political Revolution, 1913–1918 (Lanham, MD, 2007).
25 Gallus, review of Gerwath's November 1918, 148.
26 Klaus Theweleit, Male Fantasies, 2 vols, trans. Erica Carter and Chris Turner (Cambridge, 1987–89; German original, 1977–78).
27 Yuval Noah Harari, 'Vladimir Putin has already lost the war in Ukraine', Guardian, 1 March 2022, Journal, 3.
28 Gallus, Die vergessene Revolution.
29 Julian Aulke, Räume der Revolution: Kulturelle Verräumlichung in Politisierungsprozessen während der Revolution 1918–1920 (Stuttgart, 2015); Mark Jones, Founding Weimar: Violence and the German Revolution of 1918–19 (Cambridge, 2016); Nadine Rossol (ed.), Kartoffeln, Frost und Spartakus: Weltkriegsende und Revolution 1918/19 in Essener Schulaufsätzen (Berlin, 2018); Michael Brenner, Der lange Schatten der Revolution: Juden und Antisemiten in Hitlers München 1918–1923 (Berlin, 2019).
30 Klaus Weinhauer, Anthony McElligott and Kirsten Heinsohn (eds), Germany 1916–1923: A Revolution in Context (Bielefeld, 2015).
31 Dillon and Wünschmann, Living the German Revolution.
32 Moritz Föllmer, 'The Unscripted Revolution: Male Subjectivities in Germany, 1918–1919', Past and Present, 240 (2018), 161–92.
33 See, for instance, Joachim Kappner, 1918 – Aufstand für die Freiheit: Die Revolution der Besonnenen (Munich, 2017); Andreas Platthaus, Der Krieg nach dem Krieg: Deutschland zwischen Revolution und Versailles 1918/19 (Berlin, 2018); Lars-Broder Keil and Sven Felix Kellerhoff, Lob der Revolution: Die Geburt der deutschen Demokratie (Darmstadt, 2018); Christoph Regulski, Die Novemberrevolution 1918/19 (Wiesbaden, 2018); Klaus Gietinger, November 1918: Der verpasste Frühling des 20. Jahrhundert (Hamburg, 2018); and Volker Weidermann, Träumer: Als die Dichter die Macht übernahmen (Cologne, 2017).
34 E. J. Hobsbawm, The Age of Capital, 1848–1875 (London, 1975), 13–14, 304.

35 Susan Buck-Morss, *Dreamworld and Catastrophe: The Passing of Mass Utopia in East and West* (Cambridge, MA and London, 2000), 11–12, 67, 107. On dance crazes in particular, see Martin H. Geyer, *Verkehrte Welt: Revolution, Inflation und Moderne, München 1914–1924* (Göttingen, 1998), 72, 101; and Christina Ewald, '"As Long as People Are Dancing, They Are Pleased": Everyday Life and Leisure in Revolutionary Hamburg 1918–19', in Dillon and Wünschmann, *Living the German Revolution*.

36 See here Kathleen Canning, 'Gender and the Imaginary of Revolution in Germany', in Weinhauer, McElligott and Heinsohn, *Germany 1916–23*, 103–26.

37 See Ingrid Sharp and Matthew Stibbe, '"In diesen Tagen kamen wir nicht von der Straße …": Frauen in der deutschen Revolution von 1918/19', *Ariadne: Forum für Frauen- und Geschlechtergeschichte*, 73–4 (2018), 32–9 (35–6); and Christopher Dillon, 'The German Revolution of 1918/19', in Nadine Rossol and Benjamin Ziemann (eds), *The Oxford Handbook of the Weimar Republic* (Oxford, 2022), 27–47 (35–6). See also the work of East German historian Petra Rantzsch, discussed in Chapter 4 of this book.

38 See, for instance, Fritz Stern, *The Politics of Cultural Despair: A Study in the Rise of the Germanic Ideology* (Berkeley and Los Angeles, CA, 1961).

39 Schama, *Citizens*, 275.

40 *Ibid.*, 6.

41 *Ibid.*, 162. See also Bernhard Fulda, 'Die Politik der "Unpolitischen": Boulevard- und Massenpresse in den zwanziger und dreißiger Jahren', in Frank Bösch and Norbert Frei (eds), *Medialisierung und Demokratie im 20. Jahrhundert* (Göttingen, 2006), 48–72 (65–6).

42 Joachim Petzold, *Parteinahme wofür? DDR-Historiker im Spannungsfeld von Politik und Wissenschaft*, ed. Martin Sabrow (Potsdam, 2000), 192.

43 Mark Edele, *Debates on Stalinism* (Manchester, 2020), 6.

44 See also the approach taken to historiography in Franka Maubach and Christina Morina (eds), *Das 20. Jahrhundert erzählen: Zeiterfahrung und Zeitforschung im geteilten Deutschland* (Göttingen, 2016).

45 Achim Kurz, *Demokratische Diktatur? Auslegung und Handhabung des Artikels 48 der Weimarer Verfassung 1919–25* (Berlin, 1992), 25.

46 See *Gesetz über die vorläufige Reichsgewalt*, Article 6, reproduced in Ernst Rudolf Huber (ed.), *Dokumente zur deutschen Verfassungsgeschichte*, Vol. III, *Dokumente der Novemberrevolution und der Weimarer Republik 1918–1933* (Stuttgart, 1966), 69–70 (70).

47 *Ibid.*, Art. 9. See also the archival materials in Staatsarchiv Hamburg, 215–1/A1: Das außerordentliche Kriegsgericht in Hamburg – Sammelakten betreffend Belagerungszustand.
48 See Martin H. Geyer, 'Grenzüberschreitungen: Vom Belagerungszustand zum Ausnahmezustand', in Niels Werber, Stefan Kaufmann and Lars Koch (eds), *Erster Weltkrieg: Kulturwissenschaftliches Handbuch* (Stuttgart, 2014), 341–84; and Stefanie Middendorf, *Macht der Ausnahme: Reichsfinanzministerium und Staatlichkeit (1919–1945)* (Berlin, 2022), 54, 98–104.
49 See Dillon, 'The German Revolution', 42.

Part I

The thirty years war:
The Revolution as contemporary
history, 1919–48

1

The German Revolution in the Weimar Republic

The academic history profession under the Weimar Republic (1919–33) showed a great deal of continuity with the history profession of the pre-1918 era, especially when it came to social profile and political attitudes. The vast majority of history professors came from upper-middle-class backgrounds and remained wedded to what Fritz K. Ringer calls the 'German "mandarin tradition"'.[1] The historiography they produced was 'national-conservative' in form and 'statist' in content. Its focus was on the preservation and extension of sovereign power over what, until German unification in the 1860s and 1870s, they considered to have been politically disorganised territories and peoples within the German-speaking realm. In the 1920s, they tended to vote for conservative, anti-republican parties such as the Deutschnationale Volkspartei (German National People's Party (DNVP)) and its south German equivalents (the Bayerische Volkspartei in Bavaria or the Württembergische Bürgerpartei in Württemberg). In the early 1930s, some were tempted by Nazism while remaining wary of its non-traditional, non-statist aspects. With varying degrees of intensity, they disliked parliamentarism and government by multiparty coalition; the Weimar Constitution (which they denounced as a 'western import'); socialists; and 'non-German' minorities, including Jews and Poles.[2]

Yet the survival of the national-conservative 'mandarin tradition' within the German academic profession into the 1920s and beyond should not be taken to mean that members of the historical guild were unaffected by the events of 1918–19. Emotionally, the collapse of the Kaiserreich was a deeply traumatic experience, especially for those historians who had seen military service during the First World War.³ It represented a loss of (masculine) self-assuredness and sense of class superiority from which it was difficult to recover. Few, however, thought that the Revolution was a subject worthy of scholarly investigation. Military historians were the exception. For them, the Revolution offered an alibi, in other words a convenient way of explaining why Germany had lost the war instead of achieving the victory that historical developments since Bismarck were pointing towards. The events of November 1918, in their view, had robbed the army and navy of their ability to fight on to achieve an 'honourable' peace in the face of American President Woodrow Wilson's unacceptable armistice terms.⁴

This chapter will first investigate the studies produced by the Reichsarchiv and the Marinearchiv, the bodies charged with writing the official military and naval histories of the war. It will then contrast these with publications emanating from the German left. Weimar-era socialists and anti-militarists were of course keen to exonerate the Revolution of blame for military defeat, but equally they were concerned to put forward theories to explain why the unity between the two main social democratic parties in November 1918 had so quickly vanished in the winter of 1918–19. A final section in the chapter will explore the views of those anti-republicans who sought an explanation for the Revolution in the realms of biology and criminal psychology, and who drew for their ideas on pamphlets written by more respectable academics, welfare experts and physicians.

Military historiography and the German Revolution

The Reichsarchiv was formally established in September 1919 following a recommendation in a memorandum produced by Hans von Seeckt, the head of the new Truppenamt der Reichswehr (Troop Office of the German Armed Forces), in July of that year. Seeckt's proposal was to bring together the old war-historical department of the general staff with other military records, and to add to this eye-witness accounts from front-line officers.⁵ This would form the basis for an official history of the land war, which eventually extended to fourteen volumes, published between 1925 and 1956.⁶ The Reichsarchiv was based in Potsdam, just outside Berlin. It was close to the Garnisonkirche (Garrison Church), last resting place of Prussian kings including Frederick the Great and, in the Weimar era, a site of pilgrimage for right-wing veterans' groups such as the Stahlhelm and the Kyffhäuserbund.[7] Under its first director, General Major Hermann Ritter Mertz von Quirnheim, an independent Historical Commission was brought in to advise the Reichsarchiv, made up of State as well as military officials, including academically trained civilians.[8] However, among the Reichsarchiv's permanent employees in the early 1920s, a mere 'thirteen civilian historians ... were confronted by a hostile majority of fifty-two former officers'.[9] Among the latter was Otto Korfes, who had risen to the rank of major before he left active army service, joined the Reichsarchiv in 1920 and went on to marry Mertz's daughter, Gudrun.[10] The Truppenamt was the replacement for the general staff, whose dissolution had been stipulated under Article 162 of the Treaty of Versailles (signed by Germany on 28 June 1919) but whose wartime *esprit de corps* lived on in the Reichsarchiv's various research departments.[11] However, as a state institution, the Reichsarchiv was formally the responsibility of the Reich Ministry of Interior. In this sense, it differed from the Marinearchiv, whose series The War at Sea 'was not under civilian control' and was 'written [exclusively] by active and inactive naval officers'.[12] Only in the mid-1930s, under the Nazi regime, was the Reichsarchiv's Historical Commission abolished and its work placed under the direct control of the Reichswehr Ministry.[13]

Already by 1922 the Reichsarchiv had collected 41,000 eye-witness reports and diaries from veteran officers.[14] Much of its published research related to operational matters or individual battles, and had little bearing on the issue of why Germany had lost the war overall. However, as far as the ex-military employees of the Reichsarchiv were concerned, the answer to the latter question had already been provided beyond doubt on 18 November 1919, when the former commander-in-chief Paul von Hindenburg appeared before the fourth subcommittee of the Constituent National Assembly (now sitting in Berlin, not Weimar), which had been charged with investigating the causes of the war and of Germany's 'inner collapse' in 1918. Hindenburg refused to answer directly any of the questions put to him by the subcommittee, claiming that it was not for politicians to judge military decisions. He nonetheless gave his own account of his experience as head of the supreme command between August 1916 and November 1918:

> At the time we still hoped that the *will to victory* would dominate everything else. When we assumed our post we made a series of proposals to the Reich leadership which aimed at combining all forces at the nation's disposal for a quick and favourable conclusion to the war; at the same time, they demonstrated to the government its enormous tasks. What finally became of our proposals, once again partially because of the influence of the parties, is known. I wanted forceful and cheerful cooperation and instead encountered failure and weakness.[15]

The chairman of the subcommittee had already interrupted to accuse Hindenburg of failing to provide an objective account. Instead he was offering 'value judgment[s], against which I must enter a definite protest'.[16] But the Field Marshal ignored this and continued his monologue, amid much 'shouting and commotion' from the public gallery:

> An English general said with justice: 'The German army was stabbed in the back.' No guilt applies to the good core of the army. Its achievements are just as admirable as those of the officer corps. Where the guilt lies has clearly been demonstrated. If it needed more proof, then it would be found in the quoted statement of the English general and in the boundless astonishment of our enemies at their victory.[17]

Here was the essence of what rapidly became known as the 'stab-in-the-back legend', the notion that Germany's defeat had been caused not by any shortcomings on the part of the military but by civilian politicians at home – the so-called 'November criminals' – who had failed to cover the army's back.[18] Interestingly, Hindenburg was still prepared to use the term 'revolution' to describe what happened in November 1918. Yet his testimony lent legitimacy to others who denied that it was even a revolution in the conventional political sense. Instead, it was put down to a sudden 'loss of nerve', or a breakdown of tutored, masculine spirit. Many military officials referred to it as an *Umwälzung*, again a word that suggested a kind of spinning out of control or an involuntary, weak-kneed 'convulsion'.[19] For others it was a straightforward case of treason. Hermann von Kuhl, called as one of the expert military witnesses to the subcommittee on the basis of his wartime service as chief-of-staff to the army group Crown Prince Rupprecht, was particularly vocal in pointing the finger of blame at the USPD and its 'subversive activities' (*Wühlarbeit*) at home and at the front.[20] As the wartime USPD had included leading socialist politicians such as Eduard Bernstein, Hugo Haase and Karl Kautsky, as well as the assassinated Bavarian Minister-President Kurt Eisner, this was a charge that was bound to magnify existing political divisions.

Naval historiography was equally, if not even more, hostile to the Revolution. Although naval historians after 1918 were divided between straightforward monarchist and pro-Tirpitz perspectives – the latter a reference to the former Reich Secretary of State for the Navy turned fierce critic of (ex-) Kaiser Wilhelm II – all were agreed in defending the reputation and honour of the naval officer corps against left-wing charges that they had been indifferent to the hardships faced by ordinary crew.[21] Typical in this respect was a piece published in the Bremen-based newspaper the *Weser-Zeitung* in early 1919 by the former German naval attaché in Washington, DC, Captain Karl Boy-Ed. According to the latter:

> Because a few were clumsy and neglectful it is not fair to condemn the whole corps. For decades German Naval Officers have been engaged in training their crews in ceaseless perseverance and with disinterested love of their profession. In spite of the English efforts and in spite of the shameful behaviour of some of our men since 31 October of last year the glorious results of that work and their faithfulness will always be included amongst the most beautiful pages in the history of the late German empire ... The ingratitude of the Fatherland adds bitterness to their sorrow at the destruction of their life['s work].[22]

Over the next two to three years, the 'stab-in-the-back' legend developed even more extreme forms, becoming mixed up with antisemitism in narratives produced by the Nazis and other far-right groups. Instead of the USPD and the Spartacists, some of whose Jewish leaders were alleged by Boy-Ed to have been in the pay of the Bolsheviks and the British propagandist Lord Northcliffe,[23] it was now German Jews across the board who were cast as traitors. This had real-life consequences when Walther Rathenau, the Weimar Republic's Foreign Minister, was assassinated by a gang linked to the right-wing terrorist group Organisation Consul in Berlin in June 1922.[24] Rathenau, a member of the left-liberal German Democratic

Party (DDP), was regarded as one of the leading 'November criminals', and his Jewishness made him an even bigger target. His murderers – two of whom were killed in a subsequent shoot-out with the police – were condemned as traitors by all mainstream Weimar politicians, led by the Reich Chancellor Joseph Wirth.[25] Even the Communists joined in the protests at his killing. However, the assassins were regarded as heroes on the extreme right, and after Hitler came to power in 1933 their 'martyrdom' was recognised by the State through the unveiling of the kind of tomb – covered with steel helmets – that was normally reserved for fallen soldiers in the war.[26]

In fact, so toxic did the 'stab-in-the-back' legend become that some more moderate conservative military historians, notably Gerhard Ritter and Karl Demeter, later sought to claim that they had never endorsed it or believed in it[27] – unlike representatives of the older generation of national-conservative historians such as Dietrich Schäfer, Johannes Haller, Karl Alexander von Müller and Erich Marcks, who had.[28] In particular Ritter and Demeter now criticised the staging of the so-called 'stab-in-the-back' trial in Munich in 1925, at which nationalist opponents of the Weimar Republic 'tried to demonstrate publicly the guilt and complicity of the left' in the 'alleged treason against Germany' in 1918.[29] They also distanced themselves from naval versions of the 'stab-in-the-back', represented above all by two articles published by retired Vice Admiral Adolf von Trotha and retired Rear Admiral Magnus von Levetzow in the April 1924 edition of the Munich-based conservative-nationalist journal the *Süddeutsche Monatshefte*.[30] In 1951 Ritter wrote regretfully that it was 'blind hatred against the so-called Versailles system' that had 'plunged us into the arms of [the] violent adventurer [Hitler]'.[31] Possibly he had Levetzow, among others, in mind, for the latter joined the Nazi Party in 1931, helped establish contacts between the party and members of the ex-Prussian royal family between 1928 and the end of 1932, and went on to play a leading role in the Nazi seizure of power as Police President of Berlin and organiser of the 'hunt against communists' (*Kommunistenjagd*) in the German capital from February 1933 to July 1935.[32] The liberal historian Friedrich Meinecke went even further in his 1946 book *The German Catastrophe*, singling out the 'stab-in-the-back' myth as 'the fatal turning point' for modern Germany and in particular for its middle class, causing the latter to 'close its mind more and more against the democratic idea'.[33]

The writings of Ritter, Demeter and Meinecke were an important aspect of the de-Nazification and thus the rehabilitation of military and naval history in West Germany after 1949, particularly in the run-up to the latter's entry into the North Atlantic Treaty Organization (NATO) in 1955. By contrast, those, like Otto Korfes, who returned to Potsdam, now in East Germany, to help rebuild the military archives there, had less immediate cause to break with the 'stab-in-the-back' theory. Typically, they belonged to a group of nationalist officers with a conservative-Protestant world view, the *Bund deutscher Offiziere*, who converted to a 'patriotic' form of opposition to Hitler and Nazism whilst in Soviet captivity during the Second World War. Upon their release, they became loyal East German citizens, although their version of anti-fascism 'also remained ... closely linked to military virtues' and 'Prusso-German traditions'.[34] Ritter's long-term association with Korfes and the Reichsarchiv – which continued into the early 1950s – indeed suggests that, like many other German historians who had fought as officers in the First World War, he still took for granted that the general thrust of the official Weimar-era military history was correct. In other words, the army had suffered total collapse in 1918 not because it was defeated in the field but because of inadequate discipline on the home front, culminating in (but not beginning with) the November Revolution. Echoes of this view could still be found in 2006 in the work of the right-wing historian Ernst Nolte, who referred to what happened at the end of the First World War as 'the revolution that broke Germany internally' ('die deutsche Zusammenbruchsrevolution').[35]

The left and the Revolution

Not surprisingly, left-wing publicists in the Weimar years strongly opposed the stab-in-the-back legend and other anti-republican narratives put forward by conservative-military historians. An early example would be a pamphlet issued by the SPD in the Prussian port city of Altona, near Hamburg, in the second half of 1919:

> Germany's impending defeat was unstoppable well before the revolution broke out. It was caused by the unfulfilled expectations of the U-boat war, the heavy losses experienced during the retreat on the western front, which had been going on for three months, and

the capitulation of Germany's allies. Germany stood alone against a whole world, against enemies, above all America, whose resources were still increasing, while home and front were led to believe that the enemy's reserves were almost exhausted. Severe hunger was raging in the interior of Germany and critical raw materials were increasingly unavailable. Our opponents, on the other hand, enjoyed an enormous material superiority.[36]

However, aside from this, the left-wing parties were fundamentally disunited in their views. In particular, they could not agree on what kind of revolution had taken place in November 1918, or how it measured up against other revolutions (1789, 1848, 1917). Some argued that the Revolution was caused by social tensions and abuses within the army, and the failure of the supreme command adequately to address this problem. This was the position, for instance, of the 'outspoken republican' Martin Hobohm, one of the few civilian historians employed in the Reichsarchiv and author of a detailed report on 'social grievances in the army', which he was commissioned to write in the late 1920s for the parliamentary subcommittee investigating the causes of Germany's collapse.[37] More militant leftists – such as the one-time leader of the revolutionary shop stewards' movement and first chairman of the executive committee of workers' and soldiers' councils in Berlin (*Berliner Vollzugsrat*), Richard Müller – claimed that it was a revolution staged not only against the social injustices caused by the war and the old imperial system, but also against the SPD itself and its policy of supporting the military's efforts to end strikes and isolate strike leaders in 1917–18.[38] However, perhaps the biggest area of disagreement was over how and why the apparent revolutionary unity of early November 1918 among the SPD, the USPD and politically non-aligned workers organised in the councils movement had unravelled in the months that followed.

While the USPD had indeed split from the SPD in April 1917 over the issue of the latter's continuing support for the war effort, it should not be forgotten that there was still common ground between them on many other policies, and at least some potential for wartime divisions to be healed in the moment of revolution in November 1918. Both parties agreed to govern through a Council of People's Deputies on the basis of parity of membership on that six-member body. And the leaderships of both parties were highly suspicious of Lenin's regime in Russia, objecting to its dictatorial methods and its insistence on one-party rule. There was no dissent from the USPD when it was decided not to include representation for the tiny Spartacist League on the Council of People's Deputies. And a few days before the Revolution, on 1 November 1918, Eduard Bernstein told the left-liberal Berlin journalist Theodor Wolff that he and Karl Kautsky, the two dominant intellectual figures in the USPD (and one-time fierce opponents in prewar debates about the future of Social Democracy) were both 'resolute' in their opposition to 'Bolshevism'.[39]

The events of December 1918 and January 1919 led to a strong leftward shift in the USPD, which from 29 December was no longer in any power-sharing agreement with the SPD. Over the course of the following weeks, Bernstein and Kautsky both resigned from the USPD, and while its leader, Hugo Haase, maintained a sceptical line towards the Bolsheviks and left-wing elements within his own party, his main ire was now directed towards Ebert and the SPD. After Haase's death on 7 November 1919, a direct result of an assassination attempt carried out a month earlier by a right-wing extremist, the USPD moved even closer to Bolshevik positions, eventually voting (by a two-thirds majority among delegates at a party conference in Halle in October 1920) to affiliate to the Moscow-based Third International (Comintern) and to merge with the much smaller German Communist Party (KPD). The new 'United Communist Party of Germany' (which quickly dropped the 'United' from its title and reverted simply to calling itself the KPD) now emerged as a mass movement and the dominant challenger on the left to the SPD.[40] A smaller 'centrist' rump of the USPD – whose members included the future East German Minister-President Otto Grotewohl and the future Mayor of (West) Berlin, Ernst Reuter – continued in existence until 1922, before applying for readmittance to the SPD.

Representatives of the KPD after 1920, especially many former USPD members, were determined to expose what they saw as the SPD's 'betrayal' of the Revolution. Paul Frölich, one of the founders of the KPD in December 1918, was lead author of a critical left-wing pamphlet that first appeared in 1924 under the title *Zehn Jahre SPD (Ten Years SPD)*.[41] By ordering soldiers in the army to continue to obey orders from their officers, by allowing courts to continue to operate without oversight from the workers' and soldiers' councils, and by ordering the disarming of revolutionary militias attached to the workers' and soldiers' councils, all in the period 12 November to 14 December 1918, the leaders of the SPD and the right wing of the USPD were accused of failing to 'protect' the Revolution from the regrouped forces of German 'militarism' and of allowing the restoration of 'bourgeois class justice' under the pretence of upholding judicial independence:

> The initial measures taken by the [Council of] People's Deputies already amounted to emasculation of the revolution, marginalisation of the Red Guard, suppression of the rights of the soldiers' councils ... restoration of the powers of the old officer corps and thus the start of the counterrevolution.[42]

A later edition of the pamphlet, published in 1928, included new contributions from Albert Schreiner, a member of the Spartacist League in Stuttgart during the war and (for six days) Minister of War in the first Government of the Free State of Württemberg.[43] He resigned on 15 November 1918 after local Spartacist leaders withdrew their support for the new revolutionary Government, but continued to have a major influence on the development of the early KPD in Württemberg and on Communist military policy nationally, emerging as the first leader of the Roter Frontkämpferbund (Red Front Fighters' League (RFB)) in 1924.[44]

In 1928, the tenth anniversary year of the Revolution, Schreiner was co-author of another important publication, the *Illustrated History of the German Revolution*, written from a KPD perspective and addressed to 'German workers' who were invited to view it as a 'weapon in the struggle for proletarian freedom'.[45] The 'duplicity' of Ebert, Scheidemann and other right-wing Social Democrats (*Rechtssozialisten*) was again denounced, with the argument that they had not really wanted revolution in November 1918 but had 'smuggled themselves' into the workers' and soldiers' councils in order to disarm them. Ebert was quoted as allegedly saying, on the morning of 9 November, that he 'hated revolution like sin'; he and Scheidemann were referred to as 'Kaiser socialists' whose main concern was to ensure that 'the rapport they had established with [representatives of] the old order did not break down'.[46] Even so, Schreiner, as former War Minister in Stuttgart, also had something to say about the role of the proletarian masses themselves in the

Revolution, something that reflected his own military interests and thinking (he had undergone military training in Moscow in 1924).

> The onset of the workers' revolution was brought to a standstill but only after the proletariat had temporarily held political power in their hands ... With the heightened class consciousness of a class that was used to ruling but now felt its power to be under threat, the bourgeoisie sought out the Achilles heel of the proletarian revolution. The key strategic goal which the counterrevolution set its sights on was the disarmament of the revolution. In other areas they made concessions to the workers, but on the question of disarmament they showed that they were not joking ... And once the counterrevolutionaries had forced through the disarmament of the revolution, the revolution itself was slain.[47]

Not all Communists agreed with the Frölich–Schreiner line, however, especially as it seemed to lend support to the idea of 'revolutionary putschism', i.e. of a transition to socialism by means of an armed uprising without first building up a band of Comintern-trained, politically-conscious cadres capable of winning over the masses. Attempts to seize power in this way had been tried, and seen to fail, during the 'March Action' in Halle-Merseburg in 1921 and the Hamburg Uprising in October 1923, with Frölich taking part in the former event and Schreiner centrally involved in the latter. Tensions also arose because Schreiner and Frölich were former Spartacists and/or members of the ultra-left International Communists of Germany (Internationale Kommunisten Deutschlands, IKD), a group operating from 1917–18 in Bremen, Hamburg and other towns, whereas the KPD after 1920 was increasingly dominated by those who had decided to follow the 'Moscow' or Comintern line on the path to socialist revolution (including during the latter's Stalinist phase from 1924, and especially from 1928). Many of the most fervent supporters of the Stalinisation of the KPD under its new leader, Ernst Thälmann, after 1925 were in fact former USPD members who had opposed the IKD and were convinced that the left wing of the USPD and the councils' movement had been insufficiently 'Bolshevik' and 'disciplined' in 1918–19. This included Thälmann himself; Wilhelm Koenen, a revolutionary strike leader in central Germany in 1919 and future party secretary for the Halle-Merseburg region; and Walter Ulbricht, a USPD/KPD official from Leipzig, Saxony, who went on to become the first secretary of the East German Socialist Unity Party (SED) after 1946.[48]

By contrast, Frölich had an on-off relationship with the top figures in the KPD, being expelled from the party in December 1920 for 'revolutionary dilettantism', but making a come-back the following year.[49] He was expelled again in 1928 and joined first the KPD-O (Communist Party-Opposition), and then in 1931 the SAPD (Socialist Workers Party).[50] Schreiner, like a number of other former Spartacists, was also forced out of his party and RFB functions in 1928, and ended up, at least for several years, in the KPD-O, a decision that came back to haunt him in the GDR of the 1950s.[51] Meanwhile, the Stalinists inside the KPD adopted the far-left line against the 'opportunists' and 'revisionists' inside the SPD and its right-wing USPD allies, but took a more negative view of the events of November 1918–August 1919. This had been a 'bourgeois' revolution from start to finish; the proletariat never held the reins of power, not even on 9 November. Germany was not ready for a socialist revolution, because at that time it still lacked a disciplined Marxist-Leninist party of the type built by the Bolsheviks in Russia (and by Thälmann in Germany after 1925). By extension, the Spartacist Uprising had been just that: a premature rebellion without any realistic chance of success, not only because the KPD was then still in its infancy, but because the majority of the January 1919 rebels had refused closer links with Moscow and 'opposed Lenin's plans to establish a Communist International'.[52] As early as May 1919, the left-wing satirist Kurt Tucholsky wrote in the socialist magazine *Die Weltbühne*: 'We have not had a revolution in Germany – but we have had a counterrevolution.'[53] This was close to his views ten years later, when he belittled the events of November 1918 as a 'coup' ('Umsturz') that 'took place in the assembly hall' ('im Saale stattgefunden hat').[54] One part of the bourgeoisie had been overthrown by another. The German working class in 1918–19 had had its radical spokesmen and -women, in other words, but unlike Lenin (and Stalin) they were not real proletarian revolutionaries able to mount a decisive move against the fortress of bourgeois power.

Where did the moderate and centrist left stand on these issues? Like Tucholsky, they were very critical of the role played by the Spartacists in 1918–19, but from a completely different ideological perspective. Kautsky, the great Marxist theoretician, wrote a pamphlet in 1919 attacking the Bolsheviks in Russia as 'terrorists', comparing Lenin and Trotsky to the radical Jacobin leaders Robespierre and Saint-Just during the French Revolution, and defending the decision not to give their German counterparts any role in the Council of People's Deputies after 9 November 1918.[55] He also claimed to have fallen out with Rudolf Hilferding, another leading thinker on the Marxist left and a future Reich Minister of Finance, over the question of whether the role of the councils should be temporary or, as the latter suggested, lasting: 'As much as I value Hilferding as an economist', he wrote to Bernstein in 1921, 'his political maxims always provoke my sharpest protest'.[56] In an article published in 1924, he went even further in challenging Leninist interpretations of recent German history. November 1918, he argued, was a 'proletarian revolution', and the failure to ensure the permanent institutionalisation of the councils did not change that. By contrast, the Russian Revolution, 'which, according to th[at] country's economic structure, could only be a bourgeois one', had confused the rest of the world by pretending to be able to introduce socialism by means of political terror. In particular, it had split the German Social Democrats at a crucial moment when 'only close-knit unity could keep the proletariat in power'.[57]

Bernstein's views, which were not too dissimilar to Kautsky's, were expressed in a series of short articles and other pieces, culminating in two book-length works published in 1921: *The German Revolution* and *How a Revolution Died*. In *The German Revolution*, he spoke of the growing recklessness of Spartacist agitation in Berlin in November–December 1918, which threatened the new-found unity on the left, especially when Karl Liebknecht called for the removal of the SPD from office and the handing of full executive powers to the councils.[58] The pro-Spartacist newspaper *Die Rote Fahne* printed 'a tissue of *lies*' and was bent on 'turning as large a number of Berlin workers as possible against the Social Democrat representatives in the new Government'.[59] The SPD and the moderates in the USPD were right to believe that if this agitation were allowed to continue unchecked, it could spread into the ranks of the army and lead to full-scale revolutionary (civil) war, of the type that had already broken out in Russia between Reds and Whites.[60]

Yet Russia was not the only negative influence. From Bernstein's point of view, Rosa Luxemburg's decision to endorse the politics of violent struggle after her release from prison on 9 November 1918 was a mistake on a par with the calls of the Blanquists for the physical overthrow of the moderate republican Government in France after the February 1848 Revolution. It had made the split on the German left, and thus the 'perishing' of the 1918–19 Revolution, inevitable, just as it had led to the victory of the National Guard and the conservative, property-owning republicans over the radical protagonists of the 'social question' during the 'June days' in Paris in 1848.[61] Even so, and in an apparent contradiction with the notion of the Revolution's demise, Bernstein felt that its final outcome remained open, a point he made with growing confidence after 1920. He also spoke more highly of Luxemburg than of Liebknecht, referring to her as a 'selfless fighter' whose brutal death was a great loss to the social democratic cause, and insisting that, had she made different decisions in 1918–19, she 'could have rendered invaluable services to the Republic'.[62] The tragedy was that she and other leftist socialists had failed to see the opportunity presented in November 1918 to participate in the creation of a genuine social and democratic workers' republic.

The SPD's 1921 Görlitz Programme – on whose drafting committee Bernstein sat – pointedly celebrated the 'political upheavals' at the end of the First World War, which had 'swept away rotten systems of government' and 'brought democratic rights to the masses'.[63] A 'vastly strengthened workers' movement', it claimed, had risen up to claim its place as capitalism's evenly matched and morally superior opponent.[64] Fighting for the Görlitz Programme's extensive list of social reforms was a way of 'extending his critique of Bolshevik and Blanquist tendencies within the left-wing of the USPD and the KPD', to cite Marius S. Ostrowski's apt summary of Bernstein's reading of the 'lessons' of 1918–19 in 1921.[65] In a 1922 article, 'Four Years On', Bernstein continued to celebrate the Revolution's concrete achievements in advancing 'the political rights of Germany's working classes and their social-legal status [*soziale Rechtsstellung*]', adding that:

> The German Republic proclaimed on [9 November 1918] by the workers of Berlin is not yet a workers' republic [*Republik der Arbeiter*]. Yet that does not already make it a bourgeois republic [*Bourgeois-Republik*] – rather, it is a civic republic [*bürgerliche Republik*] in the old democratic conception of the word.[66]

Yet as the 1920s continued, and as the SPD, now reunited with the right wing of the USPD, consolidated itself as the chief political voice for social democracy in Germany, there was a tendency to avoid 'owning' the Revolution as a major landmark event in the party's – and nation's – history. The party's 1925 Heidelberg Programme, while underlining a commitment to the 'democratic republic' as a 'form of government whose maintenance and improvement is an absolute imperative in the struggle for liberty', said nothing about the events of 1918–19. In terms of domestic policy, its stronger anti-capitalist thrust and demand for immediate workers' control of the economy reflected the requirements of SPD–USPD reunification rather than the notion of building a 'civic' republic in organic alliance with reformers from outside the socialist camp. Bernstein was again on the drafting committee, but his voice was now weaker. If he had any influence, it was now on foreign policy, including statements on the 'pursuit of peace', the creation of a 'United States of Europe' and the 'democratisation of the League of Nations'.[67]

In the anniversary year, 1928, SPD figures and members of the republican paramilitary group the Reichsbanner, who wanted something more than a purely anti-capitalist programme on the Heidelberg model and were interested in the theoretical and practical enhancement of centre-left and social democratic ideals, looked to the March 1848 revolutions in central Europe rather than the Revolution of 1918–19 (or France in 1789).[68] Two major projects were launched in 1928 that sought to present the Weimar Republic as a continuation of the civic and social ideals of the revolutionaries of 1848. Ironically, they were both written by men who had connections with the Reichsarchiv – albeit as civilian experts appointed by the Reich Ministry of Interior to serve on its Historical Commission, rather than as former soldiers.[69] Ludwig Bergsträsser was commissioned to work on a (never completed) study of the Frankfurt Parliament of 1848–49 after giving up his own Reichstag seat, which he had held since 1924 for the left-liberal DDP. By 1930 he had joined the SPD. He was forced to abandon his work in the Reichsarchiv's external branch in Frankfurt in 1933, but made a political and academic comeback in West Germany after 1945, serving as the first US-appointed civilian head (*Regierungspräsident*) of the new State administration in Hesse (until 1948); as an SPD member of the Parliamentary Council (in 1948–49); and as a university professor in Darmstadt, Frankfurt and Bonn.[70] Meanwhile, also in 1928, Veit Valentin, another left-leaning DDP member, was tasked by the Reichsarchiv's Historical Commission with writing a two-volume study of the German Revolution of 1848–9, using its holdings of sources from that period. He completed this in 1930–1, before being forced into exile after 1933, first in London, and then in Washington, DC, where he died in 1947.[71]

Interestingly, then, the Reichsarchiv's structures did allow for some defence of democratic and parliamentary values, albeit by State-appointed 'outsiders' with (unusually) progressive values rather than by regular employees (Hobohm being almost the sole exception there). Valentin was a member not only of the DDP, but also of the Reichsbanner and of the German League for Human Rights (Deutsche Liga für Menschenrechte).[72] Both he and Bergsträsser campaigned alongside the KPD and the SPD for the dispossession of the former princely households in the (rather impressively run but ultimately unsuccessful) national referendum on this issue in June 1926.[73] Yet it is noticeable that two years later, in 1928 – a time when the centre-left and centre-right gained ground against 'extremist' candidates in the Reichstag, and the SPD was able to lead a 'grand coalition' Government at national level for the first time since 1920 – the two main republican parties seemed to feel that the cause of democracy and parliamentarism was best served by commemorating 1848, not 1918–19. In the late Weimar period, for instance, Eduard Bernstein accepted invitations from Social Democrat groups to speak on the annual memorial day for the Berlin *Märzgefallene* (March Fallen) of 1848, but not, as far as is known, on the anniversary of 9 November 1918.[74] This was in marked contrast to the situation in 'Red Vienna' in the 1920s and early 1930s, where, as Veronika Helfert has shown, the revolution that overthrew the Habsburg monarchy and paved the way for the founding of an Austrian republic on 12 November 1918 was celebrated in style by socialists young and old as 'a spectacle, an event that ha[d] to be read and interpreted as a performance'.[75]

Biology and the medicalisation of the German Revolution

One final view of the Revolution that became academically and politically influential in the early Weimar Republic stemmed from attempts to cast it as a biological or criminological-psychological phenomenon. As early as 1919 four prominent medical experts, Hugo Marx, Helenefriderike Stelzner, Eugen Kahn and Emil Kraepelin, published articles in scientific and literary journals espousing this line of thought. Marx and Stelzner were based in Berlin and wrote largely against the background of events in the capital city since November 1918. Stelzner had gained a certain notoriety during the First World War when, having been told that the Prussian army would not accept women doctors, she volunteered for the Habsburg army instead. The description of her in some online biographical dictionaries as a champion of women's rights may require substantial revision, however, given her published views on the November Revolution discussed below.[76] The second two medical experts, Kahn and Kraepelin, held positions in Munich and drew for their observations on records of court proceedings against revolutionaries staged in the aftermath of the Munich Councils Republic of April–May 1919. Kraepelin in particular was a world-famous expert on psychiatric illness, which he attributed to genetic and biological defects rather than to the psychodynamic interplay of conscious and unconscious thoughts and emotions. His works had already been translated into several languages before 1914, in spite of, or maybe because of, the fact that his theories were at odds with those of Sigmund Freud.[77] Needless to say, Kraepelin's essay endorsing the arguments made by Marx, Stelzner and Kahn was significant in lending credibility to medicalised views of the Revolution of 1918–19, particularly as it was published in the highly respected *Süddeutsche Monatshefte*, the house journal of literary and artistic anti-modernism and national conservatism in Munich since 1904 (and, as we saw above, a strong promoter of the anti-republican stab-in-the-back legend after 1919).[78]

Hugo Marx, whose article was the first to appear, in March 1919, following a lecture he gave at the Berlin-based Association for Forensic Medicine (Forensisch-medizinische Vereinigung) on 21 February, was keen to underline that he was taking not a *political* standpoint against the Revolution, but a *criminal-anthropological* and *biological* one.[79] His concern was with what the Revolution told urban physicians such as himself about the physical and mental health of the national body, or *Volkskörper*. The prognosis was not good, Marx argued, but the situation could still be remedied if only the 'healthy' elements were rescued from the 'unhealthy' influence of 'pathological' elements, and at the same time given adequate housing and enough to eat. Interestingly, his explanation of why the Revolution took place steered clear of blaming the home front in general; if anything, he was willing to recognise the enormous material and psychological suffering of Berlin's population under the impact of the war and the Allied economic blockade.

> Hardships can be observed in all revolutionary situations, but they must appear doubled in a period of revolution like ours, because the general causes of [wartime] debilitation persist and the exhaustion psychosis threatens to continue indefinitely. Badly nourished brains come under the control of suspect ideas ... unfounded hostilities arise, and every stratum of the nation threatens to lose all understanding of other strata.[80]

This focus on the suffering of the German people stood at odds with the findings of a report published shortly afterwards by the American nutritional experts Vernon Kellogg and Alonzo Taylor to the Inter-Allied Supreme Economic Council in Paris, insisting that Germany had been defeated in summer and autumn 1918 on the battlefield, and not by dint of the hunger caused by the economic blockade.[81] For Marx, indeed, defeat could only be explained by wartime deprivations and a short-term loss of nerve or 'exhaustion psychosis' on the home front as the fifth winter of the war approached. The temporary psychological weakness of the people had made them vulnerable to the depraved charms of criminal-deviant types, i.e. the kind of people who in normal times would be dismissed as cranks and mentally disturbed.

> I am thinking of the great class of psychopaths. These personalities rise easily enough from the wave of revolution, and now they can freely follow their innate inclinations. It must be said that they make the most unrestricted use of this freedom. They were and are a tremendous danger to our public life in a time when the social inhibitions that could otherwise put shackles on them appear to have been lifted.[82]

Marx noted that politicians needed to pay more attention to the socio-economic condition of the masses, thereby distancing himself from the views of arch-conservative politicians such as Count Kuno von Westarp, who had already written disparagingly about the 'revolutionary madness of the masses' and their 'raging in the streets' in an article in the reactionary *Kreuzzeitung* on 10 November 1918.[83] In all likelihood he had paid attention to the warnings delivered by various welfare experts during the war who had called on the Government to plan ahead for the coming peace in order to offset a looming threat to societal order in the shape of accelerating rates of moral degeneracy and collapsing levels of physical and mental fitness. One specialist in this area wrote in 1917:

> The World War has inflicted the greatest upheaval on our nation ... In the space of a few years, economic and social changes have taken place ... that we could never have foreseen ... The concentration of all production efforts on war material and feeding the nation has had a profound effect on the everyday outlook of our people. In addition, the mass experience of millions of troops fighting on fronts far from home ... [and] the extraordinary expansion of women's work to all areas of economic activity ... has significantly altered the social mindset of the entire population. Today a different Germany is emerging from the one that, with youthful enthusiasm, marched victorious through northern France in August 1914.[84]

However, in 1919 Marx went much further than this, calling for medical experts to have a direct scientific input into the welfare and criminal justice systems. This was the only way, in his view, to come to 'a proper therapeutic treatment of the societal [and biological] deterioration' that four-and-a-half years of military conflict, followed by revolution and the breakdown of law and order, had supposedly caused.[85]

Ethnological views of revolutionaries as pathological 'criminals' and 'tyrants' had in fact already been popularised by the Italian physician Cesare Lombroso and his colleague Rodolfo Laschi in their late-nineteenth-century studies of key personalities from the Paris Commune of 1871 and other supposed moments of extreme psycho-political disturbance.[86] Robert Lansing, who served as US Secretary of State under Woodrow Wilson from 1915 onwards, described the Bolsheviks as 'a crew of murderers ... appealing to the criminal and the mentally unfit'.[87] Matthias Erzberger, progressive Catholic Centre Party politician and Reich Finance Minister from June 1919 to March 1920, labelled Bolshevism an 'Asiatic disease' in a statement to the Constituent National Assembly on 8 July.[88] And in August 1919 even Social Democrat Eduard

Bernstein referred to one-party Communist rule in Russia as a 'monstrous miscarriage' and an unnatural deviation from the progressive 'laws of [organic] development':

> Already now, Bolshevism's main strength is a militarism that recalls the former janissary economy in Turkey ... [Its] economic and social policy is a web of screaming contradictions: the most sweeping idealism alongside downright oriental despotism ... The bureaucratic apparatus is likewise growing beyond measure. Parasitism is rising, not falling; on the contrary, what is falling is production and with it the people's prosperity.[89]

Yet Hugo Marx was the first physician to advocate not just an ethnological-anthropological *interpretation*, but a material-biological *solution* to the 'problem' of revolutions. His colleagues Stelzner, Kahn and Kraepelin took up this call, but added their own take on how to identify and remove from society certain 'pathological types' who represented a danger to the nation's health. Kahn – whose article was based on an address to the annual conference of the Bavarian Association of Psychiatrists in Munich on 3 August 1919, felt it necessary to draw attention to the number of Jews he found among sixty-six Communist 'ringleaders' ('Radelsführer') charged with political offences after the fall of the Munich Councils Republic.[90] Basing his evidence on a more detailed examination of fifteen of these cases, he came up with a list of four 'pathological personalities' that were present in revolutionary situations, but were otherwise kept on the margins of society by the 'healthy' majority: 'ethically defective psychopaths', 'hysterical personalities', 'fanatical psychopaths' and 'manic depressives'.[91] He placed the twenty-three-year-old ex-sailor Rudolf Eglhofer, co-founder of the Bavarian KPD and 'Red Army' Commandant of Munich at the end of April 1919, in the first category, also labelling him an 'asocial psychopath ... of moderate intelligence' who had supposedly been 'shot while attempting to flee'.[92] In fact, Eglhofer was summarily executed by 'White' Government troops on 3 May 1919.

Of all the writers discussed here, however, Stelzner is perhaps the most interesting, albeit hitherto underrated, contributor to the medicalisation of interpretations of the 1918–19 Revolution. Not only did she endorse all of her Berlin colleague Hugo Marx's views, as well as those of Kahn and Kraepelin, but she showed a particular interest in the supposed psychopathology of female revolutionaries, including the eighteen-year-old Hilde Kramer, charged with high treason because of her role as Eglhofer's secretary during the military battles in and around Munich in the second half of April 1919. Like her male colleagues, Stelzner based her arguments not on clinical observations, but on court proceedings and associated newspaper reports. Among other things, she commented in a lecture delivered on 12 May 1919 to the Berliner Gesellschaft für Psychiatrie und Nervenkrankheiten (Berlin Society for Psychiatry and Nervous Diseases), later written up as an article for the *Zeitschrift für die gesamte Neurologie und Psychiatrie*, on the supposed 'manly appearance' of those women such as Kramer who were suspected of having participated in acts of 'Bolshevik' savagery:

> A certain Hilde K. took part in the Munich Uprising, hoping to sway others through the example of her actions. The daily press describes her as a two-metre-long man-woman [*Mannweib*] with short-cut hair. She was arrested with other women who were related to her. [At any moment in historical time], revolutionary movements may be directed by such sexually abnormal persons.[93]

Even so, she attributed the current situation less to a threat to heterosexual relations through the supposed growth of homosexuality during the war and the absence of 'healthy' men at the front, and more to a widespread 'erotic abandon' ('erotische Hemmungslosigkeit') on the part of young people of both sexes, combined with an unhealthy lust for 'enjoyment' and 'pleasure' rather than discipline, order and work. Left-wing agitators in the big cities had supposedly encouraged this as part of a broader, psychologically depraved plan to create chaos. So too had the female deputies elected to the Constituent National Assembly in January 1919; their 'dainty appearance' and 'masculinised exterior' in most cases suggested something opposite to the 'virginal' propriety of earlier women's movements.[94] Once again the masses were not to blame; they merely needed something or someone to guide them back to health.

> [In November–December 1918] the moment of general uncertainty had arrived, threatening honour, property and life ... and putting enjoyment [for its own sake] in their place ... The psychological stress and tension are vividly expressed in the dramatic images used

in street art and posters. On the one hand, the menacing Bolshevik gorilla appears, trampling on house and home in a giant boot, and on the other hand, under the new guarantees of freedom from censorship, you see particularly saucy, street-wise couples dancing the latest fashions.[95]

The proponents of the biological view of the German Revolution insisted that they were interested not in (party) politics but in issues of 'health' and psychological harmony only. However, in fact they had an even more important – albeit hitherto less well documented – impact on the Nazi interpretation of 1918–19 than the standard tropes about the army having been 'stabbed in the back' by traitors at home. Certainly biological interpretations of recent (and ancient) history helped to distinguish National Socialism as a political ideology from more conventional forms of conservative or militarist nationalism in the 1920s and beyond.[96] In particular, Nazi policies towards Communists, gay and bisexual men, early Jewish concentration camp inmates, 'habitual criminals', and the 'work-shy' in the period 1933–38 contained strong echoes of the myth that wartime 'shirking' had led to a 'reverse Darwinism' whereby, as in the case of the events leading to the fall of Ancient Rome, the 'fit', masculine elements in German society had been killed off in large numbers, and the 'weakest' elements saved themselves through selfish, egotistic means.[97] Germany under the Third Reich, it was now proudly proclaimed, would finally be 'cleansed' of all the 'sick' and 'degenerate' elements that had allegedly caused the 'criminal act' of November 1918.[98]

Even so, it would be wrong to assume that there was no push back against this racial-medicalised view of the Revolution in the early years of the Weimar Republic. Its ideological underpinnings were directly lampooned in the expressionist film *Nerven*, directed by Robert Reinert, which premiered in the *Kammerlichtspiele* in Munich in December 1919 and was in all likelihood a direct response to the ideas expressed by Kraepelin in the June 1919 edition of the *Süddeutsche Monatshafte*.[99] In Reinert's film, as Benjamin Ziemann has shown, it was the bourgeoisie – in the figure of the industrialist Roloff – who needed treatment for pathological nervousness. Roloff has his hysterical imperialist dreams of power and emotional claims to leadership put to test during the war; what he wants, and cannot get, is ownership of the future, which, since the Revolution, belongs to the mass of ordinary people 'mourning over bloody battlefields'.[100] The message – that it was the bourgeoisie that was the parasitical, volatile element in the German nation, not the November revolutionaries – was later taken up by propagandists for the East German regime in the 1950s and beyond.[101] But the notion that all the masses wanted was 'bread' and not 'power' also probably sat uneasily with the GDR's future rulers, who, like Lenin, saw centralised control by a vanguard party as one of the essential pillars of the new socialist order. And as we shall see in the next chapter, the message of Reinert's film also stood at odds with more general attempts after 1933 to create a unified anti-fascist left that would prioritise patriotic composure, political realism, and the coordinated military and ideological defeat of Nazism as necessary preconditions for the restructuring of socio-economic relations in Germany.

Notes

1 Fritz K. Ringer, *The Decline of the German Mandarins: The German Academic Community, 1890–1933* (Cambridge, MA, 1969), 82.
2 See Hans Schleier, *Die bürgerliche deutsche Geschichtsschreibung der Weimarer Republik* (East Berlin, 1975), esp. 45–68.
3 Christoph Cornelißen, 'Die Frontgeneration deutscher Historiker und der Erste Weltkrieg', in Jost Dülffer and Gerd Krumeich (eds), *Der verlorene Frieden: Politik und Kriegskultur nach 1918* (Essen, 2002), 311–37.
4 See also Boris Barth, 'Dolchstoßlegende und Novemberrevolution', in Gallus, *Die vergessene Revolution*, 117–39 (131).
5 Karl Demeter, *Das Reichsarchiv: Tatsachen und Personen* (Frankfurt am Main, 1969), 6–8.
6 See also Markus Pöhlmann, *Kriegsgeschichte und Geschichtspolitik: Der Erste Weltkrieg. Die amtliche deutsche Militärgeschichtsschreibung 1914–1956* (Paderborn, 2002).
7 Middendorf, *Macht der Ausnahme*, 281.
8 Demeter, *Das Reichsarchiv*, 14–15, 50.
9 Benjamin Ziemann, *Contested Commemorations: Republican War Veterans and Weimar Political Culture* (Cambridge, 2013), 227.
10 Demeter, *Das Reichsarchiv*, 30, 48 n. 18.
11 *Ibid.*, 6, 16.

12 Keith W. Bird, 'The Origins and Role of German Naval History in the Inter-War Period 1918–1939', *Naval War College Review*, 32.2 (1979), 42–58 (47). On the role of the Marinearchiv see also Christian Lübcke, '"Hat nichts mit Wahrheitsfindung zu tun": Der Kieler Matrosenaufstand von 1918 und die deutsche Militärgeschichtsschreibung', *Vierteljahrshefte für Zeitgeschichte*, 68.4 (2020): 505–33; and Daniel Horn, *The German Naval Mutinies of World War I* (New Brunswick, NJ, 1969), xi.
13 Demeter, *Das Reichsarchiv*, 14–16, 41.
14 Winfried Baumgart (ed.), *Von Brest-Litovsk zur deutschen Novemberrevolution: Aus den Tagebüchern, Briefen und Aufzeichnungen von Alfons Paquet, Wilhelm Groener und Albert Hopman. März bis November 1918* (Göttingen, 1971), 15.
15 Paul von Hindenburg, 'The Stab in the Back' (18 November 1919), reproduced in Anton Kaes, Martin Jay and Edward Dimendberg (eds), *The Weimar Republic Sourcebook* (Berkeley, CA, 1994), 15–16.
16 *Ibid.*, 15.
17 *Ibid.*, 16.
18 See also Barth, 'Dolchstoßlegende und Novemberrevolution', esp. 133.
19 See, for instance, Bundesarchiv Berlin, R 3001/6664, 50–2 (50), Reich Military Attorney-General Bernhard Knappmeyer to State Secretary in the Reich Ministry of Interior Theodor Lewald, 24 January 1919.
20 Benjamin Ziemann, 'Introduction', in Bernd Ulrich and Benjamin Ziemann (eds), *German Soldiers in the Great War: Letters and Eyewitness Accounts*, trans. Christine Brocks (Barnsley, 2010; German original, 1997), 1–19 (5).
21 Bird, 'The Origins', 45.
22 Kapitän zur See K. Boy-Ed, 'Revolution der Marine', *Weser-Zeitung*, exact date unknown [March 1919], copy, with English translation, in The National Archives, Kew, London (TNA), ADM 137/3849, 76–82 (82).
23 *Ibid.*, 77.
24 Thomas Hüetlin, *Berlin, 24. Juni 1922: Der Rathenaumord und der Beginn des rechten Terrors in Deutschland* (Cologne, 2022).
25 Robert Gerwarth, *November 1918: The German Revolution* (Oxford, 2020), 216.
26 Mosse, *Fallen Soldiers*, 169.
27 Gerhard Ritter, *Carl Goerdeler und die deutsche Widerstandsbewegung* (Stuttgart, 1955), 227, 396; Karl Demeter, *Das deutsche Offizierkorps in Gesellschaft und Staat 1650–1945* (Frankfurt am Main, 1962), 175.
28 Wolfgang Niess, *Die Revolution von 1918/19 in der deutschen Geschichtsschreibung: Deutungen von der Weimarer Republik bis ins 21. Jahrhundert* (Berlin, 2013), 109.

29 Horn, *The German Naval Mutinies*, x. On the 1925 Munich *Dolchstoß* trial, see also George S. Vascik and Mark R. Sadler, *The Stab-in-the-Back Myth and the Fall of the Weimar Republic: A History in Documents and Visual Sources* (London, 2016), esp. 159–76.
30 See Adolf von Trotha, 'Der Dolchstoß auf der Flotte'; and Magnus von Levetzow, 'Der letzte Akt', *Süddeutsche Monatshefte*, 21.7 (April 1924): 49–54 and 55–71 respectively.
31 Cited in Hedwig Richter, *Demokratie: Eine deutsche Affäre* (Munich, 2020), 211.
32 On Levetzow, see Stephan Malinowski, *Die Hohenzollern und die Nazis: Geschichte einer Kollaboration* (Berlin, 2021), 234, 262–3, 303–4; and Teresa Walch, 'With an Iron Broom: Cleansing Berlin's Bülowplatz of "Judeo-Bolshevism", 1933–1936', *German History*, 40.1 (2022), 61–87 (70).
33 Friedrich Meinecke, *The German Catastrophe: The Social and Historical Influences which Led to the Rise and Ruin of Hitler and Germany*, trans. Sidney B. Fay (Boston, MA, 1950; German original, 1946), 31.
34 Frank Biess, 'Men of Reconstruction – the Reconstruction of Men: Returning POWs in East and West Germany, 1945–1955', in Karen Hagemann and Stefanie Schüler-Springorum (eds), *Home/Front: The Military, War and Gender in Twentieth-Century Germany* (Oxford, 2002), 335–58 (346).
35 Ernst Nolte, *Die Weimarer Republik: Demokratie zwischen Lenin und Hitler* (Munich, 2006), 49–57.
36 *Was ist in Deutschland geschehen? Eine Übersicht über die Revolutions-Ereignisse*, undated SPD pamphlet [1919], 3–4, copy in Staatsarchiv Hamburg, 424-24/99: Wohlfahrtsamt Altona.
37 The report was published in 1929; see 'Soziale Heeresmißstände als Teilursache des deutschen Zusammenbruchs von 1918: Gutachten des Sachverständigen Dr. Martin Hobohm', in *Das Werk des Untersuchungsausschusses der Verfassunggebenden Deutschen Nationalversammlung und des Deutschen Reichstages 1919–1930: Verhandlungen, Gutachten, Urkunden*, Series 4, Der innere Zusammenbruch, Vol. II (Berlin, 1929). On Hobohm as one of the few permanent staff in the Reichsarchiv with 'undoubted republican credentials' see also Ziemann, *Contested Commemorations*, 225–34.
38 Richard Müller, *Die Novemberrevolution* (West Berlin, 1973 [1925]), esp. 16–17. On Müller see also Ralf Hoffrogge, *Working-Class Politics in the German Revolution: Richard Müller, the Revolutionary Shop Stewards and the Origins of the Council Movement* (Leiden, 2014).
39 Theodor Wolff, *Tagebücher 1914–1919: Der erste Weltkrieg und die Entstehung der Weimarer Republik in Tagebüchern, Leitartikeln und Briefen des Chefredakteurs am 'Berliner Tageblatt' und

Mitbegründers der 'Deutschen Demokratischen Partei', ed. Bernd Sösemann (Boppard am Rhein, 1984), Vol. II, 640.
40 Ralf Hoffrogge and Norman Laporte (eds), *Weimar Communism as Mass Movement, 1918–1933* (London, 2017), introduction, 1–24 (6).
41 Paul Frölich, *10 Jahre SPD*, ed. Kommunistische Partei Deutschlands (Berlin, 1924).
42 *Ibid.*, 45–7 (quote on 46).
43 Paul Frölich and Albert Schreiner, *Die deutsche Sozialdemokratie: Vierzehn Jahre im Bunde mit dem Kapital* (Berlin, 1928).
44 On Schreiner see Klaus Latzel, 'Geschichten der Novemberrevolution: Historiographie und Sinnbildung im geteilten Deutschland', in Maubach and Morina, *Das 20. Jahrhundert erzählen*, 87–141 (109–17). Also Mario Keßler, *Albert Schreiner: Kommunist mit Lebensbrüchen* (Berlin, 2014).
45 *Illustrierte Geschichte der Deutschen Revolution*, written by a collective of authors including Albert Schreiner (Berlin, 1928), 1.
46 *Ibid.*, 208.
47 *Ibid.*, 512.
48 See Norman LaPorte, 'The Rise of Ernst Thälmann and the Hamburg Left, 1921–1923', in Hoffrogge and LaPorte, *Weimar Communism*, 129–49 (131); and Mario Frank, *Walter Ulbricht: Eine deutsche Biografie* (Berlin, 2001), 59–77. On Koenen in particular see Ottokar Luban, 'The Role of the Spartacist Group after 9 November and the Formation of the KPD', in Hoffrogge and LaPorte, *Weimar Communism*, 45–65 (53).
49 Florian Wilde, 'Building a Mass Party: Ernst Meyer and the United Front Policy, 1921–1922', in Hoffrogge and LaPorte, *Weimar Communism*, 66–86 (67).
50 Gerhard Engel, 'The International Communists of Germany, 1916–1919', in Hoffrogge and LaPorte, *Weimar Communism*, 25–44 (40–1).
51 Petzold, *Parteinahme wofür?*, 82–3.
52 Luban, 'The Role of the Spartacist Group', 55–6.
53 Jörn Leonhard, *Der überforderte Frieden: Versailles und die Welt, 1918–1923* (Munich, 2018), 1224.
54 Kurt Tucholsky, 'Novemberumsturz' (1928), reproduced in Kurt Tucholsky, *Gesamtausgabe: Texte und Briefe. Vol. 10: Texte 1928* (Reinbek bei Hamburg, 2001), 496.
55 Karl Kautsky, *Terrorismus und Kommunismus: Ein Beitrag zur Naturgeschichte der Revolution* (Berlin, 1919).
56 Kautsky to Bernstein, 15 April 1921, in Eva Bettina Görz (ed.), *Eduard Bernsteins Briefwechsel mit Karl Kautsky (1912–1932)* (Frankfurt am Main and New York, 2011), 89–93 (91).

57 Karl Kautsky, 'Die Aussichten der Gegenrevolution in Deutschland', *Der Kampf*, 17 (1924), 1–10, cited in Görz, *Eduard Bernsteins Briefwechsel*, 107 n. 7.
58 Eduard Bernstein, *Die deutsche Revolution: Geschichte der Entstehung und ersten Arbeitsperiode der Deutschen Republik*, ed. and intro. Heinrich August Winkler (Bonn, 1998 [1921]), 107–10.
59 *Ibid.*, 115. Italics in the original.
60 *Ibid.*, 185, 207.
61 See Eduard Bernstein, *Wie eine Revolution zugrunde ging: Eine Schilderung und eine Nutzanwendung* (Stuttgart, 1921), 8.
62 Bernstein, *Die deutsche Revolution*, 236. Some of the English translations and analysis in the two paragraphs above are taken from Marius S. Ostrowski (ed.), *Eduard Bernstein on the German Revolution: Selected Historical Writings* (London, 2019), 1–28, 259.
63 *Protokoll über die Verhandlungen des Parteitags der Sozialdemokratischen Partei Deutschlands, abgehalten in Görlitz vom 18. bis 24. September 1921* (Berlin, 1921), at www.marxists.org/deutsch/geschichte/deutsch/spd/1921/goerlitz.htm (accessed 9 February 2022).
64 *Ibid.*
65 Ostrowski, *Eduard Bernstein*, 14–15.
66 Eduard Bernstein, 'Four Years On', *Breslauer Volkswacht*, 9 November 1922, reproduced in Ostrowski, *Eduard Bernstein*, 415–17 (416).
67 *Sozialdemokratischer Parteitag 1925 in Heidelberg: Protokoll mit dem Bericht der Frauenkonferenz* (Berlin, 1925), at www.marxists.org/deutsch/geschichte/deutsch/spd/1925/heidelberg.htm (accessed 9 February 2022). On the Görlitz and Heidelberg Programmes see also Stefan Berger, *Social Democracy and the Working Class in Nineteenth and Twentieth Century Germany* (Harlow, 2000), 117–18.
68 See Eric Bryden, 'Heroes and Martyrs of the Republic: Reichsbanner *Geschichtspolitik* in Weimar Germany', *Central European History*, 43.4 (2010), 639–65; and Peter Friedemann, 'Französische Revolution und deutsche sozialistische Arbeiterpresse 1918–1933', *Tel Aviver Jahrbuch für deutsche Geschichte*, 18 (1989), 233–48 (247).
69 Demeter, *Das Reichsarchiv*, 33–7.
70 On Bergsträsser see Elisabeth Fehrenbach, 'Ludwig Bergsträsser', in Hans-Ulrich Wehler (ed.), *Deutsche Historiker* (Göttingen, 1971–82), Vol. VII (1980), 101–17.
71 Veit Valentin, *Geschichte der deutschen Revolution von 1848–49*, 2 vols (Berlin, 1930–31). On Valentin see also Elisabeth Fehrenbach, 'Veit Valentin', in Wehler, *Deutsche Historiker*, Vol. I (1971), 69–85.

72 On the Reichsbanner see Ziemann, *Contested Commemorations*.
73 Matthew Stibbe, 'Coalition-Building and Political Fragmentation, 1924–1930', in Rossol and Ziemann, *The Oxford Handbook of the Weimar Republic*, 72–94 (85).
74 Görtz, *Eduard Bernsteins Briefwechsel*, 411 n. 2.
75 Veronika Helfert, *Frauen, wacht auf! Eine Frauen- und Geschlechtergeschichte von Revolution und Arbeiterräten in Österreich, 1916–1924* (Göttingen, 2021), 23.
76 See, for instance, the entries on Stelzner at www.deutsche-biographie.de/sfz126554.html and https://peoplepill.com/people/helenefriederike-stelzner (both accessed 9 February 2022).
77 Kurt Kolle, *Kraepelin und Freud: Beitrag zur neueren Geschichte der Psychiatrie* (Stuttgart, 1957).
78 Emil Kraepelin, 'Psychiatrische Randbemerkungen zur Zeitgeschichte', *Süddeutsche Monatshafte*, 16 (June 1919), 171–83. See also Eliza Ablovatski, *Revolution and Political Violence in Central Europe: The Deluge of 1919* (Cambridge, 2021), 213–16.
79 Hugo Marx, 'Aerztliche Gedanken zur Revolution', *Berliner klinische Wochenschrift: Organ für praktische Aerzte*, 12 (24 March 1919), 279–80 (279).
80 *Ibid.*, 280.
81 Even so, Kellogg and Taylor still pleaded for a lifting, or easing, of the economic blockade in February 1919, and put forward evidence that shortages in Germany had got worse since the armistice, with a complete 'breakdown of food distribution' possible by 1 May unless things changed. See Mary E. Cox, *Hunger in War and Peace: Women and Children in Germany, 1914–1924* (Oxford, 2019), 260–1.
82 Marx, 'Aerztliche Gedanken', 280.
83 Graf Kuno von Westarp, 'Die innere Politik der Woche', *Kreuzzeitung*, 10 November 1918, cited in Daniela Gasteiger, *Kuno von Westarp (1864–1945): Parlamentarismus, Monarchismus und Herrschaftsutopien im deutschen Konservatismus* (Berlin, 2018), 148.
84 Direktor Dr. Blaum (Strasbourg), *Die Übergangsfürsorge vom Krieg zum Frieden: Vorschläge* (Munich and Leipzig, 1917), 1, copy in Staatsarchiv Hamburg, 351-2 II, Allgemeine Armenanstalt, 146, Band 1.
85 Marx, 'Aerztliche Gedanken', 280.
86 Cesare Lombroso and Rodolfo Laschi, *Delitto politico e le rivoluzioni in rapporto al diritto, all'antropologia criminale ed alla scienza di governo* (Turin, 1890), translated into German as *Der politische Verbrecher und die Revolutionen* (Hamburg, 1891).

87 Cited in Alexandra Richie, *Faust's Metropolis: A History of Berlin* (London, 1998), 297.
88 Middendorf, *Macht der Ausnahme*, 59.
89 Eduard Bernstein, 'Lassalle and Bolshevism', *Vorwärts*, 31 August 1919, reproduced in Ostrowski, *Eduard Bernstein*, 381–4 (383–4).
90 Eugen Kahn, 'Psychopathen als revolutionäre Führer', *Zeitschrift für die gesamte Neurologie und Psychiatrie*, 49 (1919), 90–106 (92).
91 *Ibid.*, 92–3.
92 *Ibid.*, 94.
93 Helenefriderike Stelzner, 'Psychopathologisches in der Revolution', *Zeitschrift für die gesamte Neurologie und Psychiatrie*, 49 (1919), 393–408 (403).
94 *Ibid.*, 404.
95 *Ibid.*, 402.
96 On 'biological materialism' as a key component of Nazi ideology, albeit 'not the whole explanation' for the Holocaust, see Tim Mason, 'Open Questions on Nazism', in Raphael Samuel (ed.), *People's History and Socialist Theory* (London, 1981), 205–10 (208).
97 Ablovatski, *Revolution and Political Violence*, 213.
98 See, for instance, Julia Hörath, *'Asoziale' und 'Berufsverbrecher' in den Konzentrationslagern 1933 bis 1938* (Göttingen, 2017); Kim Wünschmann, *Before Auschwitz: Jewish Prisoners in the Pre-War Concentration Camps* (Cambridge, MA and London, 2015); and Götz Aly, Peter Chroust and Christian Pross, *Cleansing the Fatherland: Nazi Medicine and Racial Hygiene* (Baltimore, MD and London, 1994).
99 Kraepelin, 'Psychiatrische Randbemerkungen'.
100 Ziemann, 'The Missing Comedy'.
101 See, for instance, Paul Wandel, *Der deutsche Imperialismus und seine Kriege: Das nationale Unglück Deutschlands* (East Berlin, 1955).

2

Alternatives to fascism: The 1918–19 Revolution and efforts to construct a unified left, 1933–48

The fierce divisions on the German left, which were already manifest in 1918–19 and the early 1920s, and which reappeared with renewed force after 1928, were held by many after 1933 to have been one of the major factors in explaining Hitler's rise to power. The German Revolution featured in these divisions insofar as Thälmann's KPD became more and more dogmatic in its insistence that 1918–19 had been a 'failed bourgeois revolution' that was completely lacking in socialist content and had even fallen short of the democratising impulses of 1789 and 1848. Events such as the 'Blutmai', or 'Bloody May', in Berlin in 1928, when security police controlled by the SPD-led Prussian Government fought three days of violent battles against the KPD for control over the working-class districts of Neukölln and Wedding, seemed to confirm the Communists' view that they were already living in a proto-fascist state.[1] Meanwhile, the KPD also had to contend with the growing presence in these same working-class districts of the breakaway KPD-O, which manifestly took a different line on the 1918–19 Revolution. In a pamphlet published in 1930, the KPD-O boldly declared that the upheavals of November 1918 had been 'proletarian in origin', with real power briefly held by the working class through its representative organs, the soldiers' and workers' councils.[2] This message was one that appealed to ex-Spartacists opposed to the growing 'bureaucratisation' of the KPD under Thälmann, especially those with memories of what had actually happened in the streets of the German capital in the autumn and winter of 1918–19.

Both the KPD and the KPD-O dismissed the SPD leadership as out-and-out 'social fascists', although their strategies for appealing to the SPD rank-and-file were somewhat different.³ For its part, the SPD refused all offers of 'united fronts' against fascism coming from far-left groups. Only after 1933, and particularly after 1935, did a certain amount of rethinking take place. By the mid-1930s, not only had the Nazi regime consolidated its hold over Germany, but it had also completely smashed all left-wing opposition. If not in hiding or in concentration camps, German Communists, dissident Communists and Social Democrats found themselves in exile, with the KPD setting up its headquarters in Paris and the SPD in Prague. Movement towards a common position against fascism and in favour of a democratic-revolutionary transformation in Germany to complete the (supposedly) unfinished business from both 1848 and 1918 was slow, however, and subject to sudden, periodic reversals. If the Revolution's tenth anniversary, in 1928, had highlighted the splits on the left, the twentieth anniversary brought with it even less cause for celebration. On 9 November 1938 the Nazi regime launched its nationwide pogrom against the Jewish population, known subsequently as *Kristallnacht*, or the Night of Broken Glass. War in Europe, narrowly averted by the Munich Agreement of 30 September 1938, now seemed once again very much on the cards. Exiled German leftists in Prague made arrangements to leave the Czechoslovak capital as soon as possible, as a Nazi takeover of Bohemia and Moravia, in contravention of the Munich Agreement, seemed imminent.⁴ The mood was very dark, as indeed it was to remain for most of the next ten years.

 This chapter will focus on attempts to construct a united German left between 1933 and 1948, attempts that ultimately failed but nonetheless bequeathed an important legacy for the development of historiography on the German Revolution of 1918–19 lasting well into the Cold War era and beyond. It begins by exploring the work of dissident Communist historian Arthur Rosenberg in the mid-1930s and its impact among exiled German leftist communities in the West. It then moves on to explore debates during the Second World War about Germany as a 'country without revolution', before ending with sections on the memory of 1918 at the 'zero hour' in 1945, and again on the thirtieth anniversary of the Revolution in 1948.

Arthur Rosenberg's *History of the German Republic* (1935)

Arthur Rosenberg had an unusual life, both before and after the events of 1918–19. He was born into a middle-class Jewish family in Berlin in 1889, and at first seemed destined for an academic career as a classicist, studying at the Friedrich-Wilhelms-Universität (today's Humboldt University) and gaining a Ph.D. in Roman constitutional history in 1911. His conversion to left-wing politics seems to have come only at the end of the war. In 1918 he joined the USPD and in 1920 the KPD, situating himself firmly on the party's ultra-left.[5] In 1924 he became an elected Reichstag deputy for the KPD, but left the party in 1927 after disagreeing with its direction under Thälmann, and sat as an independent. Upon quitting parliament in 1928, he sought unsuccessfully to rebuild his academic career by taking on a number of teaching positions in ancient history. He also published his first work on contemporary history, *Entstehung der deutschen Republik 1871–1918* (*Birth of the German Republic, 1871–1918*).[6] In 1933 he was forced into exile, travelling first to Switzerland and then to Prague. By the time his most famous book, *Geschichte der deutschen Republik* (*History of the German Republic*) was published in the Czech town of Karlsbad (Karlovy Vary) with the support of the Sudeten German Social Democrats in 1935, he had already moved on to England.[7] He taught ancient and modern history at the University of Liverpool between 1934 and 1937, and then at Brooklyn College, New York, from 1937 until his death in 1943.[8]

Rosenberg's central argument was that the German Revolution of 1918–19 had been anti-war rather than socialist in character, and had led to the creation of a 'bourgeois-democratic state' in opposition to the military dictatorship created by Hindenburg and First Quartermaster General Erich Ludendorff in 1916, not to a dictatorship of the proletariat against the bourgeoisie.[9] The victors were the soldiers and workers; the peasants and the urban middle class; and Catholic voters in small towns and villages, the 'overwhelming majority' of whom wanted an end to the war and now stood behind the new Government of workers' and soldiers' councils. Meanwhile, the losers were neither the capitalists and higher civil servants, nor the old-fashioned trade unions and consumer organisations, nor the army supreme command, all of whom quickly came to terms with the Revolution. Rather, the losers were the old East Elbian nobility, whose powers were swept away when the new Government replaced the three-class franchise in Prussia with universal suffrage, and the ruling houses in each of the federal states, who 'already in October 1918 found themselves in as powerless a position as [Kaiser] Wilhelm II'. In this sense, 'the November Revolution swept away the dynastic houses but otherwise did not fundamentally change the structure of the German State'.[10]

The Spartacist leaders Luxemburg and Liebknecht, he suggested, had had 'no illusions' on this score and were quite clear that the German proletariat was not ready for a socialist revolution in 1918–19.[11] Yet he also rejected the KPD notion that Germany's new rulers in 1918 had *failed* at bourgeois revolution. Rather, the SPD leaders had already ensured the *success* of the bourgeois revolution when they oversaw and participated in the formation of a parliamentary government in October 1918, and when they co-opted the USPD into this mix in November. The Revolution that Germans got in late 1918 was the revolution that they wanted, a bourgeois-democratic one, and paradoxically, it was the revolution that they already had achieved, even before 9 November. What had gone wrong was an exaggerated fear of Bolshevism among the leaders of the SPD and the right wing of the USPD after 9 November, causing them to refuse to arm the people against the danger of a counterrevolution from the right. The violence of winter 1918–19 had destroyed the solid bourgeois foundations laid in October–November 1918, and had provided the Bolsheviks on the left and the Freikorps on the right with a significant support base that they otherwise would not have had. Most Spartacists, he noted, had supported the call for parliamentary elections – at least until the Council of People's Deputies, using the dictatorial powers that it had assumed on 9 November, had turned against them and their allies in the Volksmarinedivision (People's Naval Division) on 24–25 December.

> By giving the sailors an easy victory, the Government made itself look completely helpless. Any chancer now believed he could risk taking a shot at the Government. The vote of confidence in the Council of People's Deputies passed by the General Congress of Workers' and Soldiers' Councils impressed nobody, because it was not backed up by any armed force ... By the end of December the two wings of

German Social Democracy were already heading towards fragmentation as the *Noskepolitik* [the hard-line anti-Communist policies named after Reichswehr Minister Gustav Noske] came into effect.[12]

Rosenberg's 1935 book is interesting because it foreshadows much of the historiography that was to emerge on the western left in the 1960s, such as the American former naval lieutenant Richard M. Watt's 1969 book *The Kings Depart*, whose premise was almost exactly the same.[13] It was also the first work on the German Revolution to bridge two worlds: the largely inward-looking world of German leftist sectarian politics and the largely anglophone world of international liberal-progressive scholarship outside Germany, a world that nonetheless embraced refugee historians from central Europe – both older ones such as Rosenberg and younger ones such as Francis L. Carsten and Raimund Pretzel (a.k.a. Sebastian Haffner).[14] *A History of the German Republic* appeared in English translation as early as 1936, and was read as widely in London and New York as it had been in Prague. It was a major contribution to anti-fascism not because it was *pro*-Communist (if anything, Rosenberg now sympathised with the left wing of the SPD)[15] but because it was anti-*anti*-Communist. Its main theme was that the supposed Communist threat had been exaggerated, to the detriment of building a broader movement for social and economic change 'in the spirit of 1848', and in particular in the spirit of Marx and Engels, who, as revolutionary democrats and political realists, had 'always regarded State and society as a single entity'.[16] Rosenberg had already made this point in a speech to the Reichstag in July 1927, shortly after he had left the KPD. Here he openly mocked the 'revolutionary romanticism' of the Thälmann leadership:

> On the basis of my knowledge of the Communist Party I can emphasize with all stress: there is no responsible communist who thinks in any way of deeds of violence or actions against the law, even in the slightest way. What remains is only a certain romantic phraseology which does not constitute the slightest real threat to the existing political order ... Through this romanticism millions of workers are prevented from pursuing their interests in a realistic and factual way.[17]

In the 1930s, however, with the rise and then consolidation of the Nazi regime, debates about the German Revolution were becoming not only less sectarian and more scholarly, but also more transnational. Rosenberg's book was at the forefront of this. Among exiled Social Democrats it was judged to be the best explanation of why the Revolution had failed to prevent the rise of fascism in Germany.[18] This positive reception continued into the postwar period, with a pamphlet produced by the SPD's executive committee (*Parteivorstand*) in Bonn in 1962 describing Rosenberg as 'one of the most level-headed and knowledgeable historians of the Weimar Republic'.[19]

Writing in the mid-1950s, the conservative (West) German scholar Karl Dietrich Erdmann also acknowledged the pioneering role of Rosenberg's work and its importance in stimulating new, more extensive academic research in the émigré German- and English-speaking realms after 1935. While disagreeing profoundly with its conclusions, he nonetheless remarked that the book's publication had marked the beginning of 'serious scholarly research on German history in the years 1918 to 1933'.[20] In particular he praised Rosenberg's careful use of the unpublished protocols of the meetings of the Council of People's Deputies: 'This alone makes his work indispensable for the study of the period between the November Revolution and the gathering of the National Assembly [in Weimar].'[21] And twenty-five years later, in 1980, Erdmann's former student Hagen Schulze continued to recognise Rosenberg as one of the outstanding left-wing 'émigré German scholars' who had made a conscious effort to produce 'less partisan forms of analysis', admittedly 'without being able to resist entirely the temptation to go for over-simplistic formulations'. In so doing, he had placed the 'missing [social] revolution' of 1918–19 at the centre of post-1945 research on the failure of the Weimar Republic.[22]

Germany as a 'country without revolution'

While Rosenberg's book reached English-language as well as German-language academic audiences, interwar transnational debates about 1918–19 were also heavily influenced in a more immediate sense by the worsening international situation after 1936, and by the evident failure of the German people to develop any form of mass resistance to the Hitler regime. Anti-German feeling also became stronger in the West after the outbreak of war in

September 1939 (and in the Soviet Union after the Nazis reneged on their non-aggression pact with Stalin in June 1941). Critical views of the 'failure' of the Revolution to lay the foundations for a stable, fascist-proof democratic or socialist political system in Germany now became mixed up with claims, often made by wartime Allied propagandists, that the Germans were simply a 'non-revolutionary people', as the novelist Thomas Mann, then still in his conservative-romantic phase, had claimed in his essay *Betrachtungen eines Unpolitischen* (*Confessions of a Non-Political Man*), written between 1915 and 1918.[23] The notion of a positive *Sonderweg*, or special path, in German history, developed by nineteenth-century nationalist German historians such as Heinrich von Treitschke and continued by artistic thinkers such as Mann into the early years of the twentieth century, was revived in the 1930s and 1940s outside Germany, but with its meaning up-ended to give it a negative, anti-German connotation. The special path was now associated with the traits of militarism, authoritarianism, racial intolerance and anti-Enlightenment thinking, problems that the Revolution of 1918–19 had not been able to overcome.[24]

A prominent example of this was Lord Robert Vansittart's 1941 pamphlet *Black Record: Germans Past and Present*, based on seven radio broadcasts that Vansittart, a retired senior British diplomat, had made in 1940 for the BBC's overseas programme. Vansittart assured his listeners and readers that 'tortures are practised in modern Germany on a scale that puts the Middle Ages into the shade'.[25] The barbaric German 'soul', although not absolutely *unchangeable*, constituted an ongoing menace to the world because the German people themselves had 'not yet really tried' to find a 'cure' for their 'national egotism'.[26] In this sense 1918–19 was no different from other lost opportunities:

> After the Napoleonic wars there was a moment [in the 1830s and 1840s] when it seemed that Prussia might lead Germany into liberalism. But the flicker went out, and the new movement had about as much chance as the Weimar Republic after the last war. Germany as a whole has always been hostile and unsuited to democracy. Hitler had this old instinct to play on.[27]

Many German anti-fascist exiles agreed with this diagnosis, or at least felt reluctant to oppose it whilst the war was still on. The

BBC's (and Lord Vansittart's) voice was a powerful one, and for several months after the French surrender in June 1940, Britain and its empire stood alone in the fight against National Socialism. Even so, some exiled German leftists still felt that it was important to defend the humanitarian core of the German soul, which, they argued, had only been placed in temporary abeyance by the Hitler regime. In Britain, their efforts were led by the Free German League of Culture, founded in London in 1939 and revived after 1941.[28] Others developed what might be described, only partially with tongue in cheek, as 'revolution envy', questioning whether Germans were the only advanced nation which had problems with enacting lasting, world-changing social revolutions.[29] One example of this was the curious controversy that developed between the German Marxist economic historian Jürgen Kuczynski, then living in exile with his family in London, and the Oxford-based British Communist scholar Christopher Hill over the class character of the English Revolution of the mid-seventeenth century. In a pamphlet published in 1940, as the Battle of Britain raged, Hill presented a short Marxist overview of the English Revolution to mark the 300th anniversary of 1640, and, as R. C. Richardson notes, to act as his 'political testament should he die in the Second World War'.[30] The English Parliament, he argued, by waging 'class warfare' against the 'despotism of Charles I' and the established Church, had brought together a 'great social movement like the French Revolution of 1789'. In the midst of this, 'the state power protecting an old order was violently overthrown, power passed into the hands of a new class, and so the freer development of capitalism was made possible'.[31] Even the return of Charles I's son as Charles II in 1660, he suggested, was 'by no means a restoration of the old régime'. This was because the 'prerogative courts were not restored' and 'the King had no power of taxation independent of Parliament'.[32] Furthermore, 'the returned Royalists had perforce to adapt themselves to the new free market conditions, i.e. to turn themselves into *capitalist* farmers or lessors of their estates, or they went under in the competitive struggle'.[33]

Yet Hill's boldest claim was that the English Revolution had even anticipated an era *beyond* capitalism. True, there was no organised working-class movement in mid-seventeenth-century England, and thus no proletarian revolution. The demands of the Levellers 'were those of the petty bourgeoisie, a class always unstable and difficult to organise because of its dependence, economic and ideological, on the big bourgeoisie', the so-called 'Grandees'.[34] However, apart from the Levellers there were smaller, more radical groups such as the 'True Levellers' or Diggers, led by Gerrard Winstanley, who built a colony on common lands in Surrey in 1649–50. The Diggers had openly championed 'the interests of the propertyless', proclaiming 'The poorest man hath as true a title to the land as the richest man.' The year 1940 – the year in which Britain's war against Hitler became an anti-fascist 'people's war' – was, in Hill's view, already 'glimpsed' in Winstanley's prophetic words from the time of the English Revolution: 'Wherever there is a people united by common community of livelihood into oneness it will be the strongest land in the world, for they will be as one man to defend their inheritance.'[35] It was these claims that Kuczynski, then a hard-line Stalinist and one of the few German Communists in Britain who had managed to avoid internment as an enemy alien during the mass round-up of Jewish and left-wing refugees from central Europe in May–June 1940 (in fact he had been interned earlier, in January 1940, but was released in April, just before the increase in anti-alien restrictions), set out to challenge.

Kucyznski, born into a 'bourgeois progressive' Jewish family in Berlin in 1904, was only fourteen when the November 1918 Revolution broke out, but his father, the radical statistician Robert René Kuczynski, had important contacts with leading political figures of the day. A variety of public figures, ranging from Karl Liebknecht to Walther Rathenau, were guests in the Kuczynski household.[36] Kuczynski followed an academic career in the 1920s, including an extended stay in the USA, but returned to Germany and joined the KPD in 1930. The party ordered him to London in 1936, where he became its leading representative, but he also made enemies among other German leftist exiles in the British capital, particularly those arriving from Prague in 1938–39.[37] His view of the German Revolution of 1918–19 was actually very close to the orthodox Stalinist position (a 'compromised', or in other words incomplete, 'bourgeois revolution', as it was described in the official *History of the Communist Party of the Soviet Union (Bolsheviks): Short Course*, first published in 1938 – with the SPD and right wing of the USPD cast as 'compromisers of the type of the Russian Mensheviks' who turned the workers' councils into an 'obedient tool of the bourgeois parliament').[38] However, in 1940–41, a time of intense in-fighting among German Communists in London over issues such as how, if at all, to defend the Nazi–Soviet Pact, it was easier for Kuczynski to argue this case by proxy, in other words by taking the English Revolution of 1640–60 as a parallel example of a 'failed bourgeois revolution'.

Under the pseudonym P. F. (Peter Forster), Kuczynski wrote a stark critique of Hill's book for the October 1940 issue of *Labour Monthly*, the chief theoretical organ of the Communist Party of Great Britain (CPGB), whose editorial board he belonged to.[39] He used a pseudonym partly because, as leader of the KPD in London, he had been ordered not to involve himself in internal debates in other national Communist parties, and in particular in the party of the host country, Britain. As 'Peter Forster' he nonetheless sparked a furious debate that went on for several months in *Labour Monthly* and drew in many other figures from the future CPGB's historians' group, including Dona Torr, Maurice Dobb and Douglas Garman. Eventually, this led to the intervention of the then party general secretary, Ranjani Palme Dutt, followed by a statement issued by the editorial board of *Labour Monthly* in March 1941 'regret[ting] the publication of the review ... which advanced several incorrect propositions [and] challenged several fundamental Marxist ideas on the subject of the State'.[40] The CPGB leadership, in other words, decided in favour of Hill but also tried to shut the debate down. Neither Hill nor Kuczynski would let the matter go, however, and when the two Marxist scholars met again in person in 1971 in Oxford, where Hill was now Master of Balliol College, they both enquired – using almost identical language – whether the other still 'stood by the false position' he had adopted in 1940.[41]

Essentially Kuczynski challenged Hill's claims that 1640 had witnessed a revolution in England of world-historical importance on a par with 1789 in France. First he suggested that the bourgeoisie had a great deal of economic power in England from the Tudor period onwards, with the 'capitalist spirit' already 'victorious' there well before the 1640s. And second – with even greater significance for parallel interpretations of the German Revolution – he suggested that the English Parliament and its 'Grandee' allies had failed to eradicate harmful vestiges of feudalism that continued to exist in England even after they had beaten the Royalist armies and executed the King in 1648–49. In short, they failed to revolutionise and democratise England, and in so doing opened the door to the gradual return of political reaction, first in the shape of Oliver Cromwell, suppressor of the Levellers and representative of the independent landed gentry, and then in the guise of Charles II, king by divine right of England, Scotland and Ireland.[42] In a rejoinder to a critique of his critique, written by Garman for the December 1940 edition of *Labour Monthly*, Kuczynski made clear the contemporary class relevance of his 'dispute' with Hill's book:

> The lesson to be drawn from [1640] is: even if a system is decayed, it is by no means already dead and harmless. Stalin would have advised the revolutionary leaders of 1640: Beware of the feudal elements in bourgeois society! [A]nd he would have given this advice not in 1640 but considerably earlier.[43]

Kuczynski's broader point was that the German people in the early twentieth century, just like the English people in the mid-seventeenth century, were not to be castigated for their supposed 'non-revolutionary' character. They did not have a 'reactionary' soul and were not 'unsuited to democracy'. Rather, the revolutions they had begun, in pursuit of justice and freedom, had been thwarted first by their 'compromiser' leaders who talked revolution but (unlike Lenin and Stalin) failed to follow through, and second by their class enemies: the 'reactionary sections of the bourgeoisie' who allied themselves with absolute monarchy and the established Church in mid-seventeenth-century England, and the aristocrats, armaments manufacturers and big capitalists who joined forces with fascists and antisemites in Weimar and Nazi Germany.[44] The German people and their English counterparts did not need utopian thinkers such as Winstanley, or free revolutionary spirits such as Rosa Luxemburg. Instead, they needed an organised, disciplined, Leninist party.

However, Kuczynski was a minority voice in the exile community, even in the KPD in London at this time, which in May 1941 removed him as *Pol.-Leiter* (political leader) following his dispute with Hill and his advocacy of Communist support for a revolutionary strike wave in British industries. Indeed, the idea of organising strikes against the Churchill–Attlee Government was in direct opposition to the gradual shift in Communist exile circles towards backing the 'anti-defeatist', 'people's war' line. Only Hitler's overthrow could save the revolution. The new, post-Kuczynski KPD leadership in London in fact went further than speaking out in favour of a 'people's war'. It actively embraced the alliance between the Soviet Union and the West after June 1941, welcomed Britain's repudiation of the Munich Agreement in August 1942, took courage from the Soviet victory at the Battle of Stalingrad in January–February 1943, and supported the resolutions of the 'Big Three' (Churchill, Roosevelt, Stalin) at Tehran on 1 December 1943 concerning border changes in eastern Europe at Germany's expense and the formation of a new international organisation (the future United Nations) to replace the 'failed' League of Nations of the interwar years.[45] By now there was even some surprising support among exiled Communists for the late Eduard Bernstein's view of the English Revolution, as set out in his *Cromwell and Communism*, originally published in 1895 and reappearing in an English translation in 1930, some two years before his death.[46] Bernstein of course recognised the historical and material limitations of an abstract idea of social democracy that had emerged in a preindustrial era in which the productivity gains and class interests to be reaped from fully developed capitalism were yet to be realised. Nonetheless, using as an example the late-seventeenth-century writings of the post-Restoration English social activist and Quaker John Bellers, he argued that the English Revolution of 1640, like the French Revolution of 1789 and perhaps even the German Revolution of 1918–19, had made it

> possible to launch a sharper criticism of society and its tendencies, [to offer] not only a moral condemnation of the inequalities pervading society, but also a denunciation of the economic powers that were in the ascendancy and of society's own inability to direct its productive forces in the interests of the whole.[47]

Significantly, then, the writings of the 'revisionist' Marxist Bernstein on seventeenth-century England seemed – at least from a post-Stalingrad perspective – to allow history to follow a path of continuously unfolding, materially based reason, leading societies to come ever closer together, social conflicts to be straightened out and (democratic) nations to be united in common interest. At the international level multilateralism should prevail – as seen at Tehran.

This appeared not only as politically desirable to various shades of émigré socialist opinion in 1943 and the first half of 1944, but also as a historical necessity. It was, in short, the only logical outcome of developments in the world since 1917–18, and in particular of the 'greater influence which the [global] struggle [against fascism] had given to the working classes'.[48]

Even so, and particularly after the failed assassination attempt against Hitler in July 1944 (the 'Stauffenberg plot'), more and more voices on the exiled German left – those in the Soviet Union as well as those in London and the USA – also began to ask why the workers in the Third Reich were not rising up to end the murderous Nazi regime.[49] Perhaps Vansittart had been right when he claimed that it would take 'at least a generation' before the Germans were ready to enter the ranks of the civilised nations.[50] A revolution at the end of this war, as at the end of the last war, even if it were to come, might not be enough to redeem the German people, and particularly the German working class, from the charge of having collaborated with National Socialism. Rather, in all likelihood Germany would have to face years of foreign military occupation, coupled with territorial losses and reparations bills that would completely surpass the more punitive clauses of the Treaty of Versailles. With the fighting in Europe slowly coming to an end, and with much of Germany's basic infrastructure destroyed by the never-ending demands of the Nazi war economy and the relentless Allied bombing campaigns, few German leftists were expecting – let alone hoping for – a rerun of November 1918. Instead the mood was summed up by Albert Schreiner in a book review published in *The German American* on 1 September 1944. Here the one-time War Minister in revolutionary Stuttgart in early November 1918 turned Communist dissident and anti-Nazi exile in France and the USA confessed that he could see no hope of any immediate improvement:

> We ... are almost choking to death on Germany's present shame. It is as if history, before making a grand turn for the better, has decided to combine together all the misery of the German past and all of human madness to create the greatest scar on humanity, embodied in Hitler and his system.[51]

This *Katastrophenstimmung*, or sense of dire gloom, was in fact present across the German left in the final months of the Third

Reich and in the period immediately following its collapse. As late as December 1947, the Bavarian Social Democrat Max Drechsel could still warn in an editorial for the *Mittelbayerische Zeitung* that 'we have yet to secure democracy as a fixed part of our national life' and, worse still, that 'the prospects of winning over our politically uneducated people to democracy are hardly favourable'.[52] Only very briefly, in summer 1945, were hopes revived of a new-found democratic unity on the left; but these hopes were soon crushed by the emergence of the Cold War and fresh divisions between East and West.

1945: Zero hour and the opportunity for a new start

German exiles in 1945 had often not seen Germany for many years. Many were Jewish and had lost relatives in the Holocaust; others, particularly those from Communist backgrounds, had family members who had been incarcerated, and perhaps had died, in the vast Nazi concentration camp system. 'The governing spirit of these returning exiles', writes Martin Conway, 'as well as many of those who had lived through the events of the war years within [continental] Europe, was one of disabused sobriety. They did not want to return to the past but [wanted to] escape it.'[53] Many also now lived in countries with a very negative view of German history – what Kuczynski called the 'Ehrenburg-Vansittart' line in reference not only to the British author of *Black Record*, but also to the Soviet poet and propagandist Ilya Ehrenburg, who had called on Red Army soldiers to regard Germans as 'non-human'.[54] In 1945, the latest addition to this international genre was the British historian A. J. P. Taylor's *The Course of German History*, which argued that Germany's chances of developing into a liberal democracy by means of revolution had effectively died in 1848, the point at which 'German history failed to turn'.[55] The 'November Revolution' in 1918, he went on, had 'ended in defeat ... in February 1919, as soon as the Constituent National Assembly came together in Weimar.

> The Weimar [National] Assembly was a repetition, almost a parody, of the Frankfurt Parliament of 1848 ... In 1848 the liberals still hoped for success and believed in their own system; in 1919 even the men of Weimar despaired of their own ideals. In 1848, with the crumbling of

the dynasties [of central Europe], the liberal intellectuals represented all the energies of the middle class; in 1919 the great capitalist middle class was tarred with the 'national' disaster [of defeat in war], and the intellectuals, impotent and ignored for forty years, were alien to and repudiated by it. By a strange but inevitable paradox, the Weimar Constitution was the work of the smallest of the parties in the Assembly. The Democrats [DDP]; a party without force and almost without backing, but possessing to the full the 'spirit of 1848' ... They were protected from radicalism by the Free Corps, the members of which would have liked nothing better than to massacre these liberal idealists.[56]

In fact, Taylor was wrong in his characterisation of the DDP; in the January 1919 elections it had won 18.5 per cent of the vote nationally, making it the third largest party in the Constituent National Assembly, just behind the Catholic Centre Party on 19.7 per cent and well ahead of the USPD and smaller centre-right and right-wing parties.[57] Nor were its leaders 'idealists'; many were hard-nosed realists, such as the jurist Hugo Preuß – author of the 10 February 1919 Law on the Provisional Authority of the Reich and, subsequently, of the Weimar Constitution – and the future Foreign Minister Rathenau, who negotiated the Treaty of Rapallo with the Soviet Union before his assassination in June 1922. Taylor's views nonetheless typified a certain strain of anti-German feeling in Britain in the late 1940s, shared also by many leading figures in the Labour Government of that time, including Chancellor of the Exchequer Hugh Dalton and Foreign Secretary Ernest Bevin.[58]

The end of the Nazi regime in May 1945 and the liberation of the last concentration camps nonetheless allowed some German leftists to start hoping again for a better future. The KPD, re-established in the Soviet zone of Germany in June 1945 and led by former Moscow exiles such as Walter Ulbricht and Wilhelm Pieck, officially distanced itself from darker readings of German history, doubtless helped by Stalin's decision to order his ideology chief, Georgy Alexsandrov, to publish a critique of Ehrenburg in the official party newspaper, *Pravda*, on 14 April 1945, just as the war was coming to an end.[59] In its first proclamation since the collapse of the Third Reich, circulated in Berlin on 11 June 1945, the Central Committee of the KPD made no mention of socialism, but declared:

With the destruction of Hitlerism, it is also important to complete the democratization of Germany, that bourgeois-democratic transition that began in 1848, to completely remove the last vestiges of feudalism and of reactionary, old-Prussian militarism, with all its economic and political offshoots.[60]

Although the explicit reference here was to 1848, the (negative) experience of November 1918 was also implied as a point of comparison. Just as Kuczynski had criticised the English revolutionaries of the mid-seventeenth century for failing to do away with the 'last vestiges of feudalism' when they had the chance in 1640, so the leaders of the SPD and USPD were being charged with the same omissions in the immediate aftermath of the First World War:

> Today, at the end of the 'Third Reich', after all the suffering and misfortune, all the shame and disgrace, after the darkest era in German history, the Social Democratic German worker will agree with us that the fascist plague was only able to spread through Germany because in 1918 those who were responsible (for the war), and those who had committed war crimes, went unpunished, because the struggle for a genuine democracy was not waged, because the Weimar Republic gave free rein to reactionary forces, because the anti-Soviet agitation of a few democratic leaders paved the way for Hitler, and because the rejection of a unified anti-fascist front paralyzed the people.[61]

A very similar position was now also taken by three German Communists living in exile in the United States – Gerhart Eisler, Albert Norden and Albert Schreiner – in a book published in English in 1945. On 9 November 1918, they argued, the German republic – the republic established by the peace- and freedom-loving German people, including 'workers, peasants, and urban middle classes' – looked for leadership from the social democratic left. Its two main parties, the SPD and USPD, were faced with momentous decisions:

> The German republic would either triumph over the reactionary elements – or become their victim. It would either undermine the economic basis of the reactionaries – or lose all power itself. It would either resolutely sweep away the supporters of Pan-Germanism, the big industrialists, the bankers, and the Junker landlords – or be swept away by them. It would either destroy Prussian militarism – or eventually be itself destroyed. Only in the struggle against the reactionaries could the republic exist, develop, and triumph.[62]

What happened in 1918–19, they continued, must not be allowed to happen again. From December 1918:

> The new rulers of the young republic allowed the discredited Pan-German imperialists to crawl out of their holes, form legal political parties, and, thanks to wealthy backers, monopolize the press. They made an alliance with the munitions-makers at a moment when the German people were ready to take the sharpest action against them.[63]

In 1945, however, the socialist parties would not let the people down. They would help them to root out the true enemy by cleansing the nation of 'every reactionary institution, tradition and individual'.[64] And they would do this in the knowledge that Vansittart, Taylor and others were wrong to castigate the German people for the historical crimes of omission and commission undertaken in their name: 'There is no law of hereditary sin in the evolution of nations and classes. Sins which human beings have committed can be atoned for by human beings, once they uncover the sources of these sins and root out the unholy sinners and their institutions.'[65] The SPD, in its first postwar proclamation, issued in Berlin on 15 June 1945, interestingly did not make any reference to 1848 or 1918, although it did put forward an action programme that went further than the KPD when it came to enacting socialist measures, including 'nationalization of banks, insurance companies, and natural resources; nationalization of mines and the power industry [and] seizure of large-scale landholdings, viable large-scale industry, and all war profits for the purposes of reconstruction'.[66] Tensions between Social Democrats and Communists in 1945–46 were in fact not policy-related; rather, they reflected the growing suspicion of the former regarding the Stalinist methods used by the latter to achieve 'organizational unity' of the working class. Whereas in summer 1945 the SPD had been keener than the KPD on the idea of a unification of both parties, by the beginning of 1946 the tables had turned. What many SPD members saw as a 'forced' merger of the two parties to create the SED was implemented in April 1946, but only in the Soviet zone of Germany and the Soviet sector of Berlin. Here, as the SPD noted with increasing concern, the SED's programme of 'destroy[ing] the remnants of Hitler fascism and liquidat[ing] militarism and imperialism' was targeted not just at 'reactionary' elements.[67] Rather, Social Democrats, members of centre-right parties, and former supporters of dissident left groups such as the KPD-O and SAPD who had joined the SED in 1946 were also increasingly caught up in the new wave of Stalinist terror.[68]

These developments also made the SPD suspicious of claims made by Alexander Abusch, a leading figure in the SED responsible for cultural policy in the Soviet zone, that the newly merged party was still committed to the principle that each country should follow its own path to socialism, determined by the 'peculiarities of its national development', rather than having to following the path set out by the Soviet Union.[69] Abusch, born into a Jewish family in Krákow, Poland, in 1902, and a member of the KPD since 1918, had spent the Nazi period in exile, first in France and then in Mexico. In early 1946 he published what was to become one of the most important early postwar books on German history, *Der Irrweg einer Nation* (*A Nation on the Wrong Track*). Abusch wrote passionately about the cultural achievements of the German people – expressed in the humanist legacy of Herder, Goethe and Alexander von Humboldt – but also suggested that they owed it not only to the world, but also to themselves, to reset their politics.

> A long-lasting occupation by the armies of the United Nations will give the German nation a unique opportunity to renew itself from top to bottom. It will mean taking the most urgent lessons from its history and transforming them into new ways of behaving and completing the revolutions of 1848 and 1918 in one go. The redistribution of landed estates among the smaller peasants and the full dismantling of imperialist monopoly capitalism are historic necessities that will allow the completion of a democratic revolution, even without barricades. By means of extensive surgery on Germany's former structures, the face of the nation can be changed.[70]

The SPD, however, did not accept the need for a long military occupation, believing that it would allow the abuse of Soviet power in particular. Under its first postwar leader, Kurt Schumacher, it was less critical, although not altogether accepting either, of the presence of the western Allies.[71] 'Today in Germany', Schumacher told the party's first postwar congress in Hanover in the British zone in May 1946, 'democracy is no stronger than the Social Democratic Party. All of the others needed the war potential and supremacy of the Anglo-Saxon powers for their hearts to discover democracy. We did not need them for that. We would be democrats if the English and Americans had been fascists.'[72] As for the KPD, he already noted in summer 1945 that it was 'the only party in Germany which confesses the guilt of the whole German people for Nazism and thus for the war'. This was a 'reactionary formula' and a 'naïve propaganda of contrition' designed to serve the Soviet Union's agenda on reparations: 'We want to deliver reparations ... but we do not want to commit suicide ... One cannot excuse the injustice of today by pointing to past injustice ... The Nazi policy of plunder must not be a model for the policy of the United Nations.'[73] Already by 1945–46, then, significant cracks were beginning to appear in the optimistic belief in working-class unity that had been evident in some émigré anti-Nazi circles after 1942. Even so, complete rupture did not become inevitable until 1948.

1948: Which revolution to celebrate, and where?

The year 1948 is significant for our study for two main reasons. First, it marked the real beginning of the Cold War in Europe. In February, the Czechoslovak Communists seized power in Prague, casting aside the previous multi-party Government that they had led since 1945, and in March the (non-Communist) Czechoslovak Foreign Minister Jan Masaryk died in what appeared to be a suicide attempt but was seen in the West as an act of foul play. In June, Stalin launched an eleven-month blockade of the western sectors of Berlin in response to the West's introduction of a new currency in those parts of Germany that they controlled. And finally, in September 1948, the SED formed a new city Government in East Berlin to rival the office of the governing mayor for the whole city, Ernst Reuter of the SPD. The latter, who was re-elected by 64.5 per cent of voters in West Berlin in November 1948, was forced to take up new headquarters in the Rathaus Schöneberg in the American sector.[74]

Second, 1948 also happened to be the thirtieth anniversary of the 1918 Revolution and the centenary year of the 1848 Revolution, both events being marked in a Germany now effectively divided between East and West, or pro-Soviet and pro-American spheres. On 9 September 1948 Reuter addressed a large crowd of anti-Communist Berliners in front of the burned-out building of the

Reichstag, in the British sector, and declared them to be a sovereign people in the spirit of 1848 and 1918:

> When today hundreds of thousands of representatives of the people of Berlin have risen up, then we can be assured that the entire world can see this Berlin. No longer can its fate be determined by negotiations between generals or by bargains struck by cabinets. Behind what is happening stands the will of free nations who have recognised that here, in this city, a bulwark, an outpost of freedom has been established, which nobody can abandon with impunity.[75]

The thirtieth anniversary of the November Revolution should have been a happier time for German leftists than the twentieth, in 1938. Then, Europe had stood on the brink of world war. Now it had been liberated from fascism, and Hitler and Mussolini were both dead. However, in an atmosphere dominated by talk of a possible third world war, or 'a new dark age' and 'a further descent into chaos', interpretations of 1918–19 suddenly took on fresh relevance.[76] This may also have been because, compared to 1848, 1918–19 offered a more admonitory tale, which suited the mood of the second half of the 1940s. Indeed, as Conway argues, '[t]he Europe of 1945–[48] had little of the euphoria of 1848, and democracy was viewed, especially by those in positions of authority, with a mentality of caution'.[77] If this was the case in the western zones of Germany, as well as in the rest of western Europe, however, it is also important to consider the unique circumstances of postwar Berlin. Here, during the resistance to the Soviet blockade in 1948, the 'political will' of the city's inhabitants was expressed 'for the first time since the war',[78] and this inclined Social Democrats – not just Reuter, but others, such as Paul Löbe, the former President of the Reichstag in the Weimar years – to invoke the fraternal heroism of the barricades of 1848 as opposed to the disunity and splits of 1918–19. Löbe thus urged an audience in West Berlin on 18 March 1948 to regard the centenary of 1848 as a spur to opposing Soviet proposals for a 'people's congress' or 'national referendum' on Germany's political future: 'Do not expect the victory of socialism to come from institutions and organisations, from laws and regulations alone, but rather soak your work above all with that spirit of brotherhood, goodness and love for people, which is the real basis of our socialist convictions.'[79] The Communists in the eastern half of the city were not slow to respond to what they saw as the Berlin SPD's 'hostile' assemblage of arguments about the relevance of 1848 and 1918 to Germany's political future. For instance, one week after Reuter's speech, on 16 September 1948, the SED's ruling body issued a set of twenty-five theses on 'The November Revolution and its lessons for the German workers' movement'. German social democracy, it claimed, had been split three ways in 1918, among 'opportunists and revisionists' in the SPD, 'centrists' in the USPD, and a tiny 'left wing' led by Liebknecht and Luxemburg.[80] The 'lack of a [proper] revolutionary party' in Germany, combined with the 'counterrevolutionary role of the right-wing Social Democratic leaders', had led November 1918 to remain an 'incomplete bourgeois revolution'.[81]

The lessons to be drawn from this were presented as self-evident by the SED: a successful social revolution could only be achieved in Germany by ridding the workers' movement of all forms of *Sozialdemokratismus* and instead building up a 'party of a new type' based on the Bolshevik model of democratic centralism as practised by Lenin and Stalin in the Soviet Union and by the SED from 1948–49 onwards: 'It has to be a party that brings under one roof the best elements of the working class, that is grounded in Marxism-Leninism and in which a tight discipline rooted in a shared commitment of all members holds sway.'[82] Here the SED was in effect using the supposed 'lessons' of November 1918 to justify not only the enforced fusion of the KPD and SPD in the Soviet zone in April 1946, but also the decision to roll back on the promise made at that time that former Social Democrats and Communists would have parity of representation and esteem in all bodies of the new party. It was also attempting to justify the wave of purges that were already taking place, and were to continue until 1953, at all levels of the party. By the end of this process, the original fourteen-member Central Secretariat of the SED, with seven members each from the old KPD and SPD, had been replaced by an eleven-member Politburo, on which one former Social Democrat, Otto Grotewohl, sat alongside ten Communists.[83] In fact, Grotewohl had already accepted the basic fundamentals of Marxism-Leninism, and had thereby purged himself of his social democratic past, in 1948. In August of that year he wrote, in the pamphlet *November 1918 – Thirty Years Later* – produced with the help of Erich Paterna and

Karl Polak of the SED's new Parteihochschule Karl Marx (Party Academy Karl Marx) – that he no longer believed, as he had in the 1920s, that 'one can avoid a takeover of the State apparatus by the workers' party and still achieve socialism'.[84] The 'lessons' of November 1918 were important to him as a German, he claimed, but also relevant to fraternal Communist parties as well. Here the significance of what had happened in the Yugoslav party, which had been expelled from the Soviet bloc in June 1948 for deviating from the Marxist-Leninist line, came to the fore:

> Through a series of pseudo-radical measures the Yugoslav party sought to speed up the systematic building of socialism and has only discredited itself [in the process] ... If the Yugoslav comrades fail to understand the impact of their go-it-alone strategy, then Yugoslavia will be driven into the arms of the imperialists, thereby losing its independence and being degraded into a purely bourgeois state.[85]

This, in Grotewohl's view, is also what had happened to the once great German Social Democratic Party in 1918–19. It had failed to grasp the laws of history, or to come to terms with the need for a single socialist party permeated with Leninist ideas in order to secure proletarian power in the State.

Yet the problem for Grotewohl and other leading lights in the SED was that the SPD was still very much alive, in spite of the growing persecution of its members and former members in the Soviet zone. What's more, in the western parts of Germany and in West Berlin it had renewed its commitment to Marxism, but not Bolshevism, and had found new leaders in Schumacher and Reuter, ready to take on not only the Communists in the East, but the Christian Democrats and their allies, who were about to come to power in Bonn, capital of the new West Germany. The scene was set for a new era in the debate over the German Revolution.

Notes

1 On the 'Blutmai' see Chris Bowlby, 'Blutmai 1929: Police, Parties and Proletarians in a Berlin Confrontation', *Historical Journal*, 29.1 (1986), 137–58; and Axel Weipert, *Das Rote Berlin: Eine Geschichte der Berliner Arbeiterbewegung 1830–1934*, 2nd edn (Berlin, 2019), 144–6.

2. *Plattform der Kommunistischen Partei Deutschlands (Opposition)* (Berlin, 1930), 19.
3. On the KPD-O see Ben Fowkes (ed.), *The German Left and the Weimar Republic: A Selection of Documents* (Leiden, 2014), esp. 336, 353–5.
4. See Charmian Brinson and Marian Malet (eds), *Exile in and from Czechoslovakia during the 1930s and 1940s* (Amsterdam, 2009).
5. See Francis L. Carsten, 'Arthur Rosenberg: Ancient Historian into Leading Communist', *Journal of Contemporary History*, 8.1 (1973), 63–75.
6. Arthur Rosenberg, *Imperial Germany: The Birth of the German Republic*, trans. I. F. D. Morrow (Oxford, 1970 [1931]; German original, 1928).
7. Arthur Rosenberg, *A History of the German Republic*, trans. I. F. D. Morrow and L. M. Sieveking (London, 1936; German original, 1935).
8. The best biographical study is Mario Keßler's *Arthur Rosenberg: Ein Historiker im Zeitalter der Katastrophen (1889–1943)* (Cologne, 2003).
9. Quotes taken from the new post-1945 German edition, published as Arthur Rosenberg, *Geschichte der Weimarer Republik*, ed. Kurt Kersten (Frankfurt am Main, 1961), 5.
10. Ibid., 6.
11. Ibid., 23.
12. Ibid., 48.
13. Richard M. Watt, *The Kings Depart: The Tragedy of Germany. Versailles and the German Revolution* (London, 1969).
14. Haffner, *Failure of a Revolution*; Francis L. Carsten, *Revolution in Central Europe, 1918–19* (London, 1972).
15. Niess, *Die Revolution von 1918/19*, 549.
16. Rosenberg, *Geschichte der Weimarer Republik*, 11, 92.
17. Carsten, 'Arthur Rosenberg', 71.
18. Niess, *Die Revolution von 1918/19*, 548–50.
19. Willi Eichler, *100 Jahre Sozialdemokratie*, ed. Parteivorstand der SPD (Bonn, 1962), 47.
20. Karl Dietrich Erdmann, 'Die Geschichte der Weimarer Republik als Problem der Wissenschaft', *Vierteljahrshefte für Zeitgeschichte*, 3.1 (1955), 1–19 (5).
21. Ibid., 6. Erdmann's objections to Rosenberg's actual conclusions are dealt with in Chapter 3 of this book.
22. Hagen Schulze, 'Das Scheitern der Weimarer Republik als Problem der Forschung', in Karl Dietrich Erdmann and Hagen Schulze (eds), *Weimar: Selbstpreisgabe einer Demokratie. Eine Bilanz heute* (Düsseldorf, 1980), 23–41 (24).

23 Thomas Mann, *Betrachtungen eines Unpolitischen* (Berlin, 1918). By the mid-1920s, Mann had come to repudiate many of his former views, and declared himself in favour of the Weimar Republic.
24 On the *Sonderweg* idea see Jürgen Kocka, 'German History before Hitler: The Debate about the German *Sonderweg*', *Journal of Contemporary History*, 23.1 (1988), 3–16.
25 Robert Vansittart, *Black Record: Germans Past and Present* (London, 1941), 10.
26 *Ibid.*, 55.
27 *Ibid.*, 24.
28 Charmian Brinson and Richard Dove, *Politics by Other Means: The Free German League of Culture in London, 1939–1946* (London, 2010).
29 On this concept see James Krapfl, 'Afterword: The Discursive Constitution of Revolution and Revolution Envy', in Kevin McDermott and Matthew Stibbe (eds), *The 1989 Revolutions in Central and Eastern Europe: From Communism to Pluralism* (Manchester, 2013), 271–84.
30 R. C. Richardson, *The Debate on the English Revolution*, 3rd edn (Manchester, 1998 [1977]), 125–6.
31 Christopher Hill, *The English Revolution 1640: An Essay* (London, 1940), 6.
32 *Ibid.*, 57.
33 *Ibid.*, 58. Italics in the original.
34 *Ibid.*, 50.
35 *Ibid.*, 51–2.
36 Jürgen Kuczynski, *Memoiren: Die Erziehung des J. K. zum Kommunisten und Wissenschaftler* (East Berlin and Weimar, 1981), 17, 32.
37 On Kuczysnki see also Mario Keßler, *Exilerfahrung in Wissenschaft und Politik: Remigrierte Historiker in der frühen DDR* (Cologne, 2001), 91–145.
38 See *Stalin's Master Narrative: A Critical Edition of the 'History of the Communist Party of the Soviet Union (Bolsheviks): Short Course'*, ed. David Brandenberger and Mikhail Zelenov (New Haven, CT and London, 2019 [1938]), 420.
39 Brinson and Dove, *Politics by Other Means*, 6.
40 See the relevant documents in the Labour History Archive and Study Centre, Manchester, CP-IND-DUTT, 08–08.
41 Kuczynski, *Memoiren*, 327–8. See also Kuczynski to Hill, 27 October 1971, in Stadtbibliothek Berlin, Nachlaß Jürgen Kuczynski, Ku 2–1, H-1790.

42 P. F. [i.e. Jürgen Kuczynski], 'England's Revolution', *Labour Monthly*, October 1940, 558–9.
43 P. F., 'Rejoinder', *Labour Monthly*, December 1940, 653–55 (655).
44 *Ibid.*, 654.
45 Kuczynski, *Memoiren*, 376–7.
46 Eduard Bernstein, *Cromwell and Communism: Social Democracy in the Great English Revolution*, with an introduction by Eric Heffer, MP (Nottingham, 1980; first published in English in 1930; original German edition, 1895).
47 *Ibid.*, 282.
48 *Ibid.*, 17.
49 See Franka Maubach, '"Wie es dazu kommen konnte": 1933 als Fluchtpunkt deutsch-deutscher Ursachensuche im frühen Kalten Krieg', in Maubach and Morina, *Das 20. Jahrhundert erzählen*, 142–89 (149–59).
50 Vansittart, *Black Record*, 55.
51 Albert Schreiner, 'Die deutsche Misere von Weimar bis Hitler. Zu Paul Merkers Buch: *Deutschland: Sein oder Nichtsein?*', *The German American*, 1 September 1944, copy in Stiftung Archiv der Parteien und Massenorganisationen der ehemaligen DDR im Bundesarchiv Berlin (henceforth SAPMO-BArch), Nachlaß Paul Merker, NY 4102/31, 223.
52 Max Drechsel, '85:63 für Demokratie', *Mittelbayerische Zeitung*, 2 December 1947, 1, cited in Till van Rahden, *Demokratie: Eine gefährdete Lebensform* (Frankfurt am Main, 2019), 30.
53 Martin Conway, *Western Europe's Democratic Age, 1945–1968* (Princeton, NJ, 2020), 16.
54 Matthew Stibbe, 'Jürgen Kuczynski and the Search for a (Non-Existent) Western Spy Ring in the East German Communist Party in 1953', *Contemporary European History*, 20.1 (2011), 61–79 (72).
55 A. J. P. Taylor, *The Course of German History: A Survey of the Development of German History since 1815* (London, 1945), 71.
56 *Ibid.*, 216–17.
57 Gerwarth, *November 1918*, 160.
58 T. D. Burridge, *British Labour and Hitler's War* (London, 1976).
59 Stibbe, 'Jürgen Kuczynski', 69 n. 35.
60 Proclamation of the Central Committee of the KPD, 11 June 1945, English translation at http://ghdi.ghi-dc.org/docpage.cfm?docpage_id=3253 (accessed 23 February 2022).
61 *Ibid.*
62 Gerhart Eisler, Albert Norden and Albert Schreiner, *The Lesson of Germany: A Guide to Her History* (New York, 1945), 76.

63 *Ibid.*, 83.
64 *Ibid.*, 209.
65 *Ibid.*, 217.
66 'German Social Democratic Party, Call to Rebuild the Party Organization (June 15, 1945)', English translation at http://ghdi.ghi-dc.org/docpage.cfm?docpage_id=3293 (accessed 23 February 2022).
67 'Principles and Aims of the Socialist Unity Party of Germany (April 21, 1946)', English translation at http://ghdi.ghi-dc.org/docpage.cfm?docpage_id=3246 (accessed 23 February 2022).
68 See Matthew Stibbe, 'East Germany, 1945–1953: Stalinist Repression and Internal Party Purges', in Kevin McDermott and Matthew Stibbe (eds), *Stalinist Terror in Eastern Europe: Elite Purges and Mass Repression* (Manchester, 2010), 57–77.
69 Alexander Abusch, *Der Irrweg einer Nation: Ein Beitrag zum Verständnis deutscher Geschichte* (Berlin, 1946), 270.
70 *Ibid.*, 268.
71 On Schumacher see Victor Sebestyen, *1946: The Making of the Modern World* (London, 2014), 48, 236.
72 Jeffrey Herf, *Divided Memory: The Nazi Past in the Two Germanys* (Cambridge, MA and London, 1997), 250.
73 *Ibid.*, 248.
74 Stibbe, 'East Germany, 1945–1953', 64.
75 Ernst Reuter's speech before the Reichstag building in Berlin, 9 September 1948, text available at www.berlin.de/berlin-im-ueberblick/geschichte/artikel.453082.php (accessed 23 February 2022).
76 Sebestyen, *1946*, xviii, 369.
77 Conway, *Western Europe's Democratic Age*, 16.
78 Norman M. Naimark, *Stalin and the Fate of Europe: The Postwar Struggle for Sovereignty* (Cambridge, MA, 2019), 192.
79 Paul Löbe, *Erinnerungen eines Reichstagspräsidenten* (West Berlin, 1949), 172–3. On Löbe's speech on 18 March 1948, which took place in the Städtische Oper in the British sector, see also Paul Steege, 'Holding on in Berlin: March 1948 and SED Efforts to Control the Soviet Zone', *Central European History*, 38.3 (2005), 417–49 (417, 443 n. 83).
80 'Die Novemberrevolution und ihre Lehren für die deutsche Arbeiterbewegung: Beschluß des Parteivorstandes vom 16. September 1948', reproduced as an annex to Otto Grotewohl, *Dreissig Jahre später: Die Novemberrevolution und die Lehren der Geschichte der deutschen Arbeiterbewegung* (East Berlin, 1948), 147–67 (150–1).
81 *Ibid.*, 158.
82 *Ibid.*, 167. For a further discussion see also Jürgen John, 'Das Bild der Novemberrevolution 1918 in Geschichtspolitik und

Geschichtswissenschaft der DDR', in Heinrich August Winkler (ed.), *Weimar im Widerstreit: Deutungen der ersten deutschen Republik im geteilten Deutschland* (Munich, 2002), 43–84 (56–60).
83 Stibbe, 'East Germany, 1945–1953', 57–8.
84 Grotewohl, *Dreissig Jahre später*, 144. Like Grotewohl, Paterna was a former Social Democrat who joined the SED in 1946. See Dietrich Orlow, *The Parteihochschule Karl Marx under Ulbricht and Honecker, 1946–1990: The Perseverance of a Stalinist Institution* (Cham, 2021), 7.
85 Grotewohl, *Dreissig Jahre später*, 144–5.

Part II

Divided Europe and the politics of history: '1918' in the two Germanys

3

Revolution betrayed or democracy saved? West German debates, 1949–79

The Cold War, which developed apace after 1949, was a truly worldwide phenomenon. Its global reach was underlined by events such as the Korean War of 1950–53, the testing of the first H-bomb in 1952, the Sino-Soviet split from 1960 and the Cuban Missile Crisis of 1962. Nonetheless, it also came to have a special ideological and symbolic significance in central Europe, where two German states – the Federal Republic founded in May 1949 and its Communist rival, the German Democratic Republic, established in October of the same year – stood on what for much of the 1950s and the early 1960s seemed to be the brink of all-out war. From 1955 they were also integrated into rival military alliances – the American-led NATO in the case of the FRG and the Warsaw Pact in the case of the GDR.

Just as the German nation was split in half after 1949, so too was the German history profession. However, the timeline for this did not follow the course of the Cold War exactly. In the early 1950s there were still some on both sides who hoped that there was enough common understanding to allow for the maintenance of a single professional body for German historians. The final split came in the mid-to-late 1950s. West Germans such as the conservative Gerhard Ritter, President of the Verband der Historiker Deutschlands (German Historians' Association (VHD)), refused to accept the new East German journal the *Zeitschrift für Geschichtswissenschaft*, founded in 1953, as a 'scientific' publication, denouncing it as Marxist propaganda. Very few western historians would write for it. Then, at its annual conference in Trier in September 1958, the VHD forbade three East German historians – Ernst Engelberg, Max Steinmetz and Leo Stern – to speak if they appeared as official representatives of the Deutsche Historiker Gesellschaft (German Historians' Society (DHG)), the new East German body that had been founded a few months before. The DHG ordered a full-scale walk-out, and henceforth instructed all of its members to resign from the VHD.[1] Finally, in the run-up to the eleventh International Congress of Historical Sciences in Stockholm in August 1960, Ritter successfully pressed the Swedish organisers not to allow an official delegation from the GDR to attend, insisting that there was only one legitimate body for German historians – the VHD.[2] The split was now complete, and indeed at its most intense during the early 1960s. This was not helped, of course, by the building of the Berlin Wall in 1961 and the deaths of would-be escapers that followed.

From this short summary it should be clear that most of the debates conducted in West Germany in 1949–79 were among West German scholars, and not between East and West. In a direct sense, GDR historiography had little impact on what was said in West German controversies about the Revolution of 1918–19 – that is, at least until the opening of limited dialogue in the late 1980s, as we shall see in Chapter 5. However, this did not make West German scholarship narrow or inward-looking. Over time, it increasingly opened up to influences from the wider world and from Britain and America in particular, a process aided by the presence of many German-born émigré historians there, by scholars who emigrated back to Germany from English-speaking countries in the late 1940s and the 1950s, and by cultural and academic exchange programmes that helped to internationalise critical social science methodologies.[3] Furthermore, work in the GDR indirectly shaped how West German historians developed their own increasingly diverse intellectual approaches. This applied in particular to 'anti-authoritarian' Marxists in the late 1960s student movement who sought to differentiate themselves from orthodox Marxist-Leninist positions.[4] This chapter will further explore the question of external influences, direct and indirect, on West German scholarship. It will look first at the situation in the 1950s, at the height of the first phase of the Cold War, before moving on to the emergence of New Left views in the early 1960s; the impact of the student protest movements of 1966–68; and the return to more pragmatic, social-liberal views (borrowing from Marx 'without being Marxists', as German-American scholar Georg Iggers put it) in the 1970s and early 1980s.[5]

The 1950s

The conservative historians who dominated the profession in West Germany in the 1950s had – with a few exceptions – remained in Germany under National Socialism. Some, like Gerhard Ritter, emerged as resistance heroes because of their involvement in the July 1944 plot against Hitler.[6] Many others, particularly those born between 1902 and 1927, had fought in the Second World War.[7] Although they remained conservative in their methodology and, quite often, their political beliefs, the one thing that the experience of the 1930s and 1940s had taught them was that they could no longer avoid addressing issues in contemporary history if they wished their profession to be taken seriously and if they hoped to create an alternative set of narratives to that being developed in the GDR. Somehow they also had to draw in prominent German scholars who had gone into exile after 1933 and now taught in American universities, such as Hans W. Gatzke at Johns Hopkins University, Baltimore; Felix Hirsch at Bard College, New York; and Hans Rothfels, who returned to Germany in 1951 after posts as an émigré scholar at St John's College, Oxford, Brown University in Providence and the University of Chicago, Illinois. This was the background to the emergence of the Institut für Zeitgeschichte (Institute for Contemporary History (IfZ)), established in Munich in 1949. Alongside its house journal, the *Vierteljahrshefte für Zeitgeschichte* (founded in 1953 under the editorship of Rothfels and Theodor Eschenburg), the IfZ became the leading vehicle in the Federal Republic for professional research on German history since the First World War.[8]

It was in the Rothfels–Eschenburg journal that a landmark article was published in 1955 setting out the new orthodox West German view of the 1918–19 Revolution. It was written by Karl Dietrich Erdmann, professor at the University of Kiel since 1953, whose previous academic career under the Nazis had been stymied because of doubts about his wife's 'Aryan' ancestry. It is likely that

Erdmann himself held fairly pro-Nazi views in the 1930s, but he did not join the party. He was thus able to emerge without much of a 'brown' past after 1945, although after his death in 1990 there was some controversy about his exact relationship with and attitudes towards the Third Reich.[9] More importantly to Rothfels, Erdmann shared his commitment to saving the cause of moderate conservative nationalism from the taint of National Socialism.[10]

Erdmann began with the claim that the most important scientific question to ask of the Weimar Republic was why it failed.[11] The events of 1918–19 were relevant here because of the argument made by Arthur Rosenberg in his 1935 book that a different course taken in those years, namely towards the implementation of social revolution, might have placed the republic on more solid democratic foundations. For Erdmann, Rosenberg had asked the right questions but had provided the wrong answer. There was, he said, no alternative path that Germany could have taken in 1918–19 other than parliamentary rule (already conceded by the monarchical system in October 1918) or Communist dictatorship. Ebert and the other SPD leaders had not been strong enough to maintain power on their own. Having abandoned the monarchy under American duress, they needed an ally, and the choice, quite simply, had been one 'between a red army and an army based on leadership by the officer corps of the old imperial order'.[12] As such, the parliamentary republic was in fact saved at the very point that Rosenberg claimed it was destroyed, through an alliance between moderate Social Democrats and 'national-conservative elements' in the old officer corps. This alliance was improvised on both sides, but was also entirely necessary in view of the palpable threat of Communist insurgency.[13]

Erdmann's claims were backed up by memoir literature published in the 1950s, in particular the account given by Wilhelm Groener, Ludendorff's successor as First Quartermaster General, of his 'pact' with Ebert on 10 November 1918.[14] However, what is interesting about Erdmann's article is not only its stark anti-Communism – typical of nearly all professional German historians from the 1920s through to the 1960s – but his insistence that his conclusions were founded on scientific objectivity, not partisan belief. In the conclusion, he welcomed the 'emergence of [a] certain distance' from the events of 1918–19, which had helped scholars to move beyond earlier, politicised accounts of the Revolution, but qualified this by referring to his own 'alertness to a drama ... that still touches us directly, because the questions that arose then have resurfaced with fresh urgency today'.[15] The drama in question was the supposed threat to western civilisation posed by the Bolshevik Revolution of 1917, made worse since the end of the Second World War by the spread of Communist ideology over large parts of Europe and East Asia.

As far as domestic politics in West Germany was concerned, this threat was greatly exaggerated. The KPD, relegalised after 1945, had won a mere 5.7 per cent of the vote in the federal election of September 1949, falling to 2.2 per cent in September 1953. Furthermore, moves were already in train to have it banned, a process completed by a ruling made by the Federal Constitutional Court in August 1956.[16] Smaller dissident leftist parties escaped prohibition but were pushed to the margins by dint of being isolated from the political mainstream.[17] However, for Erdmann, and many of his conservative West German colleagues, this was not reassuring enough. Communism, in their view, was still a threat even if it was supported only by small groups of activists. In particular, it preyed on states that 'are not firmly established'.[18] West Germany might appear stable, particularly after the Christian Democrat Chancellor Konrad Adenauer won a handsome victory in the 1957 federal election on the slogan 'No Experiments!', but two problems appeared on the horizon: would the Christian Democrats still hold together as a party once Adenauer had left the stage, and would the West German electorate continue to support a foreign policy that placed western integration above the possibility of national reunification? On the other hand, Adenauer was right, in Erdmann's view, to claim that Communism also preyed on states that engaged in radical political experiments, as was the case in 'Red' Bavaria before and after the assassination of Kurt Eisner in February 1919. The new 'Bonn Republic' thus still had a lot to learn from the mistakes of its Weimar-era predecessor. The latter had allowed itself to be infiltrated and undermined by small extremist parties of left and right. In particular, the problem

> lay in the presence of Communist votes [in the post-1920 Reichstag] that made it impossible for both parliamentary combinations, the Weimar coalition and the coalition of right-leaning parties, to form

stable majorities, not least as the Communists rejected both combinations in equal measure.[19]

What was new in Erdmann's conservative account, then, was the absence of any condemnation of the November Revolution as such, and any reference to politicians stabbing the army in the back. Equally, though, Erdmann refused to draw any link with past democratic revolutions – whether 1789 or 1848. Instead, the decisions made in October and November 1918 were presented as *unavoidable*, both for conservative groups and for the Social Democrats. If they had stuck more firmly to the choices they made in late 1918, the two camps could have continued to govern Germany indefinitely, alternating between government and loyal opposition. The problem came after 1920, both with the transformation of the KPD into a permanent force on the back of its merger with the left wing of the USPD, and with the 'self-abandonment' ('Selbstausschaltung') of responsible parliamentarians in the face of this threat.[20] In the 1950s, it was the job of West German politicians, both the governing Christian Democrats and the loyal opposition in the guise of the SPD, to avoid repeating these mistakes.

For much of the late 1940s and the 1950s, the SPD indeed continued to be almost as fiercely anti-Communist as the Christian Democrats. Veteran SPD activists published or republished memoirs that underlined this.[21] True, the party under its first two postwar leaders, Kurt Schumacher and Erich Ollenhauer, continued to oppose West German membership of NATO, and to insist that they were still Marxists, formally committed to the 1925 Heidelberg Programme. However, after suffering another major defeat in the 1957 federal election, the SPD began to distance itself from doctrinaire anti-capitalist positions, a move enshrined in its November 1959 Bad Godesberg Programme.[22] Social Democrats henceforth accepted the 'social market economy', the impossibility of German neutrality in the Cold War, and membership of the Federal Republic in the West's economic and military alliance structures. Their main research and educational institute, the Friedrich-Ebert-Stiftung (Friedrich Ebert Foundation (FES)), was already named in 1925 after the man whose decision to enter into an improvised alliance with the army in 1918–19 was now considered by Erdmann and much of the historical establishment in West Germany to have been unavoidable. Interestingly, the FES chose to keep that name – and the educational mission to preserve the memory of German Social Democracy while remaining formally independent of the party's structures – when it was reconstituted in Bonn in 1954.[23]

In the first decade or so of the Federal Republic's existence, then, anti-Communism manifested itself on at least two different levels. It was evident in the continued suspicions of the Christian Democrats, the smaller right-wing and centre-right parties, 'patriotic' conservative historians, and the security establishment towards the SPD as the harbinger of 'godless' Marxism.[24] At the same time, it was founded on a cross-party consensus that included the SPD, at least as far as (non-) cooperation with the KPD at home and (non-) pursuit of political and cultural relations with the GDR and other Soviet bloc countries abroad were concerned.[25] This common hostility towards the East German state – along with the ban on the KPD in 1956 – also profoundly influenced the way in which the events of 1918–19 were now interpreted. The Council of People's Deputies, an SPD pamphlet noted in 1962, had acted wholly in line with social democratic principles and policies when it chose to reject 'Bolshevik' methods and restrict its executive decrees in November and December 1918 to issues around 'social policy, labour rights and ... democratisation of the voting laws'.[26] In contrast to their enemies on the far left and reactionary right, they 'did not want to impose their views' by a diktat and instead 'trusted in the healthy instincts of the people', as expressed through parliamentary elections.[27]

Friedrich Stampfer, who in 1918 had been a member of the SPD's national executive and editor of its daily newspaper, *Vorwärts*, was even more forceful in his view of the events of 1918–19 when he came to publish his memoirs in 1957, just under a decade after his return to West Germany from US exile:

> The social revolution is a continuation of the bourgeois revolution, not its opposite. Workers fought on the barricades for so-called 'bourgeois' democratic rights, and they were right to do so, since this represented the first steps towards their own advancement [as a class]. Not through the destruction of democracy, but only through its improvement, can the foundations be laid for a social order worthy of the name socialism.[28]

And yet even in the second half of the 1950s, there were some dissenting voices who opposed the dominant post-1949 narrative, and were willing to develop an alternative line, one that questioned mainstream anti-Communist views without developing explicitly pro-Communist or pro-Soviet ones. By the early 1960s, the protagonists of this New Left position had begun to make a mark on the academic debate on the German Revolution, not only through their revival of the writings of Arthur Rosenberg and other exiled anti-Nazi writers from the 1930s and 1940s, but also as a result of their own empirical research and theoretical insights.

The New Left

Politically, the origins of the New Left in West Germany can be found in the opposition to Adenauer's policy of rearmament before and after the Federal Republic's entry into NATO in 1955.[29] As the SPD moved towards a more centrist line in the late 1950s, abandoning Marxism and accepting the FRG's membership of NATO, criticism of the new consensus mounted. In contrast to both Communism and social democracy, however, the New Left was largely an intellectual phenomenon without deep roots in or attachments to the labour movement. When it came to reinterpreting the German Revolution of 1918–19, its arguments were often theoretical and/or sociological rather than historical. In western Europe generally, as Martin Conway notes, the New Left 'had no single political definition', and many of the class, racial and gendered injustices it claimed to oppose were global rather than European in nature.[30] Nonetheless, it was deeply influenced by events in Hungary in October–November 1956, when a momentous but short-lived revolt against the Government of the People's Republic helped to undermine the assumption that workers' councils were inevitably tied to Communism in its dictatorial, Soviet form.

In the United States, the New Left was associated above all with the sociologist C. Wright Mills, while in Britain some of its key adherents were former Communists who resigned their membership of the CPGB following the Soviet invasion of Hungary in November 1956, including John Saville and E. P. Thompson.[31] In West Germany, by contrast, its protagonists typically had no prior attachments to the KPD or dissident offshoots such as the KPD-O, but were either activists on the left wing of the SPD or younger academics without formal political affiliation. Among those who became engaged in studies of the 1918–19 Revolution, Walter Tormin and Peter von Oertzen (born in 1923 and 1924 respectively) were SPD members, whereas Eberhard Kolb, Reinhard Rürup and Ulrich Kluge (born in 1933, 1934 and 1935 respectively) were not involved with any particular party. The latter group completed Ph.D.s in the 1950s and their *Habilitationsschriften* (the German second dissertation) in the 1960s, before moving on to permanent university chairs.[32] Standing between these two groups was Helga Grebing, born in 1930 and a member of the SPD since 1948, who established herself as a leading academic expert on the German labour movement through a book published in 1966.[33] Her childhood experiences of Nazi and early Cold War Berlin (she was raised in Pankow, in the eastern part of that city) made her a staunch critic of Soviet-style Communism, albeit from a strongly leftist, working-class perspective.[34] In the 1970s and 1980s she held professorial chairs in labour history at several West German universities and was a leading member of the SPD's Historical Commission.

Arthur Rosenberg had already anticipated some of the New Left's ideas in 1935. However, his main interest was in the decisions taken by the Council of People's Deputies and the division of the left into three main streams represented by the SPD, USPD and KPD. In the late 1950s and early 1960s, the focus of attention shifted instead to the workers' and soldiers' councils, building on an earlier book published by Walter Tormin in 1954.[35] And one of the first discoveries of this new research was that the model Rosenberg had provided of three different streams of socialism, while it worked for understanding the development of organised political parties, did not map so easily onto the councils' movement. The classic example, stressed in particular by Peter von Oertzen in his 1963 study of workplace councils, was the announcement made by the soldiers' and workers' council in Essen on 9 January 1919 regarding the immediate nationalisation of the Ruhr mining industry. 'Party' had played no particular role in this demand, given that the SPD, USPD and KPD were all equally represented on the Essen council and were all equally committed to the nationalisation issue.³⁶ At stake here, in other ways, was not the party-political definition of socialism in Germany, but the class basis of the State.

In a variety of studies published in the 1960s and 1970s, Kolb, Oertzen, Rürup and Kluge all advanced the argument that the Weimar Republic could have been developed on a more solid proletarian basis in 1919 if only the councils had been allowed a greater say, particularly over economic decisions, such as nationalisation of the mines.³⁷ A 'third way' had existed between capitalism and Soviet-style socialism, they insisted.³⁸ This 'third way' would have involved an element of power-sharing between the socialist- (but not Communist-) dominated councils and the non-socialist majority in the Constituent National Assembly. An important opportunity had been lost in 1918–19 to revolutionise German society and the economy. Even those who voted for non-socialist parties, such as the peasants and lower middle class, it was claimed, could have been won over for a programme of confiscating the property of big capitalists and big landowners. This missed opportunity was important, in the sense that the big capitalists and big landowners were the very people whose loyalty to the new republic was most in doubt. For Kolb, it was the SPD leaders' obsessive fear of Communism – not force of circumstance, as Erdmann had suggested in 1955 – that was responsible for narrowing the Government's options down to a binary either–or choice between parliamentary democracy or Bolshevik dictatorship:

> Even if the SPD leaders had calculated that the creation of a mood of panic around Bolshevism would bring them political advantages, and even if they saw it as a political necessity, this did not mean that they had to succumb to their own propaganda. Rather, their objective should have been to examine the real situation and take into account the actual, not the over-blown, dangers. But in fact the SPD leaders ... [were] blinded by fear of Bolshevik dictatorship in Germany.³⁹

Kolb's notion of an anti-Communist 'psychosis' that had narrowed down policy options and dominated mainstream newspaper headlines at the expense of a more sober assessment of realities may well have been understood by some readers of his book as a critique both of Adenauer's hard-line stance towards the Soviet bloc, and the tendency of the SPD in the late 1950s in particular to 'tolerate' and perhaps even encourage domestic anti-Communism at the expense of developing constructive alternatives. In her 1966 survey of the history of the German labour movement, Grebing – who cited Kolb, alongside Tormin and Rosenberg – noted, among other things, how an exaggerated fear of Communism had led the SPD leadership in January 1919 to misinterpret the goals of the miners' movement in the Ruhr and the majority demands of the Essen workers' council. The latter were striving not for Bolshevism but merely for 'socialisation, by which they meant the introduction of co-determination [*Mitbestimmung*] in industry and its maintenance by works councils'.[40] Talk of 'missed opportunities', or of what Grebing, quoting Rosenberg, referred to as the unfulfilled possibility of 'a new republic of the common people' ('einer neuen, volkstümlichen Republik'), had deep political implications in the 1960s, especially when linked to the still very live question of a 'third way' between capitalism and socialism.[41] Even so, Kolb insisted that his aim had been to produce an 'entirely historical account of the German workers' councils of 1918–19 in their concrete forms and manifestations, as determined by the unique historical circumstances that first gave rise to their development'.[42] In this sense, at least, he agreed with Erdmann on the desirability of academic 'distance' from the events in question.

Yet here is where the similarities ended. The grounds on which Kolb and colleagues such as Oertzen, Grebing, Rürup and Kluge disagreed with Erdmann are complex, but can be reduced to two underlying claims, one more plausible than the other. More plausible, because rooted in empirical research, was the notion that the workers' and soldiers' councils had never been dominated by Communists, but remained – from late 1918 through to 1920 – in the hands of SPD, USPD and non-affiliated workers. Furthermore, even when individual Communists were present in leadership positions within councils in particular regions or industries, they were not necessarily the most radical voices. Those pushing hardest for nationalisation of the Ruhr mining industry, for instance, had little interest in political parties at all, and few, if any, ties to Moscow. The failure of the SPD leadership around Ebert and Noske to recognise this, and their use of the military and Freikorps to crush labour unrest in the early months of 1919, drove the councils leftwards and made an alliance between them and the new State increasingly unlikely.[43] Or, as the British historian A. J. Ryder put it in his 1967 study, which was influenced by the new West German scholarship and by his own findings, 'the majority in the workers' councils, and nearly all the members of the soldiers' councils, were SPD supporters, so that by allowing them greater scope in the transition period Ebert need not have let the situation get out of control'.[44]

The second, and more questionable, claim was that without Ebert and Noske's hard-line anti-Communism, some kind of power-sharing arrangement might have been possible between the councils and the Constituent National Assembly. In order to understand why this is unconvincing, we first need to say a little more about what the councils were, and how they differed from standard trade unions. Trade unions exist to defend their members' interests, and to negotiate with employers over issues of mutual concern, such as hours, wages, productivity norms and so on. These negotiations, even in cases where they lead to industrial conflict, rely on a degree of mutual recognition and obligation.[45] Furthermore, in a constitutional state, where powers are separated between the executive, the legislature and the judiciary, both trade unions and employers are obliged to operate within a legal framework established through parliamentary legislation, and/or within a set of political compromises reached through ministerial intervention or independent arbitration and open – on all sides – to contestation in the courts.

In Germany, trade unions had strengthened their political position during the war, especially in view of the growing cooperation between the social democrat trade unions, led by Carl Legien, and big business, led by the Ruhr steel and shipping magnate Hugo Stinnes. For instance, the two worked with the supreme command on the drafting of the Auxiliary Service Law of December 1916, which allowed labour conscription under the wartime emergency, and on plans for deregulation and demobilisation after the war. The Stinnes–Legien Agreement of 15 November 1918 emerged out of this process, although it was also a response to the unexpected outbreak of revolution in early November. In essence, the unions agreed to distance themselves from the nationalisation agenda of the councils in return for certain concessions from the employers, notably the introduction of the eight-hour day and collective

Revolution betrayed or democracy saved? 93

bargaining in larger workplaces. Industrialists also agreed not to return to the prewar practice of hiring 'yellow labour' (strike-breakers), while union leaders achieved reaffirmation of their status as contractually recognised representatives of the workforce, which had already been partly conceded during the war. Finally, both sides agreed to the establishment of a consultative body, the Zentralarbeitsgemeinschaft (Central Working Association), which functioned as an information bureau and attempted to set common standards for wage claims and collective bargaining processes across the different sectors of industry.[46]

Workers' and soldiers' councils, on the other hand, appeared spontaneously on the eve of the Revolution. They were an improvised solution to the sudden collapse of political authority in many towns and cities, and to the need to maintain law, order and food supplies.[47] They were not anchored in law, and had no ties of mutual obligation to representatives of the old regime, whether this be officers in the army and navy; the owners of industry; or the unelected county administrators, the *Landräte*.[48] They also reacted with suspicion when peasants and middle-class groups sought to form their own (anti-socialist) councils, or *Bürgerräte*.[49] Admittedly, they did have some ties of *political* obligation to the new National Assembly, in the sense that on 19 December 1918 the first Reich Congress of Soldiers' and Workers' Councils had voted overwhelmingly in favour of staging parliamentary elections at the earliest possible date, i.e. 19 January, with 400 for the motion and only fifty against.[50] However, this vote was taken in the expectation that the elections would lead to a healthy majority for the two main social democratic parties, the SPD and the USPD. Indeed, in support of this, Rürup notes that the December congress had also passed a resolution calling for an effective end to the Stinnes–Legien Agreement and for the 'nationalisation of all key industries, in particular the mines' – a slap in the face to the official trade unions, but politically an entirely realistic goal if one were to bank on a socialist victory at the polls.[51] When the SPD and USPD ended up with only around 45 per cent of the vote between them in the January election, however, the possibility of achieving this by parliamentary means was gone.

Nationalisation of the mines and other industries might have been possible before 19 January on the basis of revolutionary decrees issued by the Council of People's Deputies. But after that date it would have been impossible to achieve except by proroguing the new National Assembly, in other words by usurping its legislative functions in the sphere of economics and property rights. Critics of a councils dictatorship feared that such a regime would lack any safeguards against abuse of power, whether over the judiciary, the legislature or other independent pillars of democracy, such as the media and culture. Besides this, the SPD and the established trade unions were opposed to immediate nationalisation of industry and, in the case of the Ruhr coalfields, appointed a three-member commission made up of the mining director Arnold Röhrig, the industrialist Albert Vögler and the trade unionist Otto Hué to draft a report on their future. Without a socialist majority, the Constituent National Assembly would never agree to share its law-making powers with a body – the Essen workers' and soldiers' council and its equivalents in other industrial regions – that only represented one part of the German nation, namely (a portion of) its working class.[52] Whereas the Council of People's Deputies had used its executive powers to introduce universal suffrage for Reich and State elections on 12 November 1918, elections to soldiers' and workers' councils did not take place within any existing legally recognised framework, and were restricted in the sense that only wage-earners could vote, meaning that large parts of the middle and upper class, as well as women who did not work for wages, were excluded. The SPD had made this clear as early as 9 November 1918 in response to Spartacist and USPD calls to place 'all executive, legislative and judicial power exclusively in the hands of representatives of the working people and the soldiers'. The radical left's demand, it said, was 'tantamount to calling for a dictatorship of one portion of one class, without the support of the majority of the people. It follows that we should reject this demand, because it stands in opposition to our democratic principles.'[53]

 If their claims about the possibility of a 'third way' have not stood the test of time, the empirical findings of Tormin, Kolb, Grebing, Rürup and others nonetheless opened the way for greater understanding of the councils movement itself. In particular, they shifted attention away from the first Reich Congress of Workers' and Soldiers' Councils and the supposed finality of its vote on 19 December for elections to a Constituent National Assembly, and towards the changed circumstances in which the second Reich Congress took place in Berlin in April 1919. Here, radical voices such as those of Ernst Däumig and Richard Müller, who had been in a minority in December 1918, now clearly had more influence.[54] Müller, for instance, demanded the formal anchoring of the councils in the new constitution, and a reorganisation of the economy so that:

> All those who work for wages are required to join single closed-shop organisations [*Zwangsorganisationen*]. The existing trade unions and professional associations should be merged with these new bodies, or rather should serve as the basis for their formation. Rural workers and farmers who are not in permanent waged employment should join their own closed-shop organisations. Workers' councils will then control and direct all sales and technical aspects of the running of the business, or in case of a collection of small, nominally independent enterprises, a single council can be formed by creating an overall body elected by several different workforces. All matters relating to the production process can only be determined with the approval of the relevant workers' councils.[55]

This was a call not for power-sharing, but for a prorogation of parliamentary powers. Yet it was also a call conditioned by the new circumstances of spring 1919 – the failure to win a socialist majority in the National Assembly and the SPD-dominated Government's continued use of violence against the left.[56] It is worth noting, however, that Däumig and Müller were members not of the KPD, but of the USPD. Indeed, as Kolb discovered, the KPD had even called for a boycott of council elections ahead of the second Reich Congress, and its candidates, where they did stand, had little success. For this reason, 'the radicalisation process that materialised from January [1919] onwards came to benefit the USPD almost exclusively'.[57] This radicalisation was caused, primarily, by the SPD's own narrowing of its options to the point where cooperation with the USPD at national level was no longer possible. Where the KPD contributed to radicalisation, it was more in the negative sense that its utterly partisan and politically self-interested approach to involvement in councils, including its refusal to suspend publication of its newspaper *Die Rote Fahne* in the interests of a joint campaign for socialist democracy in the factories and coalfields, actually put many workers off, and drove them either towards the utopian left of the USPD or towards new forms of (semi-) independent workplace activism.[58]

The year of revolt: 1968

In the second half of the 1960s, big political changes took place in West Germany. Adenauer resigned as Federal Chancellor in 1963, and his successor, Ludwig Erhard, turned out to be less suited to the top position in government than he had been to the role of Economics Minister, an office he had held since 1949. In December 1966, the centre–right coalition he led was replaced by a 'grand coalition' government between the Christian Democrats and the SPD. Parliamentary opposition was reduced to a small number of deputies for the business-friendly Free Democratic Party (FDP), but meanwhile protest was coming from a new source: the Ausserparlamentarische Opposition (Extra-Parliamentary opposition (APO)), an umbrella name given to a movement on the anti-authoritarian left headed by the Sozialistische Deutsche Studentenbund (Socialist Student League). With strongholds on campuses throughout the FRG, and especially in Frankfurt am Main and West Berlin, the APO called for greater sexual and personal freedoms, an 'authentic' reckoning with the Nazi past, and an end to capitalism. It also led campaigns against the Vietnam War (including West Germany's support for US involvement there), pro-western dictators from Third World countries, the Soviet-led Warsaw Pact invasion of Czechoslovakia in 1968 and the mainstream media at home.[59] Although the APO embraced the ideas of Marx and Engels – and in particular their *Communist Manifesto* from 1848 – it rejected the *Parteikommunismus* (Communism directed by a hierarchically led political party) of the SED in East Germany and of the Deutsche Kommunistische Partei (German Communist Party, DKP). The latter was legally (re)constituted in West Germany in September 1968 as the political successor to the old KPD, and received funds from the SED.[60]

As Timothy Scott Brown has claimed, the '1968ers' in West Germany differed from old-style Communists in many ways, including in their taste for theatricality and their predilection for instant 'self-historization' and 'self-theorization'.[61] Appearing in court as part of a group charged with setting fire to two department stores in Frankfurt in protest at the Vietnam War in April 1968, the activist Thorwald Proll gave his date of birth as '1789'. His attorney, Horst Mahler, explained:

> When [the accused] cites the year of the French Revolution as his date of birth, this is intended to lend weight to his claim that this event is of decisive importance in the development of his political awareness. It should not be held negatively against the accused that the court has not understood this statement in the sense that it was meant.[62]

Other revolutionary events were also important to the '1968ers', including the Paris Commune of 1871; St Petersburg in 1905, 1917 and 1921 (the Kronstadt Uprising); the two 'Red Years' in Italy from 1918 to 1920; Spain, and particularly Barcelona, in 1936–37; China in 1949; Budapest in 1956; and Cuba in 1959.[63] Yet the German Revolution of 1918–19 appeared less frequently in their 'self-historization', and not only because their frame of reference was 'global', or at least transnational as opposed to Germano-centric.[64] When the Chinese Prime Minister Zhou Enlai reputedly told Henry Kissinger during the latter's secret visit to Beijing in July 1971 that the outcome of the French Revolution was still too early to call, some confusion arose over whether this exchange related to 1789 or to the 'May Events' in Paris in 1968.[65] But the outcome of the German Revolution of 1918–19 was already seen by most '1968ers' and their less prominent heirs in the 1970s as a closed book owing to the 'betrayals' of Ebert and other SPD leaders. As the jurist-turned-journalist Sebastian Haffner – himself from a much older generation than that of the '1968ers' but in many ways speaking their language – put it in his famous 1969 work *Failure of a Revolution*:

> The collective hero of the Revolution, the German working class, never recovered from the blow. Socialist unity, for which they had fought and bled so bravely, was lost for ever in 1918. From that great betrayal dates the great schism of Socialism and the inextinguishable hatred between Communists and Social Democrats – a hatred as between wolves and dogs. (A dog, of course, was once a wolf, domesticated by man for his own purposes. The Social Democrats were once a workers' party, domesticated by capitalism for its own purposes).[66]

There were nonetheless some exceptions to this damning verdict that the democratic socialist dreams of the German workers had been 'lost for ever' in 1918–19. One example would be the book published by Dieter Schneider and Rudolf Kuda in 1968.[67]

Schneider, born in 1931, and Kuda, born in 1940, were both senior functionaries in the IG-Metall trade union, headquartered in Frankfurt and, since its founding in 1949, one of the largest trade unions in West Germany. Their interest was primarily in the idea of a 'pure councils system' (*das Konzept des reinen wirtschaftlichen Rätesystem*) as put forward by Däumig and Müller at the second Reich Congress of Workers' and Soldiers' Councils in April 1919.[68] Such a system, they explained, constituted not a kind of 'third way' between parliamentary democracy and Bolshevik dictatorship, but rather an anti-authoritarian alternative to both systems that went much further than either in its search for a grass-roots, socialist democracy. In this system, proletarian dictatorial power would rest solely in the hands of the councils at regional and local level, run by permanently recallable representatives of the workforce. Authoritarian state bureaucracies of the capitalist or Soviet kind would disappear and hierarchically organised political parties would either be banned or cease to be relevant, as everything would be decided by the councils themselves.[69] Universities, trade unions and other public bodies could be run on similar lines, making them democratic institutions rather than institutions run by the (authoritarian-capitalist or authoritarian-Communist) State.

For Schneider and Kuda, the 'pure councils system' had one further theoretical advantage. It would help to decide the age-old conflict between indirect or parliamentary democracy and direct democracy (democracy as a daily plebiscite). In other words, this was no 'third way' solution, but, in Marxist terms, a new synthesis. True, they acknowledged the claims made by the German-born American political theorist Hannah Arendt that parliamentary democracy and councils democracy were both, in different ways, 'democratic' and therefore the opposite of (Soviet) 'totalitarianism', the authoritarian system (re)imposed by military force in Hungary in 1956. However, they went further, by arguing that 'councils democracy' was the purer form. This was because it overcame the need for parties, which were inevitably hierarchical and run by self-serving bureaucracies.[70]

Schneider and Kuda had nothing but criticism for the *Parteikommunismus* of the early KPD. The real radical dynamic in 1918–19 had come from the far less hierarchical USPD. The latter's merger with the KPD in late 1920 had spelled the death knell for the 'pure councils system'.⁷¹ Däumig and Müller had joined the KPD temporarily, but soon left once they realised that the merger was in effect a Bolshevik takeover.⁷² Yet they had represented only one strand of USPD thinking, also linked with the Marxist theoretician Karl Korsch. Most of those on the left of the USPD who joined the KPD in 1920 rejected Korsch's ideas. The 'pure councils system' was not suited to the economic and political circumstances of 1919, and was largely dropped, even by the surviving remnants of the USPD, after the merger of 1920.⁷³ However, for Schneider and Kuda it was a glimpse of a possible future that had much relevance for the more affluent but still very socially unequal and authoritarian West Germany of 1968.⁷⁴

The critique of *Parteikommunismus* contained in the Schneider/Kuda account should not be taken to mean that they rejected the view of Ebert and Scheidemann as counterrevolutionaries. Far from it: in this reading of the events of 1918–19, the SPD's anti-Communism had not only narrowed options for maintaining unity between parties on the left or for removing the economic power of big business and big landowners; in a more direct and visceral way, it had betrayed democracy in its purist form, the democracy of the ordinary workers.

> The Council of People's Deputies shied away from any direct intervention in the economy ... They failed to recognise that a people's government that wants to survive must base itself on the real will of the people. This led them to oppose the councils system and, with overdue haste, to bring about the election of a National Assembly ... The abandonment of the elementary democratic forces that lay dormant in the councils movement weakened the young republic from its very beginning and provided the forces of reaction with a strong, perhaps even decisive, foothold [in the new system].⁷⁵

Such rhetoric at least contained within it the possibility that, in spite of the many setbacks of 1918–19, the outcome of the Revolution was still (partly) open. It therefore differed in many ways from Haffner's more populist work, which simply – and rather repetitively – accused Ebert and Noske of 'betrayal' and cast the revolution as an outright 'failure'.⁷⁶ And yet the fact remains that the councils movement, even in its 'pure', economic form from April 1919 onwards, was no more successful than the SPD or the

National Assembly at becoming a vehicle for empowering ordinary workers. Certainly it could support recurring social protest. And certainly the grinding poverty of the immediate postwar years gave workers much to protest about. But the 'pure' councils movement lacked the organisational power, and the alliances with other social movements, to drive through a concrete political programme based on the liberation of society from capitalism and the alienation from life and work that it gave rise to. So too, ultimately, did the APO in West Germany and similar leftist movements in France, Italy and elsewhere in 1966–68.

The return to realism: The 1970s

Following the federal election in West Germany in September 1969, the 'grand coalition' Government was replaced by a 'social–liberal' coalition between the SPD and FDP. The FRG was now ruled by two Social Democratic Chancellors in succession: Willy Brandt (1969–74) and Helmut Schmidt (1974–82). 'Normal' practices of parliamentary rule returned, with the Brandt and Schmidt Governments both facing strong opposition from the Christian Democrats. In spite of this, the social–liberal coalition was able to push through significant changes in West Germany's relationship with the Communist East, a policy known as the *neue Ostpolitik* (new eastern policy). As much of the sting was taken out of the West German anti-Communism of the 1950s and 1960s, the historic split of the German left into the three streams identified by Arthur Rosenberg seemed increasingly to be a question of distant history rather than of contemporary politics. The student and extra-parliamentary opposition movements also gradually ebbed away after 1968. The break with the Marxist past taken by the SPD at Bad Godesberg in November 1959 finally seemed to have paid off with the election (and, on three further occasions in a row, the re-election) of SPD-led federal governments.

Social Democrat-supporting historians also increasingly interpreted the East–West conflict in non-party and non-partisan/ realist terms. It was not a fight between the SPD and the KPD/SED/ DKP for the heritage of German socialism, but between two entirely different value systems that nonetheless had to find a way of living alongside each other for the sake of European peace and security. This view reached its classic expression in the meeting between Helmut Schmidt and his SED counterpart, Erich Honecker, in the East German cathedral town of Güstrow on 13 December 1981. On this day, Europe and the world were put on high alert by the declaration of martial law in Poland following the growing success there of the independent trade union movement Solidarity. But Schmidt wanted to draw attention to something else: never again must wars be fought on German soil, whether they be caused by disputes over borders, territory, religion or ideology. Peace came first, even if it had to be a peace backed up by the NATO nuclear deterrent.[77]

Even so, 1978 was hardly a calmer, more sober anniversary than 1968. True, as Rürup put it in an essay published in 1983, 'what was still heavily contested in 1964 was widely accepted by 1979 as established fact'.[78] There was now considerable agreement that Ebert and other SPD leaders had exaggerated the threat of Communism in 1918–19 and had used 'disproportionate force' when trying to suppress it.[79] It was also recognised that the councils had not been vehicles for Bolshevik dictatorship. Rather, their vision, while diffuse and subject to change, was more one of decentralised, democratic socialism.[80] Where disagreement still existed, however, was over whether this democratic socialist vision had had any realistic chance of success, in other words whether it was a viable 'third way'. Wolfgang J. Mommsen and Heinrich August Winkler took issue with Rürup and others on this score. Mommsen, writing in 1978 on the sixtieth anniversary of the Revolution, described the notion of a 'third way' as 'overstated' and a reflection of 'utopian thinking'.[81] Winkler was even clearer on this score:

> The SPD cannot ... be criticised for having rejected the option of dual authority between the councils and parliament, as parts of the USPD called for. Such a system would have led to a progressive hollowing out of parliamentary democracy and would have been both costly and inoperable ... The installation of organs of economic co-determination as a constituent part of representative democracy would only have worked as a social extension of this form of government, not as the basis of a new kind of regime in its own right.[82]

Rürup hit back in 1983, noting that the notion of one single 'third way' was largely an invention of critics of the new research, and that if the concept was to be given a fair hearing 'then for the sake of accuracy, one should speak of several different possible "third ways"', not all of which were anti-parliamentary in nature.[83] In particular, the rejection of the utopian 'pure' councils system put forward by Däumig did not rule out the viability of alternative schemes bringing together 'self-organisation and grass-roots democratic elements … with a democratic parliamentary constitution'.[84]

Nonetheless, all parties – Rürup, Winkler and Mommsen – could agree that a revolution had taken place in November 1918; that it was a revolution in protest against the old regime and its refusal to end the war; and that it was therefore a significant political event, not just a 'primitive rebellion of the masses', as Gerhard Ritter had once dubbed it.[85] The conservative notion advanced by Theodor Eschenburg in 1954 and repeated by Karl Dietrich Erdmann in 1955 that the Revolution had been 'unnecessary' (*überflüssig*), as the monarchy had already conceded parliamentarism in October 1918, was no longer accepted.[86] Even Erdmann had changed his language by now, implicitly conceding that a revolution to overthrow the monarchy had been unavoidable in November 1918, while still insisting that Ebert had had no other choice, if he wanted to prevent a Bolshevik takeover, than to ally with the old conservative elites, thereby ruling out social revolution as a political option.[87]

The end of the 1970s was thus the point where the bulk of West German historians began to 'own' the Revolution as a part of the Federal Republic's democratic heritage and national history, and not just as a backdrop to the 'chaos' of Weimar and the rise of Hitler. For Winkler in particular, November 1918 had paved the way for significant social reforms that favoured the cause of labour. Socialism, however, had been impossible in 1918–19, as it had been in 1848.[88] But this time it was impossible for different reasons: not just because (as Erdmann said) there was an anti-socialist majority in the National Assembly, but because the largest party, the SPD, did not consider that the *economic* conditions were right for its immediate introduction and was at the same time opposed to the alternative, *political* option of using dictatorial means to impose it on the German people.[89] Paradoxically, then, the advanced state of Germany's democratic values in 1918–19 – represented above all by the SPD's belief in a non-violent, parliamentary road to socialism – also made it 'too advanced' to achieve either a classic social revolution à la 1789 or a Bolshevik-style leap from absolutism into socialist revolution.[90]

The differences among Erdmann, Rürup, Mommsen and Winkler in the late 1970s and early 1980s were admittedly still real and prevented the realisation of any binding consensus on the historical meaning and significance of the 1918–19 Revolution in West Germany. But at least the ground was beginning to shift. No longer was the Revolution seen as a 'national' embarrassment, either because it was 'primitive' (the argument of the conservative right), 'unnecessary' (the view of Eschenburg and Erdmann in 1954–55) or 'incomplete' and an outright 'failure' (the position adopted by the radical left in the 1960s). Instead, the direction of travel was towards a more balanced and nuanced recognition that it had created a democracy of sorts, however unsatisfactory, messy, too-timid or too-formalistic that democracy might have been. For Rürup in particular, this was of lasting importance. Writing shortly before his death in April 2018, he noted that research since the 1970s had led to a 'differentiation of the picture of the revolution, but not to any decisive change in factual understanding'.[91] The 1918–19 Revolution, he continued, was owed a 'place of honour in the history of German democracy' alongside, but in a different way from, the Revolution of 1848.[92]

Notes

1 Ilko-Sascha Kowalczuk, *Legitimation eines neuen Staates. Parteiarbeiter an der historischen Front: Geschichtswissenschaft in der SBZ/DDR 1945–1961* (Berlin, 1997), 276.
2 Christoph Cornelißen, *Gerhard Ritter: Geschichtswissenschaft und Politik im 20. Jahrhundert* (Düsseldorf, 2001), 452–7.
3 Winfried Schulze, *Deutsche Geschichtswissenschaft nach 1945* (Munich, 1989), 130–44; Georg Iggers, *The Social History of Politics: Critical Perspectives in West German Historical Writing since 1945* (Leamington Spa, 1985), 26–7.
4 Timothy Scott Brown, *West Germany and the Global Sixties: The Antiauthoritarian Revolt, 1962–1978* (Cambridge, 2013), esp. 41–9.
5 Iggers, *The Social History of Politics*, 26.

6 Cornelißen, *Gerhard Ritter*, 335–69.
7 Christina Morina, 'Triumph und Demütigung: Der zweite Weltkrieg in der doppelten deutschen Geschichtsschreibung', in Maubach and Morina, *Das 20. Jahrhundert erzählen*, 190–244.
8 Theodor Eschenburg, *Letzten Endes meine ich doch: Erinnerungen 1933–1999* (Berlin, 2000), 201, 204; Iggers, *The Social History of Politics*, 21.
9 See Hans-Ulrich Wehler, 'Nationalsozialismus und Historiker', in Winfried Schulze and Otto Gerhard Oexle (eds), *Deutsche Historiker im Nationalsozialismus* (Frankfurt am Main, 1999), 306–39. Also the contributions to the special issue of *Geschichte in Wissenschaft und Unterricht*, 61.12 (2010), on the theme 'Karl Dietrich Erdmann: Geschichtswissenschaft und Politik'.
10 Niess, *Die Revolution von 1918/19*, 123. Hans Rothfels's own views were set out in his book *The German Opposition to Hitler: An Appraisal* (Chicago, IL, 1948).
11 Karl Dietrich Erdmann, 'Die Geschichte der Weimarer Republik', 5.
12 *Ibid.*, 7.
13 See also Theodor Eschenburg, *Die improvisierte Demokratie der Weimarer Republik* (Munich, 1954).
14 Wilhelm Groener, *Lebenserinnerungen: Jugend, Generalstab, Weltkrieg* (Göttingen, 1957).
15 Erdmann, 'Die Geschichte der Weimarer Republik', 19.
16 Patrick Major, *The Death of the KPD: Communism and Anti-Communism in West Germany, 1945–1956* (Oxford, 1997).
17 Mario Keßler, 'Zwischen Kommunismus und Sozialdemokratie, zwischen Ost und West: Die marxistischen Kleingruppen auf dem Weg in die deutschen Nachkriegsgesellschaften', in Arnd Bauerkämper, Martin Sabrow and Bernd Stöver (eds), *Doppelte Zeitgeschichte: Deutsch-deutsche Beziehungen 1945–1990* (Bonn, 1998), 251–66 (263–5).
18 Erdmann, 'Die Geschichte der Weimarer Republik', 5.
19 *Ibid.*, 17.
20 *Ibid.*
21 See, for instance, Otto Braun, *Von Weimar zu Hitler* (Hamburg, 1949 [1940]); Gustav Noske, *Erlebtes aus Aufstieg und Niedergang einer Demokratie* (Offenbach, 1947); Paul Löbe, *Erinnerungen eines Reichstagspräsidenten* (West Berlin, 1949); Friedrich Stampfer, *Erfahrungen und Erkenntnisse: Aufzeichnungen aus meinem Leben* (Cologne, 1957).
22 Berger, *Social Democracy*, 170.

23 Patrik von zur Mühlen, *Die internationale Arbeit der Friedrich-Ebert-Stiftung: Von den Anfängen bis zum Ende des Ost-West-Konflikts* (Bonn, 2007), 48, 89.
24 See '"Adenauer war jedes Mittel recht": Der Zeithistoriker Norbert Frei über die illegale Ausforschung des SPD-Vorstandes durch den BND', *Die Zeit*, 13 April 2022, 17.
25 Major, *The Death of the KPD*, 8.
26 Eichler, *100 Jahre Sozialdemokratie*, 50.
27 *Ibid.*, 51.
28 Stampfer, *Erfahrungen und Erkenntnisse*, 290.
29 See Holger Nehring, *Politics of Security: British and West German Protest Movements and the Early Cold War, 1945–1970* (Oxford, 2013), 156–82. Also Michael Frey, *Vor Achtundsechzig: Der Kalte Krieg und die Neue Linke in der Bundesrepublik und den USA* (Göttingen, 2020).
30 Conway, *Western Europe's Democratic Age*, 283.
31 Nehring, *Politics of Security*, 108.
32 Latzel, 'Geschichten der Novemberrevolution', 99–108; Heinrich August Winkler, 'Ein umstrittener Wendepunkt: Die Revolution von 1918/19 im Urteil der westdeutschen Geschichtswissenschaft', in Winkler, *Weimar im Widerstreit*, 33–42 (35). Like Frey, *Vor Achtundsechzig*, this chapter takes the line that the New Left was already established in West Germany in the late 1950s and early 1960s. For the alternative view – that the New Left proper only really began in the Federal Republic and West Berlin in 1966–68, and that historians such as Kolb and Oertzen, who published their first books in 1962 and 1963 respectively, are best described as coming from the 'Old Left' – see Ralf Hoffrogge, 'Remembering the Revolution. Neo-Marxist Interpretations of the German Revolution 1918/1919: A Challenge for Cold War Historiography', in Stefan Berger and Christoph Cornelissen (eds), *Marxist Historical Cultures and Social Movements during the Cold War: Case Studies from Germany, Italy and Other Western European States* (London, 2019), 115–39 (127–8).
33 Helga Grebing, *History of the German Labour Movement: A Survey*, rev. edn, trans. Edith Körner (Leamington Spa, 1985; German original, 1966).
34 See her memoirs, published as Helga Grebing, *Freiheit, die ich meinte: Erinnerungen an Berlin* (Berlin, 2012).
35 Walter Tormin, *Zwischen Rätediktatur und sozialer Demokratie: Die Geschichte der Rätebewegung in der deutschen Revolution 1918/19* (Düsseldorf, 1954).

36 Peter von Oertzen, *Betriebsräte in der Novemberrevolution: Eine politikwissenschaftliche Untersuchung über Ideengehalt und Struktur der betrieblichen und wirtschaftlichen Arbeiterräte in der deutschen Revolution 1918/19* (Düsseldorf, 1963), 113.
37 Reinhard Rürup, 'Einleitung', in Reinhard Rürup (ed.), *Arbeiter- und Soldatenräte im rheinisch-westfälischen Industriegebiet* (Wuppertal, 1975), 7–31. See also Eberhard Kolb, *Die Arbeiterräte in der deutschen Innenpolitik 1918/19* (Düsseldorf, 1962); Reinhard Rürup, *Probleme der Revolution in Deutschland 1918* (Wiesbaden, 1968); Ulrich Kluge, *Soldatenräte und Revolution: Studien zur Militärpolitik in Deutschland 1918/19* (Göttingen, 1975); and Ulrich Kluge, *Die deutsche Revolution 1918/19: Staat, Politik und Gesellschaft zwischen Weltkrieg und Kapp-Putsch* (Frankfurt am Main, 1985).
38 Reinhard Rürup, 'Demokratische Revolution und "Dritter Weg": Die deutsche Revolution von 1918/19 in der neueren wissenschaftlichen Diskussion', *Geschichte und Gesellschaft*, 9 (1983): 278–301.
39 Kolb, *Die Arbeiterräte*, 406.
40 Grebing, *History of the German Labour Movement*, 103.
41 *Ibid.*, 104.
42 Kolb, *Die Arbeiterräte*, 404.
43 Tormin, *Zwischen Rätediktatur*, 113.
44 A. J. Ryder, *The German Revolution of 1918: A Study of German Socialism in War and Revolt* (Cambridge, 1967), 263.
45 See, for instance, Amerigo Caruso, *'Blut und Eisen auch im Innern': Soziale Konflikte, Massenpolitik und Gewalt in Deutschland vor 1914* (Frankfurt am Main and New York, 2021).
46 Richard Bessel, *Germany after the First World War* (Oxford, 1993), 56, 107–8; Gerald D. Feldman, *The Great Disorder: Politics, Economics, and Society in the German Inflation, 1914–1924* (Oxford, 1993), 107.
47 Rürup, 'Einleitung', 21; Rürup, *Probleme der Revolution*, 20.
48 Dillon, 'The German Revolution', 34.
49 *Ibid.*, 35. On the *Bürgerräte* see also Chapter 6 of this book.
50 Bernstein, *Die deutsche Revolution*, 135–8.
51 Rürup, 'Einleitung', 27.
52 Wolfgang J. Mommsen, 'The German Revolution, 1918–1920: Political Revolution and Social Protest', in Mommsen, *Imperial Germany*, 233–54 (244–5).
53 Eichler, *100 Jahre Sozialdemokratie*, 49.
54 Ryder, *The German Revolution*, 180–1.
55 Richard Müller, 'Forderungen für die Räteverfassung', in Richard Müller, *Was die Arbeiterräte wollen und sollen* (Berlin, 1919), 31–2.
56 Jones, *Founding Weimar*.

57 Kolb, *Die Arbeiterräte*, 305.
58 See also Mommsen, 'The German Revolution', 248.
59 Nehring, *Politics of Security*, 185–6; Brown, *West Germany and the Global Sixties*, 9.
60 Stephen L. Fischer, *The Minor Parties of the Federal Republic of Germany: Toward a Comparative Theory of Minor Parties* (The Hague, 1974), 125–6.
61 Timothy Scott Brown, *Sixties Europe* (Cambridge, 2020), 189, 199.
62 Matthias Jahn and Sascha Ziemann, 'Da war es noch Theater: Wie 1968 der Frankfurter Kaufhausbrandstifter-Prozess zum Schauplatz politischer Inszenierung wurde', *Die Zeit*, 9 July 2020, 18.
63 Brown, *Sixties Europe*, 118.
64 See also Norbert Frei, *1968: Jugendrevolte und globaler Protest*, new edn (Munich, 2018 [2008]).
65 Rowan Callick, *The Party Forever: Inside China's Modern Communist Elite* (New York, 2013), 232.
66 Haffner, *Failure of a Revolution*, 200.
67 Niess, *Die Revolution von 1918/19*, 232.
68 Dieter Schneider and Rudolf Kuda, *Arbeiterräte in der Novemberrevolution: Ideen, Wirkungen, Dokumente* (Frankfurt am Main, 1968), 9.
69 *Ibid.*, 7.
70 *Ibid.*, 35–8, 61–2. See also Hannah Arendt, 'Epilogue: Reflections on the Hungarian Revolution', in Hannah Arendt, *The Origins of Totalitarianism*, 2nd edn (New York, 1958 [1950]), 481–510.
71 Schneider and Kuda, *Arbeiterräte*, 10.
72 *Ibid.*, 33.
73 Mommsen, 'The German Revolution', 250.
74 Schneider and Kuda, *Arbeiterräte*, 58–60.
75 *Ibid.*, 26.
76 Haffner, *Failure of a Revolution*.
77 Neil MacGregor, *Germany: Memories of a Nation* (London, 2014), 540–1.
78 Rürup, 'Demokratische Revolution', 278.
79 Mommsen, 'The German Revolution', 253.
80 Winkler, *Die Sozialdemokratie*, 29, 59–63.
81 Mommsen, 'The German Revolution', 237, 241.
82 Winkler, *Die Sozialdemokratie*, 64.
83 Rürup, 'Demokratische Revolution', 290.
84 *Ibid.*, 292.
85 Ritter, *Staatskunst und Kriegshandwerk*, Vol. IV, 465–6.
86 Eschenburg, *Die improvisierte Demokratie*, 35. See also Erdmann, 'Die Geschichte der Weimarer Republik'.

87 Karl Dietrich Erdmann, 'Versuch einer Schlußbilanz', in Erdmann and Schulze, *Weimar: Selbstpreisgabe einer Demokratie*, 345–58 (349).
88 Winkler, *Die Sozialdemokratie*, 64. See also Heinrich August Winkler, *Von der Revolution zur Stabilisierung: Arbeiter und Arbeiterbewegung in der Weimarer Republik 1918 bis 1924* (Bonn, 1984), esp. 19–26.
89 Winkler, *Die Sozialdemokratie*, 65. Cf. Erdmann, 'Versuch einer Schlußbilanz', 349.
90 Winkler, *Von der Revolution zur Stabilisierung*, 26.
91 Reinhard Rürup, *Revolution und Demokratiegründung: Studien zur deutschen Geschichte 1918/19*, ed. Peter Brandt and Detlev Lehnert (Göttingen, 2020), 14.
92 Ibid., 18.

4

Who were the Spartacists? East Germany's '1918'

While it was only in the late 1970s and early 1980s that West German historians really came to 'own' the Revolution as part of the prehistory of the Federal Republic, in East Germany the opposite was the case. Here, 1918–19 was already claimed in the 1950s as a crucial moment in the prehistory of the GDR, and indeed a moment that belonged exclusively to the 'progressive' side in the Cold War. The FRG, by contrast, had in East German eyes inherited the forces of the counterrevolution – which, in this narrative, unsurprisingly included Ebert and the SPD, along with the 'bourgeois' liberal and clerical parties, business owners, the landowning elite, the military, and so forth.[1] The USPD and the councils movement stood somewhere outside this, containing some 'reactionary' elements (notably the 'revisionist' Bernstein and the 'renegade' Kautsky) and some more 'progressive' voices. The only truly revolutionary force, however, was the KPD, founded on 30 December 1918.[2] As Joachim Streisand put it in a 1956 essay, it was this party alone that understood the specific historical and material conditions under which the modern German 'national character' was formed and could thus be *re*formed. Since its formation it had stood at the vanguard of the most socially forward-looking elements in the population, the workers. The latter in turn had consistently battled against the dominant reactionary trends in German history since the late eighteenth century, namely '[t]he ... absolutist regimes within state-territorial frameworks, the [post-1820] ... re-feudalisation of the bourgeoisie, the [choice of a] Prussian path to capitalism, and, after the defeat of the 1848 revolution, [political] unification through a revolution from above.'[3] When the 1918–19 Revolution failed not only to realise socialism, but even to accomplish the bourgeois-democratic aims of the 1848ers, the KPD inherited the task of completing both. This was the message of its 1945 political programme and the commemorations it launched in 1948.[4] During the next important anniversary year, in 1958, East German leader Walter Ulbricht published a new set of theses in the *Zeitschrift für Geschichtswissenschaft* that characterised November 1918 as a 'failed bourgeois revolution carried out in part by proletarian means', while emphasising that the KPD had been the only party not to betray the workers and their bourgeois-progressive allies.[5]

The foregrounding of the KPD in East German narratives of the 1918–19 Revolution did not mean, however, that their assessment of the role of the Spartacists was all positive. The latter had sought to press forward with a series of violent attempts to seize power in Germany (most notably in Berlin in January and March 1919) at the wrong point in time – in other words, without first having secured the backing of an organised, mass movement, led by a disciplined cadre of Marxist-Leninist revolutionaries. As soon as they realised that they lacked mass support and the ability to publicise their beliefs to the workers in an organised fashion, they gave up of their own accord. They had lacked Lenin's insight 'that socialism could be attained only *after* the working class was in full control of political power' and of the media.[6] This was a historic error, but one that some ex-Spartacists, even after the development of the KPD into a mass movement after 1920, failed to recognise.

Memories of splits in the late 1920s, and in particular the founding of the KPD-O in 1928, still haunted the KPD in 1945, and its successor, the SED, after 1946. On the surface, former KPD-O members were welcomed into the ranks of the KPD/SED in 1945–46 if they had not already rejoined the party in the late 1930s. Some, it is true, had disappeared into the Soviet Gulag during the Stalinist terror, which had also reached into the ranks of émigré Communists from central Europe living in Moscow in 1936–38.[7] But nobody talked about them in 1945. The darker sides of Stalinist rule were forgotten, denied or suppressed in a moment of proletarian anti-fascist unity, which lasted until around mid-1948. Thereafter, however, a wave of purges in East Germany also came to target former *Abweichler* (dissident Communists) who were now held to stand in the way of the SED's transformation into a Marxist-Leninist party of a new type, in line with the broader postwar Sovietisation of eastern Europe.[8] Unity was now to be imposed from above via the appointment of a Central Party Control Commission, and, in the 1950s, by the development of various hierarchically organised departments of the SED's Central Committee responsible for ideological questions, cadre training, and relations with universities and research institutes.[9] This also made it difficult, and at times downright dangerous, to adopt narratives about historical events that stood outside the established party line.

This chapter will examine how the GDR's approach to the Revolution of 1918–19 developed from the 1950s through to the late 1970s. Without ignoring the role of Communist dogma and cases of direct and indirect party interference in the creation of historical knowledge, it will also look at spaces where greater nuance and independent thought were possible. The chapter does not seek to compare East German historical writing with that of the West, because the conditions in which it was produced were entirely different. Neither, however, does it treat East German historical narratives as a separate 'other', completely divorced from trends in the West. Rather, following the model suggested by Christoph Kleßmann, it looks for examples of asymmetric entanglement and mutual dependency, as well as estrangement, between the two German historiographies.[10]

The character of the November Revolution

The GDR as a brand new state in 1949 required a greater degree of legitimation than the FRG, which willingly accepted that it was the legal heir of the Third Reich and enjoyed much wider diplomatic recognition and trade relations across the globe in the 1950s and 1960s than its eastern neighbour.[11] Ulbricht's 1958 intervention into the debate on the November Revolution had a strange parallel with the claims made by Karl Dietrich Erdmann in his 1955 essay for the *Vierteljahrshefte für Zeitgeschichte* in the sense that both postulated that there had been, and continued to be, no alternative or 'third way' between parliamentary democracy and Soviet-style Communism. This very much fitted the binary mentalities of the early Cold War. At the same time, Ulbricht's claim to have defined the character of the November Revolution once and for all was part and parcel of reinforcing the GDR's legitimacy as a *socialist* German state and heir to all the progressive forces in Germany's past on four different levels.

First, it allowed the GDR to take advantage of the fact that the FRG's elder generation of senior historians seemed to want to cast the Revolution as something surplus to requirements, at least as far as creating a new national identity for West Germans was concerned. If the East Germans wanted to claim the Revolution as 'theirs', in the 1950s and 1960s it was there for the taking. The central party newspaper *Neues Deutschland* did not let the opportunity pass, its headline on 9 November 1968, the Revolution's fiftieth anniversary, straightforwardly proclaiming 'Legacy of 1918 fulfilled by us'.[12] True, by the 1970s, with the developments in West German historiography discussed in Chapter 3, questions of ownership were more fluid. Even so, in a 1978 publication marking the Revolution's sixtieth anniversary, the East German expert Wolfgang Ruge reasserted the GDR's proprietorial claims (as well as the antiwestern implications of the Revolution's 'lessons'):

> The November Revolution was the most potent revolutionary uprising of the German people since the peasants' war of the sixteenth century ... This was the point when the most forward-looking forces in the German nation first raised their weapons against imperialism and militarism and made their destruction the key historic task of the day. The revolutionary workers, soldiers and sailors fought for the interests of all wage-earners, whose exploitation and subjugation had reached particularly inhumane dimensions and unbearable levels during the imperialist First World War.[13]

Second, Ulbricht's theses on the November Revolution underpinned a State-endorsed narrative about the post-1918 role of the KPD and post-1946 role of the SED. Their historic task had been to 'correct' past failures and complete long-overdue political and social changes by concentrating all progressive energies in the German nation into a disciplined, centralised, avant-garde party of the working class. The KPD was the only party in Germany that had drawn the correct lessons from the failure of 1918–19. Bolshevism had triumphed in Russia a year earlier not because that country was more backward and agricultural, but because its leaders, first and foremost Lenin, had been able to generate a gigantic leap forward in human development – equivalent to the leap made by the bourgeoisie in 1789 – by successfully solving the power question in favour of the industrial proletariat and its peasant allies. In his foreword to a book published by Hans Beyer in 1957 on the November Revolution and Councils Republic in Munich, Ernst Engelberg – an increasingly dominant figure among Marxist historians in the GDR – contrasted Lenin's success in these areas with the failings of Bavaria's Independent Socialist leader Kurt Eisner:

> Eisner represented the German form of Jacobinism in all its positive features and in its limitations. He took a leading role in the November Revolution and adopted a consistent and brave stand against Prusso-German militarism and the nationalist drivel that emerged from all sections of society. [But he showed] his limitations when he opposed the extension of the new Soviet power [in the East] and the development of the revolution [in Bavaria] towards the goal of full-scale proletarian socialism. On top of this he nourished illusions about the supposed democratic and peaceful intentions of the imperialist West.[14]

The SED directed similar criticisms against supporters of the Hungarian Revolution in October–November 1956, including the Marxist philosopher György Lukács, who served as Education Minister in the multi-party Government of Imre Nagy (24 October–4 November). By the end of 1956, Nagy stood accused of having lost faith in Soviet power and of having wilfully underestimated the threat posed by NATO to the entire eastern bloc when he unilaterally took Hungary out of the Warsaw Pact on 1 November. This made him a traitor to 'proletarian internationalism' and justified the subsequent Soviet invasion.[15]

Third, Ulbricht's theses (re)legitimised the internal party purges both of the 1925–45 period and of the late 1940s and the 1950s in the sense that it showed how a 'liberal' attitude towards deviationist tendencies could spell disaster for the KPD/SED and the workers who needed its leadership and proletarian steadfastness. This was possibly an even more important message after February 1956, when the Communist world was turned upside down by the revelations of Stalin's crimes contained in Nikita Khrushchev's speech to the twentieth congress of the Communist Party of the Soviet Union (CPSU). The lip-service that the SED leadership paid to de-Stalinisation after 1956 could in no way be allowed to signal that it was renouncing the use of purges as a means of cleansing the party of 'unreliable' elements. Indeed, on 27 November 1956 the SED Politburo had ordered the arrest of a number of party intellectuals, including the philosopher Wolfgang Harich, the journalist Manfred Hertwig and the economic historian Bernhard Steinberger, followed on 6 December by the director of the Aufbau publishing house, Walter Janka, and in March 1957 by the editors of the journal *Sonntag*, Heinz Zöger and Gustav Just, and the radio commentator Richard Wolf. In trials in March and July 1957 the 'Harich–Janka group' were convicted of founding a 'counterrevolutionary platform aimed at the restoration of capitalism in the GDR' and sentenced to long terms in prison.[16] Their 'crime', in effect, had been to engage in discussions with Lukács, among others, about a possible 'third way' between western parliamentary democracy and Soviet-style Communism.[17]

Finally, Ulbricht's theses helped to provide a framework for disciplining (and, if necessary, punishing) historians in the present who strayed too far from the party line. In the late 1950s and early 1960s, Communist veterans, many of whom had membership cards going back to 1919 or 1920, were asked to write their memoirs for the Institute for Marxism-Leninism (IML), a body attached to the SED's Central Committee. In part this was as a means of preserving the KPD's pre-1946 history, but it was also a tool for ensuring that veterans could be guided into remembering the past in a way that suited the SED's current purposes.[18] Herta Geffke, in the 1950s a senior figure in the Central Party Control Commission and a hardline Stalinist, dictated her memoirs of the November Revolution in 1963 in a manner that conformed perfectly to how the party expected her, a former USPD-turned-KPD member from Stettin (Szczecin) in Prussian Pomerania, to present her less enlightened, pre-Leninist self:

> Through news of and written reports about the socialist October Revolution [in Russia] we developed greater clarity in our thinking about certain problems. But our knowledge of Lenin's revolutionary theories remained very weak. Thus our struggle for proletarian revolution in Germany was still driven by emotional instinct. True, we had understood enough about the October Revolution to appreciate the importance of destroying the reactionary state apparatus and arming the workers. But we still failed to grasp the relevance of

forming alliances with the peasantry, and such connections that did exist were very weak. We had some influence among the rural proletariat, who now began to organise themselves in trade unions and to hold public meetings. I can still remember many of these meetings, from which I came away with strong impressions of the simplicity and warmth of the peasantry, but also the joy that they expressed that at last enlightenment had been brought to them, even down to the remotest village.[19]

Geffke's memoir remained unpublished, but others written for the IML appeared in special anthologies, including one brought out in 1958 for the November Revolution's fortieth anniversary with the title *Vorwärts und nicht vergessen (Forwards and Never Forget)*.[20] A three-volume collection of source materials published by the IML in 1958 also provided a documentary account of the splits on the German left during the First World War, the formation of the KPD in December 1918 and its merger with the left wing of the USPD in 1920.[21] Even the newly formed East German Ministry of Defence, responsible for moulding a new generation of class-conscious soldiers, brought out a special issue of its journal *Militärwesen (Military Affairs)* to mark the forty years since the founding of the KPD.[22] Professional historians, particularly those trained in the GDR, had to come to terms with the fact that the IML had prerogative rights when it came to the writing of the party's own history and the broader history of the German labour movement.[23] The party archive was indeed housed in the same building as the IML in East Berlin.[24] According to Wolfgang Niess, the above-mentioned Wolfgang Ruge, as a rehabilitated party veteran who was employed by the Institute for History in the GDR Academy of Sciences after returning from the Soviet Union in 1956 (where he had spent many years in the Gulag), was obliged – against his inner convictions – to adopt an 'ever more militant tone' and to cling 'even more closely' than the IML's staff to Ulbricht's 1958 theses in the works he wrote in the 1960s and 1970s on the 1918–19 Revolution and the Weimar period.[25]

The corrective function of Ulbricht's theses, and the role played by the IML, the SED Central Committee, and district branches of the SED, can also be seen in two particular cases of individual experts on the November Revolution who fell foul of party dogma and were accused of 'revisionism'. The first concerns the party veteran Albert Schreiner: Minister of War in Stuttgart for five days in November 1918; co-founder of the KPD in the following month; and, for a brief period from 1928 to around 1933, a member of the dissident offshoot party the KPD-O. When he returned to East Germany from US exile in late 1946, Schreiner joined the SED and launched a new career for himself as a historian and academic, penning a book in 1952 on German foreign policy under the Kaiserreich that was written from a strictly Marxist perspective.[26] Already appointed to a chair at the University of Leipzig in 1947, he suffered a brief period out in the cold during the party purges against ex-KPD-O members in the late 1940s and early 1950s, but by 1952 had managed to secure a new position at the German Historical Museum in East Berlin, responsible for building the section on the period 1918–45. His work in the museum completed, in 1956 he joined the Institute for History in the Academy of Sciences, again taking charge of research on the years 1918–45 (and effectively becoming Ruge's first boss).[27] But in 1957 disaster struck when he produced a work on the fortieth anniversary of the Bolshevik Revolution in Russia that clashed with the conventional position being developed by Ulbricht. Schreiner provocatively insisted that Germany had experienced a proletarian, rather than a bourgeois, revolution in November 1918, albeit one that the left failed to bring to completion.[28] This was a view he also expressed in his closing address to a joint conference of East German and Soviet historians at the University of Leipzig in November 1957.[29] In an essay co-written for the fortieth-anniversary volume with one of his junior colleagues in the Institute for History, Günter Schmidt, Schreiner asserted that the Russian Revolution, together with the foundation of the USPD in April 1917, had led to a significant growth of socialist consciousness in Germany.

> This development ... was the outward expression of the willingness of the masses to engage in revolutionary struggle and a demonstration that the slogans of the left had reached far and wide. The police authorities in Düsseldorf even claimed that they could no longer dismiss the possibility that 'countless' members of the middle class, tradesmen, independent artisans and small business owners were 'succumbing to radical influences'. It therefore contradicts the facts when Tormin claims that the working masses, the SPD and the majority of the USPD saw their goal in October–November [1918] as

being parliamentary democracy ... [I]t is absurd to say that the revolution that was coming did not go further in its goals than 'what the new government in October [1918]' had already achieved.[30]

Schreiner's argument was at least in part based on his own experiences in Stuttgart as a member of the Spartacist League and subsequently of the KPD, experiences that put him in a different position from Ulbricht, who had been a member of the USPD in Leipzig until December 1920. As Mario Keßler puts it: 'Those, like Schreiner, who had fought in the Spartacist League could not come to terms with the idea that they had put their lives on the line for a "bourgeois" revolution.'[31] Indeed, Schreiner's work took a very sharp line not only against the SPD and the USPD 'moderates', but also against the left wing of the USPD, which he suggested had dragged the councils movement in an inward-looking, counter-revolutionary direction in 1919, thus burying its international socialist potential.[32] For him, as for Ulbricht, there was quite simply no 'third way' between capitalism and Communism – a lesson that they also both drew from their experiences of the Weimar period, the Nazi era and the early Cold War. The difference between them lay largely in their competing claims over what it meant to be a party veteran. For Ulbricht, it meant recognition that the party was always right. Schreiner agreed insofar as more recent generations of SED members were concerned: 'The younger comrades, who are unable to make judgements on the basis of their own life experiences, should verify their findings with the help of the party and of older comrades.'[33] Yet in 1957–58 he was still determined to have his own experiences validated as part of the process of writing party history and the history of the labour movement – at least until massive pressure from the SED forced him into a public retraction in late 1958.[34]

Schreiner's run-in with the party ended with his gradually being frozen out of his roles within the Academy of Sciences, and eventually with his retirement in 1960. He was unable to complete the planned second volume of his study of German foreign policy, covering the years 1918–45. An altogether different experience was had by Willibald Gutsche, born in 1926 (and thus thirty-four years younger than Schreiner) and somebody who came to academic studies as a mature student in East Germany in the 1950s. Gutsche belonged to what Mary Fulbrook calls the '1929er generation', that section of the population born between 1926 and 1932 whose teenage years and early adulthood were shaped by the Second World War and the events of 1946–49.[35] As a young man from a lower-middle-class family in the town of Erfurt, Gutsche fought as a soldier in 1944–45, was a prisoner of war until late 1946, and then took a teacher training course with the recently established Ministry of Education in the Soviet zone of Germany. By 1948 he was a history teacher at a grammar school in Erfurt, also studying in his spare time for a master's degree. Having completed this, in 1956 he enrolled on the Ph.D. programme at the University of Jena as a mature student. His subject was the November Revolution in Erfurt.[36]

Gutsche submitted his dissertation in 1959 but, because of the intervention of the district leadership of the SED in Erfurt, was forced to defend it at a public meeting in the town, rather than at a traditional academic viva (oral defence) in a university setting. The chief problem was his failure to make his findings on Erfurt fit with Ulbricht's characterisation of November 1918 as a 'failed bourgeois revolution carried out in part by proletarian means'. As his wife Birgitte later wrote:

> Numerous party functionaries and members turned up [at the viva] and during the proceedings persistently sought to prevent a successful defence of the dissertation. They accused the author of having 'deviant tendencies' and of underestimating and therefore falsely representing the role of the KPD. Only the delicate, and for that time not entirely unhazardous, interventions of his supervisors, Professor [Max] Steinmetz and Professor [Heinz] Herz, prevented the candidate from failing. There followed a series of critical attacks in the party's central organs ... One or two functionaries in the district leadership of the SED were dismissed. The whole affair was planned in advance and was part of the intensifying political-ideological struggle in many spheres of public life in the second half of the 1950s, not least in the teaching profession, a phenomenon that caused Willibald Gutsche increasing unhappiness in his chosen career.[37]

The intervention of his academic supervisors did allow Gutsche to receive his Ph.D., demonstrating that party hegemony had certain limits. Even so, he had to rewrite sections of it before it could be published in full. His position as a teacher in Erfurt was also undermined, and in 1961 he was forced to switch jobs, taking up a research post in the Institute for History in the Academy of Sciences, where he joined a team working on a three-volume history of Germany in the First World War.[38] The impact of these developments on him was not only material (although his pay at the Academy of Sciences was initially lower than that of a teacher and he had to spend many hours commuting between Erfurt and East Berlin); in the 1970s and 1980s he became one of the GDR's foremost experts on the First World War and was awarded a professorial chair in 1976. However, he was still held back by his earlier run-ins with the party in Erfurt, and had to take great care over what he published and how he managed his contacts with western scholars. In a letter to the British historian John Röhl in October 1991 he commented on how much he regretted the limited nature of the exchanges he had had with colleagues on the other side of the Iron Curtain during the Cold War. This had prevented him 'from judging received ideas in a more differentiated manner'.[39] Although he continued to produce work on the local history of his home town, Erfurt, he made sure that this did not clash with party directives.[40] More to the point, after publishing the revised version of his Ph.D. thesis in 1963 he never again took up the topic of the November Revolution.[41]

Who were the Spartacists?

While Ulbricht's theses on the November Revolution in 1958, and the capitulation of Schreiner, resolved some problems for the SED, other questions remained. The most important of these was how to cast the role of the Spartacists in 1916–18, now that the Revolution was definitively identified as 'bourgeois'. Walter Bartel, born in 1904 – a Communist resistance fighter and former inmate of the Buchenwald concentration camp who had nonetheless briefly been expelled from the KPD while in Czechoslovak exile in the 1930s, only to be rehabilitated – wrote the first major East German study of the radical left in Germany during the First World War, published in 1958.[42] Yet, as he would have been fully aware, in the late 1950s the question of who the Spartacists were was not just a historical one. It was also a question about power in the present. On one level, it mattered that the current First Secretary of the SED, Ulbricht, had not been a member of the Spartacist League. Admittedly, some ex-Spartacists did rise to very high positions in the early GDR, most notably East Germany's State President, Wilhelm Pieck, who like Ulbricht spent a great deal of time in Moscow after 1936. Yet the problem went much further than that. The purges in the KPD between 1925 and 1945, while often very arbitrary and following no consistent pattern in terms of who was targeted, had nonetheless affected a disproportionately large number of ex-Spartacists. This was particularly the case during the most murderous phase of the purges, namely in Moscow exile in the years 1936–38. Of the several hundred victims, many were shot or did not survive the Gulag.[43] But some – around 400 or so, if dependants are included – did survive. And after Stalin's death in 1953, they re-emerged from the Soviet concentration camp system and sought repatriation to Germany. This was an extremely delicate situation for the SED. It did not wish to talk about Stalinist-era crimes, but also could not refuse rehabilitation to those party members who had been expelled from the KPD and imprisoned or banished to the Soviet Far East in the late 1930s and the 1940s, and who now turned up at the East German embassy in Moscow, their convictions overturned by Soviet organs and their sights now set on entry into the GDR.[44]

The solution was to appoint a rehabilitation commission, which would look carefully into each case. This commission began its work in October 1955 and concluded it in July 1962. Altogether 257 persons were approved for restoration of party membership, sixty-six of them posthumously.[45] The politically rehabilitated and their surviving relatives would also be cared for socially and economically, their repatriation, housing, health and employment needs all catered for by the SED. Moreover, their party record would be completely restored, beginning with the date that they joined (usually in 1919 or the early 1920s) and with all trace of their expulsion – even if it had lasted for twenty years – being erased. The *quid pro quo*, however, was that such rehabilitated party members would not be allowed to mention their bad experiences in the Soviet Union (including the loss of parents, children or spouses), and instead would have to cut this entire period of their lives from their personal life-stories. When it came to writing memoirs for the IML, returnees from the Soviet Union to the GDR in the post-1953 period were usually encouraged to write about their earliest revolutionary experiences, in the 1900s, 1910s and 1920s – and to gloss over the period 1936–53. For ex-members of the Spartacist League, this typically meant focusing on the First World War era, and the events of 1918–19 in particular.

One early example of this rewriting of individual biographies came in 1958. On 28 October the official SED newspaper *Neues Deutschland* carried an article by the veteran communist Martha Globig, who recalled how, as a seventeen-year-old activist in the Spartacist League, she had taken part in the founding conference of the Freie Jugend Groß-Berlins (Free Youth of Greater Berlin) on 5 May 1918, the centenary of Karl Marx's birth, and in an anti-war march in the German capital on 28 October 1918 in defiance of local ordinances. The protestors were blocked by armed police, but

> the young people at the head of the march would not allow themselves to be intimidated and sought to break through the cordon. Arrests followed. When we sought to free the prisoners, the police shot at us at point-blank range ... The crowd pulled back but then surged forward again with renewed determination ... In this way, the delegates representing young workers from across Germany had not only organised a spirited conference, but stood shoulder to shoulder with their comrades from Berlin in the battle for the streets.[46]

For the co-writer of the *Neues Deutschland* piece, this made Globig a role model for socialist youth in the GDR:

> The heroism and sacrifice of young workers in the decades-long revolutionary struggle has paved the way for what we have and take for granted today. Because the working class holds the reigns of power, because it has smashed the power of the militarists, the old rulers are also no longer able to control education [and] our young people now have equal rights and opportunities for development.[47]

What the article failed to mention, however, was that Globig had spent almost twenty years as a Gulag prisoner in the Soviet Union. Her conviction had been quashed by a Moscow court in December 1955, and she had been able to return to Germany in April 1956. Her formal rehabilitation and enrolment in the SED were subsequently ratified by the Central Party Control Commission in October 1956, which agreed to backdate her party membership to before 30 December 1918, the day of the KPD's foundation.[48] She was given a job in the IML, and an extract from her memoirs of the revolutionary struggles in the years 1917–18 was included in the IML's publication *Vorwärts und nicht vergessen*. Here she was recognised as an 'active participant in the November Revolution in Berlin'.[49] However, although her carefully reconstructed past was now held up as an inspiration to East German youth, and although she was called upon by the IML to record her autobiographical memories for the benefit of the 'memoir section' of the IML in 1962, it was made clear to her – and she accepted – that these memoirs would never be published in full in the GDR.[50]

A second example would be Hugo Eberlein, co-founder, alongside Karl Liebknecht, Rosa Luxemburg, Franz Mehring and Ernst Meyer, of the Spartacist League in 1916 and of the KPD in December 1918. In 1937 Eberlein was arrested in Moscow as a suspected traitor, and, after several years of interrogation, torture and prison camps, was shot in October 1941. On 15 October 1956 the Central Party Control Commission decided on his posthumous rehabilitation.[51] His son Werner, who was separated from his stepmother and deported to the Soviet Far East in 1941, returned to what was to become the GDR in 1948. From 1956 he experienced a rapid rise in the SED, becoming Ulbricht's chief Russian interpreter during the latter's visits to the Soviet Union and joining the Central Committee in 1960. In 1983 he became party First Secretary in Magdeburg, and from 1986 to 1989 served in the SED Politburo.

Werner Eberlein's memoirs, written just before his death in 2002, bore the title *Born on 9 November*, a reference to the fact that his birth in 1919 fell on the first anniversary of the November Revolution.[52] His account begins with the story that his father left Berlin for Moscow in March 1919, not knowing that his wife was already a few weeks pregnant with their first son. Hugo Eberlein was chosen to represent the KPD at the founding conference of the Comintern, in place of the now murdered Rosa Luxemburg.[53] Initially he shared Luxemburg's view that, while a new organisation should eventually be founded to replace the defunct Second International, which had collapsed in 1914, it would be premature to move immediately in that direction. On the third day of the congress, however, he changed his mind, having been convinced by Lenin that the time was ripe. His mandate had been to vote against the Comintern's formation, but now he decided to abstain, alongside making a statement that he was sure that the KPD would formally endorse the congress's resolutions once he had brought news of them back to Berlin. In this way, Eberlein was responsible for ensuring the KPD's early membership of the Comintern.[54]

Hugo remained a member of the KPD central executive until 1929, and thereafter worked for the Comintern. By then, however, he had made a number of enemies within the party, which may explain why he was denounced and then arrested during the terror wave of 1936–38 in Moscow. In his memoirs, Werner Eberlein also noted one further interesting anecdote about his father's position, as a former Spartacist, in the KPD of the 1920s. Citing from the memoirs of Rosa Meyer-Leviné, widow of both Eugen Leviné (the Munich revolutionary leader executed in June 1919) and Ernst Meyer (leader of the KPD in 1921–22, who died in 1930), he drew attention to the conflict lines that existed between those who had founded the KPD in December 1918 and those who had only come to the party two years later, via the USPD. Meyer-Leviné wrote, with respect to the election of the Stalinist Ernst Thälmann to the position of KPD leader in October 1925:

> I once said that the highly experienced and educated Eberlein, who enjoyed the same advantage of proletarian birth and who, in contrast to Thälmann, had been one of the early Spartacists, would have been a much better candidate for the role. Whereupon Eberlein replied that he knew his own limitations and would never have put himself forward.[55]

Globig and Eberlein are examples of purged Spartacists who were eventually rehabilitated in the mid-1950s. In July 1961 Globig was even honoured with an official announcement of her sixtieth birthday in *Neues Deutschland*, a mark of recognition reserved for esteemed party veterans.[56] Eberlein was given his due in Walter Bartel's 1958 book as co-founder of the Spartacist League.[57] He also received several mentions in the IML's eight-volume *Geschichte der deutschen Arbeiterbewegung* (*History of the German Workers Movement*), published between 1966 and 1968. However, his death was wrongly given as 1940, and there was no mention of how or why he died.[58] Other purge victims remained 'non-persons' and therefore unmentionable in the GDR, at least until the late 1980s. Among them were Heinz Neumann (shot in 1937) and Hermann Remmele (executed in 1939), both senior functionaries in the KPD from 1920 onwards.⁵⁹ Wolfgang Duncker, son of Hermann and Käte Duncker, who were both founder-members of the Spartacist League in 1916 and of the first central executive committee of the KPD, elected in January 1919, was posthumously rehabilitated on 15 October 1956.⁶⁰ However, his presumed death in the Soviet Union following his arrest in Moscow in 1938 was still a taboo subject in East Germany, broken only when Jürgen Kuczynski – whose father, Robert René, had been a family friend of the Dunckers – mentioned it in his 1983 book *Dialog mit meinem Urenkel* (*Dialogue with My Great-Grandson*).⁶¹

Fritz Globig, Martha Globig's husband and himself a Soviet purge victim who was rehabilitated and readmitted to the party a year before her in November 1955, is listed as one of the co-authors of the above-mentioned *Geschichte der deutschen Arbeiterbewegung*.⁶² Volume V even included a passage about his work for the Spartacist League in the working-class Neukölln district of Berlin in 1916–18 alongside other youth activists, including his girlfriend/wife-to-be, then known as Martha Jogsch. At least one of their comrades from that time, Leo Flieg, was shot in Moscow in the late 1930s.⁶³ None of this could be mentioned. On the other hand, in the same volume that discussed the work of Flieg, Globig and their comrades in Neukölln, the IML's *Geschichte der deutschen Arbeiterbewegung* deliberately – and perhaps wisely – gave the false impression that the young Walter Ulbricht had been a prominent contributor to the post-1914 revolutionary workers' movement in Leipzig. This was by dint of his having belonged to an 'opposition group' that had established close contact with Liebknecht from an early stage in the war.⁶⁴ All in all, then, the GDR found it very difficult to provide an open answer to the question 'Who were the Spartacists?'.

The (bourgeois-) progressive elements of the Revolution

The history of the Spartacist League caused problems to East German chroniclers of the First World War because it could hardly be left to western scholars to write up, but at the same time threatened – if dealt with openly – to tarnish the subsequent history of the KPD. It was something that the SED had to own, but also tightly control. However, it should not be forgotten that the

GDR claimed to represent all 'progressive' forces in German history, not just those linked to the labour movement directly. Some hints of this could already be found in publications in the 1950s. Ernst Engelberg, for instance, in his above-mentioned forward to the 1957 book by Hans Beyer on Munich in 1918–19, reminded readers that the GDR owed much to the bourgeois-progressive writer Heinrich Mann, older brother of Thomas and author of the famous satirical novel critiquing the German empire *Der Untertan* (*Man of Straw*), published in 1918. In Engelberg's words, 'It was none other than Heinrich Mann who on 16 March 1919 in Munich gave an oration at the funeral of the murdered Kurt Eisner; and it was the same Heinrich Mann who after 1933 became a friend of the Soviet Union and an ally of the Communist Party of Germany.'[65]

Given such accolades, it is not so surprising that the GDR's main literary essay prize, awarded by the East German Academy of Arts from 1953 onwards, was called the Heinrich-Mann-Preis. Mann himself died in California in 1950, without ever having visited the GDR, but his name – and his association with the November Revolution – belonged to that part of German history which was claimed by the new East German state.[66] Another 'bourgeois progressive' from that time who was much in favour in the GDR was the artist and sculptor Käthe Kollwitz, famous for her depictions of parents grieving for sons lost to war. Her 1920s cycle of woodcut prints, *Krieg* (*War*), and her 1919 woodcutting *In memoriam Karl Liebknecht*, were frequently used as illustrations in GDR textbooks.[67] In 1947 a square and street were named after her in the East Berlin borough of Prenzlauer Berg, close to the house where she had lived for fifty-two years before her evacuation from the German capital and subsequent death in 1943–45; and in 1960 a bronze monument, designed by the sculptor Gustav Seitz, was erected in her honour on the square.[68] Engelberg's definition of the 'bourgeois-progressive' was actually very narrow and included only those non-party but pro-socialist middle-class revolutionaries in 1918–19 with a record of never having criticised the Soviet Union or the KPD. But other historians, particularly those who wished for greater dialogue between East and West, saw an opportunity in this concept to free up some space for more rigorous academic research outside the tight controls imposed by the SED. The most prominent of these scholars was Fritz Klein, from 1959 director of the Arbeitsgruppe Erster Weltkrieg (Research Group on the First World War) in the Academy of Sciences. Like Engelberg, Klein was a member of the SED. However, their views on how historical scholarship might benefit the East German state were entirely different. This ended in trouble for Klein in 1965 when the more senior Engelberg denounced him for his alleged 'lack of dialectical thinking' and his 'pseudo-Marxist liberalism'.[69] The background to this was a report written by Klein in June 1962, criticising the current state of GDR research on the First World War era and warning that it could soon be overtaken by the West in terms of academic quality:

> Historical scholarship in the GDR has hitherto almost completely ignored those social forces in the nation which lie somewhere between the two extremes of reactionary imperialism and the labour movement. However, the development of a national understanding of history requires – not least in relation to the First World War, a period which is linked by so many threads to our contemporary world – an examination and analysis of all classes and social strata. We currently have no studies of the lower middle classes and their political organisations, whether in relation to the [urban] bourgeoisie or the peasantry. And as yet we have produced no historical works on ... the middle-class peace movement, the middle-class youth movement, the middle-class women's movement – all of which played an important role in the life of the nation. We need a careful investigation of all of these phenomena in order to understand their impact, positive or negative, on the nation's struggle for a future based on peace and social justice.[70]

Klein never wrote directly on the November Revolution himself. His main interest was in the origins and early history of the First World War. But as his career recovered from the setbacks it had suffered as a result of Engelberg's attacks on him in 1965, and as he moved towards a greater interest in contemporary East–West relations in the 1970s and 1980s, he also developed a passion for what he called 'peace history', in other words the history of peace movements in the twentieth century. The scientific study of peace initiatives, he claimed, could be fitted around a Marxist-Leninist framework without succumbing to a dogmatic insistence that the only true force for peace in the world since 1917 was the Soviet Union.[71] This was potentially dangerous territory ideologically, and

Klein opened himself up – not for the first time in his career – to attacks as a 'sham-Marxist' who had abandoned the first principle of 'proletarian internationalism' – namely that the USSR was always right. However, he persisted, and by the mid-1980s his views were beginning to become a little more mainstream in the GDR, without fully being accepted by party hard-liners.[72]

An important example relating to the November Revolution would be a pioneering journal article published by Ursula Herrmann in the March 1985 edition of the *Zeitschrift für Geschichtswissenschaft* on the role played by Social Democrat women in Germany in peace movements before and during the First World War.[73] Not only did this essay represent the first published assessment of the relationship between the hunger protests led by women in twenty big cities in Germany in 1915–16 and the development of the anti-war movement.[74] For all its nods to standard tropes in East German historiography since 1958, it also marked a shift away from the view of 1918–19 as a 'failed bourgeois revolution' and a willingness to consider new angles. Class was not the only lens through which to see social protest and collective struggle. Rather, according to Herrmann,

> the revolutionary mass upheaval also changed the position of women. The November Revolution ended the First World War and liberated women from the scourge of war. It gave women back the social protections that they had been robbed of during the war. It forced through universal suffrage [including] equal suffrage for women. And it ensured the insertion [of important clauses] into the Weimar Constitution ... regarding the formal equality of all citizens before the law, the eight-hour day, the right to holidays, and a number of other social and economic rights.[75]

Herrmann's article was followed in September 1988 by a conference at the Pädagogische Hochschule Clara Zetkin in Leipzig on 'Women and the November Revolution', organised by the research group Geschichte des Kampfes der Arbeiterklasse um die Befreiung der Frau (History of the Workers' Struggle for the Liberation of Women). The nine published papers included contributions on 'the relationship between the bourgeois and proletarian women's movements' (by Hans-Jürgen Arendt), women in the workers' and soldiers' councils (by Peter Kuhlbrodt), and women's contribution to the creation of the KPD in Leipzig (by Martina Siere). However, the most striking, because it took up Klein's interest in 'peace history', was the paper by Petra Rantzsch on feminist-pacifists on the left wing of the 'bourgeois' women's movement. Rantzsch was interested, among other things, in the proposal for the creation of separate women's councils (*Frauenräte*) in Munich in early 1919, made by female activists in the local USPD and supported by Bavarian Minister-President Kurt Eisner. This was of course anathema to the KPD and to Communist women such as Clara Zetkin, who insisted that women should be drawn into the mainstream (and male-led) workers' councils and should not organise separately, lest this dilute the class struggle.[76] Yet Rantzsch's approach was more sympathetic to the cause of the *Frauenräte*:

> While feminist tendencies obviously came to the fore here, it is also important not to equate the rejection of the 'male parties' with a narrow-minded hatred of men. The close cooperation of women such as Anita Augspurg, Lida Gustava Heymann, Gertrud Baer and others with the men involved in the Munich Councils movement would suggest the opposite. It was more a case of rejecting the militaristic and reactionary politics of the past, when men had called all the shots.[77]

These publications from 1985 and 1988 are interesting not only for what they say about the evolution of GDR historical writing in the 1980s and the opening up of new, albeit still very limited, spaces for thinking about the social and economic aspects of the Revolution. Rather, the shift towards looking at women's history, and doing so in a way that went beyond the tired old questions about whether 1918–19 was a 'failed bourgeois' or a 'failed socialist' revolution, pointed towards new ground on which East and West German perspectives might gradually converge. Indeed, Herrmann's journal article on Social Democrat women was written for delivery at the sixteenth International Congress of Historical Sciences in Stuttgart, West Germany, in August 1985, where it was to form part of an international panel session with the title 'Frauen und Friedensbewegung im Atomzeitalter' ('Women and Peace Movements in the Age of the Bomb'). Furthermore, an earlier version was read out at a conference in Toronto, Canada, in September 1984.[78] Of course, the future was still open in

1984–85, and there was as yet no inevitability about the collapse of the GDR and German reunification half a decade later. The politics of the East–West conflict still dominated historiography in the mid-1980s.[79] But nor should we imagine that the events of 1989–90 caused a sudden, sharp, overnight change. As far as historical writing in both East and West Germany on 1918–19 is concerned, the bigger changes came earlier, in the period after 1979, as well as later, in the years after 2009–10.

Notes

1 Andreas Dorpalen, *German History in Marxist Perspective: The East German Approach* (London, 1985), esp. 476–8, 484, 493–7.
2 *Ibid.*, 35, 316.
3 Joachim Streisand, 'Das Problem des Nationalcharakters', in Fritz Klein and Joachim Streisand (eds), *Beiträge zum neuen Geschichtsbild: Zum 60. Geburtstag von Alfred Meusel* (East Berlin, 1956), 27–34 (34).
4 John, 'Das Bild der Novemberrevolution', 56–60.
5 Walter Ulbricht, 'Über den Charakter der Novemberrevolution', *Zeitschrift für Geschichtswissenschaft*, 6.4 (1958), 717–29 (729).
6 Dorpalen, *German History in Marxist Perspective*, 322. Italics in the original.
7 Hermann Weber, *'Weiße Flecken' in der Geschichte: Die KPD-Opfer der Stalinschen Säuberungen und ihre Rehabilitierung*, 2nd edn (Frankfurt am Main, 1990 [1989]).
8 Keßler, 'Zwischen Kommunismus und Sozialdemokratie', 260–3; Stibbe, 'East Germany, 1945–1953', 61–3.
9 See Andreas Malycha and Peter Jochen Winters, *Die SED: Geschichte einer deutschen Partei* (Munich, 2009).
10 Christoph Kleßmann, 'Verflechtung und Abgrenzung: Aspekte der geteilten und zusammengehörigen deutschen Nachkriegsgeschichte', *Aus Politik und Zeitgeschichte*, B29–30 (16 July 1993), 30–41.
11 William Glenn Gray, *Germany's Cold War: The Global Campaign to Isolate East Germany, 1949–1969* (Chapel Hill, NC and London, 2003).
12 'Vermächtnis von 1918 bei uns erfüllt', *Neues Deutschland*, 9 November 1968.
13 Wolfgang Ruge, *Novemberrevolution: Die Volkserhebung gegen den deutschen Imperialismus und Militarismus 1918/19* (East Berlin, 1978), 174.

14 Ernst Engelberg, foreword to Hans Beyer, *Von der Novemberrevolution zur Räterepublik in München* (East Berlin, 1957), XV.
15 Malycha and Winters, *Die SED*, 137.
16 Ibid., 135–6.
17 Ibid., 129, 138.
18 On the IML's 'memoir section' see Catherine Epstein, *The Last Revolutionaries: German Communists and Their Century* (Cambridge, MA, 2003), 194–9.
19 SAPMO-BArch, SgY 30/0257/1, Herta Geffke, *Einige Erinnerungen aus dem Bezirk Pommern über die Entwicklung der USPD und ihre politische Arbeit bis zum Vereinigungsparteitag Dezember 1920*, unpublished memoir written in 1963, 31–2.
20 Institut für Marxismus-Leninismus beim ZK der SED (ed.), *Vorwärts und nicht vergessen: Erlebnisberichte aktiver Teilnehmer der Novemberrevolution 1918/19* (East Berlin, 1958).
21 Institut für Marxismus-Leninismus beim ZK der SED (ed.), *Dokumente und Materialien zur Geschichte der deutschen Arbeiterbewegung*, 3 vols (East Berlin, 1958).
22 *Zum 40. Jahrestag der Novemberrevolution und der Gründung der KPD, Militärwesen*, special issue (1958).
23 See, for instance, Fritz Klein, *Drinnen und Draußen. Ein Historiker in der DDR: Erinnerungen* (Frankfurt am Main, 2000), 224.
24 Epstein, *The Last Revolutionaries*, 194.
25 Niess, *Die Revolution von 1918/19*, 356–7.
26 Albert Schreiner, *Zur Geschichte der deutschen Aussenpolitik, 1871–1945*, Vol. I, *1871–1918: Von der Reichseinigung bis zur Novemberrevolution* (East Berlin, 1952).
27 On Schreiner see Latzel, 'Geschichten der Novemberrevolution', 113; and Niess, *Die Revolution von 1918/19*, 338–52.
28 Albert Schreiner, 'Einleitung', in Albert Schreiner (ed.), *Revolutionäre Ereignisse und Probleme in Deutschland während der Periode der Großen Sozialistischen Oktoberrevolution 1917/1918: Beiträge zum 40. Jahrestag der Grossen Sozialistischen Oktoberrevolution* (East Berlin, 1957), VII–XIV (X).
29 Albert Schreiner, 'Schlußwort', in Kommission der Historiker der DDR und der UdSSR (ed.), *Protokoll der wissenschaftlichen Tagung in Leipzig vom 25. bis 30. November 1957*, Vol. I, *Die Oktoberrevolution und Deutschland. Referate und Diskussionen zum Thema: Der Einfluß der Großen Sozialistischen Oktoberrevolution auf Deutschland* (East Berlin, 1958), 488–91.
30 Albert Schreiner and Günter Schmidt, 'Die Rätebewegung in Deutschland bis zur Novemberrevolution', in Schreiner, *Revolutionäre Ereignisse und Probleme in Deutschland*, 231–308 (quotation

on 306). The quote at the end was taken from Tormin, *Zwischen Rätediktatur*, 56.
31 Keßler, *Exilerfahrung*, 193.
32 Schreiner and Schmidt, 'Die Rätebewegung in Deutschland', 242–3.
33 Schreiner, 'Schlußwort', 489. Also cited in Latzel, 'Geschichten der Novemberrevolution', 114.
34 Keßler, *Exilerfahrung*, 195. See also Petzold, *Parteinahme wofür?*, 125–61.
35 See Mary Fulbrook, *Dissonant Lives: Generations and Violence through the German Dictatorships* (Oxford, 2011), esp. 251–3.
36 On Gutsche see Matthew Stibbe, 'Flüchtige Allianzen: Der Erste Weltkrieg als Erwartungshorizont und Explanandum', in Maubach and Morina, *Das 20. Jahrhundert erzählen*, 32–85 (70–80).
37 'Kurze Biographie von Willibald Gutsche, unveröffentlichtes Manuskript von Birgitte Gutsche', cited in Stibbe, 'Flüchtige Allianzen', 73–4.
38 See Fritz Klein, Willibald Gutsche and Joachim Petzold, *Deutschland im Ersten Weltkrieg*, 3 vols (East Berlin, 1968–69).
39 Gutsche to Röhl, 26 October 1991. Letter in the private possession of Professor John Röhl.
40 See, for instance, Willibald Gutsche, *Geschichte der Stadt Erfurt*, new edn (Weimar, 1989 [1986]); and Willibald Gutsche, *Erfurt: Ein Führer durch die Blumenstadt und ihre 1200jährige Geschichte* (Erfurt, 1967).
41 Willibald Gutsche, *Die revolutionäre Bewegung in Erfurt während des 1. imperialistischen Weltkrieges und der Novemberrevolution* (Erfurt, 1963).
42 Walter Bartel, *Die Linken in der deutschen Sozialdemokratie im Kampf gegen Militarismus und Krieg* (East Berlin, 1958).
43 In 1989, Hermann Weber listed 305 dead or missing KPD members from the period 1936–53, while reckoning there were many more 'blank spots'. By no means all the victims were former Spartacists or participants in the events in Berlin in 1918 and early 1919, but some were. See Weber, '*Weiße Flecken*', 66–99.
44 For further details see Matthew Stibbe, 'The Limits of Rehabilitation: The 1930s Stalinist Terror and Its Legacy in Post-1953 East Germany', in Kevin McDermott and Matthew Stibbe (eds), *De-Stalinising Eastern Europe: The Rehabilitation of Stalin's Victims after 1953* (Basingstoke, 2015), 87–108.
45 *Ibid.*, 95.
46 'Vor 40 Jahren an der Weberwiese: Zum Jahrestag der Gründung der Freien Sozialistischen Jugend', *Neues Deutschland*, 28 October 1958. On the Freie Jugend Groß-Berlins see also Walter Sieger, *Die junge*

Front: Die revolutionäre Arbeiterjugend im Kampf gegen den Ersten Weltkrieg (East Berlin, 1953), 148.
47 'Vor 40 Jahren an der Weberwiese'.
48 Josef Gabert, Lutz Prieß, Peter Erler and Jutta Finkeisen (eds), *SED und Stalinismus: Dokumente aus dem Jahre 1956* (East Berlin, 1990), 156.
49 Martha Globig, 'Weiße haben hier nichts zu suchen!', in Institut für Marxismus-Leninismus beim ZK der SED, *Vorwärts und nicht vergessen*, 300–9 (300).
50 The memoirs were recorded in two sittings in January and July 1962, and covered her life from her involvement in the young workers' movement in the First World War up to 1943, but remained hidden away in the party archives until 1990. They were subsequently published in Ulla Plener (ed.), *Leben mit Hoffnung in Pein: Frauenschicksale unter Stalin* (Frankfurt an der Oder, 1997), 231–79. The original transcript can be found in SAPMO-BArch, SgY 30/0278.
51 Gabert *et al.*, *SED und Stalinismus*, 154.
52 Werner Eberlein, *Geboren am 9. November: Erinnerungen* (Berlin, 2000).
53 See also Werner Müller, 'Die KPD in ihrem ersten Jahr', in Gallus, *Die vergessene Revolution*, 160–86 (169–70).
54 Eberlein, *Geboren am 9. November*, 12–15.
55 *Ibid.*, 18. See also Rosa Leviné-Meyer, *Inside German Communism: Memoirs of Party Life in the Weimar Republic*, ed. David Zane Mairowitz (London, 1977), 69.
56 'Martha Globig 60 Jahre', *Neues Deutschland*, 9 July 1961.
57 Bartel, *Die Linken in der deutschen Sozialdemokratie*, 239–40, 270.
58 See Institut für Marxismus-Leninismus beim ZK der SED (ed.), *Geschichte der deutschen Arbeiterbewegung*, 8 vols (East Berlin, 1966–68), Vol. V, 30, 64, 67, 79, 85; Vol. VI, 64, 117, 154, 168, 179.
59 Weber, '*Weiße Flecken*', 39, 86–7, 90.
60 Gabert *et al.*, *SED und Stalinismus*, 154. See also Weber, '*Weiße Flecken*', 72, 106.
61 Jürgen Kuczynski, *Dialog mit meinem Urenkel: Neunzehn Briefe und ein Tagebuch* (Weimar, 1983), 80–1.
62 Gabert *et al.*, *SED und Stalinismus*, 155.
63 Institut für Marxismus-Leninismus beim ZK der SED, *Geschichte der deutschen Arbeiterbewegung*, Vol. V, 4, 29. See also Weber, '*Weiße Flecken*', 74, 101.
64 Institut für Marxismus-Leninismus beim ZK der SED, *Geschichte der deutschen Arbeiterbewegung*, Vol. V, 29, 80–1.
65 Engelberg, foreword to Beyer, *Von der Novemberrevolution zur Räterepublik*, XV–XVI.

66 Jörg Bernhard Bilke, 'Heinrich Mann in der DDR', in Klaus Matthias (ed.), *Heinrich Mann 1871/1971: Bestandaufnahme und Untersuchung* (Munich, 1973), 367–84.
67 See, for example, Ruge, *Novemberrevolution*, 6, 143.
68 Klaus Grosinski, *Prenzlauer Berg: Eine Chronik* (Berlin, 2008), 192, 332.
69 See Stibbe, 'Flüchtige Allianzen', 63–5.
70 *Ibid.*, 62.
71 See, for instance, Fritz Klein, 'Einig im Willen, den Krieg zu verhindern', *Neues Deutschland*, 3 November 1983; and Fritz Klein, 'Aufgaben der Historiker im Friedenskampf', *Zeitschrift für Geschichtswissenschaft*, 32.12 (1984), 1092–101.
72 See also Matthew Stibbe, 'Warum Kriege? Wozu Geschichte(n) von Kriegen? Der Erste Weltkrieg in der wissenschaftlichen Geschichtsschreibung der DDR', in Emmanuel Droit and Nicolas Offenstadt (eds), *Das Rote Erbe der Front: Der Erste Weltkrieg in der DDR* (Berlin, 2022), 273–305.
73 Ursula Herrmann, 'Sozialdemokratische Frauen in Deutschland im Kampf um den Frieden vor und während des ersten Weltkrieges', *Zeitschrift für Geschichtswissenschaft*, 33.3 (1985), 213–30.
74 *Ibid.*, 223.
75 *Ibid.*, 229–30.
76 See, for instance, Clara Zetkin, 'Richtlinien der Kommunistischen Internationale für die kommunistische Frauenbewegung', *Die Kommunistin*, 3.2 (January 1921), 1.
77 Petra Rantzsch, 'Linke Kräfte der bürgerlichen Frauenbewegung in der Novemberrevolution', in Pädagogische Hochschule Clara Zetkin (ed.), *Die Novemberrevolution 1918/19 und die Frauen: Kolloquium der Forschungsgemeinschaft 'Geschichte des Kampfes der Arbeiterklasse um die Befreiung der Frau' am 27. September 1988. Referate und Diskussionsbeiträge* (Leipzig, 1988), 45–53 (49).
78 Herrmann, 'Sozialdemokratische Frauen', 213.
79 See Dorpalen, *German History in Marxist Perspective*; Iggers, *The Social History of Politics*.

5

1989 and all that: The German Revolution of 1918–19 and the passing of the GDR

While the thirteen months between September 1989 (beginnings of the peaceful collapse of the East German state) and October 1990 (German reunification on western terms) certainly constitute a major turning point in twentieth-century German history, it is worth noting that afterwards, the events of this time were rarely constructed with the same continuous timelines that had dominated accounts of earlier revolutions (1918–19 as well as 1789 and 1848) during the Cold War era. 'Ours is an age of instant history', wrote Marla Stone in her introduction to a compilation of public-facing texts written in immediate reaction to German reunification that she co-edited with her Princeton colleague Harold James in 1992.[1] The question of 'being' in the present – and especially putting oneself 'out there' – was now given priority over establishing links with the past. Historical change could no longer be measured simply by reference to the 'false universalism' of class interest; ideological struggle; political thought; or supposedly singular, world-changing events such as the French Revolution of 1789 or the Bolshevik Revolution of 1917. Instead, fragmented narratives of the past came to be seen as a more open-ended and more authentic way of revealing the richness of human experience and the ambiguous meanings it threw up.[2] On top of this, scholars increasingly followed French philosopher Michel Foucault's approach to the 'historical operations of power', seeking to uncover the hidden archaeology behind present-day notions of what is considered 'normal' or 'rational' within the 'established disciplines of knowledge' – meaning sociology, anthropology, psychiatry, medicine, criminology and other branches of the post-Enlightenment 'human sciences'.[3]

In fact, the shift towards what Foucault called the 'history of the present' did not simply begin overnight in 1989–90. Much of the groundwork was already laid in the preceding decade, beginning around 1979. The Iranian Revolution of that year had been a revolt against the West that was not based on any ideological attachment to Soviet-style Communism or any desire for adherence to Moscow, Beijing or the movement of non-aligned countries led by Tito's Yugoslavia. Rather, the creation of the Islamic Republic and its rejection of 'western' rationality rooted in the Enlightenment opened up new ways of seeing the relationship among identity, social being and religious belief in the (post-) modern era.[4] Even East German social scientists recognised, as the organiser of a conference in East Berlin in March 1981 remarked, that the challenges of late modernity required them

> to pay more attention to the relative independence of the superstructure or parts of the superstructure and to research it in a more differentiated manner (including, for example, the historicity of irrational ideologies such as religious fanaticism, which, as developments in Iran since 1979 show, is also a question of practical politics).[5]

Yet at this time the eyes of the world and of the international academic community were not just on Iran. The Solidarity crisis in Poland in 1980–81 also challenged previous assumptions about the foundations of modern political, social and cultural life. A mass movement of workers, intellectuals and Catholics had mobilised against a Communist state, but also sought the latter's recognition as a negotiating partner. The talk was of an entirely new phenomenon, the 'self-limiting revolution'.[6] Meanwhile, in West Germany the Green Party had entered the Bundestag for the first time in the 1980s and increased its vote share from 5.6 per cent in 1983 to 8.3 per cent in 1987. The Greens were a centre-left party, founded in 1980 and with roots in the 1968er movement, but compared to the Social Democrats, their agenda was less ideologically grounded in History with a capital 'H' and more focused on the immediacy of current political issues (climate change, feminism, gay rights, atomic power and the nuclear arms race).[7] Where they differed from socialist traditions was also in their refusal to foreground 'mastery and control over the material world' as the defining feature of societal progress and the best measure of human creativity.[8]

As this chapter will show, the implications of these broader developments for historical debates on the Revolution of 1918–19 were both profound and difficult to pin down. Change happened in an asymmetrical and asynchronous manner, coming more sharply and profoundly to historians in the East compared to those in the West. But in both cases it came very quickly, and indeed with giddying speed as the decade of the 1980s reached its remarkable end. To quote Marla Stone again, in the late twentieth century making sense of contemporary events necessitated 'adaptation to a postmodern appetite for immediate action' while at the same confronting the 'emotional challenge' of sudden loss of rootedness in history and certainty about the future.[9]

The chapter will first examine what it meant to throw off the baggage of the Cold War in the 1980s in the context of historical interpretations of the November Revolution. This will include both an analysis of broader shifts towards cultural and gendered approaches to reconstructing the past, and a brief discussion of cross-border dialogue between SPD and SED historians at two unique meetings in Bonn in March 1987 and East Berlin in May 1989. The second part of the chapter moves on to look at the more direct challenge posed by the events of 1989–90 to conventional readings of the 'problem' of revolution in modern German history, and seeks to explain why – with the exception of the post-Communist left – scholars tended to shy away from the topic of November 1918 in the first two decades after German reunification.

Casting off the baggage of the Cold War

What did casting off the baggage of the Cold War actually mean in the 1980s and 1990s? First, it implied acceptance that there was no scientific way of measuring historical experience. 'Objectivism', meaning the stress on external structures, processes or events as the proper 'object' of historical enquiry, merely reinforced the power-claims and inequalities that hid behind modern notions of knowledge, reason and progress.[10] For postmodernists, 'historical truth' had to be reframed in ways that embraced the existence of subjectivities, counternarratives, and 'hidden' or 'disobedient' histories.[11] More to the point, 'the very notion of a consistent ego or self' had to be 'historically problematized'.[12] In this sense, subjective accounts were of value not because of their greater authenticity ('authenticity' itself being a relative concept) but because they 'provide insights into changing conceptions of historical selfhood and emergent discourses of self-representation across time'.[13] In West Germany, the cultural historian and theorist Reinhart Koselleck drew on a particular example here, namely changing conceptions of personal 'realms of experience' and discordant shifts in 'horizons of expectation' emerging from (and leading to) changing perceptions of *historical* time and time to come, as he uncovered in his 1979 study *Futures Past*.[14]

The second scholarly development concerned gender. Women's history had already begun to establish itself, albeit in the face of a great deal of male hostility, in parts of western academia in the 1960s and 1970s. But it was not until December 1986 that the American scholar Joan W. Scott published a landmark essay on gender in the mainstream *American Historical Review*. Here she advanced what was then a novel idea, but which from today's perspective appears entirely self-evident: namely that gender – a word used to indicate partial or wholesale rejection of 'biological determinism' in relation to sex in favour of an understanding that distinctions between male and female are socially, culturally and linguistically constructed – is a useful category for analysing all kinds of historical phenomena, including revolutions.[15] *Gendering* history, a challenge subsequently taken up by scholars on both sides of the Atlantic,[16] required a new way of thinking and a new set of heuristic priorities. In Scott's own words:

> We need a refusal of the fixed and permanent quality of the binary opposition [male/female], a genuine historicization and deconstruction of the terms of sexual difference. We must become more self-conscious about distinguishing between our analytic vocabulary and the material we want to analyze. We must find ways ... to continually subject our categories to criticism, our analyses to self-criticism ... [T]his criticism means analyzing in context the way any binary opposition operates, reversing and displacing its hierarchical construction, rather than accepting it as real or self-evident or in the nature of things.[17]

Since revolutions, like other historical events, construct and are constitutive of gender, Scott's methodology opened the door to a whole new way of viewing 1918–19, one that decentred class and challenged the gendered hierarchies that class-based narratives of the past helped, both by default and design, to reproduce.[18] The social self was now also a gendered self, and class no longer determined all.

The third issue related more one-sidedly to East Germany. As the 1980s progressed, the ruling party there gradually lost confidence in its own rigid narratives about the past. As the GDR historian Wolfgang Ruge put it retrospectively, the increasingly 'chaotic character' of the world and the sheer 'diversity of circumstances that shape society' led many in the profession after 1979, himself included, to lose their faith in the ability of the natural and social sciences to shape forthcoming events:

> Engels's fundamental belief, which underlies the entire idea of socialism, that humans will be able to take control of processes of development once they have recognised the laws of movement in society, began to look like an illusion. The dreams of the planned construction of a society based on the future gradually melted away.[19]

The new uncertainties were partly the result of the East German regime's growing estrangement from the Soviet Union under Mikhail Gorbachev, symbolised above all by the decision to ban the perestroika-friendly Soviet magazine *Sputnik* in the GDR in November 1988.[20] In the same month, on the occasion of the seventieth anniversary of the Revolution, the SED was noticeably less forward in claiming 'ownership' of 1918–19 than it had been on previous anniversaries. In fact, it largely ignored the November anniversary. Instead, the headline news story in the party newspaper *Neues Deutschland* on 9 November 1988 was the staging of a minute's silence in the East German Parliament, the *Volkskammer*, in honour of the victims of the 'fascist pogrom' of 1938 (known in the West as *Kristallnacht*) and, by extension, in remembrance of all the victims of the Nazi regime, 'including the six million murdered Jews'.[21] When it came to 1918–19, the party instead chose to mark the seventy years since the founding of the KPD in December 1918, which now appeared as the only really 'positive' aspect of the upheavals of 1918–19 that the GDR wished to commemorate. Indeed, the KPD's anniversary was the subject of a new set of theses published in June 1988 by a commission of historians and functionaries appointed by the SED Central Committee.²² This was accompanied by a statement issued by SED ideology chief Kurt Hager, noting that 'We are not part of the CPSU and our course is derived from our own decisions. This point must be firmly upheld by our social scientists.'²³ Celebrations continued throughout that year, with the history of German Communism now increasingly being rewritten as an East German, rather than Soviet or global, phenomenon. The creation of the KPD was, according to the front page of *Neues Deutschland* on 30 December 1988, a 'moment of huge historic importance in the struggle for the welfare of our nation'.²⁴ As Peter Grieder shrewdly notes, 'pointing up "national peculiarities" in East Germany's development' in this way had, by the late 1980s, become the standard symbolic means of communicating the GDR's sense of alienation from Gorbachev and the current leadership of the Soviet Union while confirming its historical commitment to socialism.²⁵

As far as the November Revolution was concerned, however, the SED no longer seemed particularly interested in recognising it as part of the 'history of the present'. This allowed space for some critical GDR historians, notably Ruge and a younger colleague, Werner Bramke, to dare to challenge a number of the more outlandish interpretations decreed by senior figures in the party – or what Ruge dubbed the 'Politburocracy'.²⁶ As we saw in the previous chapter, in 1978 Ruge had written the latest GDR text on the November Revolution, in which he repeated the essentials of Ulbricht's 1958 theses. Already in 1980, however, before fellow members of the SED group among the historians in the Academy of Sciences, he complained openly about party interference in the writing of history, noting in particular that 'we place too much emphasis on the exposure of reactionary elements in the SPD' and 'we spend more time than is necessary bludgeoning the SPD'.²⁷ The informer who passed this information on to the Stasi (secret police) also observed that Ruge had failed to admit any 'errors' in his political thinking when called upon to do so by fellow party members:

> In the course of the discussion, RUGE made direct reference to his personal experience of ten years' imprisonment in the USSR. RUGE returned from the USSR in 1956 and was given every imaginable assistance to progress in his academic career. Even today he has not

been required to take on any administrative roles, in order that he can concentrate on strengthening his scholarly profile without being distracted![28]

In 1988 Ruge contributed a chapter on the November Revolution and the Weimar Republic to a new university textbook on German history edited by Joachim Herrmann. In his 1978 book, Ruge had already described November 1918 as a 'popular uprising against imperialism and militarism' without explicitly pointing out where his account contradicted Ulbricht's characterisation of it as a 'failed bourgeois revolution'.[29] Now he went further, suggesting that the initial socialist potential of this popular revolt had placed it on a par with the Bolshevik Revolution in Russia:

> The extent to which the most active workers had understood the significance of the Russian model, or at least – to follow Lenin's later formulation – 'had grabbed hold of it with the instinct of a revolutionary class', can be seen by the sudden appearance and enormous growth of the councils movement.[30]

In particular, the USPD in the weeks and months before November 1918 needed to be seen in a more nuanced light. Its left wing was 'borne by a great sympathy for the October Revolution in Russia'. Many of the ordinary workers who joined the USPD also embraced militant labourism and 'identified emotionally with the Spartacist group', even if their grasp of theoretical and organisational issues was no match for the Bolsheviks.[31] This was very different to Ruge's portrayal of the USPD in 1978. Here he quoted Lenin's disparaging remarks on Kautsky and the negative assessment of the USPD read out at the illegal Spartacist conference held in Berlin on 7 October 1918: 'Favourable experiences of collaboration with the USP[D] are not forthcoming anywhere ... The independents' agitation in favour of parliamentarisation is a diversion that distracts us from the actual goal of the proletarian movement, namely the staging of revolution.'[32]

Bramke's revisions went even further. In an article jointly written with Ulrich Heß for the December 1988 edition of the *Zeitschrift für Geschichtswissenschaft*, he acknowledged Lenin's point about 'the absence of a strong revolutionary party' in Germany but insisted that Lenin had still given the 'proletarian revolution [here] a good chance'. This was not only because 'socialism was the immediate goal of the majority of German workers, even the social democratic ones',[33] but also because of the unique moment in time that the Revolution took place: 'It remains to this day the only attempt by workers in a large, advanced capitalist country to overthrow imperialism and to establish a democracy of an entirely new type [*eine Demokratie ganz neuen Typs*] by their own efforts.'[34] Ruge and Bramke, in other words, were now both free to say that November 1918 was a failed socialist revolution and at the same time the world's first popular uprising against imperialism. In so doing, they showed a new-found ability to imagine how socialist histories of the Revolution of 1918–19 might free themselves from the ideological dogmas of the twentieth century.[35] This was an extremely significant development in GDR historiography, albeit one that was swiftly forgotten in the aftermath of German reunification in 1989–90.

East–West dialogue 1987–89

Less important than these internal developments, but still of some significance, were attempts at dialogue between SPD and SED historians across the Cold War divide in the late 1980s. The SPD had been out of power at federal level in West Germany since October 1982 but was still important as the main opposition party and as the dominant coalition partner in several state governments. From 1984 it began exploratory talks with the SED on a number of matters, leading to the publication of a joint statement on 'ideological differences and security concerns' in August 1987.[36] Also from around 1984, the first tentative moves were made towards contacts between scholars (and students) working on contemporary historical themes, although at first the focus was almost entirely on links between the SPD's Commission on Fundamental Values and the SED Central Committee's Academy of Social Sciences.[37] This changed in March 1987 when, in a separate but related move, the Historical Commission attached to the SPD executive committee invited six SED historians – Ernst Engelberg, Dieter Fricke, Walter Schmidt, Gustav Seeber, Manfred Weißbecker and Walter Wimmer – to take part in a conference in Bonn on the history of the German labour movement, whose results were later published in West Germany.[38] The event was attended by over 600 delegates,[39] and began with an address by Willy Brandt, who noted, among other things, that there could be little doubt that 'the weaknesses of the left ... and in particular the divisions within the labour movement have weighed heavily on developments in Germany ever since the First World War'.[40] After a two-year hiatus, a further 'discussion forum' was held in East Berlin at the end of May 1989, attended by around 170 academics and students from the GDR, as well as a delegation of ten academics from the SPD's Historical Commission, including Helga Grebing, Susanne Miller, Hans Mommsen, Heinrich Potthoff, Reinhard Rürup, Klaus Schönhoven and the former Communist turned arch-critic of the KPD Hermann Weber. This time, journalists were allowed in from both sides (sixteen from the FRG, thirteen from the GDR) and the papers and subsequent discussions were reported in the press as well as in academic journals.[41]

The subject of the November Revolution appeared as one of a number of discussion points in both 1987 and 1989, and was still a difficult area on which to reach common agreement, not least, as Walter Wimmer from the IML conceded, 'because of [its] place... in the self-image of our socialist republic'.[42] Indeed, Helga Grebing, one of the key participants on the West German side, made known her concerns in March 1987 about the tendency of East German historiography to draw false 'lines of continuity' from earlier episodes in the history of the labour movement to the foundation of the GDR, while shutting out the possibility of alternative, more democratic paths that could have been taken,[43] and in December 1987 she repeated these concerns in a critical article on the joint SED–SPD statement on 'ideological differences and security concerns' published in Bonn.[44] At the May 1989 symposium in East Berlin, she and her colleague Reinhard Rürup continued to put forward the position of the left of the SPD, namely (in Rürup's words) 'that we do not believe in a simple either–or between "imperialism" and "socialism" but rather grant the possibility of intermediate forms' between the two.[45] Against this, the SED historian Joachim Petzold put the standard East German case, namely 'that the basic shortcoming of the November Revolution was that it failed to create the right material conditions for the construction of a socialist society in regard to ownership of property and the question of power'.[46] This had been a shortcoming rectified in the GDR after 1949, ensuring the emergence of an entirely different, more just society than that in the FRG.

Indeed, perhaps the most positive thing that can be said about the May 1989 symposium was that it happened at all. In East Berlin, the SPD's Historical Commission was no longer seen – or at least was no longer regarded entirely – as the anti-Communist 'enemy', even by members of the IML such as Wimmer.[47] Between March 1987 and May 1989 there were also some tentative moves towards East–West contact at the individual level, for instance when Werner Bramke invited Heinrich August Winkler to give a lecture on 'The November Revolution and the Problem of Continuity in German History' at the University of Leipzig in 1988.[48] Writing ten years later, after the end of the Cold War, Bramke insisted that these and other 'East–West contacts were desired by both sides' and should be judged more for what they say about the greater 'political discernment' in the GDR in the late 1980s than about the supposed fundamental incompatibility between the two German historiographies.[49] At the end of 1988, as we have seen, Bramke and his colleague Heß published a piece in the *Zeitschrift für Geschichtswissenschaft* that partly accepted the thesis of a 'third way'. If November 1918 was not a successful proletarian revolution, it was at least *more* than a failed bourgeois one.[50]

Bramke may have been further encouraged to challenge established Communist orthodoxies by hints of a shift in the CPSU's ideological position on the November Revolution, as witnessed during a joint conference of East German and Soviet historians held in East Berlin in September 1988.[51] In his keynote address to the conference, Ernst Diehl, himself a long-standing member of the SED Central Committee as well as deputy director of the IML, received applause when he explicitly parted company with Ulbricht's 1958 definition of the Revolution as 'bourgeois'. According to Joachim Petzold, this intervention came as something of a surprise not only to the historians present but even to ideology chief Hager, who was not quite ready to accept the alternative thesis that it had been an 'anti-imperialist-democratic revolution'.[52] In other respects, though, Bramke's ideas went further than Diehl's and were reminiscent of the concept of a *democrazia di tipo nuovo* first developed by the Italian Communist Party leader Palmiro Togliatti in the 1930s and 1940s as an alternative to insurrectionist and narrowly sectarian forms of *Parteikommunismus*.⁵³ However, it was still not possible for him to say what a 'democracy of a new type' might have looked like, had it succeeded in 1918–19. Would it have guaranteed freedom of speech and other individual rights? Would it have agreed to operate within a parliamentary framework? Or would it have extended more power to workers in the social sphere? Or perhaps both? As an SED historian, Bramke could hardly join the 200 East German dissidents on 15 January 1988 and the 300 East Berlin protestors on 15 January 1989 who used the occasion of the anniversary of Liebknecht and Luxemburg's murder to demand an end to censorship in the GDR, quoting Luxemburg's famous dictum that 'freedom is always and exclusively the freedom to think differently'.⁵⁴ This would have been a step too far. Even in its final years, the Honecker regime did not make it easy for its Marxist scholars to find a 'third way' between outward displays of loyalty to the party line and open political dissent.⁵⁵ In short, while SED historians such as Bramke and Heß, and their counterparts such as Winkler, Rürup and Grebing, may have found some unique, if rather awkward opportunities for dialogue in 1987–89, there was never going to be a mutual coming together over the meaning, value and historical roots of democracy. By extension, there was also no prospect of common agreement across the Berlin Wall on the character and legacy of the Revolution of 1918–19, whether for the working class of that particular city or for the German and European labour movements as a whole.

1918–19, 1989 and the 'problem' of revolution in Germany

The events of September 1989–October 1990, when the GDR was people-protested, voted and finally negotiated out of existence, were more or less instantly characterised as Germany's 'peaceful revolution'⁵⁶ and, in official discourses at least, this is also how these events are still remembered on significant anniversaries.⁵⁷ The SED's power simply imploded, facilitated by divisions between pro- and anti-Gorbachev voices within its leadership and by a mass exodus of ordinary rank-and-file members who no longer believed that the party had a future. After the fall of the Berlin Wall on 9 November, the party's fate was sealed in the final weeks of 1989; by January 1990 it had already renamed itself the Partei des Demokratischen Sozialismus (Party of Democratic Socialism (PDS)) and on 18 March 1990, led by the reformer Hans Modrow, it won only 16.4 per cent of the vote in the first free elections ever staged in East Germany. The March poll also arguably settled the debate about whether the GDR should continue to exist as a separate state or merge as soon as possible with the FRG. Parties supporting a swift merger, led by the Christian Democrat-dominated Alliance for Germany, won a decisive majority; aside from the PDS on 16.4 per cent, dissident groups still advocating some kind of socialism and gathered together in the left-leaning coalition Bündnis 90 (Alliance 90) took a mere 2.9 per cent of ballots cast. Modrow was forced to resign as East German Minister-President on 12 April, and his successor, Lothar de Maizière, spent the next few months settling the terms of the GDR's liquidation. Reunification finally took place on 3 October 1990.

The reality of a peaceful revolution with a decisive, democratic outcome also changed the terms on which the 1918–19 Revolution was debated and interpreted. Perhaps the most important development here was its decoupling from notions of a separate national path of historical development in Germany, leading up to the Nazi seizure of power in January 1933. Non-violent revolutions happened all over the world in the late twentieth century; Germany was no exception.[58] But nor did it any longer have to feel ashamed over its past 'failed' revolutions, or envious of countries that had managed to produce more successful ones. An opportunity was opened to see the 1918–19 Revolution as part of a broader European story of battles for workers' rights, paths to women's suffrage, and/or struggles against fascism and tyranny.[59]

Yet this denationalisation of historical discourse also carried with it the danger that the 1918–19 Revolution might simply move into the shadows, displaced by new concerns with the Weimar Republic as a globally significant 'laboratory' of cultural modernity.[60] Weimar was now at the heart of debates not only about Germany in the 1920s and early 1930s, but about the transnational spread of ideas, fashions, styles and icons. 'Weimar was Berlin, Berlin Weimar', as American historian Eric D. Weitz put it in an engaging study published in 2007.[61] The old world had vanished and a new world was dawning. Now was the time when 'The center of gravity had shifted to the city with its cacophony of sounds and images, to the factories and mines pounding out the products of an advanced industrial economy, and to the tensions and excitements of "mass society".'[62] Against this image of a world city in constant flux, it was perhaps not surprising that Weitz dealt with the Revolution of 1918–19 in one short chapter, which he titled simply 'A Troubled Beginning', before moving to the subject that really interested him, namely Weimar Berlin's 'vibrant, active spirit' and its opening of 'one of the greatest periods of artistic and intellectual creativity in the twentieth century'.[63]

Indeed, the passing of the Cold War, and the 'cultural turn' in historical studies, made debates about the class character and even the 'success' or 'failure' of the 1918–19 Revolution seem redundant. The bigger question, as another American historian, Peter Fritzsche, suggested in 1996, was whether Weimar itself had 'failed' or whether in fact some of its experimentalism lived on into the Third Reich and beyond.[64] Yet the very manner in which Fritzsche posed this question also suggested new ways of framing historical debate. Concepts such as 'success' or 'failure', 'crisis' or 'opportunity', 'violence' or 'non-violence', and even 'historical time' and 'social history', were now being deconstructed and critically interrogated. Much like the concepts 'male' and 'female', they were being rethought as non-binary and unstable concepts, ripe for historicisation and critical re-evaluation.[65]

Under these circumstances, the 1918–19 Revolution simply fell out of favour as a subject worthy of historical investigation in its own right. It gave rise to few debates that cultural historians were interested in and did not appear to lend itself well to transnational and comparative studies. The seventy-fifth and eightieth anniversaries in 1993–94 and 1998–99 were remarkably low-key affairs, and seem even more so in retrospect. In the 1990s, the big historical controversies in and about Germany were centred on the Holocaust, a trend already started with the original West German *Historikerstreit* (Historians' Quarrel) of 1986–87 over the uniqueness of the Nazi genocide against the Jews.[66] In 1996 the claim of American historian Daniel Jonah Goldhagen, in his book *Hitler's Willing Executioners*, that most 'ordinary' Germans had enthusiastically supported Hitler's 'exterminatory antisemitism' was the subject of huge debate within and beyond the Federal Republic.[67] At the end of the decade, the Holocaust again became the centre of political discussion when the new Green Foreign Minister, Joschka Fischer, and other members of the recently elected 'Red–Green' coalition Government, referred to it when justifying Germany's decision to participate in the NATO-led bombing of Serbian forces in Kosovo.[68] The meaning of the post-1945 pacifist slogan 'Never again war' was thereby transformed in a more 'interventionist' direction by adding to it, as Fischer did at an extraordinary party conference of the Greens in Bielefeld in May 1999, the higher moral imperative 'Never again Auschwitz'.[69] In an article published in *History and Memory* in 2005, Helmut Walser Smith also identified not 1918–19, 1933 or 1939, but the last months of the year 1941 and the beginning of the year 1942 – when the gas chambers were unleashed in the extermination camps of occupied Poland – as the true 'vanishing point' in modern German history.[70] Auschwitz, in other words – using the metaphor of an artist's painting – was now the 'point on the canvas' that was considered 'decisive for structuring the whole'.[71] Meanwhile, in mainstream academic and media discussions, nobody seemed to have anything new to contribute – or indeed much to say at all – about the November Revolution, a situation that continued, more or less unchanged, until at least the end of the first decade of the twenty-first century.

What remained: 1918 and alternative views of the past in the 1990s and beyond

There were of course some exceptions to this, particularly in relation to historians from the former East Germany who were less content with the 'success story' being told about German reunification. In the years immediately following the collapse of the GDR, virtually all of the institutions that had funded and hosted East German research were closed down, and many of their employees were pensioned off or sacked.[72] Some nonetheless continued to find ways of bringing their interest in alternative, socialist narratives of the recent past to public attention. Werner Bramke, for instance, formerly a professor at the University of Leipzig and SED member, sat as a PDS deputy in the Saxon Parliament between 1994 and 2003 and, after stepping down from formal political life, wrote a regional study of Leipzig during the 1918–19 Revolution together with a younger colleague, Silvio Reisinger.

Bramke's aim, as he explained in the opening chapter, was 'to stimulate the drawing of comparisons between the popular uprisings of 1918 and 1989'. Leipzig was a good case study to choose for this, because it had remained an industrial city with a long tradition of labour militancy through much of the twentieth century, only succumbing to deindustrialisation and a shift away from left-wing politics in the aftermath of reunification in the 1990s. Events in that city in both 1918–19 and 1989–90 – including the overthrow of an authoritarian regime while avoiding descent into the kind of chaos that could only harm the workers' interests – disproved the idea of the 'futility of revolutions in modern industrial societies'. They also posed a question that had been overlooked by mainstream historiography since 1990, namely about the original thrust of the 1989 Revolution. Was it simply an anti-Communist rising undertaken to achieve rapid reunification with the West and integration into its capitalist economy? Or was it possible to challenge the claims of those who never tired of insisting that there were 'no alternatives' to the current free market system?[73]

Oddly enough, and without explicitly stating it, Bramke was reviving the notion of a 'third way' between western-style parliamentary democracy and authoritarian state socialism, but this time with a glance towards 1989 as well as 1918. During the First World War, Leipzig had been a stronghold of the USPD, and indeed the city's industrial workers remained loyal to that party throughout the period November 1918–August 1919 and even beyond, seeing it not as a radical break with the past but as a vehicle for the achievement of a Marxist programme in continuity with the old SPD of the immediate pre-1914 period. In October 1920, around 60 per cent of USPD members in Leipzig voted *against* merger with the KPD, whereas the national average was two to one in favour. In December 1920, only 11,400 out of the 60,000-strong USPD branch in Leipzig applied to join the new 'United Communist Party', and only 3,250 went the other way, towards the SPD. The remainder stuck with the continuing USPD.[74]

What explained this atypical attachment to the USPD until its final dissolution in 1922 in Saxony's largest city? According to

Bramke, it was the unique bond of trust developed between the party base and its local leadership, underpinned by contacts with trade unions as well as councils, and by a common commitment shared by all to bring industry into public ownership.[75] At the same time,

> There was agreement with the Communists on questions of fundamental principle, but not on the stance to be taken towards elections. This difference was not only tactical in nature, but rather was the clearest demonstration of the commitment of the Leipzig Independents to a democratic form of socialism.[76]

This democratic socialism was one that the PDS claimed to represent, and one that they argued would certainly have been taken more into consideration in the discussions leading up to reunification with the West if it had not been for the indoctrination of East German voters with slogans about the lack of real, positive alternatives to post-industrial, market-based capitalism. Even after reunification had taken place, there was still a role – perhaps even a duty – for historians to present other possible outcomes:

> In reality, the reunification of 1990 should have stimulated a reopening of the debate around the November Revolution. After all, it could be argued that the developmental course that began in Germany in 1918–19 and pointed towards the establishment of parliamentary democracy found its provisional conclusion in the 'peaceful revolution' [of 1989]. The obvious thing would have been to have a discussion about this, in continuation of the debates that were broken off by the founding of the two German states after the Second World War ... It is clear that political reasons were behind the fact that such a discussion did not take place between historians or among the general public after reunification had taken place.[77]

Yet as in 1989, so also in 2009, there was still a great deal of vagueness on what a democratic socialism would look like. How would the voice of the people be represented, if not indirectly through elected deputies in the Bundestag and in state parliaments? Could democratic socialists and labour militants work together with non-socialist parties? And how would a democratic socialist state safeguard against abuses of authority by separating out the powers of the executive, legislative and judicial branches of government? The veteran West German social historian Jürgen Kocka already raised these questions in an essay published in 2000. Certainly, he conceded, there were 'elements of radical, participatory and consensus-oriented democracy in the mass demonstrations and round table negotiations' held between the SED and opposition groups in the GDR in late 1989. But 'these elements were different from and alien to the West German constitutional system that would later be extended to the East'. And, more importantly for Kocka, 'nothing came of them' because the SED's lack of commitment to reform meant that they had little 'chance to be routinized and endure'.[78] Revolution, in other words, was necessary in East Germany in 1989 because there was no other way of enacting domestic political change. This is where the similarities with 1918–19 became evident. According to Kocka, writing on the tenth anniversary of German reunification:

> Whether one chooses the term 'revolution' or not is partly a semantic, partly a political question. It should not become a scholastic one. German history is not rich in revolutions, particularly not in successful ones. Seen against this background, the East German turn [*Wende*] was quite revolutionary even if it contained many reformist traits.[79]

Helga Grebing, meanwhile, was even more dismissive of the PDS's attempt to redefine the notion of a 'third way' between Soviet-style state socialism and SPD-style social democracy. For her, the 'missing' element that might have made 1918–19 a success in revolutionary terms – in other words might have represented the absent 'third possibility' – was 'a clearly formulated social democratic policy which would embrace all aspects of state and society', not something to the left of it.[80] Writing in 1998, she argued that the programme informally drawn up by East German dissidents and SED 'moderates' in autumn 1989 'to bring about a fundamental reform of the socialist system without blowing a hole in the system itself' very quickly turned out to be 'in practice illusionary'.[81] As for the historic split on the left, going back to 1918–19, Grebing saw no hope of this being healed through the process of German reunification:

> It was already clear by [the beginning of 1990] that the meaning of democratic socialism as understood in the social democratic tradition was never going to be compatible with the concept drawn up by the PDS and other 'successor parties'. For Social Democrats, democratic

socialism is a governing principle, not some 'third way' [between capitalism and Communism] drawn up at the 'last minute'.[82]

In 2007 the PDS merged with various pro-trade union/anti-welfare reform organisations from western Germany to form a new party, Die Linke (The Left). Henceforth, the argument for a continued socialist reading of the 1918–19 Revolution became more of a joint enterprise between hitherto competing leftist traditions, and as such a little less rooted in debates about the specific political culture of the GDR and its place in the 'new' Germany. A common theme was opposition to what was dubbed the prevailing 'neo-liberal consensus', symbolised by the (anti-socialist) policies of the 'Red–Green' coalition of 1998–2005 and the centrist 'grand coalition' between the Christian Democrats under Angela Merkel and the SPD from 2005.[83] The notion that there was still a genuine left-wing political alternative to neo-liberalism was also mirrored in the approach taken by supporters of Die Linke to the writing of history, which still owed a great deal to classical Marxist theorists, albeit perhaps less to Lenin and more to Engels, Luxemburg and Marx himself.

In 2009, for instance, Ulla Plener of the Leibniz Association in Berlin edited a collection of essays on the November Revolution sponsored by the Rosa Luxemburg Foundation that included contributions by veteran socialist/East German academics such as Werner Bramke and Ingo Materna as well as younger scholars working at universities and research institutes in both eastern and western Germany.[84] Materna, an author of and contributor to numerous GDR works on the history of the workers' movement in Berlin, broke with previous orthodoxies when he now wrote, among other things:

> The formation of the KPD at the end of 1918 in the Prussian House of Representatives once again draws attention to the central role played by Berlin in the emergence and ultimately the creation of an alternative left-wing party. It was certainly an important event, albeit not quite so outstandingly important and historically significant as was repeatedly claimed in GDR publications ... In this regard, it is vital to remember that [the KPD] did not succeed in winning over the most progressive elements of the Berlin workers' movement [in the early months of 1919] ... and thus failed to exert a greater influence over moves in the direction of a councils democracy.[85]

The contribution that really stands out, however, is Plener's own on the relationship between democratic and socialist elements in the November Revolution. Here she sought to link the idea of a people's republic to broader trends in European history, while also abandoning the Leninist argument that German workers 'failed' in their contribution to these trends by dint of their lack of a disciplined revolutionary party before November 1918. Rather, the example of the flawed Soviet experiment *since* 1918–19 had taught that Lenin was wrong and that socialism 'can only be achieved through a broad and strong movement "from below", one that emerges from and through society'.[86] Bolshevism, at least in its post-1918 guise, was an aberration from a prouder European tradition of democratic socialism, in other words, although the Russian Revolutions of 1905 and 1917 still belonged in that lineage:

> The democratic and socialist aspirations of the workers' movement are founded on 'humanity's innate drive for freedom' and on the 'explosive force of democratic ideas'. So wrote Engels in 1853 in relation to the French Revolution of 1789. [Democratic socialism] is a matter of the unfolding of the creative spirit of humanity, of its self-determination, a question that has particular meaning for the class of wage earners, for it is their work that creates the material basis for the inventiveness of the human race. The drive for freedom is the mainspring of the pursuit of democracy among the working and labouring classes. It was in their ranks that the democratic principles of freedom, equality and fraternity were first taken up and transformed into the demand for the social freedom and social equality of all men – what we now call socialist democracy. This was precipitated in 1848 in the call of the Parisian proletariat for a 'social republic'. The particular form that fixed [the social republic] found its first expression in 1871 in the Paris Commune and then in 1905 and from February 1917 in the workers' soviets set up in Russia. The councils established in Germany and elsewhere in Europe in 1918–19 followed the same model.[87]

This was written in 2009, the year in which Die Linke achieved what to date is its best ever result in a nationwide election, with 11.9 per cent of votes cast. In two states in the old East, Saxony-Anhalt and Brandenburg, it even emerged as the largest party, with 32.4 per cent and 28.5 per cent respectively.[88]

In the 2010s, however, discussions of 'social history' and its relevance to the future of democracy became even more decoupled from mid-twentieth-century historical perspectives and notions of class. Meanwhile, the collapse of the neo-liberal consensus following the world financial meltdown in 2008–9 and the Syrian refugee crisis from 2015 enhanced the growing sense of marginalisation for the poorest groups in society, and a feeling of powerlessness often expressed through right-wing populism or the distorting lens of a dehistoricised identity politics. As the GDR-born writer Jenny Erpenbeck put it in an interview in 2020:

> When the refugees [from Syria] came, some of those [East Germans] who had just about managed to keep afloat financially experienced an existential fear that boiled over and ended up being directed at the wrong people [i.e. refugees]. I had a feeling that the East liked giving the rest of the country a scare. If you can't be the good child, then you should try to be the bad child and start screaming. Suddenly the west was forced to listen and engage with how people in the former GDR felt.[89]

In fact, slogans such as 'Freedom', 'First integrate *us*!' and 'Empowerment Ost' have so far benefited the populist right more than the democratic left, even if they have recently been reclaimed by Erpenbeck and other progressive voices looking for ways of rebuilding civil society and historical consciousness in the face of the neo-nationalist challenge in Saxony and elsewhere.[90] Meanwhile, the alternative, socialist reading of the 1918–19 Revolution offered by Die Linke has not had a great deal of impact on mainstream interpretations, either of 1918–19 itself, or of 1989. In 2021 Robert Habeck, Green Party co-chairperson and future Economics Minister and Vice-Chancellor in the 'Traffic Light' coalition Government, conceded that 'our present builds on the experiences and often enough on the ruins of the past', but went on to insist that the future would have to be 'different from here on out'. What Germany needed in the 2020s, he continued, in a clear pitch for the centre ground and away from classical leftist ideas, was not a revolution but 'a different culture … We shouldn't want to go back to what was considered normal; we shouldn't want to go *back* at all.' More important was reinventing Germans and German politics in the here-and-now.[91]

That said, one important legacy of twentieth-century mindsets that has survived – at least until the full-scale Russian attack on Ukraine in 2022 forced a major rethink of previous assumptions about non-violence[92] – is the general abhorrence felt by many left-liberals as well as socialists towards the practice of war and militarism. In 1989, GDR expert on 1918–19 Wolfgang Ruge wrote in a contribution to an East German volume devoted to reflections on war and peace since 1500: 'Subjectively, Ebert and Scheidemann certainly had no intention of preparing for a return of the most extreme reactionaries. However, objectively, by positioning themselves as shields for the military, they gave the go-ahead.'[93] Likewise, in 1991 the retired West German historian Fritz Fischer, a well-known critic of German war aims in the First World War, wrote to his Berlin-born British colleague Francis Carsten to congratulate him on the appearance of his new biography of prewar SPD leader August Bebel:

> You are quite right to pose the question: what would Bebel have done in 1914 or in 1918–1919 [had he not died in 1913]? The unconditional support that the SPD gave to the [military and the imperial Government] during the war led to a split that paralysed [the workers' movement], especially after Ebert, out of 'fear of Bolshevism', unleashed the Freikorps in such a brutal way that in the end many moderate elements on the left went over to the KPD. What had been the strongest party in Germany before 1914 [now] entered the [Weimar] Republic in a weakened and divided state.[94]

Eighteen years later, there were echoes of these concerns in a paper written by Werner Bramke to mark the ninetieth anniversary of the November Revolution, an occasion for retrospective thinking that, he claimed, had been largely overlooked in the Federal Republic.

> In the days leading up to 9 November 2008 nothing in the media suggested that there would be any acknowledgement of the significance of the revolution that ninety years ago opened the way for a democratic republic [in Germany] … The November 1918 Revolution was painted into the corner of representative [rather than participatory] democracy by the Majority Social Democrats, albeit with the help of the same military that later proved to be the gravedigger of Weimar democracy. The accusation that such an alliance was unnecessary, and that its fatal consequences for democracy were predictable in advance, has never been convincingly refuted … It is high time that the revolution of 1918–19 be placed under renewed scrutiny, so that we can identify its successes and analyse those aspects that promised much but remained underdeveloped.[95]

Carsten died in 1998, Fischer in 1999, Ruge in 2006 and Bramke in 2011. In the 2010s, Bramke's calls for a revival of critical discussion of the 1918–19 Revolution were to some extent met, and indeed by scholars working outside Germany as well as within its national borders. The result was movement and change, although perhaps not quite in the direction that Bramke and others on the socialist and anti-militarist left had hoped for on the Revolution's ninetieth anniversary.

Notes

1 Marla Stone, 'Introduction', in Harold James and Marla Stone (eds), *When the Wall Came Down: Reactions to German Unification* (London and New York, 1992), 17–30 (17).
2 Richard Vinen, *A History in Fragments: Europe in the Twentieth Century* (London, 2000).
3 Gunn, *History and Cultural Theory*, 89–90.
4 Afshin Matin-Asgari, 'Iranian Postmodernity: The Rhetoric of Irrationality?', *Critique: Critical Middle Eastern Studies*, 13.1 (2004), 113–23.
5 Günther Rose, 'Modernisieriungstheorien und bürgerliche Geschichtsschreibung', in Akademie für Gesellschaftswissenschaften beim ZK der SED (ed.), *Zur theoretisch-methodologischen Analyse und historiographischen Umsetzung bürgerlicher Modernisierungstheorien: Materialien der 4. Tagung der Fachkommission 'Theorie, Methodologie und Geschichte der Geschichtswissenschaft' am 26. März 1981 in Berlin* (East Berlin, 1982), 7–39 (39).
6 Neal Ascherson, *The Polish August: The Self-Limiting Revolution* (London, 1982); Jadwiga Staniszkis, *Poland's Self-Limiting Revolution*, ed. Jan T. Gross (Princeton, NJ, 1984).
7 See the various contributions to Margit Mayer and John Ely (eds), *The German Greens: Paradox between Movement and Party* (Philadelphia, PA, 1998).
8 Sheila Rowbotham, *Daring to Hope: My Life in the 1970s* (London, 2021), 245.
9 Stone, 'Introduction', 17.
10 Michel Foucault, *The Archaeology of Knowledge*, trans. A. M. Sheridan Smith (London, 1972; French original, 1969).
11 See, for instance, Jane Schneider and Rayna Rapp (eds), *Articulating Hidden Histories: Exploring the Influence of Eric R. Wolf* (Berkeley,

CA, 1995); and Keith Jenkins, *At the Limits of History: Essays on Theory and Practice* (London and New York, 2009).

12 Mary Fulbrook and Ulinka Rublack, 'In Relation: The "Social Self" and Ego-Documents', *German History*, 28.3 (2010), 263–72 (267).

13 *Ibid.*, 268.

14 Reinhart Koselleck, *Futures Past: On the Semantics of Historical Time* (Cambridge, MA, 1985; German original, 1979).

15 Joan W. Scott, 'Gender: A Useful Category of Historical Analysis', *American Historical Review*, 91.5 (1986), 1053–75 (1054).

16 See, for example, Barbara Caine and Glenda Sluga (eds), *Gendering European History, 1780–1920* (Leicester, 2000).

17 Scott, 'Gender', 1065–6.

18 For further discussion see Matthew Stibbe, Corinne Painter and Ingrid Sharp, 'History beyond the Script: Rethinking Female Subjectivities and Socialist Women's Activism during and after the German Revolution of 1918–1919', in Dillon and Wünschmann, *Living the German Revolution*.

19 Wolfgang Ruge, 'Nachdenken über die Geschichtswissenschaft in der DDR' (1993), reproduced in Wolfgang Ruge, *Beharren, kapitulieren oder umdenken: Gesammelte Schriften 1989–1999*, ed. Friedrich-Martin Balzer (Berlin, 2007), 332–49 (347).

20 On the *Sputnik* ban see Peter Grieder, '"To Learn from the Soviet Union Is to Learn How to Win": The East German Revolution, 1989–90', in Kevin McDermott and Matthew Stibbe (eds), *Revolution and Resistance in Eastern Europe: Challenges to Communist Rule* (Oxford, 2006), 157–74 (165).

21 'Volkskammer der DDR trat zu einer Sondersitzung zusammen', *Neues Deutschland*, 9 November 1988.

22 Niess, *Die Revolution von 1918/19*, 364.

23 Petzold, *Parteinahme wofür?*, 329.

24 'Das Wirken unserer Partei für das Wohl des Volkes hat in dem Kampf der KPD eine reiche Tradition', *Neues Deutschland*, 30 December 1988.

25 Grieder, '"To Learn from the Soviet Union"', 165.

26 Ruge, 'Nachdenken über die Geschichtswissenschaft', 343.

27 Bundesbeauftragte für die Unterlagen des Staatssicherheitsdienstes der ehemaligen Deutschen Demokratischen Republik, Berlin, MfS HA XVIII AP 52505/92: IM-Bericht: Feindliche Diskussionen am Zentralinstitut für Geschichte der Akademie der Wissenschaften, 27 February 1980, 51–3 (52).

28 *Ibid.*, 53.

29 Ruge, *Novemberrevolution*. See also Niess, *Die Revolution von 1918/19*, 361.

30 Wolfgang Ruge, 'Novemberrevolution und Weimarer Republik 1918/19 bis 1933', in Joachim Herrmann (ed.), *Deutsche Geschichte in 10 Kapiteln* (East Berlin, 1988), 299–347 (303).
31 *Ibid.*, 302.
32 Ruge, *Novemberrevolution*, 26–7.
33 Werner Bramke and Ulrich Heß, 'Die Novemberrevolution in Deutschland und ihre Wirkung auf die deutsche Klassengesellschaft', *Zeitschrift für Geschichtswissenschaft*, 36.12 (1988), 1059–73 (1062).
34 *Ibid.*, 1064–5.
35 See also the discussion in Niess, *Die Revolution von 1918/19*, 366–7.
36 On these talks see Rolf Reißig, *Dialog durch die Mauer: Die umstrittene Annäherung von SPD und SED* (Frankfurt am Main and New York, 2002); and Timothy Garton Ash, *In Europe's Name: Germany and the Divided Continent* (London, 1994), 312–42.
37 See Martin Sabrow, 'Der Streit um die Verständigung: Die deutschdeutschen Zeithistorikergespräche in den achtziger Jahren', in Bauerkämper, Sabrow and Stöver (eds), *Doppelte Zeitgeschichte*, 113–30. Also Berger, *Social Democracy*, 170.
38 Susanne Miller and Malte Ristau (eds), *Erben deutscher Geschichte. DDR–BRD: Protokolle einer historischen Begegnung* (Reinbek bei Hamburg, 1988).
39 *Ibid.*, 7.
40 *Ibid.*, 23.
41 Hermann Weber and Gerda Weber, *Leben nach dem 'Prinzip Links': Erinnerungen aus fünf Jahrzehnten* (Berlin, 2006), 391–2.
42 See Walter Wimmer, 'Schlußwort zum 2. Podium', in Walter Schmidt and Manfred Weißbecker (eds), *Perspektive und Aktion. Erfahrungen deutscher Arbeiterbewegung: Protokoll eines Geschichtsforums am 30./31. Mai 1989* (Jena, 1989), 94–5 (94).
43 Helga Grebing, 'Ich vermag diese Vorgang "Revolution von oben" nicht zu nennen', in Miller and Ristau, *Erben deutscher Geschichte*, 109–17 (116).
44 Reißig, *Dialog*, 286. See also Helga Grebing, *Der 'deutsche Sonderweg' in Europa 1806–1945: Eine Kritik* (Stuttgart, 1986), 144–9.
45 Reinhard Rürup, 'Massenbewegungen und parlamentarische Demokratie in der Grundphase der Weimarer Republik', in Schmidt and Weißbecker, *Perspektive und Aktion*, 51–9 (59).
46 Joachim Petzold, 'Die Bedeutung von Massenaktivitäten für die Gestaltung der bürgerlich-parlamentarischen Republik von Weimar', in Schmidt and Weißbecker, *Perspektive und Aktion*, 44–50 (47).
47 See Wimmer, 'Schlußwort zum 2. Podium', 94–5. Also Weber and Weber, *Leben nach dem 'Prinzip Links'*, 389–90.

48 Werner Bramke and Silvio Reisinger, *Leipzig in der Revolution von 1918/1919* (Leipzig, 2009), 10.
49 Werner Bramke, 'Kooperation in der Konfrontation: Begegnungen in der deutsch-deutschen Geschichtslandschaft der achtziger Jahre', in Bauerkämper, Sabrow and Stöver, *Doppelte Zeitgeschichte*, 131–9 (135, 138).
50 Bramke and Heß, 'Die Novemberrevolution', 1064.
51 Latzel, 'Geschichten der Novemberrevolution', 137.
52 Petzold, *Parteinahme wofür?*, 345–6.
53 On Togliatti see Conway, *Western Europe's Democratic Age*, 52, 58–60.
54 David Childs and Richard Popplewell, *The Stasi: The East German Intelligence and Security Service* (Basingstoke, 1996), 97.
55 See, for example, Matthew Stibbe, 'A Hopeless Case of Optimism? Jürgen Kuczynski and the End of the GDR', in McDermott and Stibbe, *The 1989 Revolutions*, 213–34.
56 See, for instance, Göttrik Wewer (ed.), *DDR: Von der friedlichen Revolution zur deutschen Vereinigung* (Opladen, 1990); and Peter Neckermann, *The Unification of Germany or the Anatomy of a Peaceful Revolution* (London, 1991).
57 See, for example, '30 Jahre Friedliche Revolution und Deutsche Einheit', webpage created by the German Federal Ministry of Interior for the thirtieth anniversary in 2019–20, at www.bmi.bund.de/SharedDocs/topthemen/DE/topthema-30-jahre-einheit/topthema-30-jahre-einheit-artikel.html (accessed 14 February 2022).
58 See Sharon Erickson Nepstad, *Nonviolent Revolutions: Civil Resistance in the Late 20th Century* (Oxford, 2011).
59 See, for instance, Helga Grebing and Klaus Kinner (eds), *Arbeiterbewegung und Faschismus: Faschismus-Interpretationen in der europäischen Arbeiterbewegung* (Essen, 1990); and Geoff Eley, *Forging Democracy: The History of the Left in Europe, 1850–2000* (Oxford, 2002).
60 Peukert, *The Weimar Republic*.
61 Eric D. Weitz, *Weimar Germany: Promise and Tragedy* (Princeton, NJ, 2007), 41.
62 *Ibid.*, 4.
63 *Ibid.*, 7–39 (quotation on 39).
64 Peter Fritzsche, 'Did Weimar Fail?', *Journal of Modern History*, 68.3 (1996), 629–56.
65 See, for instance, the English-language volume of Reinhart Koselleck's essays, *The Practice of Conceptual History: Timing History, Spacing Concepts*, trans. Todd Presner (Stanford, CA, 2002).

66 On the *Historikerstreit* see Richard J. Evans, *In Hitler's Shadow: West German Historians and the Attempt to Escape from the Nazi Past* (London, 1989).
67 On the Goldhagen controversy see Geoff Eley (ed.), *The 'Goldhagen Effect': History, Memory, Nazism. Facing the German Past* (Ann Arbor, MI, 2000).
68 Heinrich August Winkler, *Germany: The Long Road West*, Vol. II, *1933–1990* (Oxford, 2007), 563.
69 Wolfgang Geiger, *Weimar – Bonn – Berlin: Lehren aus der Geschichte* (Frankfurt am Main, 2019), 136.
70 Helmut Walser Smith, 'The Vanishing Point of German History: An Essay on Perspective', *History and Memory*, 17.1–2 (2005), 269–95.
71 *Ibid.*, 270.
72 See Stefan Berger, 'Former GDR Historians in the Reunified Germany: An Alternative Historical Culture and Its Attempts to Come to Terms with the GDR Past', *Journal of Contemporary History*, 38.1 (2003), 63–83.
73 All the quotes in this paragraph are from Bramke and Reisinger, *Leipzig in der Revolution von 1918/1919*, 15.
74 *Ibid.*, 151. See also Sean Dobson, *Authority and Upheaval in Leipzig, 1910–1920: The Story of a Relationship* (New York, 2001), 289.
75 Bramke and Reisinger, *Leipzig in der Revolution von 1918/1919*, 150.
76 *Ibid.*, 151.
77 *Ibid.*, 10–11.
78 Jürgen Kocka, 'Reform and Revolution: Germany, 1989–90', in Rürup, *The Problem of Revolution in Germany*, 161–79 (174).
79 *Ibid.*, 173.
80 Grebing, *History of the German Labour Movement*, 104.
81 Helga Grebing, 'Dritte Wege – "Last Minute"? Programmatische Konzepte über Alternativen zu den beiden "real existierenden" Deutschland zwischen Ende 1989 und Anfang 1990', in Bauerkämper, Sabrow and Stöver, *Doppelte Zeitgeschichte*, 214–23 (215).
82 *Ibid.*, 223.
83 See Kate Hudson, *The New European Left: A Socialism for the Twenty-First Century?* (Basingstoke, 2012), esp. 83–98.
84 Ulla Plener, *Die Novemberrevolution 1918/19 in Deutschland: Für bürgerliche und sozialistische Demokratie* (=Rosa-Luxemburg-Stiftung, Manuskripte, Vol. LXXXV) (Berlin, 2009), available online at www.rosalux.de/publikation/id/910/die-novemberrevolution-19181919-in-deutschland/ (accessed 14 February 2022). See also the discussion in Niess, *Die Revolution von 1918/19*, 532–5.

85 Ingo Materna, 'Berlin: Das Zentrum der deutschen Revolution 1918/1919', in Plener, *Die Novemberrevolution*, 92–103 (101).
86 Ulla Plener, 'Zum Verhältnis demokratischer und sozialistischer Bestrebungen 1918/1919', in Plener, *Die Novemberrevolution*, 79–91 (86).
87 *Ibid.*, 79.
88 See 'Bundeswahlleiter, Vorläufiges Ergebnis der Bundestagswahl 2009 in den Ländern', at https://web.archive.org/web/20160115225314/https://www.bundeswahlleiter.de/de/bundestagswahlen/BTW_BUND_09/ergebnisse/landesergebnisse/ (accessed 14 February 2022).
89 Jenny Erpenbeck, interview with Philip Oltermann, *Guardian*, review section, 12 December 2020, 16–19 (19).
90 Alongside Erpenbeck see Petra Köpping, *Integriert doch erst mal uns! Eine Streitschrift für den Osten* (Berlin, 2018); and Thomas Oberender, *Empowerment Ost: Wie wir zusammenwachsen* (Stuttgart, 2020). But note too the warning from Volker Weiss, 'Wenn Rechte für die "Freiheit" kämpfen', *Die Zeit*, 19 November 2020, 52.
91 Robert Habeck, *Von hier an anders: Eine politische Skizze* (Cologne, 2021), 371; italics in the original. See also Habeck's plea for making decisions (in this instance, delivery of arms to Ukraine) 'on the basis of present necessities' rather than remaining stuck in the 'debates of the past', during an interview in *Die Zeit*, 5 May 2022, 10–11.
92 The change in thinking was marked in a speech made by SPD Chancellor Olaf Scholz in the Bundestag on 27 February 2022, three days after the Russian assault on Ukraine, in which he spoke of a *Zeitenwende* (turning point) and announced both that Germany would deliver defensive weapons to Ukraine and that it would boost annual spending on its own armed forces, the Bundeswehr, to 2 per cent of GDP on top of an immediate investment of €100 billion. Even then, as Luke Harding notes, 'Many Social Democrats preferred the party's old Russia-friendly stance' and 'left-wing intellectuals signed open letters calling for peace'. See Luke Harding, *Invasion: The Inside Story of Russia's Bloody War and Ukraine's Fight for Survival* (New York, 2022), 168–9.
93 Wolfgang Ruge, 'Die deutsche Novemberrevolution: Klassenantagonismus und Friedensalternative' (1989), reproduced in Ruge, *Beharren, kapitulieren oder umdenken*, 95–104 (101).
94 Bundesarchiv Koblenz, Nachlaß Fritz Fischer, N 1422/35, Fischer to Carsten, 28 September 1991. Cf. Francis L. Carsten, *August Bebel und die Organisation der Massen* (Berlin, 1991).
95 Werner Bramke, 'Zwei Revolutionen im November', in Plener, *Die Novemberrevolution*, 304–8 (304–5).

Part III

Forgotten or rediscovered?
Debates on the German Revolution
since the 1990s

6

The experience of revolution: Soldiers, sailors, civilians, young people

As the twentieth century gave way to the twenty-first, another trend that pushed the Revolution of 1918–19 to the margins of scholarly concern was the renewed interest in the violence of the First World War as a major 'catalyst' for political upheaval.[1] The focus was no longer just on how the war ended for Germany, but rather on how it was fought – and how it was experienced – from the very beginning onwards. Writing in 2010, for instance, the American scholar Andrew Donson noted how 'the First World War ushered in the great era of mobilizing youths and schoolchildren for extreme political movements and experiments in state building'.[2] From its start, in August 1914, the war was often now seen as a kind of revolution in its own right, a coming together of the nation in an imagined – and sometimes popularly experienced – moment of unity.[3] Even if this unity was more apparent than real, it shaped how many ordinary Germans made sense of the war.[4] They were also able to measure their own personal encounters with growing material hardship, food shortages, military rule, family separation, and loss and bereavement against the assertions of continued war enthusiasm, pending victory and other 'mobilisation myths' put out by the army supreme command and the civilian authorities.[5]

Before the 1990s, both FRG and GDR historiography had of course claimed certain events during the war as belonging to the prehistory of their particular state. West German scholars of parliamentarism, for instance, placed a great deal of emphasis on the Reichstag's growing demands to be consulted over matters of State policy, culminating in its famous Peace Resolution of July 1917.[6] Their conservative counterparts were more interested in the October 1918 constitutional reforms and the supposed missed opportunity to avoid revolution and save the monarchy.[7] Labour historians in both East and West were keen to explore the meaning and significance of the two big strike waves of April 1917 and January 1918.[8] And in the GDR, the naval mutiny of 2 August 1917, when 350 crewmen of the *Prinzregent Luitpold* in Wilhelmshaven staged a revolt that led to the execution of two ringleaders, Albin Köbis and Max Reichpietsch, and the imprisonment of several others, enjoyed an iconic status.[9] This was doubtless helped by the fact that in 1930 the expressionist playwright and revolutionary Ernst Toller published a play about this event, *Feuer aus den Kesseln* (*Draw the Fires*), which was soon afterwards banned in Germany. It was performed in English translation in Manchester in 1935 by the Marxist Theatre of Action company under the direction of Joan Littlewood, and for the first time in the GDR in 1958 in honour of the Revolution's fortieth anniversary.[10] By the 1970s it was presented in the standard East German work on Weimar-era Marxist theatre as a major contribution to 'national literature' and as a cherished part of the GDR's cultural heritage. It was a play that 'brought the revolutionary act itself to life'.[11]

From the 1990s onwards, however, the First World War was rethought. No longer was it a series of dramatic national events, lost battles for parliamentary rule or epic strikes and naval mutinies, but a diverse, four-year ordeal for individuals and families that gave rise to new, revolutionary ways of *imagining* the nation, the citizen, the soldier, the worker, the consumer, the grieving mother and so forth. These developments in *lived* and *communicated* experience were not unique to one particular nation or one particular theatre of the war, but rather 'stirred up revolutionary demands for popular sovereignty' at the Europe-wide and global levels.[12] Germany, indeed, was not the only dynastic-imperial state to be overthrown in 1917–18. The importance of the Russian case was already acknowledged, but historians after 1990 also became interested in exploring comparisons and contrasts with the fall of the multi-national Habsburg and Ottoman empires in November 1918. 'The nature of "homecoming"', as Robert Gerwarth and John Horne noted in 2012 in their landmark volume of essays on postwar paramilitary violence, was 'an important variable' in its own right, helping to shape not just national but regional and local disparities in the experience of the transition from war to peace.[13]

Even societies that did not face full-scale revolution and/or counter-revolution were nonetheless touched by incidents of political unrest; nowhere in Europe was entirely unscathed by postwar violence.[14]

In order to become an object of historical enquiry, individual and collective experiences of war and revolution had to be *communicated* by real subjects, by actual soldiers, sailors, civilians and so on.[15] Revolutionary and counterrevolutionary mindsets, it now seemed, may be less visible in institutions and parties than in the frequent if uneven contact between, and shared experiences of, those fighting in the field and their relatives and comrades back at home. This contact was made possible both by leaves of absence from the front, and by letters to and from the field, with studies of the latter revealing that local and familial concerns were often entangled with broader political questions. All in all, soldiers and civilians; fathers and sons; husbands and wives; town and country; policemen and female food rioters; and children, teenagers and parents knew far more about each other's war and immediate postwar experiences than had previously been realised.[16]

Knowledge, of course, did not always lead to mutual sympathy or understanding, and new social divisions could also appear. The image shown in Figure 6.1, for instance, of men and women casting their ballots together for the first time, which was published by the liberal *Frankfurter Zeitung*'s sister paper, *Das Illustrierte Blatt*, on 14 January 1919, might easily be presented as a celebration of the universal suffrage granted by the Revolution. Yet the objectification of voters as enlightened citizens who were now able to fulfil their 'duty' by turning out to 'create clarity [for the nation] internally and externally' was more a piece of wishful thinking than an accurate reflection of how most ordinary Germans – including those still hungry and struggling to afford food and/or those still under the minimum voting age of twenty – actually felt about the Revolution at that time. The true state of social relations in Germany, on the eve of the murders of Liebknecht and Luxemburg and five days before the election of the National Assembly, was somewhat different and certainly less uniformly rosy.

This chapter will not examine historical debate about ordinary Germans' war experiences directly. Rather, it will explore how those debates also (eventually) fed into new socio-cultural interpretations of the 1918–19 Revolution itself, including the shadow that the lost

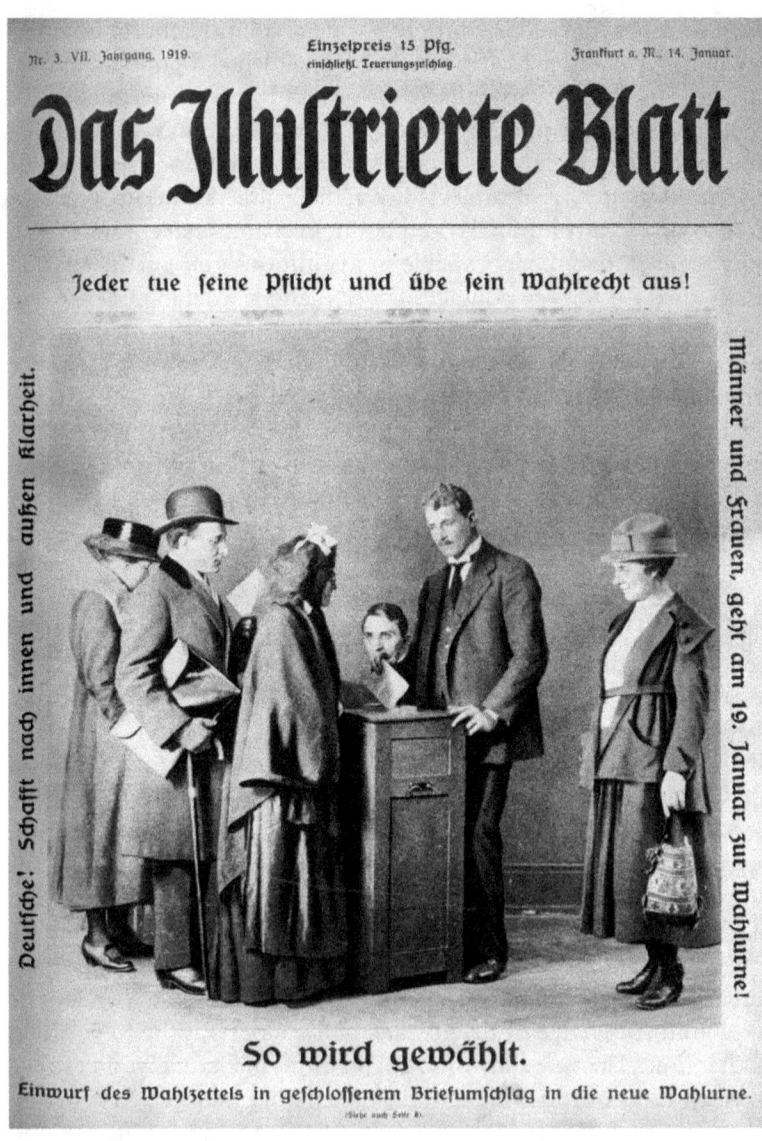

Figure 6.1 'So wird gewählt' ['This is how to vote'], front page of *Das Illustrierte Blatt,* an illustrated weekly associated with the liberal *Frankfurter Zeitung,* urging German men and women to do their 'duty' and vote in the forthcoming National Assembly elections, 14 January 1919. Wikimedia Commons.

conflict threw over popular mentalities and expectations. While the chapter is divided into sections on soldiers, sailors, civilians and young people, consideration will also be given to possible overlaps and interactions among these different categories of revolutionary subject. This is important, for, as Robert Gerwarth has argued, the 'disparate actors' in the Revolution, including the millions of female and male citizens about to vote in the January 1919 elections, 'never formed a singular force'.[17]

Soldiers

The complexity and diversity of German soldiers' war experiences between 1914 and 1918 have been documented in a vast array of new studies since the early 1990s.[18] For purposes of understanding the soldierly input into the November Revolution specifically, as opposed to post-1918 revolutionary and counterrevolutionary violence more generally, the western front and the home front have been the two principal sites of interest. Yet even these two realms were far from homogeneous spaces. Conditions varied considerably between different sectors or regions and at different times across the 1914–18 period. As Benjamin Ziemann has shown for the western front, at the most elemental level, death rates themselves fluctuated considerably, both over time and among different age groups. The highest proportion of casualties came as a result of artillery bombardment, not because of its accuracy but because of its concentrated mass application in small, targeted spaces. Furthermore, the largest numbers of deaths occurred in the first three months of the war and then again in summer 1918, with periodic spikes in-between, especially in 1916; and soldiers aged between nineteen and twenty-four were the most at risk of dying under fire.[19]

That said, there were some commonalities between all German front-line fighters in Belgium and northern France. Throughout the war, negative attitudes towards the so-called *Etappenschweine* (those who led a supposedly comfortable existence in the staging areas behind the front lines), and a hatred of army discipline and hierarchy in general, were a more or less constant feature of how combat troops interpreted 'their' war. The desire to survive the war in one piece was much more prevalent than any 'gratification or even enjoyment in the act of killing', but changing fortunes in battle also meant that the best means of survival, or what were imagined to be the best means, were also constantly shifting.[20] Some of the resentment towards officers was expressed in class terms.[21] But this did not mean that the average soldier wanted class war instead of war between nations. While support for the Reichstag Peace Resolution was strong in summer 1917, meaning that soldiers favoured a negotiated end to the fighting rather than a 'Hindenburg peace', they did not accept the case made by the USPD and the Spartacists that laying down arms now would lead to a quicker end to the war.[22] An SPD-supporting member of the German occupation force in Belgium told the manager of a factory at Klein-Bijgaarden near Brussels in June 1917 that 'it is a shame that [our] officers amuse themselves & have a good time while the men are sent to the shambles', but when asked 'Why don't you rebel?' responded simply 'We can't during war.'[23] Similar reactions greeted news of the 1918 January strike at home. 'The war won't be over a day sooner because of that', wrote one conscript serving in the Fifth Army in northern France.[24]

What had changed six months later, in July–August 1918, was that desertion or deliberate surrender to the enemy suddenly seemed like more rational survival strategies in the wake of the Allied advance, leading to what Wilhelm Deist suggests was a 'covert military strike' at the end of the war.[25] The figures indeed support this: between 18 July 1918 and 11 November 1918 some 420,000 German soldiers were killed or severely injured on the western front and a further 340,000 were reported missing or captured.[26] Even then, historians such as Alan Kramer and Benjamin Ziemann have argued that while battlefield desertion became a mass phenomenon in summer and autumn 1918, it took place as a series of individual and small-group decisions, not as a collective enterprise.[27] Furthermore, there is little evidence of Bolshevik-style subversion of military discipline by political agitators operating within the ranks of the field armies. As Ziemann notes, only a 'relatively small number' of front-line soldiers 'were inspired to desert primarily for political reasons'.[28] Momentary calculations about how to maximise personal chances of staying alive were key.[29]

What does this mean for interpretations of November 1918? Richard Bessel may be right to argue that the quintessentially human story of how morale in the armed forces of a number of dynastic states 'cracked under an unsuccessful pursuit of the war' is crucial to understanding the Europe-wide phenomenon of revolution in 1917–18. In his view, also shared by Bernd Ulrich and Benjamin Ziemann, the front-line fighters were 'the last line of defence of the old regime'. Once they refused to fight on, the game was up – especially as American President Woodrow Wilson demanded the Kaiser's abdication, and that of his son, as a condition of peace.[30] In the parallel example of the Habsburg empire, Wolfgang Maderthaner has also argued that 'as a product of war, the Revolution originated not so much in the factories but in the barracks'. But interestingly for him, as the reference to 'barracks' suggests, 'the total breakdown of military discipline' came not only at the front but among the troops garrisoned at home:

> During mass demonstrations on 30 October 1918, soldiers appeared in the streets wearing red cockades, while others wore [republican] cockades in black, red and gold ... In ever increasing numbers, soldiers and officers succumbed to the fascination of political upheaval, assuming roles in the revolutionary movement both in Vienna and Budapest. The twenty of them who appeared before the first president of the [Austrian] National Assembly, Karl Seitz, on 31 October 1918, to declare themselves representatives of the Soldiers' Council (*Soldatenrat*) had destroyed their cockades and military decorations themselves.[31]

Indeed, it is worth exploring Maderthaner's findings further to see if they are also applicable to the collapse of discipline among the troops in Germany. With one or two exceptions, few historians have done this, instead focusing on the disintegration of morale in the field armies.[32] Yet in the German case, too, when the war came to an end by no means all soldiers were serving at the front or in the staging areas. Hundreds of thousands were officially on leave, and others were lying injured in hospitals or had used periods of lighter garrison duty at home or in depots as an opportunity to desert. In Hamburg, the Senate Commission on the Administration of Justice complained as early as April 1918 about the number of civilians being arrested in the city on charges of harbouring soldiers who had failed to return to duty. Cases against such persons were clogging up the work of the courts, since convictions were usually only possible after the serviceman himself had been convicted by a court martial of going absent without leave.[33] Some deserters – an estimated 20,000–40,000 in Berlin alone – remained undiscovered until the end of the war, while all over Germany others had been caught and were in military prisons awaiting trial.[34] An even larger number of soldiers were serving permanently in the replacement army on the home front. They now found themselves 'placed in the path of the revolutionary tide' and, as quickly became clear, were 'unable or unwilling to stop the revolution'.[35]

In this sense, the focus on front-line fighters on active service in the field may underestimate the opportunities for and political meanings of fraternisation among soldiers, workers and civilians on the home front in November 1918. In the days leading up to 9 November, soldiers everywhere seemed to tear off their insignia and join the anti-war movement of sailors, workers and young people. In Stuttgart, for instance, where the Spartacist Albert Schreiner briefly served as War Minister from 9 to 15 November, real anger had greeted the decision of King Wilhelm II to shower First Quartermaster General Erich Ludendorff with military decorations after the latter's dismissal on 26 October 1918.[36] Fears grew among members of the replacement army on the home front and soldiers on leave that supporters of the old regime might launch a military coup, something akin to what General Kornilov had tried in Russia in 1917. Even though Ludendorff had concluded that there were no realistic prospects of pulling off such a coup, the anxieties were very real.[37] More than the political implications of a coup, however, soldiers on garrison duty feared being returned to battlefield duties, further fuelling the number of home-front desertions.

Historians are also now a little less certain than they were in the 1990s about the attitude of front-line soldiers in the final phases of the war. Scott Stephenson, for instance, claimed in his 2009 study that the attitude of those troops still engaged in live combat operations against the enemy remained ambiguous right up until the first week of November. In September and October 1918, although clearly in retreat and suffering from exhaustion and a longing for peace, the over 1.5 million soldiers deployed to hold up the Allied advance in northern France and Belgium were still capable of mounting fierce rearguard actions in certain contexts, if not for the fatherland, then at least for the sake of their comrades, or 'the prospect of hot rations'.[38] To a much greater degree than

Bessel and Ulrich and Ziemann, then, Stephenson emphasises the 'relative strength of the cohesion' within the front-line units, all the way up to 11 November, and thus the differences between their experiences and those of 'the remainder of the army' stationed in barracks or 'milling around the railroad stations and supply dumps' on the home front.[39] These differences are an important reminder of the dangers of making too many generalisations about the soldierly experience of the 1918–19 Revolution, although on their own they are not sufficient to challenge Deist's overall thesis of a 'covert military strike' in the last months of the war, undertaken primarily for non-political reasons but having profound political consequences nonetheless.

Sailors

Just as the French Revolution is associated with the fall of the Bastille in 1789, and the Bolshevik Revolution with the fall of the Winter Palace in Petrograd in 1917, there is little controversy that it was the naval mutinies in Kiel and Wilhelmshaven that sparked the November Revolution in Germany. Prior to 1990, though, this too was presented in historical works as a straightforward 'event' at national level rather than a complex series of developments with multiple meanings for the actors involved. Only one or two major historical works had sought to uncover the background to the mutinies through examining the wartime experiences of enlisted German sailors themselves: Daniel Horn's 1969 study *The German Naval Mutinies of World War I* and Dirk Dähnhardt's 1978 book *Revolution in Kiel*.[40] In 1967 Horn also brought out an English translation of what to this day remains the only substantial wartime diary written by an ordinary sailor to be published in full in its own right.[41] The diarist, Richard Stumpf, was an (anti-Marxist) Catholic trade unionist and imperial loyalist from Bavaria who signed up for service in the Reichsmarine in 1912 but nonetheless came to be highly critical of the German naval officer corps and the disregard it showed for the needs of the enlisted men. His journey from patriotic nationalist to anti-war rebel was completed on 8 November 1918, when he wrote that the revolutionary events in Wilhelmshaven, where he was then stationed, had wrought an 'unbelievable change ... within me, [transforming me] from a monarchist into a devout republican'.[42]

In fact, though, the change in political outlook in Germany's naval stations had been coming from at least June–July 1917 onwards, both for Stumpf and for his fellow ratings. Much of it had to do with hatred of the boredom and monotonous chores on board what were in effect prison-like squadrons of battleships that were kept in port for much of the war, combined with the petty rules and discipline, the lack of adequate food and shore leave, and high levels of abuse meted out by officers on a daily basis. The mood among the ratings became even worse in 1918. This is also reflected in information gathered by British naval intelligence, which picked up in particular on growing resentment towards younger naval officers with respect to the enforcement of discipline.[43] In January 1919 intelligence noticed an article by Hartmuth Merleker in the moderate social democrat journal *Sozialistische Monatshefte* that claimed:

> When the mate and his subordinate were at the wheel, and the officer of the watch on the bridge in his boredom turned his glances now to port, now to starboard, they knew that the mess was sitting comfortably over its drinks, that 60 men had no cares, and that more than 1,000 men, full of envious thoughts of the mess, were waiting for their next meal, cold and hungry ... They knew that when 'mails for the shore' was piped, their short missives to their dear ones at home would be read by Argus eyes at Wilhelmshaven, in order to supress every intimate connection with home, and any chatter as to the true state of the Fleet. They knew that when they had passed the locks on their way up the Jade, more and more work awaited them in harbour, that they would not be able to enjoy their time of rest like their comrades in the Army in the occupied areas, but that quarters and one coaling exercise after another awaited them.[44]

The reference to resentments that battlefield troops were left alone when on rest behind the lines, whereas sailors were subject to the same level of strict discipline when on shore as when on board their ships, is revealing. That said, Robert Gerwarth and others still insist that there was nothing planned about the naval mutinies. Even the presence in Kiel of more militant sailors from the Third Squadron sent from Wilhelmshaven by the high seas fleet command on 31 October 1918 is less important than the fact that ratings from both ports were able to mingle with dockers and shipyard workers, and with ordinary civilians. Indeed, in Kiel it was the failure of large numbers of sailors to obey the signal to return to duty from forty-eight hours of shore leave in the afternoon of 2 November that 'alerted the city's civilian population to the fact that something unusual was going on'.[45] In Wilhelmshaven a similar effect was achieved when a 'mighty throng' of sailors, refusing the order to return to their ships, 'moved along the docks ... receiv[ing] large reinforcements from all directions'.[46] Admiral Wilhelm Souchon, station commandant in Kiel, simply gave up when confronted with mounting street protests in his city and resigned on 4 November. In so doing, he handed power to the newly appointed chair of the workers' and soldiers' council, the SPD's military expert and future 'bloodhound' of the Revolution Gustav Noske, who had been despatched from Berlin to investigate the sailors' demands.[47]

Further east along the Baltic coast, at Stettin (Szczecin), the USPD and the local shop stewards' movement organised a protest in solidarity with their party comrades in Kiel, including shipyard worker and strike leader Lothar Popp, who had been overlooked in favour of the anti-radical Noske when it came to electing the chairperson of the workers' and soldiers' council there. Herta Geffke, in later life a hard-line senior SED functionary, remembered:

> We agreed that a group of armed sailors and soldiers should be placed at the head of the demonstration. During the night we had managed to get hold of some red flags. And so the demonstration set off, marching past all the public buildings, such as the town hall, the police headquarters and so on, and on top of each building the red flag was raised, to the cheers of the crowd ... [Many years later an old comrade] showed me a photograph taken in front of the town hall of four-to-five sailors standing in an open-top car, and me in the middle. I can no longer remember exactly who they were. But I do know that we had strong links to a group of sailors at the Vulkan [one of the main shipyards in Stettin].[48]

However, perhaps the most important finding on the link between naval war experiences and the events of November 1918 – already evident from the Stumpf diary, but given additional weight by the new history of experience – is the reality that most sailors, like most soldiers, were not particularly interested in or motivated by party labels. The accusation made by Admirals Adolf von Trotha and

Magnus von Levetzow in 1924 that radicals from the USPD had undermined discipline in the naval ports in 1917–18 (see Chapter 1) was both entirely self-serving and completely wide of the mark. As Horn put it in 1967, 'the men rebelled because of hunger and starvation, their mistreatment by officers, and their intense desire for peace'. If anyone was to blame, it was the navy's leaders, who 'clamored loudly for a continuation of the war for the sake of territorial annexations and ignored the agonized war-weariness prevailing in the enlisted ranks'.[49] 'My God', wrote Stumpf after witnessing the first stirrings of revolt in Wilhelmshaven in early November 1918:

> Why did we have to have such criminal, conscienceless officers? It was they who deprived us of all our love for the Fatherland, our joy in our German existence, and our pride for our incomparable institutions. Even now my blood boils with anger whenever I think of the many injustices I suffered in the navy.[50]

Civilians

The 1990s were a lean period when it came to works on the November Revolution. However, one study that did add significantly to previous knowledge, and helped to open up new avenues by decentring the role of workers' and soldiers' councils, was Hans-Joachim Bieber's monograph on middle-class 'citizens' councils' (*Bürgerräte*) and 'citizens' strikes' (*Bürgerstreiks*), published near the beginning of that decade, in 1992.[51] Bieber showed that the middle classes, far from being passive bystanders to events until being called upon to vote in the National Assembly elections of January 1919, were active participants in the Revolution, constructing their own councils, albeit modelled on workers' ones, and organising their own forms of collective protest in defence of middle-class property interests – often in opposition to 'socialism' or 'godless Marxism'. In some places, representatives of the middle class, and even capitalists, also sought to join workers' councils in order to steer them in a less revolutionary direction. The most striking case of this was the general director of the Bayer conglomerate, Carl Duisberg, who joined the workers' and soldiers' council in Leverkusen, centre of the Ruhr chemical industry.[52] Furthermore, although citizens' councils gradually disappeared from view in the second half of 1919, they returned during the Ruhr Uprising of March–April 1920 and only melted away again after the Reichswehr and Prussian security police had brutally restored 'order' ahead of the June 1920 Reichstag election.[53]

Bieber's book certainly opened up new ways of perceiving the Revolution as an event, or process, that impacted not just on particular (avant-garde) classes but on the whole of German society, and at all spatial levels, including the rural, the suburban and the communal, as well as the national, the regional and the metropolitan. The language he used – and in particular his focus on middle-class 'interests' and 'mobilisation' strategies – was nonetheless still reminiscent of the older social history of the Revolution, rather than the new cultural approaches.[54] Thus he did not have a lot to say about gender. Nor did he consider ways of imagining patriotic middle-class citizenship beyond citizens' councils, citizens' committees and citizens' militias – where masculinity and masculine power were taken for granted rather than being seen as in need of reconstruction and renegotiation.[55]

Scholarship on 1918–19 more generally was indeed falling behind the curve in this respect, especially when compared to new directions being taken in works on other modern revolutions – and in particular on 1789. Olwen Hufton, for instance, broke new ground with her 1992 study of the gendered limits to citizenship during the French Revolution, building on an earlier article she had already published in 1971.[56] Among other things, she argued that the late-eighteenth-century 'crowd' could be an unsatisfactory vehicle for the expression of women's gender-specific political aspirations, especially if that 'crowd' were generalised by (largely male) historians to be a homogeneous whole with a superficial '"mother heroine" figure' at its head.[57] This was significant, because hitherto most work on the '*sans-culottes* wives' had been undertaken by Marxist historians anxious to demonstrate – in the words of East German scholar Walter Markov in 1956 – that they did not constitute a separate 'female' political entity but were an indivisible part of the revolutionary *sans-culottes* movement overall.[58]

Simon Schama's 1989 study of the French Revolution was also among the first to consider the 'construction' of new ideas about citizenship beyond the conventional categories of class and estate.

In his view, the key cultural precursors of the violent events of 1793–94 could be found not in 1789–92 but in the 1770s and 1780s. It was during these decades that a modern, 'virile', 'masculine' understanding of what it meant to be an *active* citizen emerged in France, based partly on an elevated 'cult of Sensibility' and partly on a belief in the 'power of oratory', a belief that created an imagined yet 'powerful bond of identification between ancient and modern republicans'. What the prerevolutionary and revolutionary eras – i.e. the 1770s through to the 1790s – had in common, he argued, was an attempt by elites to 'inculcate the public virtues associated with republican Rome: patriotism, fortitude, integrity and frugality'.[59] These same virtues were also embodied in the minds of (aristocratic) French citizen-soldiers such as the Marquis de Lafayette in the much-revered (founding-) father-like figure of the American revolutionary leader and first President of the United States, General George Washington, with whom France was allied until 1783.[60]

The four years of the First World War have likewise been identified as a moment of intense debates on, and reformulations of, 'patriotic' citizenship. This does not mean that the nation was constructed through public oratory or spectacle, as Schama suggests was the case in late eighteenth-century France.[61] For one thing, after 1 August 1914 the Kaiser rarely appeared in public, and on those rare occasions when he did come forward to address the people, he did little to inspire a spirit of *Durchhalten*, or 'holding out'.[62] In retrospect, the attempt by nationalist intellectuals in 1914 to conjure up a patriotism based on the notion of the uniqueness of German *Kultur* – through appeals to the spirit of Kant, Goethe and Beethoven – was also bound to fail, as this appealed to the middle classes only.[63] By the time pro-regime elements and the military had managed to come up with a new slogan – in the form of calls for a 'Hindenburg peace' in 1917 – war-weariness had already taken hold of the home front on a large scale.[64]

Even so, attempts were made to construct a more popular and people-focused patriotism in spaces that were far removed from the sphere of public oratory. As most historians agree, from 1915 at the latest, when the British-led naval blockade of Germany began to kick in, politics on the home front largely revolved around the question of food.[65] Who was entitled to judge whether the amount of food now being made available to civilians – partly through Government agencies such as the Kriegsernährungsamt (War Food Office) and partly through middle-men – was sufficient in terms of quantity and quality, and whether it was being supplied at a reasonable price? Much of the Cold War historiography on this subject tended to revolve around the argument that food shortages simply magnified class divisions in German society.[66] More controversially, however, the American historian Belinda J. Davis, in a book published in 2000, argued that the food question created new and unexpected bonds of solidarity among social groups that hitherto were unlikely to feel that they had anything in common and were hardly predisposed to regarding each other as 'virtuous'. In so doing, she also created new – albeit contested – ways of interpreting both the civilian contribution to the November Revolution and its chronology.

In First World War Berlin, Davis argued, a new, open-ended form of 'participatory democracy' was forged in the streets, pitting consumers, especially poorer women, against food producers and the underresourced Government agencies that sought to control prices and ensure supplies.[67] The chief weapon in this battle for rights was not oratory but the 'street scene' (*Straßenbild*) itself, or in other words what Police President Traugott von Jagow called the everyday 'unpleasant' spectacle of women queuing in front of empty or half-empty shops, with anger, anxiety or 'bad humor' on their faces.[68] Since, by late 1915, almost the entire population of the capital city (and other major urban centres) was suffering from food shortages, the incompetence of the Government in this matter came to be defined politically, i.e. as an issue of the people versus the State. Furthermore, urban consumers became the visual, everyday symbol of the people and the goals that they were fighting for: a 'bread peace' rather than a 'Hindenburg peace'.[69] When they rioted and attacked shops or marched on municipal buildings – as they did with increasing frequency from October 1915 onwards – they typically elicited sympathy rather than condemnation from Berlin newspapers and even from the police officials sent to bring them back into line.[70]

Davis's work was significant for two reasons. First, historians previously associated declining morale on the home front with the terrible 'turnip winter' of 1916–17, whereas she showed that the politics of food began having an impact on attitudes towards the war as early as October 1914 and were already straining existing social relations to the limit by October 1915. Second, while women routinely feature as food rioters in most standard accounts of revolutions, demanding just prices and an end to 'unfair' profiteering, they appear far less often as active participants in political battles.[71] Rather, the right to eat is seen as a 'self-evident truth' and is thereby presented in de-ideologised and depoliticised terms. Unlike the vote, fighting for this right has not been equated historically with the politics of class conflict, with patriotic or democratic struggles, with constructions of citizenship, or indeed with any type of politics beyond the mere act of rioting.[72] Davis set out to correct this historiographical bias as far as Berlin in the years 1914–18 was concerned, and came up against fierce resistance.

'[I]t is one thing to throw flower-pots at police or to bang on shop windows demanding food', wrote Richard Bessel in a critical review in 2003, 'and quite another to bring down a political system'.[73] For Julia Sneeringer, Davis's book, by looking at actors who were not politically organised, and at events that were not controlled from above by established parties and institutions, had blurred the 'precise contours of antiwar sentiment'.[74] Even those, such as Schama, who are less interested in explaining political revolution than in tracing cultural constructions of (masculine or feminine) virtue had seen little point in studying acts of female rioting, except as a negative counterpart to Robespierre's notion of the 'sacred value of insurrection';[75] going after 'paltry merchandise' is something that people do when their stomachs are empty, not when their minds and spirits are free or yearning to be so.[76] Food rioters are also sometimes assumed not to be capable of showing empathy for the bodily and political rights claimed by others, such as the tens of thousands of medically discharged ex-servicemen from Berlin mentioned by Bessel in his review, or the adolescent youths discussed in the section below.[77] 'People in need or distress are not usually good democrats', as the German historian Hedwig Richter has recently put it.[78] This is just another way of saying that absence of virtue and free spirit within the 'amorphous mass' leads to tyranny and unfreedom, the lesson that eighteenth- and nineteenth-century reformers, and even some of the revolutionary leaders from those times, believed that they had learned from reading histories of Ancient Rome or chronicles of the years 1789–94 in Paris.[79]

But in fact the prejudice goes even further than this. Food demonstrations by the poor and dispossessed are not even defined as transgressive in a cultural or gendered sense, given that rioting when hungry, like rising up to protect one's children from predators, has been cast as 'natural' or 'impulsive', and not the outcome of reasoned or impassioned thought. It is a cry for 'primitive justice', in Schama's words, not 'social enlightenment'.[80] Even Davis herself slips up a bit when she borrows the term 'self-help' as a euphemism for the theft or illicit acquisition of food items by hungry city-dwellers during the war, 'self-help' not usually being equated with 'virtue' in the revolutionary canon.[81] Only in the 1920s did the German dramatist Bertolt Brecht cleverly turn this entrenched assumption on its head when he came up with the memorably impassioned retort in his play *The Threepenny Opera*: 'Erst kommt das Fressen, dann die Moral' – 'Food is the first thing, morals follow on.'[82] The key political message conveyed here is that when a society is rotten to the core, when all it can offer is opulence for the few and abject misery for the many, then only the violent shock of revolution can shake the people out of their paralysing sense of hopelessness and despair ('Whoever fights, can lose; whoever does not fight has already lost', as Brecht is also said to have proclaimed in the 1930s).[83]

Davis's work, like that of Hufton on the French Revolution, was primarily concerned with ideas about citizenship, not violent resistance. However, in it we not only find confirmation that the hunger on the home front in 1914–18 was real and immediate, as opposed to fake or stirred up by 'hostile' or 'alien' elements; we also find the historical spectacle of hungry women and men simultaneously being capable of passion and of rational thought, in other words of 'practising an effective form of politics – even if they were not always getting [enough] food'.[84] So why the reluctance by some historians of 1918–19 to take this seriously, in contrast to historians of 1789? Why could sailors and soldiers in late 1918 be virtuous as well as war-weary, hungry and grief-stricken, and not civilians? What was it in their experience of enlistment, departure for the front, killing, surviving battle and finally refusing to fight any more that made them more wholesome revolutionaries? These questions – and the failure of Davis's critics to answer them – are an important illustration of Joan Wallach Scott's point that gender history requires us to be alert to the gendered assumptions of historians in the present as well as to those of actors in the past.[85]

Young people

During the Cold War era, it was largely East German historiography that concerned itself with the role of young people in the 1918–19 Revolution. Accounts written in the 1950s and 1960s focused mainly on the Freie Sozialistische Jugend (Free Socialist Youth (FSJ)), founded in October 1918, which had branches in many big cities and industrial areas, including Berlin, Braunschweig, Hanover, Hamburg, Magdeburg, Stuttgart and parts of the Ruhr valley, and brought together adolescent supporters of the imprisoned Spartacist leader Karl Liebknecht. Together with the 'Free Youth of Greater Berlin', a group founded by working-class activists and university students in June 1918 to mark the centenary of Karl Marx's birth, the FSJ formed the cornerstone of what one 1950s East German account called the 'Young Front'.[86] Yet, as was typical of GDR historiography of this time, the point was also to tailor accounts of revolutionary youth movements in Germany to ensure that they fitted in with standard SED narratives. This meant resolutely denying that young people could ever be regarded as a political entity in their own right. Of course, it was considered important for young East German 'fighters for peace' to know that they had heroic forebears, particularly at a time, in the 1950s, when 'the Western Powers [were] believed … to be preparing for war' against the Soviet bloc.[87] But it was only under the umbrella of a fully fledged Leninist party 'of the new type' that they could become active participants in the forging of a peace-loving, socialist German State.

Towards the end of the Cold War, a fresh starting point for understanding and historicising 'youth' as a political category in First World War Germany was provided by the West German historian Ute Daniel in a book published in 1989 and translated into English in 1997. In it she examined how the years 1914–18 brought forth new ways of disciplining and objectifying youth on the one hand, and of licensing it to rebel on the other. This process took place in the context of mass male conscription; women's and adolescents' waged labour in branches of industrial production traditionally dominated by adult men; and popular as well as official efforts to endow the war with meaning as an 'unsettling', 'event-packed historical phenomenon' that 'create[d] waves' and 'sensation[s]' of an altogether unfamiliar kind.[88] The pacifist-anarchist campaigner Benno Scharmanski (1906–98), interviewed by the filmmaker Uli Bez for her 1989 documentary about the events of 1918–19 in Bavaria, *Es geht durch die Welt ein Geflüster* (*There's a Whisper Spreading across the World*), recalled what it was like to be a young person growing up in one of the many impoverished, female-headed proletarian households during the war:

> All the children – there were four of us – had to ensure that something was brought in. It didn't matter … how we did it. When we went out to go stealing, we said: 'Get up to steal, the neighbour has already left' … Some of us went to pick mushrooms, others to pick ears of corn, others to dig or steal potatoes. One day … I scouted out the railroad cars at the freight yard. I found a car full of wheat grain. I thought, that's good, my mother will praise me. I tore the seals open and scooped out a bucket of grain. Then I returned home and said: 'Mother, look what I've brought. It's all threshed.' – 'You're such a good boy', she said. Then she went straight to the baker with the grain and exchanged it for bread.[89]

Not surprisingly, youth crime and 'waywardness' were major matters of concern for the authorities on the German home front. As early as November 1914, the Deutscher Verein für Armenpflege (German Association for the Care of the Poor) wrote to the Reich Office of Interior to warn that the rising (and unpredictable) cost of food was proving detrimental to the ability of private and public welfare bodies to meet the growing demand for their services from poorer families with infants and teenagers to feed.[90] Over the course of the next three to four years, more and more of these families fell into want and despair. Yet paradoxically, official action institutionalised the social conflict that it was intended to combat, with lasting effects into the Weimar period, as Elizabeth Harvey demonstrated in her 1993 study of youth welfare policies in the 1920s and early 1930s.[91] Thus, while police officials often showed sympathy for women food protestors as the voice of the 'people', they reacted with considerably less understanding when adolescents became involved. Indeed, if male and female youths turned up at a street demonstration, this was often used an excuse to go in with truncheons drawn (although in the heat of the moment the police typically did not shy away from using their truncheons against middle-aged women as well).[92] A police report on street disturbances in Leipzig, Saxony, on 17 May 1916 noted:

> The riots involved completely senseless attacks on grocery stores: mainly it was the young mob of sixteen-to-eighteen-year-olds, some of whom came equipped with revolvers and cartridges. The senselessness of their destructive rage can be seen in the fact that shops that have absolutely nothing to do with food were attacked and partly demolished ... As of yesterday evening, twenty-three arrests for breach of the peace had been made.[93]

Overall, during six days of rioting between 14 and 20 May 1916, 'crowds ransacked twenty-four stores across the city' and hundreds of arrests were made.[94] Of the 124 Leipzigers eventually brought before the courts after being charged with public order offences, 106 were minors, among them teenage girls as well as boys.[95]

Family destitution was one problem. Yet working-class male adolescents with wartime jobs were also identified by the authorities as having too much money and enjoying too many illicit pleasures in their spare time, with gambling, drinking and visiting prostitutes singled out as particular causes for concern.[96] In some military districts, compulsory savings orders (*Sparzwangserlässe*) were introduced, whereby a significant proportion of teenagers' earnings were paid into closed accounts controlled by the communal authorities, proletarian mothers not being trusted to act responsibly on their sons' or daughters' behalf. In Berlin alone, the number of such forced savings accounts had risen to 104,000 by 1 April 1918, containing 8.75 million marks.[97] Yet opposition to these schemes also politicised the issue of youth and lent a certain amount of legitimacy to the idea of working-class rebellion as a necessary remedy in the face of arbitrary state regulation. An official from the political police department in Berlin thus reported in August 1916:

> As before, the liveliest propaganda against forced saving is carried out by young people, especially by the Social Democratic working-class youth as well as the radical [pro-Spartacist] Youth Education

Association. In the meetings of young people, reference is always made to the Braunschweig youth, who have worked out how to organise demonstrations to remove the need to save there. That the fathers of young people are happy with the forced saving scheme is also incorrect. My own observations suggest the very opposite, as do the many requests for repayment of savings.[98]

For Daniel, the significance of police reports like these 'lies less in [their] power of definition than in [their] power to direct action'. Labelling youths, and particularly working-class males, as '"wayward" delimit[ed] them as objects of bureaucratic and sociopolitical measures', including use of harsh prison sentences as well as 'correction' through military drill and 'patriotic' education.[99] In August 1918, the State Secretary in the Reich Justice Office admitted as much in a letter to the individual state governments. Long sentences passed by courts, he confessed, although justifiable 'on grounds of deterrence', had 'in some instances hit individual perpetrators unusually harshly in relation to their degree of personal culpability':

> This is particularly the case when it comes to young people who, through political immaturity and imprudence, have ... been incited by adults to act ... in violation of the law. In such cases, the penalties imposed are often felt by the public to be too harsh. The Reichstag has expressed similar concerns.[100]

Harvey also points to the growing confusion that police, court and welfare officials had when it came to 'defining norms of behaviour' in respect to girls. Whereas '[a]n interrupted work record could cause a youngster to be labelled as shiftless and work-shy', young females' '[d]elinquency ... was defined predominantly in terms of sexual behaviour'.[101] Yet the solution was often the same for both sexes. In wartime Hamburg, for instance, 'attempts to control [teenagers'] leisure activities included bans on attending popular shows and entertainments and even on ... smoking in public, measures which some state officials sought to retain into the postwar period'.[102] Like the compulsory savings schemes, these prohibitions proved impossible to enforce, however, not least as they did not have the support of parents.

Indeed, perhaps more than pointing to intensifying generational conflicts, for historians of First World War Germany the very existence, and failure, of such measures opens up new ways of interpreting shifting family and class relationships *across generations*, with proletarian mothers, and even fathers, tolerating, or even encouraging, their teenage children's rebellious behaviour. This was indeed a world in which working-class family life was subject to ever more intense scrutiny and critical discussion by the State, albeit not without push-back from the families and young people concerned. Andrew Donson, in his 2010 study *Youth in the Fatherless Land*, also found that 'deprivation', 'collapse of schooling' and 'dwindling controls over sex, crime, and play' in 1916–18 all contributed to the unravelling of earlier attempts by official youth groups and patriotic teachers to preserve the social body under wartime conditions.[103]

While Daniel's work was largely focused on German working-class households and the women who often headed them in the absence of fathers and husbands, Harvey's on the welfare state and its repressive as well as reforming sides, and Donson's on the way in which male youths' desire for freedom – whether of the patriotic or anarchic variety – led them to 'pit ... themselves against a[n] ... adult-led society',[104] a different perspective on male youth in war and revolution is provided by Nadine Rossol. In 2018 she published a unique collection of essays written in the immediate aftermath of the Revolution by a group of thirty-five sixteen- and seventeen-year-old boys at a Protestant teacher-training college in Essen on the instruction of their teacher, Dr Gustav Müller-Wolf. The boys did not come from the most privileged sections of society and were destined to be primary school instructors rather than grammar school teachers with university degrees. On the other hand, they were also not from labouring backgrounds, and their experience of the war and future expectations were not based on joining the largely Catholic or non-religious (i.e. socialist) industrial workforce of the Ruhr valley. One group of trainee teachers was asked to write about a trip they had made to Pomerania in eastern Germany in autumn 1918, where they helped bring in the harvest. They composed their essays on 27 November 1918. A second group was asked to reflect on their immediate experience of the November Revolution in Essen, and completed their assignments on 6 December 1918.[105]

The essays of those who had spent time in Pomerania reflected on the curious interim period between the outbreak of the Revolution at the beginning of November and the realisation that the war and the old Kaiserreich were actually over. Because of the unexpected events at national level, the group, accompanied by Müller-Wolf, decided to travel home early and by rail on 12–13 November. From Stettin they journeyed to Berlin, where they noted that the streets were eerily quiet, even though they were aware that noisy demonstrations had taken place in the previous few days, and even though, as one of the students remarked, 'almost everybody was wearing a red ribbon'.[106] They were in agreement that the sensations they had felt while working in Pomerania were radically different from those they encountered on their journey home via Berlin, and that the food they had eaten in the countryside was surprisingly less filling and fat-rich than they had expected. However, they were unable to reach any common agreement on what this all meant. Some expressed relief at being reunited with their families, and others irritation that they had had to come home early. One seemed utterly determined to demonstrate that the entire experience had not dimmed his wholehearted embrace of the Protestant work ethic: '[O]n 13 November at 3 o'clock in the afternoon we arrived in Essen, fortunately with a delay of only 1 hour. In this way, after a rest day, the work in the school could be resumed with renewed mental energy.'[107]

Those of the trainee-teachers who had remained in Essen showed an even more diverse range of reactions to events in their hometown, and this because for them, as Rossol notes, 'everything seemed to happen differently and faster than expected'.[108] Although largely hostile to the Revolution – in contrast to Müller-Wolf, who joined the SPD in December 1918 – they seemed to accept that some kind of political change was necessary and perhaps even desirable. They clearly did not identify with the working-class movement or groups such as the FSJ, and were made nervous by the sudden presence of red flags in the streets and on public buildings. Yet they were equally disoriented, and perhaps mildly reassured, by the failure of events to follow the historical precedents set by 1789 and 1848, and did not anticipate any radical changes to their own career plans or status as representatives of the Protestant urban lower middle class. Their experiences and expectations, and their manner of communicating the same, were also too varied to fit easily into narratives of a 'war youth generation' simultaneously radicalised by their rejection of the Revolution and militarised through their exposure to nationalist education.[109] As one of the teenage essayists wrote, 'Whether the revolution will be a blessing for Germany remains to be seen. Only the future can teach that. But to rebel against the new conditions would be senseless and could only damage our fatherland.'[110] Rossol's findings tally with those of Martin H. Geyer in his 1998 book on Munich during the era of revolution, inflation and modernity in the years 1914–24. On the one hand, Geyer found that State officials had a fleeting obsession with generational conflict in the early weeks of the Revolution, when even teachers at grammar schools – places where the sons of the middle classes were educated – were taken aback, as one of their number put it, by how far the war had impacted the 'mental balance' of all young people. On the other hand, he noted that 'the vast majority of grammar-school boys, just like the vast majority of Munich's [university] students, were and remained extremely conservative' in their political views.[111] The battle lines between young and old in 1918–19 seemed to be rather a matter of cultural identity and lifestyle, with youth in Munich and also in Hamburg apparently more willing to let their hair down in the weeks after November 1918 than Protestant trainee-teachers in Essen.[112] In its 29 January 1919 edition, the mass circulation *Münchner Neueste Nachrichten* even reported on the new 'dancing epidemic' ('Tanzseuche') that had seized hold of young people in the Bavarian capital, claiming that it was more accurately described as a 'pandemic' or – with allusions to the Spanish flu – a 'dancing on the abyss' ('Tanzen auf Abgrund').[113]

In short, generational identities, alongside those based on region and religion, may well have helped to inform the experiences and sensations of the Revolution as well as local, street-based and medialised reactions to the all-round atmosphere of irregularity and transgression.[114] Demographic factors may also have contributed to what Detlef Lehnert has described as the 'urban diversity' ('Städtevielfalt') of the Revolution, in other words its manifestly varied impact on cities in different parts of Germany and, within each city, on different districts and localities.[115] But they did not define political battle lines of left and right in the minds of contemporaries. Rather, events did. And, as we shall see in the next chapter, in the debate since 2010, those scholars who have taken a protest-centred and chronology-driven approach to narrating the history of the Revolution have often ended up directing attention to shifting political, rather than cultural, understandings of 'space' from late December 1918 onwards above all else.

Notes

1 Benjamin Ziemann, 'Germany 1914–1918: Total War as Catalyst of Change', in Helmut Walser Smith (ed.), *The Oxford Handbook of Modern German History* (Oxford, 2011), 378–99. See also Benjamin Ziemann, *Violence and the German Soldier in the Great War: Killing, Dying, Surviving*, trans. Andrew Evans (London, 2017; German original, 2013).
2 Andrew Donson, *Youth in the Fatherless Land: War Pedagogy, Nationalism, and Authority in Germany, 1914–1918* (Cambridge, MA, 2010), 2.
3 See, for instance, Smith, *A People's War*. Also Peter Fritzsche, *Germans into Nazis* (Cambridge, MA, 1998), 11–82; and Kruse, 'The First World War', 81–4.
4 See L. L. Farrar, 'Nationalism in Wartime: Critiquing the Conventional Wisdom', in Frans Coetzee and Marilyn Shevin-Coetzee (eds), *Authority, Identity, and the Social History of the Great War* (Oxford, 1995), 133–52.
5 Jeffrey Verhey, *The Spirit of 1914: Militarism, Myth and Mobilization in Germany* (Cambridge, 2000).
6 See, for instance, Erich Matthias and Rudolf Morsey (eds), *Der Interfraktionelle Ausschuß 1917/18* (Düsseldorf, 1959); and Klaus Epstein, 'Der interfraktionelle Ausschuß und das Problem der Parlamentarisierung 1917/18', *Historische Zeitschrift*, 191.3 (1960), 562–84.
7 See, for example, Erdmann, 'Die Geschichte der Weimarer Republik', 9–10.
8 See, for instance, Herrmann, 'Sozialdemokratische Frauen', 224–9; and Grebing, *History of the German Labour Movement*, 98–9.
9 Nicolas Offenstadt, 'Die "Roten Matrosen" von 1917: Albin Köbis und Max Reichpietsch, Helden der DDR', in Droit and Offenstadt (eds), *Das Rote Erbe der Front*, 117–64.
10 See Nadine Holdsworth, *Joan Littlewood* (London and New York, 2006), 6; and *Programmheft 'Feuer aus den Kesseln': Historisches Schauspiel von Ernst Toller. DDR-Erstaufführung anläßlich des 40.*

Jahrestag der Deutschen November-Revolution (Quedlinburg, 1958). *Draw the Fires* was also performed as a radio play in the GDR in 1977, the sixtieth anniversary of the mutiny, under the direction of Peter Groeger.

11 Stephen Lamb, 'Hero or Villain? Notes on the Reception of Ernst Toller in the GDR', *German Quarterly*, 59.3 (1986), 375–86 (381). See also Klaus Kändler, *Drama und Klassenkampf: Beziehungen zwischen Epochenproblematik und dramatischem Konflikt in der sozialistischen Dramatik der Weimarer Republik* (East Berlin, 1970), 6, 290.
12 Richard Bessel, 'Revolution', in Jay Winter (ed.), *The Cambridge History of the First World War*, Vol. II, *The State* (Cambridge, 2014), 126–44 (139).
13 Robert Gerwarth and John Horne, 'Paramilitarism in Europe after the Great War: An Introduction', in Robert Gerwarth and John Horne (eds), *War in Peace: Paramilitary Violence in Europe after the Great War* (Oxford, 2012), 1–18 (3).
14 See also Robert Gerwarth, *The Vanquished: Why the First World War Failed to End, 1917–1923* (London, 2016); and Charles Emerson, *Crucible: The Long End of the Great War and the Birth of a New World, 1917–1924* (London, 2019).
15 Benjamin Ziemann, *War Experiences in Rural Germany, 1914–1923*, trans. Alex Skinner (Oxford, 2007; German original, 1997), 10.
16 See also the contributions to Hagemann and Schüler-Springorum, *Home/Front*.
17 Gerwarth, *November 1918*, 91.
18 See, among others, Gerhard Hirschfeld and Gerd Krumeich (eds), *Keiner fühlt sich hier mehr als Mensch ... Erlebnis und Wirkung des Ersten Weltkriegs* (Essen, 1993); Bernd Ulrich, *Die Augenzeugen: Deutsche Feldpostbriefe in Kriegs- und Nachkriegszeit 1914–1933* (Essen, 1997); Anne Lipp, *Meinungslenkung im Krieg: Kriegserfahrungen deutscher Soldaten und ihre Deutung 1914–1918* (Göttingen, 2003); Alexander Watson, *Enduring the Great War: Combat, Morale and Collapse in the German and British Armies, 1914–1918* (Cambridge, 2008); Scott Stephenson, *The Final Battle: Soldiers of the Western Front and the German Revolution of 1918* (Cambridge, 2009); and Robert L. Nelson, *German Soldier Newspapers of the First World War* (Cambridge, 2011).
19 Ziemann, *Violence and the German Soldier*, 20–2.
20 *Ibid.*, 8, here critiquing Joanna Bourke, *An Intimate History of Killing: Face-to-Face Killing in Twentieth-Century Warfare* (London, 1999).
21 See, for instance, Ulrich and Ziemann, *German Soldiers*, 109.

22 Ziemann, *War Experiences*, 149–54.
23 Sophie De Schaepdrijver and Tammy M. Proctor (eds), *An English Governess in the Great War: The Secret Brussels Diary of Mary Thorp* (Oxford, 2017), 134 (diary entry for 26 June 1917).
24 Ulrich and Ziemann, *German Soldiers*, 172.
25 Wilhelm Deist, 'Verdeckter Militärstreik im Kriegsjahr 1918?', in Wolfram Wette (ed.), *Der Krieg des kleinen Mannes: Eine Militärgeschichte von unten* (Munich, 1992), 146–67.
26 Bessel, *Germany after the First World War*, 69 n. 2.
27 Ziemann, *War Experiences*, 108. See also Alan Kramer, *Dynamic of Destruction: Culture and Mass Killing in the First World War* (Oxford, 2007), 64, 272–6.
28 Ziemann, *War Experiences*, 102.
29 Ulrich and Ziemann, *German Soldiers*, 179.
30 Bessel, 'Revolution', 142. See also Ulrich and Ziemann, *German Soldiers*, 3.
31 Wolfgang Maderthaner, 'Utopian Perspectives and Political Restraint: The Austrian Revolution in the Context of Central European Conflicts', in Günter Bischof, Fritz Plasser and Peter Berger (eds), *From Empire to Republic: Post-World War I Austria* (New Orleans, 2010), 52–66 (53).
32 The exceptions include Gerwarth, *November 1918*, 91. See also the older study by Ernst-Heinrich Schmidt, *Heimatheer und Revolution 1918: Die militärischen Gewalten im Heimatgebiet zwischen Oktoberreform und Novemberrevolution* (Stuttgart, 1981).
33 See Staatsarchiv Hamburg, Justizverwaltung, 241–1 I/250, Senatskommission für die Justizverwaltung to the President of the Landgericht, 16 April 1918.
34 Schmidt, *Heimatheer*, 219.
35 Gerwarth, *November 1918*, 91.
36 Lothar Machtan, *Die Abdankung: Wie Deutschlands gekrönte Häupter aus der Geschichte fielen* (Berlin, 2008), 318.
37 Schmidt, *Heimatheer*, 359.
38 Stephenson, *The Final Battle*, 64–5.
39 Ibid., 65–6. For a mid-way position on this debate, see Holger Afflerbach, *Auf Messers Schneide: Wie das Deutsche Reich den Ersten Weltkrieg verlor* (Munich, 2018), 455.
40 Horn, *The German Naval Mutinies*; Dirk Dähnhardt, *Revolution in Kiel: Der Übergang vom Kaiserreich zur Weimarer Republik 1918/19* (Neumünster, 1978).
41 Daniel Horn (ed. and trans.), *War, Mutiny and Revolution in the German Navy: The World War I Diary of Seaman Richard Stumpf* (New

Brunswick, NJ, 1967; German original, 1927), For details of a recently discovered unpublished memoir by Carl Richard Linke, who served on the same battleship as Stumpf, the *Helgoland*, see Stephan Huck, 'Marinestreiks und Matrosenaufstände: Menetekel der Revolution?', in Sonja Kinzler and Doris Tillmann (eds), *Die Stunde der Matrosen: Kiel und die deutsche Revolution 1918* (Kiel, 2018), 78–83.

42 Horn, *War, Mutiny and Revolution*, 426.
43 See the intelligence reports in TNA, ADM 137/3849.
44 Hartmuth Merleker, 'Wie kam es zum Zusammenbruch unserer Marine?', *Sozialistische Monatshefte*, 20 January 1919, 30–3 (31–2). English translation in TNA, ADM 137/3849, 70–5.
45 Gerwarth, *November 1918*, 81, 84.
46 Horn, *War, Mutiny and Revolution*, 421.
47 *Ibid.*, 419 n. 60.
48 SAPMO-BArch, SgY 30/0257/1, Geffke, *Einige Erinnerungen*, 26.
49 Horn, *War, Mutiny and Revolution*, 11.
50 *Ibid.*, 419.
51 Hans-Joachim Bieber, *Bürgertum in der Revolution: Bürgerräte und Bürgerstreiks in Deutschland 1918–1920* (Hamburg, 1992).
52 *Ibid.*, 54.
53 *Ibid.*, 11, 361.
54 *Ibid.*, 12, 25–6, 86, 349, 361–3.
55 On *Bürgerausschüsse* and *Bürgerwehren/Einwohnerwehren* see *ibid.*, esp. 196–204; and Ziemann, *War Experiences*, 227–40.
56 Olwen H. Hufton, *Women and the Limits of Citizenship in the French Revolution* (Toronto, 1992); Olwen Hufton, 'Women in Revolution, 1789–1796', *Past and Present*, 53 (1971), 90–108.
57 Hufton, 'Women in Revolution', 90.
58 Walter Markov, 'Über das Ende der Pariser Sansculottenbewegung', in Klein and Streisand (eds), *Beiträge zum neuen Geschichtsbild*, 152–75 (167–9).
59 Schama, *Citizens*, 170–1.
60 *Ibid.*, 24–42.
61 *Ibid.*, 168.
62 See Bernd Sösemann, 'Der Verfall des Kaisergedankens im Ersten Weltkrieg', in John C. G. Röhl (ed.), *Der Ort Kaiser Wilhelms II. in der deutschen Geschichte* (Munich, 1991), 145–70.
63 Verhey, *The Spirit of 1914*, 133–4.
64 *Ibid.*, 191.
65 Kramer, *Dynamic of Destruction*, 152–4.
66 See, for example, Jürgen Kocka, *Facing Total War: German Society, 1914–1918*, trans. Barbara Weinberger (Leamington Spa, 1984; German original, 1973).

The experience of revolution 191

67 Belinda J. Davis, *Home Fires Burning: Food, Politics, and Everyday Life in World War I Berlin* (Chapel Hill, NC and London, 2000), 243.
68 *Ibid.*, 1, 5. See also Belinda J. Davis, 'Homefront: Food, Politics and Women's Everyday Life during the First World War', in Hagemann and Schüler-Springorum, *Home/Front*, 115–37 (117).
69 Davis, *Home Fires Burning*, 230.
70 Davis, 'Homefront', 120–1, 125–7.
71 See, for instance, Schama, *Citizens*, 80, 124–5, 324.
72 Richter, *Demokratie*, 37–8.
73 Richard Bessel, review of Davis, *Home Fires Burning*, *Social History*, 28.1 (2003): 132–4 (133).
74 Julia Sneeringer, review of Davis, *Home Fires Burning*, H-German, November 2000, at https://networks.h-net.org/node/35008/reviews/43634/sneeringer-davis-home-fires-burning-food-politics-and-every day-life (accessed 1 March 2022).
75 Schama, *Citizens*, 708.
76 *Ibid.*, 705–14.
77 Bessel, review of Davis, *Home Fires Burning*, 133.
78 Richter, *Demokratie*, 225.
79 Nan Sloane, *Uncontrollable Women: Radicals, Reformers and Revolutionaries* (London, 2022), 24–6.
80 Schama, *Citizens*, 198.
81 Davis, 'Homefront', 129.
82 Bertolt Brecht, *The Threepenny Opera*, trans. Ralph Manheim and John Willett (London, 1979; German original, 1928), 55.
83 Manfred Wekwerth, *Daring to Play: A Brecht Companion*, trans. Rebecca Braun (Abingdon, 2011; German original, 2009), xviii.
84 Davis, *Home Fires Burning*, 238.
85 Scott, 'Gender', 1075.
86 Sieger, *Die junge Front*.
87 Dorpalen, *German History in Marxist Perspective*, 288.
88 Ute Daniel, *The War from Within: German Working-Class Women in the First World War*, trans. Margaret Ries (Oxford, 1997; German original, 1989), 4.
89 *Es geht durch die Welt ein Geflüster*, directed by Uli Bez, 1989. Quotation taken from the relaunch version of 2018–19, to which English subtitles, created by Albert E. Gurganus, were added in 2021. See www.bezmedien.de/index.php/es-geht-durch-die-welt-ein-geflues ter (accessed 22 February 2022).
90 See Staatsarchiv Hamburg, 351–2 II, Allgemeine Armenanstalt II/146, 1, Deutscher Verein für Armenpflege und Wohltätigkeit to the Reich Office of Interior, 16 November 1914.

91 Elizabeth Harvey, *Youth and the Welfare State in Weimar Germany* (Oxford, 1993), esp. 59–61.
92 Davis, *Home Fires Burning*, 83.
93 Landesarchiv Berlin, A Pr. Br. Rep. 030, Nr. 15818, 7, unsigned police report on food disturbances in Leipzig, Saxony, on 17 May 1916.
94 Dobson, *Authority and Upheaval*, 146.
95 *Ibid.*
96 Daniel, *The War from Within*, 162.
97 *Ibid.*, 167.
98 Landesarchiv Berlin, A Pr. Br. Rep. 030, Nr. 15818, 288, report signed by Polizei-Wachtmeister Dittmann, 16 August 1916.
99 Daniel, *The War from Within*, 164.
100 See Staatsarchiv Hamburg, Justizverwaltung, 241–1 I/250, State Secretary in the Reich Justice Office to the governments of the federal states, 21 August 1918.
101 Harvey, *Youth and the Welfare State*, 163.
102 *Ibid.*, 60.
103 Donson, *Youth in the Fatherless Land*, 135, 154–75.
104 *Ibid.*, 5.
105 Rossol, *Kartoffeln, Frost und Spartakus*.
106 *Ibid.*, 136.
107 *Ibid.*, 108.
108 *Ibid.*, 9.
109 On the 'war youth generation' (*Kriegsjugendgeneration*) see Donson, *Youth in the Fatherless Land*, esp. 19, 224.
110 Rossol, *Kartoffeln, Frost und Spartakus*, 185.
111 Geyer, *Verkehrte Welt*, 70–1.
112 On Hamburg see Ewald, 'As Long as People Are Dancing'.
113 Geyer, *Verkehrte Welt*, 72. The literary scholar and diarist Victor Klemperer also contrasted the 'extreme calm' in Leipzig, where he spent the first weeks of the Revolution, with the 'extraordinary' atmosphere in Munich, the city to which he returned in mid-December 1918. Here the presence of the 'colourful and passionately Romantic' immediately hit one in the face. See Ziemann, 'The Missing Comedy'.
114 On the importance of 'medialised' reactions, especially at local level, see Ziemann, 'The Missing Comedy'.
115 Detlef Lehnert, 'Eine politische Revolution der Städtevielfalt: Die deutsche Republikgründungszeit 1918/19 auf kommunaler Ebene', in Andreas Braune and Michael Dreyer (eds), *Zusammenbruch, Aufbruch, Abbruch? Die Novemberrevolution als Ereignis und Erinnerungsort* (Stuttgart, 2019), 15–32.

7
Urban space and the political imaginary of the Revolution

By 2008–9 much important work had been done on the experience of the First World War and how that experience was communicated through languages and discourses used by and about particular social actors (soldiers, sailors, civilians, youths and so on). However, preoccupation with the collapse of the Weimar Republic in 1933 still dominated the terms of the debate about the political legacy of 1918–19, much as it had done during the Cold War. True, politics was now defined in a slightly less narrow way. It was no longer meant to refer solely to those active in formal, hierarchical institutions such as branches of the armed forces, trade unions, councils and socialist parties – most of whom were of course older men. However, the historiography of the Revolution had still not considered the ambiguous and at times contradictory and chaotic responses of different groups to the fast pace of events at street level during the critical months of late 1918 and early 1919. In particular, as Julian Aulke notes, the role of the 'politically indifferent' and those who rejected party labels was still largely unexplored.[1] So too was what nineteenth-century French specialist John Merriman calls the 'stigmatization of peripheral urban spaces', in other words the labelling of particular city neighbourhoods, and by extension their impoverished inhabitants, as either marginal to the national story or as aberrant custodians of an 'assumed [and often much feared] revolutionary tradition'.[2]

In fact, it was only after c. 2010 that writing on the German Revolution came to benefit from what, since the late twentieth century, had come to be known as the 'spatial turn' in cultural, historical and urban-geographical studies.[3] Starting with the work of the French Marxist philosopher Henri Lefebvre, the 'spatial turn' was interested in the way in which the production of real and imagined spaces impacts on how individuals and communities subjectively interpret and mentally order the world around them.[4] Modern urban space in particular is seen to have had a fast-changing effect on human consciousness. If space itself – both in its material and imagined forms – becomes unstable, contested or subject to rapid transition, then so too do identities, political orientations and the collective experience or life-worlds (*Lebenswelten*) of all, including even the most resolutely non-political sections of the population.[5]

The link between the spatialisation of experience and urban modernity has particular resonance for Germany history from the 1890s onwards because of the huge growth in the number and size of cities during this period, and related phenomena such as the rise of new transport networks, new forms of housing and new uses for electric lighting – all of which in turn generated new, often penetrating, sights, sounds and bodily sensations.[6] Indeed, the number of cities with more than 100,000 inhabitants in Germany increased from twenty-six in 1890 to thirty-three in 1900 and forty-eight by 1910, while the overall population rose from 40 million in 1872 to 56 million in 1900 and 67 million in 1913.[7] For many contemporary social observers, the urban landscape became a place of excitement and opportunity, but also of danger and risk. The individual was exposed to positive visions of science and progress, yet this was often combined with premonitions of violence and moral decay.[8] As early as 1903, sociologist Georg Simmel was writing about the effect of constant nervous overexcitement on the senses and mental outlook of Germany's city-dwellers.[9] During the First World War, police forces on the home front used emergency powers of detention that were officially about safeguarding against political subversion in order to target those they described in spatial terms as the *Großstadtgesindel* – the big-city scum.[10] Meanwhile, medical experts, demographers and criminologists cast urban working-class populations as the symbol of the darker, degenerate sides of modernity, predicting a national-biological crisis as birth rates plummeted in middle-class municipal districts while remaining high in the overcrowded inner-city slums where the poorest sections of society lived.[11] And even reformers with progressive left-liberal views often decried the stubborn inability of urban space to match their expectations of the supposed benefits of scientific planning and State-funded medical and psychiatric interventions for regulating human behaviour and curing social ills.¹²

The 'spatial turn' has also had a more direct impact on debates about the German Revolution on two levels. First, it has enlivened and nuanced scholarship on the gender of the Revolution. For Benjamin Ziemann, the predominantly male character of the Revolution is evidenced particularly through *Feldpostbriefe*, i.e. the correspondence sent between husbands and wives during the war. According to him, these reveal a deep longing for an end to the war among German women. However, their hunger for peace was expressed 'not in terms of agency or citizenship', and still less in any claim to 'spatial' presence, 'but rather in a bleak language of despair caused by economic misery and personal bereavement'.¹³ Julian Aulke, by contrast, in his study of the spatialisation of political imaginaries in the years 1918–20, points to the immediate transgressive effect when women and children are seen and heard in public spaces.¹⁴ On the one hand, their 'spontaneous, unorganised protests' clashed with the priorities of the 'predominantly male organised workforce' and its sense of how space itself should be ordered.¹⁵ On the other hand, the appearance of proletarian women and youths on the streets was also deeply unsettling to middle-class male sensibilities, not just during the war, but more particularly in November 1918 itself. Pointed references to young women boldly waving red flags from the backs of trucks as they were driven around the streets of Essen by members of the revolutionary Volksmarinedivision even appeared in one of the trainee teachers' essays on the Revolution that are reproduced in Nadine Rossol's collection.¹⁶

Second, spatialisation (*Verräumlichung*) allows us to uncover the lived experience of the Revolution not just as a literal battle between armed groups for physical ownership of urban space, but also as 'a symbolic show of force' that was often about something more than straightforward political rivalries and allegiances.¹⁷ Domination of the streets, public squares, town halls and assembly rooms – whether achieved for short or long periods of time – was accompanied by banner-waving, cheering and a variety of sensory experiences, reflecting the many and varied soundscapes and landscapes of the Revolution. This was the case, as Christopher Dillon has recently shown for Bavaria, even in smaller towns and among provincial populations.¹⁸ Here, and to an even greater extent in the big cities, seemingly minor public displays of revolutionary passion could take on enormous symbolic significance when associated with the conquest or reimagining of space. One example would be the seventeen-year-old Helene Zirkel's success in temporarily planting the red flag over the police headquarters at Berlin's Alexanderplatz on 9 November 1918.[19] A central bastion of imperial power and class repression had fallen to the city's workers. Martha Arendsee, another left-wing Social Democrat and future Communist who witnessed this, later recalled the noise made by the crowd 'as the released prisoners were led through a line of people. The cheering was indescribable.'[20]

The first section of this chapter will take a somewhat one-dimensional view of the 'spatial turn' as referring to new writing on events in the streets of revolutionary Berlin, Munich, and the towns and cities of the Ruhr valley in 1918–19, and the new sensations these gave rise to. However, the following three sections will adopt a more multi-dimensional view by examining what spatialisation can do for our understanding of the role of transport, prisons (including places of extra-judicial detention) and funerals/burial sites during the German Revolution.

Urban streets

For the Marxist urban geographer Edward W. Soja, city streets are the 'vulnerable point' in the capitalist system, a space that can bring together 'landless peasants, proletarianized petty bourgeoisies, women, students, racial minorities, as well as the working class itself'.[21] This is because urban space, as an artificial 'material product' of the modern age, both reflects and acts upon social relationships and their 'ideological content' – a phenomenon that Soja refers to as the 'social–spatial dialectic'.[22] John Merriman, writing on the Paris Commune of March–May 1871, expresses this in historical terms when he notes how, in the decade or so that preceded the downfall of the French second empire, '[w]orking-class families from proletarian neighbourhoods proudly strolled into the *beaux quartiers* of the capital, imagining a more just society, and prepared to take steps to make that a reality'.[23] The following lines, taken from his description of the Paris of Napoleon III and Baron

Georges Haussmann, could easily have been written about the situation in Berlin during the First World War:

> [In the] spacious boulevards ... [f]ancy restaurants and cafés welcomed those who could afford them. In the dilapidated and overcrowded districts of eastern and northern Paris, working people living in tiny apartments or rooming houses struggled to get by. For them, hard times never seemed to go away.[24]

Applied to the German Revolution of 1918–19, such spatially focused insights have helped to establish new lines of interpretation in two specific areas. First, a focus on the popular experience and celebratory nature of city centre protests in the first weeks of the Revolution, from early November through to mid-December 1918, has demonstrated that it was here – in the streets – that left-leaning urban Germans first made sense of the new democratic era and their place within it. This was partly a question of immediacy, of seeing the new world created by the Revolution and being surrounded by it but not quite knowing – to quote art critic John Berger in a different context – how to explain it 'with words'.[25] But it was also a question of the new horizontal solidarities and new hopes for social justice and equality invested in these sights, in other words of new ways of *seeing* power. In Hamburg, according to Klaus Weinhauer, the principal goal of the 'urban social movement' unleashed by the Revolution was to 'defend [the local population's] right to the streets': 'This was understood as a right to an unrestricted and uninhibited mobility on public streets and places ... to discuss in the open all topics of their own choice and to organize open street protests to this end.'[26] Urban studies of the Revolution have also pointed to the astonishing, if admittedly short-lived, ubiquity of visible symbols of the Revolution – above all the red flags. In Berlin in the first days of the Revolution, as photographic historian Anton Holzer notes, the city centre streets were full of 'soldiers, red flags and machine guns'. These were the words that appeared most often in diary entries recorded by the left-liberal editor of the *Berliner Tageblatt*, Theodor Wolff, in the six days between 4 and 9 November 1918.[27] In Essen in the Ruhr, even the gigantic Krupp armament works – once a proud hub of the Kaiserreich's industrial-capitalist might – was photographed with such a banner proudly waving above its roof tops.[28] Meanwhile, the first act of the soldiers' council, which drove out the old authorities on 8 November 1918 in Nuremberg, was to raise the red flag on the town hall, and by 9 November this same revolutionary emblem was also reported to be flying over the municipal headquarters in Augsburg, the city known as the 'Bavarian Manchester'.[29]

The second area in which the idea of a 'social–spatial dialectic' has had an impact is in interpretations of revolutionary and counter-revolutionary violence in the period from December 1918 through to the crushing of the Munich Councils Republic in early May 1919. Here urban spaces have been identified as sites for the expression of existing class hatreds, and at the same time for their radicalisation. Speaking in the Constituent National Assembly in the aftermath of the 'March Battles' of 1919, USPD leader Hugo Haase condemned the execution order (*Schießbefehl*) issued by Reichswehr Minister Noske for the Lichtenberg district of Berlin, noting that the residents of that neighbourhood had been arbitrarily placed by the State beyond all legal protections, simply because of where they lived. Martial law of the kind practised during the war, he argued, while a 'form of judicial proceeding that takes place with undue haste and in summary form', was at least constitutional in the sense that the accused had the 'right to defend themselves and present evidence'. Under Noske's *Schießbefehl*, on the other hand, 'soldiers are given permission to execute those captured whilst fighting with weapons in hand, without judicial proceedings' – a completely exceptional situation for which there was no precedent, except perhaps 'at the time of the collapse of Ancient Greece and Rome'.[30]

The working-class inhabitants of Lichtenberg thereby experienced the most extreme form of spatially based 'stigmatisation'. But although Haase's comparison with Late Antiquity may be apposite, in fact there was a more modern precedent, in the shape of the massacre that accompanied the crushing of the Paris Commune during the 'Bloody Week' of 21–8 May 1871. Thus, the targets of Noske's *Schießbefehle* in Berlin and Munich were also those living on the margins of urban life, both in a spatial and a social sense.[31] Often biological metaphors were used to separate them from the 'honest' working people living in more respectable (or less socialist-/Communist-dominated) residential districts. As in 1871, so again in 1919, degeneracy, sexual deviancy, 'work-shyness', large-scale migration and family breakdown were all associated with the 'red' threat and fears of a breakdown of 'order', while 'social stigmatisation' of particular groups 'led to massacre'.[32] Even in Imperial Germany between 1871 and 1914, when violence had been kept in check by reference to the ideal of a *Rechtsstaat* (state based on the rule of law) and scandalisation of breaches of the latter in the press, there had been similar tendencies towards a radicalisation of discourses around national security and the threat from the 'disorderliness' of the masses, as Amerigo Caruso has shown.[33] It was the experience of the years 1918–19, however, that intensified this medialisation (fear) of disorder and crime and fed into the extreme, extra-legal actions of Government troops and the Freikorps when confronted with 'riotous' urban spaces.[34]

Women caught up in strikes or revolutionary violence, especially those who smuggled or carried arms, were seen as a particular abomination.[35] Those with children of their own or with roles in girls' education who supposedly neglected their duty of care by involving themselves (or, worse still, encouraging their daughters or female pupils to become involved) in left-wing politics were condemned twice over – as 'reds' and as 'bad' mothers – a form of double jeopardy that was not usually faced by Communist men when they were put before civilian courts or courts martial.[36] In Munich, as we saw in Chapter 1, the young revolutionary Hilde Kramer, secretary to the 'Red' commandant Rudolf Egelhofer, was pilloried in the popular press after her arrest in mid-May 1919 on grounds of her deviant, 'mannish' looks. Eugenio Pacelli, papal nuncio in the Bavarian capital and the future Pope Pius XII, reported to the Vatican in late April that when he paid a visit to the headquarters of the then still-functioning Councils Republic, he found a 'gang of young women, of dubious appearance, Jewish like the rest of them', in charge. 'The boss of this female rabble', he claimed, 'was [Max] Levien's mistress, a young Russian woman, a Jew and a divorcée'. Levien himself, who alongside Eugen Leviné was head of the Councils Republic in its final stage, was 'also Russian and a Jew. [He was] pale, dirty, with drugged eyes, hoarse voice, vulgar, repulsive, [and] with a face that is both intelligent and sly.'[37]

Yet in many ways the class hatred coming from the counter-revolutionary side was stronger than the gender hatred, particularly when it was also mixed in with hostility towards Jews and other marginalised and persecuted minorities. On 1 April 1920 one Reichswehr commander in the Ruhr noted in his daily order to his troops:

> For what is facing us? These are not the 'German brothers' that some agitators talk about, who prudently keep themselves in the background. We are faced with a disorganised heap of unruly elements that are not indigenous to the region but have been drawn into the Ruhr through the lure of urban industry ... This includes above all the large numbers of Russian Poles who have not learned to submit to the German State order, even though they have enjoyed its advantages for long enough, [and] some of whom have brought the poison of Bolshevism with them from the East ... What we are facing, then, is a vermin that primarily seeks to gain personal benefit and enrichment from the unrest.[38]

In an earlier example, Bogislav von Selchow, an aristocratic naval officer who was stationed in central Berlin at the time of the November Revolution, noted in his diary as news of the armistice with the Allies reached the German capital: '[This] morning I went to the Reich Naval Office building [in the Bendlerstraße], on top of which the red flag was flying. In front, a Jewish Bolshevik in civilian clothes stood guard with rifle in hand.' As German military historian Wolfram Wette has recently pointed out, Selchow's assumption that the person he had observed could not have been 'German' is telling, not only of his world view in general, but also literally of how he *saw* the ideological battles ahead in spatial terms:

> Presumably he was [looking at] a member of the Volksmarinedivision. But for [him] such a figure was the personification of Russian-style 'Bolshevism' – in other words of revolution, subversion, godlessness and terror – and of 'Jewry' with its alleged determination to dominate the world.[39]

New, spatialised 'ways of seeing' (Berger) were also evident at times of civil unrest in the early months of 1919. Posters announcing local military ordinances or promoting enlistment in the armed Government security force (*Regierungs-Schutztruppe*), for instance, were an important means by which the anti-Bolshevik protectors of law and order visibly took control of the urban landscape (see Figure 7.1). Thus, after the overthrow of the left-wing Councils Republic in Bremen on 4 February 1919, the new SPD-led provisional Government plastered notices across the city announcing a

Figure 7.1 'The *Regierungs-Schutztruppe* calls you', recruitment poster for the pro-Government security force, Bremen, February 1919. Wikimedia Commons.

Figure 7.2 'Join the Anti-Bolshevik League!', recruitment poster for the Anti-Bolshevik League, Berlin, early 1919. Alamy.

further recruitment drive so that the streets could be made safe for the upcoming elections to the State Parliament, due to be held on 9 March.

Further to the right, those seeking to mobilise support behind the Berlin-based Anti-Bolshevik League produced posters such as the one shown in Figure 7.2, which depicted Bolshevism as a terrifying, devil-like red skeleton bringing fire, death and destruction to Germany's metropolitan centres. Compared to this, expressions of class hatred coming from the left were, in the main, less directly spatial and certainly far less murderous. For the Communists in particular, rhetoric in the form of newspaper articles, speeches and funeral orations came first. One of the most iconic propaganda images for the KPD in early 1919, for instance, depicted Karl Liebknecht addressing the crowds on the Siegesallee in Berlin-Tiergarten on 5 January 1919, at the start of the Spartacist Uprising (Figure 7.3). Workers, soldiers and sympathetic middle-class citizens all stand together, deeply moved by his remarkable (and yet in retrospect, as we shall come back to in the conclusion to this book, also profoundly tragic) gifts of oratory.

Urban space and the political imaginary 203

Figure 7.3 'Join the KPD! (Spartacist League)', recruitment poster for the KPD, Berlin, early 1919. Alamy.

This image stands out in another sense too, for in general the KPD was markedly reluctant to engage in poster wars and other eye-grabbing means of conquering real and imagined public space, at least in the early weeks of 1919. True, front-page articles in its daily newspaper, *Die Rote Fahne*, mobilised uncompromising opposition towards militarists and their supposed backers among the 'bourgeois' parties and the SPD, as Eduard Bernstein complained in his works on the German Revolution published in 1921 (see Chapter 1). The liberal *Frankfurter Zeitung* alleged that Liebknecht had called on his supporters to 'disperse the national assembly with force' in his 5 January speech on the Siegesallee.[40] Yet there is nothing to suggest that such words, if indeed spoken by Liebknecht, rendered revolution more *seeable* to the crowds below. In fact, as Benjamin Ziemann has suggested, it was the rhetoric rather than the visual imagery of civil war in which the Spartacists and their successors specialised.[41] When the freelance photographer Willy Römer, who owned his own picture-postcard agency, sought to take still shots of red militia storming the *Vorwärts* building in Berlin's newspaper district on 5 January 1919, they immediately stopped him.[42] Mass circulation of graphic images depicting violence was not their propaganda style. The one, extremely brief, exception came in the hours before the shooting dead of two captured Prussian soldiers and eight upper-class counterrevolutionaries, including one woman, in Munich on 30 April 1919, as Government troops encircled the city. Eliza Ablovatski thus notes that after being 'put under great pressure', the two captured Prussian soldiers had

> reportedly confessed that a bounty had been placed on the heads of the [Munich] revolutionaries and that their regiment had been involved in the assassination of the popular revolutionary leaders Rosa Luxemburg and Karl Liebknecht following their arrests in Berlin ... On the night of April 29, their captors set the stage for their executions by using the [requisitioned] presses of the [mass circulation] ... *Münchner Neueste Nachrichten* to print posters containing these incendiary allegations and then posting them throughout the city.[43]

Beyond Munich, however, the left seemed uninterested in depicting violence in action. Rather, it was much more focused on occupying symbolic sites of 'bourgeois' political and economic power, such as the city palace in Berlin, scene both of Liebknecht's declaration of a socialist republic on 9 November 1918 and of the stand made by members of the Volksmarinedivision in late December of that year; newspaper offices, such as the *Vorwärts* building in January 1919; or, following the example of the strike waves of April 1917

Urban space and the political imaginary   205

and January 1918, factories, mines and business premises. Even so, it is worth noting that an industrial stoppage called by the Leipzig workers' and soldiers' council in late January 1919 in protest against the murders of Liebknecht and Luxemburg – although it succeeded in bringing the city to a standstill and rallying over 100,000 demonstrators on the Augustusplatz – collapsed after just one day.[44] Likewise, a planned political strike, announced by the general workers' council of Greater Berlin for 5 June 1919 as a demonstration against the Reich and Bavarian authorities' failure to prevent the court-ordered execution of the Munich revolutionary leader Eugen Leviné, was called off at the last minute 'because [the] organizers feared violence from government troops'.[45]

In other ways, too, the post-1919 radical left found itself on the defensive when it came to the question of protecting urban/industrial – and therefore ideological – space. Peaceful strikes, such as the one that defeated the counterrevolutionary Kapp–Lüttwitz Putsch in Berlin in March 1920, were expressions of a desire not to occupy new public space in a physical sense, or to build new bridges with the equally anti-militaristic SPD, but to safeguard symbolic ground that had already been gained and then conceded in previous battles with the 'bourgeois'-capitalist State.[46] Furthermore, although there were also significant armed Communist uprisings in the Ruhr in March–April 1920; in Prussian Saxony in March 1921; and in Hamburg, Saxony and Thuringia in October 1923, urban space as something real and tangible to capture rather than as a symbol of an already-lost but still desperately defended revolution only really re-entered the equation during the events of 'Bloody May' in Berlin in 1929, and then in the regular street battles between leftist and right-wing paramilitaries across Germany during the early 1930s. And even in this later period, the left was more often on the defensive than the offensive.[47]

Traffic

Cultural historians have long been interested in city transport systems and hubs and their seemingly constant scientific improvement as symbols and 'signifiers' of technological prowess, as well as of modernity's obsession with imposing order on time and space.⁴⁸ Traffic in this sense is not only a question of spectacle, but a major contributor to the soundscape and 'pulse' of the early twentieth century, providing the kind of 'modernist aesthetic' associated with director Walter Ruttmann's 1927 film *Berlin: Sinfonie der Großstadt* (*Berlin: Symphony of a City*).⁴⁹ The steam railway and the electric tram made possible the rise of the suburb and commuting; established opportunities for mass tourism and leisure at increasingly affordable prices; and extended the reach of new forms of media, including commercial and political advertising through posters and leaflets. On the other hand, the dangers associated with new modes of travel – from being caught up in lethal or life-changing accidents through to unwelcome encounters with strangers and loss of property through theft or forgetfulness – helped to underpin the 'profound uncertainty' and 'concomitant desire to be released' that modernity seemed to bring.⁵⁰

Less has been written on traffic networks' association with the chaos and disorder or – depending on one's perspective – the orderly and heroic nature of the 1918–19 Revolution. Yet in fact, as Julian Aulke shows, railways and railway stations in particular were important sites of the Revolution, just as they had been important sites for the mobilisation and movement of troops during the war itself.⁵¹ Trains were the means by which members of the Volksmarinedivision spread themselves first from Kiel and Wilhelmshaven to other ports – Stettin, Lübeck, Bremerhaven and Cuxhaven – and then all over Germany in the first week of the Revolution.⁵² At the same time, representatives of the original soldiers' and workers' councils were anxious to protect railway stations from attempts to disrupt the smooth movement of peace-hungry troops returning from the battlefields of northern France and Belgium. In the industrial town of Mühlheim in the Ruhr valley, for instance, FSJ member Milli Bölke remembered how:

> [in] the November days of 1918 we believed that victory had already been won. My father Hermann Bölke, who was a member of the workers' and soldiers' council in [nearby] Oberhausen, stood guard, with rifle in hand, at the railway station and the post office. He kept watch over the prisoners of war who were being repatriated, and made sure that that they were not molested. He helped to store weapons so

that they did not fall into the hands of counter-revolutionary elements, and to monitor the fair distribution of food.[53]

The 'restrained nature' of revolutionary men's acts of violence in the early days and weeks of the Revolution is attributed by Moritz Föllmer primarily to the continued influence of working-class patterns of protest in the pre-1914 period 'which had occasionally entailed throwing stones or bottles at the police or beating up scabs, but not arson or lynching'.[54] Yet the notion of an orderly revolution may also have been reflected in, and produced by, the role of railway stations and other urban transport hubs as sites of determined, but calm, celebration of revolution and return of the soldiers. Sometimes hints of this could be found in provincial newspaper reports. On 18 November, for instance, the *Volkswacht*, the SPD's leading organ in eastern Westphalia and Lippe, provided an account of a demonstration called by the people of Bielefeld to mark the arrival of returning soldiers at the railway station and the victory of 'freedom' over 'militarism' in their town:

> Without following any particular command, thousands of men and women gathered in front of the town hall to express their joy at their new-found freedom. A huge cheer arose when the soldiers entered the town hall square, with a band at the front and the red flag flying. But in fact this was no military parade. Rather, by humbly and unostentatiously mingling with the civilians, they succeeded in giving clear expression to the feeling of unity between the people and the army. The crowd got bigger, and turned into a flood, but everyone willingly made way for the trams to get by. Soon the red flag was fluttering from the balcony of the town hall.[55]

In Essen, one of the Ruhr's biggest cities, the square in front of the main railway station was similarly decorated with red flags for the arrival home of the troops, although some of the narrower side-streets in the city centre had their share of the old Prussian colours – black, white and red. At this stage, as Nadine Rossol remarks, black, white and red did not necessarily imply opposition to the Revolution; more to the point, the red flag itself, and its appearance at Essen's main transport hub, struck fear into the hearts of the conservative sections of society. Thus the rector of the Protestant elementary school in the Altendorf district of Essen,

Richard Stahl, noted in his report on the school year 1918–19, composed for the local education authority in May 1919:

> A direct consequence of the revolution was the dissolution of our fighting capacity ... Flags, wreaths and gates of honour at the train stations – also 2 signs erected by the revolutionaries with a blood-red welcome ... We had imagined the return [of the soldiers] completely differently from this![56]

In May 1919, however, Stahl may have been thinking not only of November 1918, but of the chaos that resulted from strikes in the Ruhr, whether in the mines (coal was vital to the railways) or in the transport sector itself, in the Revolution's aftermath. Between 1918 and 1919 the average weekly wage of a skilled railway worker rose from 90.20 to 139.23 marks, and of an unskilled railway worker from 74.06 to 124.83 marks.[57] Much of this was achieved through industrial action, or the threat of it, marking a new stage in the Revolution, a shift from political to socio-economic goals. Indeed, in the first half of 1919, strikes by rail workers were a common occurrence, and became (wrongly) conflated in the minds of many reactionaries with the chaos allegedly caused by the Revolution from its very inception. Although they were usually quickly settled, transport strikes were viewed with increasing alarm by the middle classes and the SPD-led Prussian Government because they threatened essential supplies to the cities. After a fortnight of disruption in June–July 1919 in Berlin, Reichswehr Minister Noske even imposed a time-limited ban on such strikes, using emergency powers.[58] And on 13 January 1920, in a presidential decree issued by Ebert and countersigned by Noske, strikes were again prohibited, on this occasion for an unspecified amount of time (in practice until June 1920), in all 'vital industries', including railways alongside water, gas and electricity. On top of that, 'any verbal, written or other action aimed at bringing vital industries to a standstill' was completely 'forbidden'.[59]

Yet perhaps the longest hangover effect of the association of railways with social disorder in 1919 was the manner in which they supposedly allowed 'wild' youths to escape from borstals, homes for wayward girls and boys, and special educational institutions, in order to join the homeless street gangs or cliques of the big cities. This is the origin of what some youth welfare experts in the Weimar period diagnosed as a 'pathological urge to roam' (*krankhafter Wandertrieb*) among younger members of the urban underclass.⁶⁰ As Elizabeth Harvey has shown, juvenile delinquency and directionless lifestyles were seen as 'politically threatening' precisely because they were linked to the 'breakdown of authority' that had occurred in 1918–19.⁶¹ Transport police working on trains and at major railway stations in the 1920s and early 1930s were constantly on the look-out for runaway teenagers. Those who were caught were often sent back, as journalist and travel writer Maria Leitner related in her short novel *Mädchen mit drei Namen* (*Girl with Three Names*), about a female apprentice who runs away from her uncaring mother and abusive employer in provincial Cottbus and takes the train to Berlin:

> The main thing to make sure of [upon arrival in the big city] is that nobody notices that you are a stranger. When I got off [the train], I made sure that the expression on my face didn't reveal how disoriented I was from all the confusion, shouting and bustle at the railway station, which seemed absolutely enormous to me after our [small] Cottbus station. I only had an old cardboard box that I had brought to my friend the night before. I also told myself to deposit it at the left luggage counter immediately, because if you arrive empty-handed you look more like you belong.⁶²

Youths knew that they had to dodge the police and railway officials, in other words, just as their counterparts had needed to during the hunger caused by the war in 1916–18.⁶³ Some teenage boys even took to the highly dangerous trick of riding from one city to another by holding on to the undercarriage of trains and hoping not to slip between the wheels – as related in Ernst Haffner's recently rediscovered documentary novel *Blutsbrüder* (*Blood-Brothers*), which, similarly to Leitner's novel, was first published in Berlin in 1932 but had echoes of the years 1918–19.⁶⁴ Then, too, as the pacifist writer Ernst Glaeser remembered in his 1927 account of his youth, *Jahrgang 1902*, the railway stations were public spaces where the 'gendarmes were present in reinforced patrols', making it necessary for those carrying contraband or those on the run from the police to jump out of moving carriages or throw black-market goods from train windows in between stops.⁶⁵

Prisons

Arrests could of course take place in the streets or in private homes, as well as at railways stations. Civilian and military courts, both before and after 1918, were quick to impose harsh sentences on left-wing revolutionaries as well as black-marketeers and juvenile delinquents. One of the first analyses of prisons as 'political battlegrounds' during the Revolution of 1918–19 came in the shape of a 2002 journal article by Nikolaus Wachsmann on imprisonment in Weimar Germany in general. According to Wachsmann:

> in the public arena, the prison became a symbol for what communists and socialists called 'class justice'. Attacks on penal institutions by activists from the outside, and riots by the inmates on the inside became familiar events. Officials in fifteen larger penal institutions recorded no fewer than fifty-one riots and serious attacks on warders between 1919 and 1924 ... Most local prison officials reacted to the unrest in the only way they knew: even minor disturbances were answered with extreme brutality. A number of inmates were severely injured or killed during such incidents. Hundreds more were sentenced to further terms of imprisonment for rioting.[66]

Prisons also became sites of hunger strikes, one of the chief means – as Maximilian Buschmann shows – by which political prisoners on the left communicated a message both about their own confinement and about conditions in the outside world.[67] Indeed, not only did hunger strikes evoke associations with protests beyond Germany's borders – for instance anti-colonial struggles in Ireland and India, or the militant suffragette movement in prewar Britain; they also deliberately reproduced what the prisoners saw as the ideological content and material reality of urban space in the early Weimar metropolis, a space dominated by hunger and despair for the many, and vast riches for the privileged few. The publisher Wieland Herzfelde, who was arrested in Berlin on 7 March 1919 by two policemen accompanied by soldiers on suspicion of producing forbidden left-wing pamphlets attacking the new Social Democrat-led Government, was clear that his own thirteen-day protective custody (*Schutzhaft*) laid bare what Soja calls the 'territorial structure of exploitation and domination' – in other words the surface significance only of abstract concepts such as judicial independence and separation of powers.⁶⁸ Shortly after his release from Plötzensee jail on 20 March, he published a pamphlet on the actions of Berlin's *Ordnungstruppen* ('order troops') during the 'March Battles' in Berlin, and in particular their targeting of the working-class population of the Lichtenberg district.

> I was released suddenly and unexpectedly without having had any meeting with judges. As I learned after I had been freed, the public prosecutor had ordered my release on Sunday 16 March, but this could not be carried out because the officers [who had detained me] simply did not obey the public prosecutor's orders. Numerous prisoners who had been arrested simply for making critical statements or who did not even know why they were imprisoned, including a number of teenagers, were still in custody at the time of my release, and were in a completely undernourished and apathetic state. Some of the prison staff expressed their indignation at these conditions.⁶⁹

Finally, at the worst points, prisons could become sites of extra-judicial killings by Freikorps units and Government forces, most notoriously at Stadelheim jail in Munich in early May 1919. Among those summarily shot or beaten to death here in the immediate aftermath of the crushing of the Councils Republic were the former 'Red' commandant Egelhofer and the anarchist poet Gustav Landauer, who had briefly served as Revolutionary Commissar for Enlightenment and Public Instruction in April 1919.⁷⁰ Hilde Kramer, arrested as secretary to Egelhofer in mid-May and brought to Stadelheim where she was held with adult women prisoners, even though she had only just turned nineteen, wrote to two of her former school-teachers from her cell in July 1919:

> We are clearing the way for the new generation, we are preparing new times for them ... And in order to lay the ground for and initiate this goal, we need civil war ... For a ruling class cannot be expected to give up its power just like that, and if we are attacked with machine guns, we have to respond with machine guns ... The world war appeared to them as a sacred, unavoidable means of preserving the most sacred possessions; to us it is civil war [that is sacred].⁷¹

Yet it was not only prisons as parts of the official State justice system that became real and symbolic battlegrounds. So too did a variety of other sites of (extra-judicial) incarceration. Thus, on 9 November 1918, military barracks in central Berlin such as the Maikäferkazerne in the Chausseestraße were the target of protests by members of the radical-left FSJ, who sought to free soldiers detained in *Arrestzellen* for infractions of army discipline or attempted desertion.[72] In Munich, Hilde Kramer was released from Stadelheim on the orders of a judge in early August 1919 after key prosecution witnesses failed to turn up to a hearing of her case, and she was eventually acquitted in a second trial.[73] In Bavaria as a whole, however, forty-eight men and women were still being held without charge or trial under 'protective custody' orders (*Schutzhaftbefehle*) issued by the police and military, twenty-nine of them as political suspects and nineteen as social undesirables.[74] The men were detained at the Wülzburg fortress, which until late 1918 had functioned as a prisoner-of-war camp, and the women at the Strafanstalt Aichach, a penal institution-cum-workhouse for women near Augsburg, opened in 1909 and later used by the Nazis to house female political prisoners, 'dangerous habitual criminals', convicted lawbreakers and those sentenced to 'workhouse confinement'.[75]

The spatialisation of judicial and preventative detention – in other words its imagined and real function as a site of political conflict and 'class justice' – continued to reflect and impact on relations between the left and the Weimar Republic for many years. The most obvious example of this would be the above-mentioned 'Blutmai' in Berlin in May 1929, a set of pitched battles between the security police and protestors in the proletarian districts of Neukölln and Wedding and in the central districts around Alexanderplatz that ended in mass arrests as well as thirty-two deaths and 200 serious injuries.[76] Other instances from earlier in that decade would be the mass break-out from Brandenburg jail in March 1920 at the time of the Kapp–Lüttwitz Putsch;[77] the hunger strike announced by 120 prisoners at the Lichtenburg penitentiary near Halle in November 1921, most of them sentenced by special courts for involvement in the March 1921 uprising in central Germany;[78] and the similar protest launched by seventy-five Communist prisoners at the Fuhlsbüttel prison in Hamburg in 1925, many of whom had been held first in 'protective custody' and then in judicial detention following left-wing disturbances in the city in October 1923.[79] In late 1921, when the Bavarian authorities were faced with prisoners refusing to eat in protest at conditions in the fortress prison at Niederschönenfeld, which held around 100 political convicts sentenced for offences committed during the Councils Republic, including writers Erich Mühsam and Ernst Toller, they too invoked the language of the need to 'order' and 'control' public space, only in this case in the interests of the State, not the Revolution. In a memorandum on 23 December 1921 the Bavarian Ministry of Justice argued that it 'faced an emergency situation with respect to these violent prisoners'. This in turn justified use of 'all measures necessary to maintain order in the facility and to protect State security', including suspension of the prisoners' guaranteed constitutional rights.[80]

Burials and sites of remembrance

Where, in a spatial sense, were the victims of revolutionary and counterrevolutionary violence buried? Many of the latter were simply thrown into ditches, urban waterways or mass graves, another parallel with the crushing of the Paris Commune in May 1871.[81] Rosa Luxemburg's battered corpse was famously dumped in the Landwehr canal in the Tiergarten district of central Berlin, and was only discovered three-and-a-half months later, on 31 May 1919.[82] For their enemies, her death and that of other Spartacist leaders did not count as 'murder' but as a necessary act of 'pest control' [*Schädlingsmord*].[83] For their left-wing supporters, on the other hand, they were martyrs, butchered by the Freikorps and their SPD masters. This ideological polarisation is important, for, as George Mosse writes in his cultural history of the brutalising effects of the First World War, 'The [years 1914–18] and the post-war age made the death of the enemy a part of his general de-humanization ... War cemeteries and war monuments transcended the death of comrades while that of the enemy was usually final.'[84] Yet as much as this related to experiences in the trenches of the western front, it was also a polarisation tied to claims to ownership of urban space.

One revolutionary who was perhaps a bit luckier after his death than Liebknecht and Luxemburg was the Bavarian Minister-President Kurt Eisner, murdered by right-wing assassin Count Anton von Arco auf Valley in Munich on 21 February 1919. Eisner was given a proper funeral, followed by burial – as he would have wished, as a non-practising Jew – in the municipal cemetery in

Munich-East. Count Arco, meanwhile, was tried and convicted of murder. Even so, a large part of the conservative establishment and press in Munich did not attend the funeral, and false rumours were spread that Eisner was not a German citizen but a Jewish immigrant from Galicia (in fact, he was born in Berlin).[85] Michael Faulhaber, the Catholic Archbishop of Munich, refused to meet Eisner while he was still alive, or to put out flags or have church bells rung to mourn his passing. And even though he condemned the act of Eisner's killing, he was still willing to meet Count Arco shortly after his release from prison in 1925.[86]

While the case of Eisner was exceptional, in the first few weeks after 9 November 1918 even funerals of relatively unknown revolutionaries could become vehicles for the public expression of anti-militarism and solidarity with the left. In Berlin, for instance, prominent figures in the USPD and the Spartacist League held speeches at a large rally staged at the Tempelhofer Feld on 20 November, and at the municipal cemetery in the Friedrichshain district for comrades who fell during the early days of the Revolution. Among those who spoke were Hugo Haase, Richard Müller, Brutus Molkenbuhr, Karl Liebknecht, Emil Barth and Luise Zietz. This was an important claim on public space, and a declaration of continuing enmity with the old regime, for the Tempelhofer Feld was a military parade ground for the Berlin garrison of the Prussian army, and the Friedrichshain cemetery was the final resting place of many of the less prominent Berlin revolutionaries of 1848 (the so-called *Märzgefallene*) who had died on the barricades while defending the city from royalist Prussian troops.[87] Meanwhile, in the Ruhr town of Mühlheim, which was also the site of a military barracks, the above-mentioned Young Socialist and future KPD member Milli Bölke took part in late 1918 in the funeral of one of her comrades who had died as a result of injuries sustained during the war but was buried, probably at his own request, as a socialist and anti-militarist, a martyr to the revolutionary cause, not a soldier serving in a 'bourgeois' army. As Bölke later wrote for the SED party archive:

> Gerhard Bohnes, our much loved and talented youth leader ... returned [to us from the trenches] with a terrible jaw wound and reminded us constantly of the horrors of the war ... After he died

from his injuries, his burial in the cemetery at Mülheim-Broich turned into a strong demonstration of allegiance to the cause of anti-militarist youth.[88]

In this way, the unspeakable violence suffered by the soldiers at the front and their comrades at home 'took away all legitimacy from the war' and, in the eyes of a Communist such as Bölke, lent political authority to the rhetorical claim – already evident in Liebknecht's proclamations on 9 November and in the pages of *Die Rote Fahne* from 20 November 1918 – that there could be no reconciliation with the 'criminal' bourgeoisie.[89]

With the shift towards renewed Government repression against the far left and suppression of freedom of assembly from late December 1918, however, public ceremonies to honour the murdered and the dead became less of a priority than trying to support the needs of comrades in prisons, pretrial detention and 'protective custody'. As A. J. Ryder wrote in 1967, the 'subjugation of Berlin' by the Freikorps on 13–15 January 1919 'abruptly changed the political atmosphere' and led to a 'gradual elimination of [those volunteer] republican forces' willing to fight for the Revolution militarily.[90] In Munich, too, the radical left was on the defensive after May 1919, forced to channel its funds and energy into party-affiliated bodies such as the Frauenhilfe für politische Gefangene (Women's Aid for Political Prisoners) and the internationally linked Rote Hilfe (Red Aid) foundation, set up in 1921.[91] A partial exception came during the Ruhr Uprising of March–April 1920, when, at least while the fighting with Government troops continued, mass public processions to honour the fallen and murdered on the rebel side became the norm.[92] In general, however, public oratory at funerals was now less revolution-affirming than it had been in late 1918, not least as urban cemeteries themselves were becoming sites that reproduced and further developed class and ideological divisions on the left.

In Berlin, for instance, whereas the seven dead of 9 November 1918, the fourteen killed on 6 December and the eleven members of the Volksmarinedivision who had died defending the city palace during the Christmas clashes were all buried at the cemetery at Friedrichshain with permission from the municipal authorities, things changed after 4–5 January 1919. Following the Spartacist

Uprising, the new pro-republican but non-party mayor of the city, Adolph Wermuth, decided that the dead on the 'rebel' side – which of course included Liebknecht and Luxemburg, among 156 other Spartacists – did not belong in the proud democratic tradition of 1848 and could not be laid to rest at Friedrichshain. Instead, on 25 January 1919 thirty-two bodies, including that of Liebknecht, were buried in a mass grave at the 'less honourable' site at Friedrichsfelde. Alongside them was an empty coffin to represent Rosa Luxemburg (her body was only discovered and removed from the Landwehrkanal on 31 May). The funeral cortege on 25 January was also refused permission to use the organisers' preferred route along the Siegesallee, and was instead forced to take the back streets from Bülowplatz (today Rosa-Luxemburg-Platz), where the new KPD headquarters stood.[93]

In 1920–23, the Berlin police department forbade marches to Friedrichsfelde on 15 January, the anniversary of Liebknecht's and Luxemburg's deaths. Instead, the occasion was marked in different places in different years: in Hasenheide Park in Neukölln in 1920; at the Lustgarten Park opposite the city palace in central Berlin in 1921; and in Friedrichshain Park, to the northeast of the city centre, in 1922. Plans were nonetheless put in train for the erection of a monument in the cemetery, which finally came to fruition in the mid-1920s. Finished on 13 June 1926, the seventh anniversary of Luxemburg's burial, and formally unveiled on 11 July, the *Monument to the Revolution (Revolutionsdenkmal)*, by the modernist architect and subsequent director of the Bauhaus school Ludwig Mies van der Rohe, became a place of pilgrimage for German leftists in the remaining Weimar years and again after the Second World War, when that part of Berlin lay in the eastern sector of the city (Figure 7.4).[94]

Admittedly the monument itself was destroyed by the Nazis in 1933–35, but the memory of it was not so easily erased. In 1951 a new memorial stone, the *Gedenkstätte der Sozialisten*, was constructed and placed more centrally in the cemetery, inscribed with the words 'The dead admonish us' ('Die Toten mahnen uns') (Figure 7.5). Officially, Friedrichsfelde now became a collective site of remembrance for all German martyrs to the socialist cause – as the SED regime wanted it to be – but the popular association of this particular place of rest, mourning and reflection with Liebknecht

Figure 7.4 Architect Ludwig Mies van der Rohe's *Revolutionsdenkmal* (*Monument to the Revolution*), unveiled at the Friedrichsfelde cemetery in central Berlin, 11 July 1926. Wikimedia Commons.

Figure 7.5 Ceremony at the Memorial of Socialists, Berlin-Friedrichsfelde, to mark the centenary of the murders of Karl Liebknecht and Rosa Luxemburg, Sunday 13 January 2019. Getty Images.

and Luxemburg continued nonetheless.[95] Throughout the GDR period and beyond, and indeed to the present day, processions of Communists and post-Communists still visit the cemetery each year on or around 15 January to pay their respects and to assert the continued existence of this 'socialist space' constructed in the heart of Berlin.[96]

Notes

1. Aulke, *Räume der Revolution*, 22.
2. John Merriman, 'The Language of Social Stigmatization and Urban Space in Nineteenth-Century France' (1999), reproduced in John Merriman, *History on the Margins: People and Places in the Emergence of Modern France* (Lincoln, NE and London, 2018), 63–83 (76–7). My interpolation.
3. For a useful introduction see Edward W. Soja, *Postmodern Geographies: The Reassertion of Space in Critical Social Theory* (London, 1989). Also Simon Gunn, 'The Spatial Turn: Changing Histories of Space and Place', in Simon Gunn and Robert J. Morris (eds), *Identities in Space: Contested Terrains in the Western City since 1850* (Aldershot, 2001), 1–14.
4. Henri Lefebvre, *The Production of Space*, trans. Donald Nicholson-Smith (Oxford, 1991; French original, 1974).
5. Aulke, *Räume der Revolution*, 1, 15, 18–19. See also Klaus Weinhauer, 'World War I and Urban Societies: Social Movements, Fears, and Spatial Order in Hamburg and Chicago (*c.* 1916–1923)', in Stefan Rinke and Michael Wildt (eds), *Revolutions and Counter-Revolutions: 1917 and Its Aftermath from a Global Perspective* (Frankfurt am Main and New York, 2017), 287–306.
6. Anthony McElligott, *The German Urban Experience, 1900–1945: Modernity and Crisis* (London and New York, 2001).
7. See Frank-Lothar Kroll, *Geburt der Moderne: Politik, Gesellschaft und Kultur vor dem Ersten Weltkrieg* (Berlin, 2013), 69; and Volker Berghahn, *Imperial Germany, 1871–1918: Economy, Society, Culture and Politics* (New York, 2005), 38.
8. Moritz Föllmer, *Individuality and Modernity in Berlin: Self and Society from Weimar to the Wall* (Cambridge, 2013), esp. 25–47.
9. Georg Simmel, *Die Großstädte und das Geistesleben* (Dresden, 1903).
10. André Keil and Matthew Stibbe, 'Ein Laboratorium des Ausnahmezustands: Schutzhaft während des Ersten Weltkriegs und

in den Anfangsjahren der Weimarer Republik. Preußen und Bayern 1914 bis 1923', *Vierteljahrshefte für Zeitgeschichte*, 68.4 (2020), 535–73 (550–2).
11 Helen Boak, *Women in the Weimar Republic* (Manchester, 2013), 31.
12 For examples see McElligott, *The German Urban Experience*, esp. 94–6; and Harvey, *Youth and the Welfare State*, 159.
13 Benjamin Ziemann, 'Weimar was Weimar: Politics, Culture and the Emplotment of the Weimar Republic', *German History*, 28.4 (2010), 542–71 (549). See also Benjamin Ziemann, 'Geschlechterbeziehungen in deutschen Feldpostbriefen des Ersten Weltkrieges', in Christa Hämmerle and Edith Saurer (eds), *Briefkulturen und ihr Geschlecht: Zur Geschichte der privaten Korrespondenz vom 16. Jahrhundert bis heute* (Vienna, 2003), 261–82.
14 Aulke, *Räume der Revolution*, 182–92.
15 *Ibid.*, 20.
16 Rossol, *Kartoffeln, Frost und Spartakus*, 183–5.
17 Dirk Schumann, *Political Violence in the Weimar Republic, 1918–1933: Fight for the Streets and Fear of Civil War*, trans. Thomas Dunlap (New York and Oxford, 2009; German original, 2001), viii.
18 Christopher Dillon, '"The Revolutionary Flame Burns Also in the Provinces": The Bavarian Revolutions of 1918–19', in Dillon and Wünschmann, *Living the German Revolution*.
19 Boak, *Women in the Weimar Republic*, 64. Zirkel was the daughter of leading Neukölln Spartacist Max Zirkel.
20 SAPMO-BArch, SgY 30/0017, Martha Arendsee, 'Erinnerungen', n.d., 66.
21 Soja, *Postmodern Geographies*, 92.
22 *Ibid.*, 76.
23 John Merriman, *Massacre: The Life and Death of the Paris Commune of 1871* (New Haven, CT and London, 2014), 2.
24 *Ibid.*
25 John Berger, *Ways of Seeing* (London, 1972), 7.
26 Weinhauer, 'World War I and Urban Societies', 295.
27 Anton Holzer (ed.), *Krieg nach dem Krieg: Revolution und Umbruch 1918/19* (Darmstadt, 2017), 70.
28 Rossol, *Kartoffel, Frost und Sparatkus*, 39.
29 Dillon, 'The Revolutionary Flame'.
30 See Hugo Haase's speech in the National Assembly, 27 March 1919, in *Verhandlungen des Reichstags*, Vol. CCCXXVII (Berlin, 1920), 842–51 (843).
31 See Merriman, *Massacre*, esp. 146–224.
32 *Ibid.*, 210.

33 Caruso, 'Blut und Eisen', 26.
34 *Ibid.*, 86–90, 187–8. See also Ziemann, 'The Missing Comedy'.
35 Caruso, 'Blut und Eisen', 36; Merriman, *Massacre*, 156–8.
36 Ablovatski, *Revolution and Political Violence*, 178.
37 Enzo Traverso, *Revolution: An Intellectual History* (London, 2021), 302.
38 'Tagesbefehl der Gruppe Haas zur "Roten Armee" im Ruhrgebiet, 1 April 1920', reproduced in Heinz Hürten (ed.), *Die Anfänge der Ära Seeckt: Militär und Innenpolitik 1920–1922* (Düsseldorf, 1979), 119–20.
39 Wolfram Wette, 'Der Hakenkreuzzug: Vor 80 Jahren, am 22. Juni 1941, überfiel Deutschland die Sowjetunion', *Die Zeit*, 10 June 2021, 19 (including quote from Selchow's diary).
40 Jones, *Founding Weimar*, 177.
41 Ziemann, 'The Missing Comedy'.
42 *Ibid.*
43 Ablovatski, *Revolution and Political Violence*, 85–6.
44 Dobson, *Authority and Upheaval*, 219.
45 Ablovatski, *Revolution and Political Violence*, 227.
46 Johannes Erger, *Der Kapp–Lüttwitz-Putsch: Ein Beitrag zur deutschen Innenpolitik 1919/20* (Düsseldorf, 1967).
47 See Schumann, *Political Violence*, esp. 215–50.
48 Anthony McElligott, 'Walter Ruttmann's *Berlin: Symphony of a City:* Traffic-Mindedness and the City in Inter-War Germany', in Malcolm Gee, Tim Kirk and Jill Stewart (eds), *The City in Central Europe: Culture and Society from 1800 to the Present* (Aldershot, 1999), 209–38 (216–22).
49 *Ibid.*, 209.
50 Peukert, *The Weimar Republic*, 211, 240.
51 Julian Aulke, 'Eisenbahnen und Bahnhöfe', in Kinzler and Tillmann, *Die Stunde der Matrosen*, 145.
52 Dillon, 'The German Revolution', 30.
53 Milli Bölke, unpublished memoirs, 24 October 1958, 15. Cited in Stibbe, Painter and Sharp, 'History beyond the Script'.
54 Föllmer, 'The Unscripted Revolution', 173.
55 'Freiheitskundgebung', *Volkswacht*, 18 November 1918, 3. Copy in Landesarchiv Nordrhein-Westfalen, Abteilung Ostwestfalen-Lippe, Staatspräsidium Lippe, D 70/34.
56 Rossol, *Kartoffeln, Frost und Spartakus*, 40. Rossol's interpolation.
57 Winkler, *Von der Revolution zur Stabilisierung*, 157.
58 Annemarie Lange, *Berlin in der Weimarer Republik* (East Berlin, 1987), 223. See also the photographs of public transport and railway strikes in Berlin in June–July 1919 in Holzer, *Krieg nach dem Krieg*, 121–3.

59 'Verordnung des Reichspräsidenten betreffend Wiederherstellung der öffentlichen Sicherheit und Ordnung', 13 January 1920, Article 6. Reproduced in Huber, *Dokumente zur deutschen Verfassungsgeschichte*, Vol. III, 206–7.
60 Harvey, *Youth and the Welfare State*, 163.
61 *Ibid.*, 60. See also the archival material in Staatsarchiv Hamburg, Senatskommission für die Justizverwaltung, 241-1 I/859.
62 Maria Leitner, *Mädchen mit drei Namen*, ed. Helga Schwarz and Wilfried Schwarz (Berlin, 2013 [1932]), 145.
63 See Ernst Glaeser, *Jahrgang 1902* (Potsdam, 1928), esp. 302–3, 322, 340–1.
64 Ernst Haffner, *Blutsbrüder: Ein Berliner Cliquenroman*, ed. Peter Graf (Berlin, 2013 [1932]), esp. 60–75.
65 Glaeser, *Jahrgang 1902*, 341.
66 Nikolaus Wachsmann, 'Between Reform and Repression: Imprisonment in Weimar Germany', *Historical Journal*, 45.2 (2002), 411–32 (413–14).
67 Maximilian Buschmann, '"Freiheit oder Hungertod": Hungerstreiks als Protestform in der frühen Weimarer Republik', *WERKSTATT Geschichte* 80 (2018), 17–35.
68 Soja, *Postmodern Geographies*, 92.
69 Wieland Herzfelde, *Schutzhaft: Erlebnisse vom 7. bis 20. März 1919 bei den Berliner Ordnungstruppen* (Berlin, 1919), 16.
70 Winkler, *Von der Revolution zur Stabilisierung*, 190.
71 Kramer to Fräulein Fischer und Fräulein Koch, 16 July 1919, reproduced in Hilde Kramer, *Rebellin in München, Moskau und Berlin: Autobiographisches Fragment 1900–1924*, ed. Egon Günther with assistance from Thies Marsen (Berlin, 2011), 132–4 (133).
72 Stibbe, Painter and Sharp, 'History beyond the Script'.
73 Kramer, *Rebellin in München*, 70, 214.
74 Keil and Stibbe, 'Ein Laboratorium', 562.
75 Bavarian Ministry of Military Affairs (Operations Department) to the commanders of the First, Second and Third Bavarian Army Corps etc., 23 July 1919, in Bayerisches Hauptstaatsarchiv-Kriegsarchiv, Generalkommando II. Armeekorps (WK) 1327. On Aichach, see also Nikolaus Wachsmann, *Hitler's Prisons: Legal Terror in Nazi Germany* (New Haven, CT and London, 2004), 12 and *passim*.
76 Weipert, *Das Rote Berlin*, 144–5.
77 Wachsmann, 'Between Reform and Repression', 414.
78 Gustav Radbruch, *Reichstagsreden*, ed. Volkmar Schöneburg (Heidelberg, 1998), 184 n. 82.
79 Buschmann, '"Freiheit oder Hungertod"', 17.

80 *Ibid.*, 22.
81 See Merriman, *Massacre*, esp. 218–19.
82 Klaus Gietinger, *The Murder of Rosa Luxemburg*, trans. Loren Balhorn (London, 2019; German original, 2008), 92–3.
83 Mosse, *Fallen Soldiers*, 170.
84 *Ibid.*, 164.
85 Brenner, *Der lange Schatten*, 126–49.
86 *Ibid.*, 144.
87 Mark Jones, 'Die Toten der Revolution beerdigen: Politische Trauerfeiern im November und Dezember 1918', in Braune and Dreyer (eds), *Zusammenbruch, Aufbruch, Abbruch?*, 177–95 (183–91). On Friedrichshain cemetery see also Bryden, 'Heroes and Martyrs', 650.
88 Bölke, unpublished memoirs, 24 October 1958, 15. Cited in Stibbe, Painter and Sharp, 'History beyond the Script'.
89 Ziemann, 'The Missing Comedy'.
90 Ryder, *The German Revolution*, 207.
91 On these organisations see Nikolaus Brauns, *Schafft Rote Hilfe! Geschichte und Aktivitäten der proletarischen Hilfsorganisation für politische Gefangene in Deutschland (1919–1938)* (Bonn, 2003).
92 See the photographic evidence in Günter Gleising and Anke Pfromm, *Kapp-Putsch und Märzrevolution 1920*, Vol. III, *Totenliste der Märzgefallenen aus dem Rheinisch-Westfälischen Industriegebiet* (Bochum, 2010), esp. 16, 29 and the front cover.
93 See Élise Julien and Elsa Vonau, 'Le cimetière de Friedrichsfelde, construction d'un espace socialiste (des années 1880 aux années 1970)', *Le mouvement social*, 237 (2011), 91–113 (96–7).
94 Traverso, *Revolution*, 203–4.
95 Julien and Vonau, 'Le cimetière de Friedrichsfelde', 100, 107.
96 See also Ariane Jossin, 'Un siècle d'histoire politique allemande: Commémorer Liebknecht et Luxemburg au Zentralfriedhof Friedrichsfelde de Berlin', *Le mouvement social*, 237 (2011), 115–33. Around 20,000 people took part in the 13 January 2019 commemoration march in the centenary year of Liebknecht's and Luxemburg's murder. See Kate Connolly and Josie Le Blond, 'Germany remembers Rosa Luxemburg 100 years after her death', *Guardian*, 15 January 2019.

8

The German Revolution in European and global context: International and transnational perspectives

What was the state of research on the German Revolution at the end of the 2010s, including at the time of its centenary in 2018–19? In Germany itself, remarkably positive representations of 1918–19 as the 'true beginnings of our democracy' appeared in the media, museum exhibitions and works of popular history.[1] The largely sunny national narrative also appeared to be in harmony with the many community projects charged with marking the centenary of the Revolution at local level.[2] Yet behind the façade of public affirmation and civic pride lay a number of barely concealed fissures, reflecting doubts and anxieties brought on by the collapse of the neo-liberal 'Washington consensus' of the 1990s and 2000s, the intensification of the 'cultural wars' that began during that period, and the rise of right-wing populism in the 2010s. Added to this, as Paul Betts has written, the far-from-buoyant 2019 celebrations of the thirtieth anniversary of 1989 have shed new light on how the events of that year were not as straightforwardly positive for democracy and the politics of non-violence as previously assumed, but may have 'carried with [them] the seeds of illiberalism as well'.[3] Indeed, the widespread agreement about the didactic force of '1989' as the endpoint of Germany's long 'road to the West', which was present at the time of the twentieth and twenty-fifth anniversaries in 2009 and 2014, has now given way to overarching motifs of uncertainty and division, disenchantment with 'open borders' and perplexity about Europe's future.[4] Talk of cultural estrangement between *Ossis* and *Wessis*, very much evident in 1994 on the fifth anniversary of the fall of the Berlin Wall, and to some extent in 1999 and 2004 too,[5] has returned, but this time without the soothing comforts of nostalgia, either for the old 'East' or 'West' of the late Cold War era, or for the post-reunification elation of the early 1990s.

None of these themes was addressed directly in acts commemorating the centenary of the November Revolution; in fact, the 2018 retrospectives by and large played safe, and stuck to a deideologised script that echoed rather than challenged the post-Cold War message that there is no realistic political alternative to western-style liberal democracy and free markets. What was missing was the deeper lessons that come from decentring mainstream voices and exploring history from the margins, in other words from the point of view of the subjects, places and contexts that cannot be neatly pigeon-holed into 'good' or 'bad', 'light' or 'dark', 'success' or 'failure'. Instead, as Franka Maubach argued ahead of the centenary commemorations of the Revolution and the concomitant founding of the Weimar Republic, the plans in place typically followed a deradicalised, presentist and professionally marketed model of history as a mosaic that simply becomes 'ever more colourful' by adding more detail and fragments, but fails to act as a spur to deeper, coherent societal reflection.[6] The historicity and specificity of the different local revolutionary cultures of 1918–19 remained hidden, as did the inequalities in public funding that prevented them from being rendered visible and knowable to current and future generations.

And yet the remarkable events of 2020–22 have shown us that nothing stays the same for ever, and that change, when it arrives, can come very suddenly. The COVID-19 pandemic, the global resonance of the Black Lives Matter movement; the pro-democracy protests in Hong Kong, the mass demonstrations in Minsk and other cities in Belarus against the rigged presidential elections and police brutality of the Lukashenko regime, the inauguration of Joe Biden as forty-sixth US President in place of the defeated right-wing incumbent Donald Trump, the Burmese people's rejection of the military coup in Myanmar, the demonstrations undertaken by women and men across Poland against the ever stricter abortion laws enacted by the conservative Government there, the formation of a Social Democrat-led 'Traffic Light' coalition in Berlin three months after the federal elections of September 2021, and finally the full-scale Russian invasion of Ukraine on 24 February 2022 have all demonstrated that the question of democracy links Germany in multiple ways with political developments and social trends across the rest of the world. And if the Revolution of 1918–19 did indeed mark, if not quite the beginnings, then at least a major landmark in the German nation's path to self-determination as a liberal, open, equal, tolerant and postcolonial society,[7] then we should expect – perhaps even demand – that historiographical engagement with that event should also include Germany's many entanglements, then and now, with other countries.[8]

The development of international and transnational perspectives on the German Revolution, it should be noted, involves not only making comparisons across state and national borders but also looking for points of intersection and (false or accurate) recognition. To take a relatively trivial example, when in October 1923 the British *chargé d'affaires* in Berlin, Joseph Addison, referred to the former saddler-turned-President Friedrich Ebert as a 'good, honest, quiet, solid, promoted workman – a sort of German George Barnes', the parallel drawn with the right-wing Labour politician who served as a member of the Lloyd George wartime coalition Government from 1916 to 1918 may or may not have been apt at the personal level. But in fact it says a lot more about class prejudices inside the British Foreign Office than it does about the state of world politics or the transnational prospects for democracy at this time. It was designed to be reassuring from a British establishment viewpoint, rather than revealing anything more significant about the underlying character of the German Revolution some five years earlier.[9] On the other hand, as Adrian Zimmermann has shown, it was no coincidence that class tensions and industrial unrest in Switzerland and the Netherlands came to a head in November 1918, reflecting 'common economic and social problems of the two neutral states during World War I and ... the context of the global wave of protest, strike[s] and revolution between 1917 and 1920'. In particular, 'it was mainly an effect of the two neutral countries' strong connections with Germany, where the revolutionary movement of workers' and soldiers' councils put an end to both the monarchy and the war at the beginning of November'.[10] Stefan Berger takes this call for cross-border approaches even further, arguing that integrating national and regional case studies of revolutions in the early twentieth century into Europe-wide and perhaps even global histories of popular opposition to authoritarian regimes can lead to significant new insights.[11] In particular, it can embrace a wide range of at times overlapping and at other times competing transnational impulses, such as demands for social justice, democratisation and national self-determination, as well as for international peace, recognition of the rights of racial and sexual minorities, and an end to colonial and economic exploitation across the world.

This chapter examines recent debates on the transnational and international character of the German Revolution through four different lenses: decolonisation and worldwide demands for racial equality, political violence as a domestic and Europe-wide phenomenon, the removal of barriers to acceptance of female and queer sexualities beyond prevailing heterosexual norms, and the development of bodily as well as formal-political understandings of democracy. It concludes by arguing that on all of these fronts, the November Revolution was a necessary revolution that enhanced democratisation both nationally – i.e. within Germany – and across borders, albeit with less immediate and tangible success when it came to promoting the domestic and international rights of non-white people.

The German Revolution and global decolonisation

In spite of Addison's 'positive' (in his own view) assessment of Ebert as the 'German George Barnes', in reality the western Allies showed little support for the German Revolution in 1918–19.[12] Not only did they maintain the wartime economic blockade until 12 July 1919, they actually extended its provisions to ban Germans from fishing in the sea and further inhibited civilian food distribution by ordering the surrender of a large number of trucks, locomotives and railway carriages.[13] They also directed the confiscation of all German naval vessels, the merchant fleet included, and made this a condition of Germany receiving the first emergency food deliveries on 25 March 1919.[14] From December 1918 to January 1919 they continued to prevent neutral countries such as Norway from re-exporting pork to Germany.[15] Later they burdened the new republic with reparations, eventually fixed in 1921 at 132 billion gold marks.[16] Germany was denied entry into the League of Nations until 1926, and was not allowed to compete in the international Olympic Games in Antwerp in 1920 and Paris in 1924.[17] The Franco-Belgian occupation of the Ruhr in 1923 had a further, hugely destabilising effect on German democracy, not least as the French military also continued to encourage separatist movements in the Rhineland and Palatinate areas until at least 1924.[18] Meanwhile, the United States, having promoted the principle of self-determination as one of President Wilson's Fourteen Points in January 1918, opted for isolationism tempered only by an interest in debt recovery from all the European powers under a succession of Republican presidents after 1920.[19]

All in all, the western imperial powers showed far less solidarity with and willingness to consider the transnational interests of the early Weimar Republic than they had in the case of the Kaiserreich before 1914. Thus, between the 1880s and 1900s, as Sebastian Conrad notes, the 'increase in interaction and entanglement' among European empires was a key part of the 'expansion of capitalism around the world'.[20] The difference in 1918–19 was that Germany had now been excluded from this club of privileged white nations. Russian thinkers in November 1918 expected that Germany would now look east, break permanently with capitalist exploitation and imperialism, and become 'totally' Bolshevised. However, as Ilya Dementev notes, this assessment was based on Leninist 'faith … not on … knowledge: the data from Germany was fragmentary and inexact'.[21]

Far less has been written about reactions to the German Revolution on other continents, although this is slowly beginning to change. 'Self-determination' had been interpreted by some activists to mean national independence for countries in Africa, Asia and the Caribbean or, at the very least, a changed relationship between coloniser and colonised.[22] Instead, under the Paris Peace Settlement of 1919–20, Germany's overseas colonies, alongside former provinces of the Ottoman empire, were confiscated and handed to Britain, France and various white British dominions (South Africa, Australia and New Zealand) as special League of Nations mandates.[23] Racial equality was not included as a principle behind the creation of a new world fit for democracy, and the country that had sponsored that demand – Japan – was bought off by being offered erstwhile German port concessions in China instead. As a result, China was the only former belligerent power not to sign the Treaty of Versailles (the United States did sign it, but the Senate subsequently failed to ratify it by the required two-thirds majority).[24] Meanwhile, a petition sent on 18 August 1919 by twelve members of the Duala elite in Cameroon to the Allied negotiators in Paris, asking for a voice for the native inhabitants in the future administration of their once German-ruled country and a recognition of their civil rights and local customs, fell on deaf ears.[25]

What this meant is that by dint of its Revolution in November 1918, and its defeat in the First World War, Germany became the first western European country in the twentieth century to decolonise, albeit without necessarily becoming a genuinely 'postcolonial society' in the sense of fully or convincingly '"going beyond" the colonial'.[26] This had – and continues to have – a number of implications for the way in which the 1918–19 Revolution is remembered, or conversely forgotten, in what today is called the 'Global South', namely in poorer countries outside Europe and North America, and among diaspora communities, including Chinese and Indian nationalists, Black Americans, Liberians and Haitians, and Cameroonians and other germanophone Africans living in Germany or France, sometimes with German-born wives, children and grandchildren.

Already in May 1919 the Indian nationalist Virendranath Chattopadhyaya, then based in Stockholm, had used his links to Moscow to reactivate the wartime Indian Revolutionary Committee in Berlin;[27] subsequently he settled in Germany and joined the KPD.[28] In 1922 the Indian Communist Manabendra Nath Roy also relocated to the German capital, where he helped his wife, the American-born Evelyn Trent Roy, to publish a fortnightly anti-British paper, *Vanguard of Indian Independence* (later *Masses of India*).[29] In July 1930 Pan-Africanist George Padmore, originally from Trinidad, and African-American Communist James Ford were both centrally involved in organising the first International Congress of Negro Workers in Hamburg, which was also attended by the Berlin-based Cameroonian revolutionary and KPD member Joseph Ekwe Bilé.[30] In 1932 the visit to Germany of Ada Wright, part of a wider European tour that she undertook to draw international attention to the plight of her two sons and seven other 'Scottsboro Boys', victims of a major, racially motivated miscarriage of justice in Alabama in 1931, was judged to have been a success by its organisers, the New York-based, pro-Communist International Labor Defense.[31] Indeed, the visit built on the work of a 'Committee to Rescue the Scottsboro Victims' that had already been founded in 1931 and had a presence in several German cities, 'even [if] it was systematically blocked in the political sphere'.³²

More broadly, by the late 1920s Berlin had become one of the major European centres of the world anti-colonial movement, thanks largely to the fact that the League against Colonial Oppression, founded in 1926 by the German Communist and leading figure in the 1918–19 Revolution Willi Münzenberg, and renamed the League against Imperialism (LAI) in 1927, established its headquarters there.³³ According to one of Münzenberg's recent biographers, John Green, even before then

> The Weimar Republic had given asylum to a number of political refugees from the colonial world. As an example, at Berlin's university ... there were more than a hundred Chinese students, and the Chinese Kuomintang nationalist movement had its own office in the city ... The Vietnamese nationalist leader, Ho Chi Minh, who was residing in Paris at that time, would drop into Berlin regularly to see Münzenberg on his way to and from Moscow.³⁴

There is, admittedly, a greater difficulty in linking these broader developments directly to the November Revolution itself. True, the settled Black diasporic community in Germany – at most a few thousand strong before 1914 and dominated by Cameroonians from the port city of Douala, although it also included migrants from other parts of West Africa, East Africa and Namibia, as well as persons of Afro-Caribbean and African American descent – had its own voice, and its own, less internationally focused, expectations after 1918.³⁵ Through its leading spokesmen, it made its discrete political claims on the Revolution. We know this thanks to the detailed research of Robbie Aitken and Eve Rosenhaft on Black persons living in Germany at this time, most of them having arrived as young men between the 1880s and 1900s and many of them intermarried with white Germans. Thus, in June 1919, two leading representatives of the Berlin Cameroonian community, Martin Quane Dibobe and Thomas Manga Akwa, came in person to the Reich Colonial Office to deliver a '32-point set of "conditions" for [their] continued allegiance' to the former colonial power, including, as point 17, a statement that '[m]arriages between natives and whites are legitimate' and that '[w]e are determined to take our wives and children back home'.³⁶ Equal rights were demanded just as, supposedly,

Figure 8.1 Commemorative plaque on the house at Kuglerstraße 44, Berlin-Prenzlauer Berg, where Cameroon-born Martin Dibobe lived in 1918. Wikimedia Commons.

they had 'already been introduced in the English colonies'. This included, more radically, the right of native Cameroonian women who had borne children out of wedlock to white German settlers either to force the father to marry them, or at least to force him to make child-maintenance settlements – irrespective of whether Cameroon itself remained a German colony or not.[37]

In making these demands, Dibobe and Manga Akwa were in part focused on the needs of Cameroonians settled or intending to (re-)settle in Cameroon or other parts of the world, especially France. Needless to say, in 1919 the Reich Colonial Office refused to represent their views to domestic or international audiences, and permitted their continued presence in the metropole, often in difficult financial circumstances and certainly in considerably reduced numbers, only to bolster Germany's claims to having its colonial possessions restored.[38] Those who managed to leave Germany after 1919, either to return to Africa or to move to the new metropole, Paris, faced an uncertain future without diplomatic support from successive Weimar governments. Dibobe, for instance, is known to have attempted to travel to now French-controlled Cameroon in 1921 with his German-born wife, but to have ended up destitute and stranded in the Liberian capital, Monrovia. This came after over two years of campaigning to persuade the German and French authorities to support his repatriation.[39] Manga Akwa, meanwhile, was able to make one visit to Douala in 1921, but was refused entry by the French authorities in 1930, presumably because of his continued anti-colonial activities in Berlin and because the French suspected that he might be a German spy. In 1932, however, now separated from his wife, he was allowed back into Cameroon, the French having perhaps concluded that, because he was likely to be forced out of an increasingly chaotic and violent Germany before too long, it was better to have him in Douala than in metropolitan France.[40]

The fates of Dibobe and Manga Akwa are illustrative of a bigger problem in establishing any direct or lasting links between the German Revolution and hopes of Black liberation across the world. After 1920, networks of Africans in Germany and germanophone Black people in France, the United States and Africa were drawn into a diasporic politics that focused less on national and territorial questions, or issues of intermarriage and repatriation, and more on 'the global struggle against colonialism and white oppression'.[41] The growing importance of African American, Caribbean and French-Senegalese voices in these campaigns is indicative of this shift. Thus, while in 1919 the former Berlin transport worker Dibobe had emphasised his links, stretching back to the pre-1914 period, with the SPD, and his desire to take social democratic values back with him to Cameroon if the new Weimar authorities supported him and his German-born family,[42] the hope that the new Germany might act as a bridge between Europe and Africa hardly lasted beyond the end of that year. Indeed, in contrast to the links that the Trinidadian historian C. L. R. James makes between the actions of the impoverished Parisian masses in the period 1792–94 and the demands of the poor and enslaved Blacks in San Domingo/ Haiti for freedom from slavery, the Revolution of 1918–19 was a largely domestic German phenomenon that continued to uphold 'distinction[s] of colour'.[43] In other words, there was no anti-racist moment in 1918–19 that might compare with the 'horror' with which (in James's interpretation) 'the vast majority of [pro-Jacobin/

pro-republican] Frenchmen ... disapproved of slavery' after its initial abolition in the French colonies by decree of the National Convention in February 1794 and once again during a repeat wave of revolutionary upheaval in Paris in February–April 1848.[44]

Apart from the somewhat lone voice of the feminist-pacifist campaigner Lilli Jannasch – who published a pamphlet attacking the sexist and racist thrust behind the 1920–21 'Black Shame' crusade against the use of African troops among the French forces occupying the Rhineland – few white figures in Weimar Germany, and fewer still in the SPD, consciously made the link between anti-militarism and the fight against racial prejudice *in* Europe.[45] Instead, the racial abuse directed at non-white French soldiers soon developed into a more general campaign against Black Europeans and Black visitors to Europe, led by the national and international press. An appeal written by the Cameroonian Louis Brody (Bebe Mpessa) on behalf of the African Welfare Association and published in a major Berlin newspaper in May 1921 illustrates that the small number of Black residents in Germany from the former colonies were largely dependent on acts of self-help in the face of mounting hostility towards them:

> The Blacks who reside in Berlin and in the parts of Germany not occupied [by France or its allies] come from the former German colonies. They are not Asians or Blacks from the occupied territory. We therefore ask the Germans to respect these Blacks and not to continue through reports on the 'Black Shame' to agitate against them.[46]

Meanwhile, among the major political parties, only the KPD took an interest in anti-colonial nationalist movements *outside* Europe, and this largely within the strict confines prescribed by the Moscow-based Comintern (Third International), which also, in effect, steered Münzenberg's LAI. 'Hands off China', the worldwide campaign bolstered by Münzenberg at an international congress in Berlin in August 1925, was its main concern, indicating a prioritisation of the global struggle to 'unite the western with the eastern proletariat' through a strategic (and in fact short-lived) Communist alliance with the nationalist Kuomintang movement,[47] but saying much less about the possibilities of North–South solidarities. International socialist activist, British Labour MP and friend of the German left Ellen Wilkinson, invited by Münzenberg to the

LAI's opening congress in Brussels in February 1927 as one the key speakers, noted in her address to fellow delegates:

> The white workers have been content to see brown and yellow and black men butchered or enslaved in the name of 'hope and glory', and to procure markets for the goods the white man made. With terrible force, the result of their complaisance is coming home to them, in the severity of the competition of ill-paid labour of the East.[48]

And in its report on the February 1927 congress, the Reich Commissariat for Maintaining Public Order, a domestic surveillance body charged by the Weimar-era Reich Ministry of Interior with monitoring left-wing and subversive groups, noted that the KPD had organised a big demonstration in Berlin as the Chinese delegation passed through the German capital on its way to Brussels.[49]

This East–West bias, while it did not mean that the struggles of Black liberationists in Africa and the Americas were entirely ignored in favour of demands for the emancipation of Chinese, Indian and southeast Asian workers from colonial exploitation, was a notable characteristic of international anti-imperialist campaigns in the decades after the First World War. It continued at least until the era of wholesale decolonisation in Africa and the Caribbean in the 1960s, which of course took place in the very different international context of the Cold War, the Cuban Revolution and the Sino-Soviet split.[50]

Comparative perspectives on violence

Lack of support for Black liberation, then, was one of the global failures of the early 1920s that Germany – in spite of, and in some ways because of, the November Revolution – also contributed to. Another deficit was the continued presence of bloodshed and armed political conflict in many parts of Europe and the wider world, calling into question the notion that, with the defeat of the Central Powers, democracy had triumphed over 'militarism'. Stefan Berger, in a recent essay, gives a number of examples of this. Thus, in Italy during the 'two red years' of 1919–20,

> there were multiple attempts, some of them violent, to enforce land reforms, expropriations and communalisations, all taking place in temporarily ungoverned or quasi-ungoverned spaces. What appeared

to those hoping for greater social justice as years of utopian possibility was a cause of constant horror to opponents of socio-economic transformation. Their gruesome counterreactions ultimately led to the victory of Fascism in Italy [in October 1922].[51]

Why, then, did the war end but the violence fail to stop, and what light do the most recent studies shed on this? Mark Jones's 2016 monograph *Founding Weimar* was the latest in a long line of books to equate the years 1918–19 in Germany with harrowing tales of bloodshed at national level, albeit with the added twist that in his study the State's murderous suppression of leftist revolts such as the Spartacist Uprising, the 'March Battles' in Berlin and the Munich Councils Republic was accompanied by and achieved partly through widespread support in the press and among the public in general.[52] The death toll in 1919 may have reached around 5,000, including 1,200 left-wing rebels killed in Berlin in March, and over 1,000 in Munich and neighbouring areas in April–May.[53] The similarities with Fascist violence in Italy in the early 1920s, and with 1933 in Germany itself, are obvious, but Jones's findings also tally with some of the accounts that appeared in fictional representations written in the early Weimar period, long before the Nazis became significant players in German politics. For instance, at the beginning of his novella *Die Rebellion* (*Rebellion*), first published in 1924, the Polish-born, Berlin-based Austrian writer Joseph Roth had his lead character, the one-legged disabled war veteran, licensed street musician and fervent believer in the benevolence of the State, Andreas Pum, curse the 'disorder' that the November Revolution brings. But then, a short while later, after he had got over his anguish at the overthrow of the Kaiser and

> after he had learned from reading the newspapers ... that governments also took responsibility for affairs of state in republics, he calmed down. The rebels were shot at in the big cities. The pagan Spartacists gave no rest. They probably wanted to abolish the Government ... They were bad or foolish, they were shot, served them right. Ordinary people should not interfere in the affairs of the wise.[54]

Only after experiencing a run of bad luck, including being insulted on a tram by a businessman who calls him a 'fraudster', a 'malingerer' and a 'Bolshevik spy', and then losing his musician's licence after being arrested for appearing to threaten his defamer, is he transformed from a believer into a rebel against the injustices of the world. Roth's description of the scene on the tram at the time of the altercation is particularly telling:

> Unfortunately, there were petit-bourgeois citizens and women on the tram, people who had been rendered terrified, depressed, but no less bitter by the events of the revolution, who looked back with clenched teeth and tears of appreciation on a glorious past, and to whom the word Bolshevik meant nothing but robbery. It was as if a member of their family had been calling for help when they heard the cry: Bolshevik![55]

To add to this, a respectable gentleman 'of sublime cleanliness and radiant age' is heard to say aloud: 'It's got to be a Jew!'.[56]

Eliza Ablovatski, in her 2021 comparative study of the short-lived Councils Republics in Munich and Budapest in 1919, partly agrees that these traumatic political events were received by newspaper-reading contemporaries in an atmosphere shaped by 'rumor and terror', and by antisemitic and anti-leftist rage.[57] The association in the mainstream, as well as the right-wing and Christian-conservative print media of 'red terror', with Jewish interests or a 'Judeo-Bolshevik' conspiracy was indeed common.[58] Expectations of Communist-led violence, hostage-taking and mass shootings were in the air from the beginning, even though both regimes actually 'began without bloodshed in the chaos of national military defeat' and only turned murderous once the forces of counterrevolution and their right-wing paramilitary backers had decided on the use of unrestrained armed force to crush the rebels.[59]

On the other side of this debate, scholars such as Alexander Gallus, Robert Gerwarth and Christopher Dillon have made the case for a 'detoxified' view of the German Revolution, one that removes its automatic association with 'extremism' and 'terror', military defeat and national trauma, redemptive fantasises about violence, and supposed masculine obsession with sovereign (or sexual) power in general. Instead, they focus on what – compared to other countries in Europe that went through similar experiences in 1918– 19 – Germany actually managed to achieve in terms of stabilising democracy and dismantling 'inherited patterns of authority'.[60] In part, they are able to pick up a point already made by Richard Bessel in an essay published in 1988, namely that stories of the humiliation of returning soldiers by revolutionaries during the period of demobilisation in 1918–19 were largely invented by right-wing officers after the fact. In reality, civilian populations typically 'made great efforts to ensure … a festive welcome' to the rank-and-file troops who came home in November and December 1918.[61] Furthermore, the latter, at least initially, did not feel 'betrayed' by the Revolution. This is reinforced by Benjamin Ziemann, who notes that the largest veterans' association by a long way in the early Weimar years was the pro-Social Democrat Reichsbund der Kriegsbeschädigten, Kriegsteilnehmer und Kriegshinterbliebenen (Reich Association of War Disabled, War Participants and War Dependants), which was established in 1917 and counted 830,000 members at the height of its popularity in 1922.[62]

Sean Dobson, in his work on Leipzig, also emphasises the relative lack of violence in western Saxony in 1918–19, even though strikes and hostility towards established 'authority' and the military were the order of the day. True, the front pages of the city's middle-class press in early May 1919 were suspiciously full of 'identical content … claiming that the [workers' and soldiers' council under Curt Geyer] intended to take a number of Leipzig notables hostage' if Government troops invaded to forestall a planned general strike. Yet when the invasion actually came on 11 May, the workers adopted non-violent methods to resist it, in spite of huge provocations from the former Freikorps leader, now Reichswehr military commander, Georg Ludwig Rudolf Maercker, who ordered his troops to ransack trade union offices and carried out arbitrary arrests.[63] In fact, what the Leipzig workers had 'repeatedly expressed and acted on' since November 1918 was not a desire for physical confrontation with 'authority' but 'democratiz[ation of] the state apparatus and socializ[ation of] the economy'.[64] This is why they again took to the streets during the Kapp–Lüttwitz Putsch in March 1920.[65]

Some of these arguments questioning the connection between the Revolution and extreme political violence are also beginning to filter through into mainstream studies. The historian of photography Anton Holzer, in his visual history of the German Revolution, refers to 1917–23 as the 'years of violence', when 'no peace followed the war'.[66] However, he does concede that things were worse in other central European countries, notably Hungary and Poland. He also acknowledges that at least some of the revolutionaries in November

1918 were determined to establish the new political order on a peaceful basis. The workers' and soldiers' council of Berlin, for instance, published a statement on the front page of the second extra edition of *Vorwärts* on 9 November announcing that, despite revolution having broken out, 'There is no shooting!'. Underneath was a reassuring message that the handover of power was proceeding on a non-violent basis: 'The Alexander regiment and the fourth infantry brigade have just gone over to the people. The Social Democratic Reichstag deputy [Otto] Wels and others have spoken to the troops. Officers have joined the soldiers' (Figure 8.2).[67] The absence of shooting, wrote the world-famous German scientist Albert Einstein to a Swedish colleague on 14 November 1918, was 'the most surprising experience among all the surprises' that had taken place over the past few days in the German capital.[68] And in their pamphlet addressed to returning prisoners of war and civilian internees in 1919, Social Democrat activists in the northern port city of Altona, adjacent to Hamburg, proudly announced: 'The chief characteristic of the November Revolution is its extremely bloodless course.'[69]

In fact, this sensibility against violence, even if it faltered, in late December 1918 and again, very badly, in the early weeks and months of 1919, was a constant presence throughout the Revolution and made itself felt on a number of occasions. The decision by the workers' and soldiers' council of Greater Berlin to call off the strike planned for 5 June 1919, following the execution of revolutionary leader Eugen Leviné in Munich, would be a case in point, as it emerged from a desire to avoid clashes with police and Government troops.[70] Holzer also includes photographs in his collection of the huge rallies against militaristic violence that took place in Berlin in July 1922 and July 1924 under the slogan 'Nie wieder Krieg!' ('No more war!').[71] Apocryphal stories suggesting that Berliners, even in 1918–19, refused to step on the grass in public parks if signs were present telling them that this was forbidden,[72] could be interpreted in the same light: as the outward expression not of a pathological respect for authority, but of the desire for a peaceful transition to a new world. Finally, the rejection of militarism can also be seen in what Andrew Donson has described as the real and apparent reluctance to work (*Arbeitsunlust*) among older men released from the regimentation of the wartime economy by the November Revolution. For all the Government and media panic that ensued

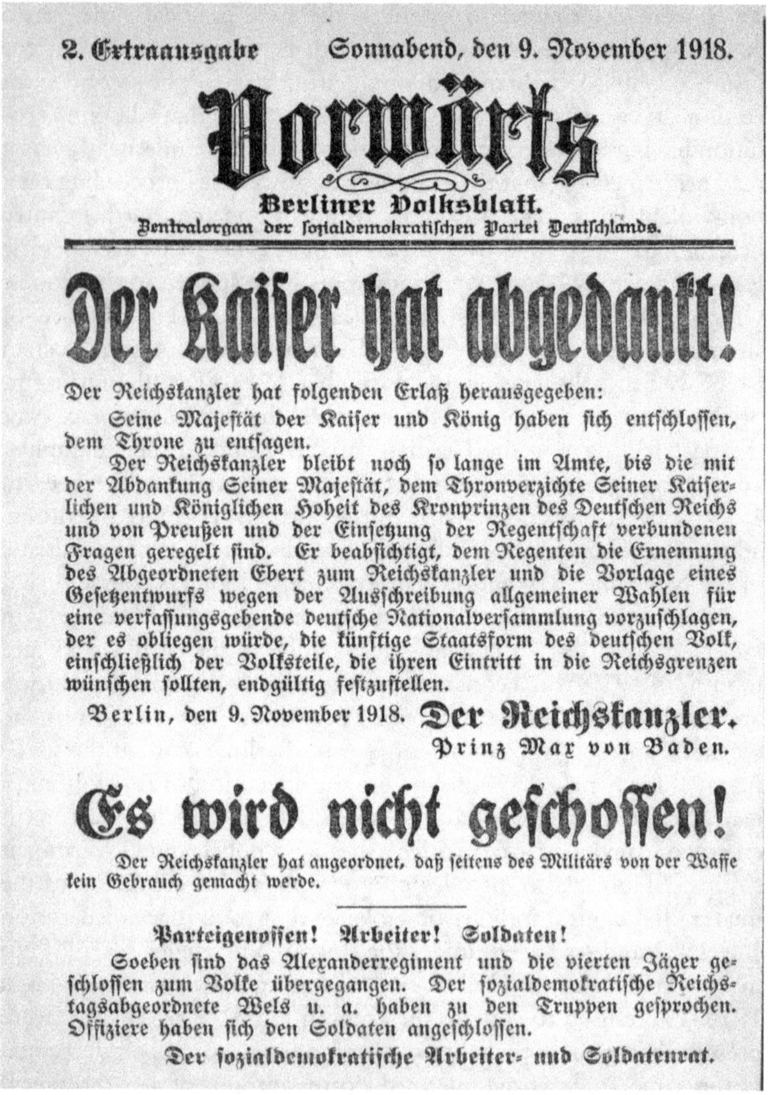

2. Extraausgabe Sonnabend, den 9. November 1918.

Vorwärts

Berliner Volksblatt.

Zentralorgan der sozialdemokratischen Partei Deutschlands.

Der Kaiser hat abgedankt!

Der Reichskanzler hat folgenden Erlaß herausgegeben:

Seine Majestät der Kaiser und König haben sich entschlossen, dem Throne zu entsagen.

Der Reichskanzler bleibt noch so lange im Amte, bis die mit der Abdankung Seiner Majestät, dem Thronverzichte Seiner Kaiserlichen und Königlichen Hoheit des Kronprinzen des Deutschen Reichs und von Preußen und der Einsetzung der Regentschaft verbundenen Fragen geregelt sind. Er beabsichtigt, dem Regenten die Ernennung des Abgeordneten Ebert zum Reichskanzler und die Vorlage eines Gesetzentwurfs wegen der Ausschreibung allgemeiner Wahlen für eine verfassungsgebende deutsche Nationalversammlung vorzuschlagen, der es obliegen würde, die künftige Staatsform des deutschen Volk, einschließlich der Volksteile, die ihren Eintritt in die Reichsgrenzen wünschen sollten, endgültig festzustellen.

Berlin, den 9. November 1918. **Der Reichskanzler.**
Prinz Max von Baden.

Es wird nicht geschossen!

Der Reichskanzler hat angeordnet, daß seitens des Militärs von der Waffe kein Gebrauch gemacht werde.

Parteigenossen! Arbeiter! Soldaten!

Soeben sind das Alexanderregiment und die vierten Jäger geschlossen zum Volke übergegangen. Der sozialdemokratische Reichstagsabgeordnete Wels u. a. haben zu den Truppen gesprochen. Offiziere haben sich den Soldaten angeschlossen.

Der sozialdemokratische Arbeiter- und Soldatenrat.

Figure 8.2 'Der Kaiser hat abgedankt! Es wird nicht geschossen!' ['The Kaiser has abdicated! There is no shooting!'], front page of the second extra edition of the Social Democratic newspaper *Vorwärts*, 9 November 1918. Archiv der sozialen Demokratie der Friedrich-Ebert-Stiftung, Bonn.

about collapsing rates of productivity, '[l]etting workers idle [actually] tamed the political revolution'.[73]

Robert Gerwarth, taking the years 1917–23 as a whole, goes even further in comparing 'the relative absence of violence' in Germany with the less favourable situation in other parts of postwar Europe.[74] Thus, the 'national revolutions within the Dual Monarchy [i.e. Austria-Hungary] soon morphed into violent upheavals in the form of both inter-state and civil wars, notably in the eastern borderlands ... [where] Polish troops conquered Lemberg' from the West Ukrainian People's Republic.[75] Many more were killed in other postwar international and domestic conflicts, including the Finnish (1918) and Russian Civil Wars (1917–20), the Anglo-Irish War (1919–21), the Irish Civil War (1922–23), the Greek–Turkish War of 1919–22, and the Bulgarian Agrarian Uprising of September 1923. The interwar South Slav State, which eventually took the name Yugoslavia, experienced 'repeated explosions of inter-ethnic violence', as did Slovenes and Croats living on the 'wrong' side of the new Yugoslav border with Italy.[76] In what had once been Russian Armenia, and was later to become Soviet Armenia, the nascent forces of the temporarily independent Democratic Republic of Armenia waged a campaign of vengeance in early 1918 during which 'close to 10,000 Muslim Turks are estimated to have been butchered'.[77] This was to avenge the deaths of up to 1.5 million Armenians during the Turkish genocide of 1915–16.

If paramilitary and state-backed political, territorial and communal violence was widespread across Europe in the years after the First World War,[78] and if the numbers killed in Germany during the November Revolution and the 1919 disturbances were relatively low compared to other countries, where does this leave debates about the murders of Liebknecht and Luxemburg after the Spartacist Uprising, Reichswehr Minister Noske's 'execution orders' in March and April–May 1919, and the at best semi-legal military courts that passed summary death sentences against supposed Communist 'ringleaders' in May–June 1919 in Munich? Gerwarth has been criticised for playing down these phenomena, and exaggerating the extent of political stabilisation and liberalisation achieved by the Weimar Republic by 1923.[79] Certainly it would be wrong to divorce them from the more general abuse of emergency powers to crush the far left, including the proactive involvement of other Social Democrat ministers (for example Johannes Hoffmann as Minister-President in Bavaria in 1919–20, and Wolfgang Heine and Carl Severing as Ministers of Interior in Prussia, the former from March 1919 and the latter from March 1920).[80] Yet the State-sanctioned extra-judicial killings and summary forms of justice that took place in Germany during this time are also probably best seen as being at the outer extremes of a wide spectrum of opportunities for State-political action in the early Weimar Republic, and not as a pointer towards any grand failure of democratisation in the aftermath of the 1918–19 Revolution.

The German Revolution and global sexual emancipation

For some female and male activists in 1918–19, the German Revolution raised issues not only about citizenship and suffrage in the political and economic spheres, and not only about civil rights in the negative sense of freedom from fear of violence, arbitrary arrest and censorship. It had also posed questions about the validity of the entire gender order, including the right of older heterosexual men to set the terms of sexual mores. The abolition of censorship by revolutionary decree in November 1918 opened up new spaces for imagining a world without traditional patriarchal structures and without formal prohibitions on the public discussion of alternative lifestyles and sexualities.[81] One early indication of this came in May 1919 with the release in Berlin of the world's first overtly gay film, *Different from the Rest* (to be discussed at the end of the chapter). This was followed in August 1919 by the launch of the first gay newspaper for public sale at the city's newsstands, *Die Freundschaft (Friendship)*.[82] Another sign would be the public protest organised by the USPD in Frankfurt am Main in December 1920 in condemnation of a speech made by Theodor Lewald, State Secretary in the Reich Ministry of Interior, defending the policy of dismissing unmarried mothers from civil service positions. The protestors pointed to several articles in the Weimar Constitution of August 1919 that rendered such outdated practices unlawful, in particular Article 128, which explicitly removed all 'special regulations' imposed on female, but not male, State employees. However, over and above this, they argued that the 1918–19 Revolution had made prejudice against women on the basis of marital status or choice of lifestyle socially unacceptable. Men were not discriminated against in the workplace for fathering children out of wedlock; neither should women.[83]

The USPD protest, which was led by the Reichstag deputy Toni Sender, is a good example of two arguments put forward by Laurie Marhoefer in her important 2015 intervention into debates on advances and reverses for sexual freedoms in the Weimar period. First, in assessing the relative stability and success of democratisation in Germany in the aftermath of the Revolution, 'there is a need to look at specific cases and issues'.[84] The question of LGBTQ+ rights would be another fitting area to consider. Second, even though discrimination against unmarried mothers in the civil service continued after December 1920, the Frankfurt protest would be an example of the Revolution having made it possible for progressive thinkers to 'act to change culture, society and politics' in new, open-ended and democracy-enhancing ways.[85] This had consequences internationally as well as nationally.

The precedent discussed by Marhoefer is the opening in July 1919 of the Berlin Institut für Sexualwissenschaft (Institute for Sexual Research), run by the physician and gay rights activist Magnus Hirschfeld, as successor to the Wissenschaftlich-humanitäres Komitee (Scientific-Humanitarian Committee) that he had set up under less favourable circumstances in the 1890s. Not only did this institute gain world renown; it also established most of the 'central principles' and much of the terminology and political strategy used in the late twentieth century to secure the aims of the gay liberation movement under conditions of mass democracy.[86] It was a triumph over what Marhoefer, quoting *Vorwärts* in 1919, calls the 'dictatorship of tradition' in the spheres of moral policing and sexuality.[87] Hirschfeld had also won the support of the Reich Ministry of Interior for the establishment of his institute, and saw this as a sign that the abolition of paragraph 175 of the Reich Penal Code, prohibiting sexual acts between men, was now possible.[88]

On the other hand, strategically speaking this success had come through separating the movement for homosexual emancipation from more radical campaigns to remove completely the dominance of patriarchal, heteronormative conservatism over State social policies. Like the sociologist Robert Michels, a pioneer of scientific research into gender politics as well as political parties, Hirschfeld's hopes for the Revolution were focused on 'the reform of sexuality, not [the] abolition [of marriage and the family] as bourgeois institutions'.[89] Thus, he by and large avoided public discussion of divorce, single parenthood, prostitution and 'free love'. It was other, more radical voices to the left of the SPD that adopted these causes. 'Never before has so much been said and written about "marriage" and "free love" as in our day', wrote Ella Lachmann in the USPD women's journal *Die Kämpferin* in October 1920.[90] And her party colleague Margarete Behrendt noted in the same journal in August 1920:

> Among our party comrades, there should not be a single case in which the 'fallen' daughters [of proletarian mothers] are judged in a cruel or derogatory manner ... After all, love and marriage are every individual's own affair. Each of us must work to have an enlightening and trailblazing influence on our closest friendship circles. Remember: every law, every moral concept is created by humans and is subject to development and transformation as times themselves change.[91]

In 1918–19, some of the most radical proponents of universal sexual freedom and abolition of marriage in Germany were also to be found in the ranks of the KPD. However, by the time of its merger with the left wing of the USPD in late 1920 the official line – which was also the Comintern line – was that sex had to be freed from economic exploitation but not from the constraints of a new socialist morality, which was heteronormative and male-defined. Above all, as the women's newspaper *Die Kommunistin* announced in January 1921, it was vital to ensure the 'protection of the health of the proletarian masses in their entirety from venereal diseases', and this could not be achieved at the same time as giving licence to 'petit-bourgeois' forms of promiscuity.[92] Earlier, in August 1920, the Reich Commissariat for Maintaining Public Order, the above-mentioned domestic surveillance body that answered to the Reich Ministry of Interior, noted in its second report that the KPD's central secretariat had recently designated 'sex-specific demands or reforms focused on individual life-styles' as a distraction from the party's main purpose, namely 'to mobilise all forces for the final assault against capitalism'.[93]

The near fatal attack on Hirschfeld by a gang of right-wing extremists in Munich in October 1920 was a further indication that attitudes towards lesbian, gay, bisexual and transgender subcultures, and towards sexual health and wellbeing in general, did not change overnight following the Revolution.⁹⁴ Paragraph 175 was not reformed in (West) Germany until 1969, even though its abolition was recommended by a fifteen-to-thirteen majority on a parliamentary committee in 1929, with representatives of the KPD, SPD and DDP all voting in favour.⁹⁵ After 1934, the new Nazi rulers launched their own murderous campaigns against male homosexuals in Germany, resulting in between 5,000 and 15,000 deaths and much suffering and abuse, mainly carried out in concentration camps.⁹⁶ Even so, recent studies have highlighted a widespread sense of optimism within the gay scene in Germany, and in particular in Berlin, during 1918–19, giving hope to LGBTQ+ communities across the world. This should not be forgotten in histories of that time, even if subsequent events cast a much darker shadow over twentieth-century Germany's treatment of its sexual minorities.⁹⁷

A necessary revolution? Reprise of an old debate

While, during the centenary in 2018–19, some scholars hailed the November Revolution as the 'beginning of Germany's present democracy', two years later, in 2020–21, a new (or rather a fresh variant of an old) controversy arose over whether the Revolution had been necessary at all, and whether it had in fact been more of a hindrance to Germany's path towards democratisation. However, whereas the 1950s discussions had focused on the supposed parlamentarisation of the Kaiserreich in October 1918, just weeks before the Revolution (see Chapter 3), the reprise of this debate concerned the bigger question of how much progress Bismarck's unified Germany had been able to make towards democratisation from its very inception in 1871. In other words, this was a debate about the Kaiserreich itself, and to some extent about Germany's political culture and transnational entanglements throughout the 'long nineteenth century' (*c.* 1780–1914). Nonetheless, it still had a bearing on how the Revolution of 1918–19 and its broader place in Germany's domestic and transnational history were being reinterpreted.

The debate centred on Hedwig Richter's 2020 book *Demokratie: Eine deutsche Affäre* (*Democracy: A German Affair*), and the definitions of both 'democracy' and 'revolution' that she applies in this study. For her, democracy is tied up not just with abstract principles of liberty, equality and fraternity, but with tangible rights to bodily autonomy, both in the negative sense of freedom from physical/sexual violation and punishments, and in the positive sense of the freedom of the individual to determine what happens to their own body. Since the late eighteenth century, reformers across the (western) world have made great progress towards the unfolding of democracy, both in a political-legislative and in a scientific-medical sense. The more empathic of them also understood that 'the emancipation of the citizen begins with respect for his body'.[98] America in the Revolutionary Era was in some ways pioneering in this respect, with Pennsylvania enacting the world's first law terminating slavery in 1777.[99] But slavery was retained in other states until the 1860s and, following the Civil War and Reconstruction periods, the South was allowed to impose racial segregation and the so-called Jim Crow laws, a situation that, in some states, lasted from the 1870s until 1965.[100] Nineteenth-century Germany also exhibited many deficits when it came to bodily autonomy, and in 1904–8 was responsible for what is now acknowledged to be the first genocide committed in the twentieth century, against the Herero and Nama populations in colonial Namibia. And yet German scientists, jurists, educationalists, traders and political thinkers – whether within Germany or as migrants and refugees in other parts of the world – made an enormous contribution to the process of democratisation around the world.[101] In this sense, according to Richter, the democratic outlook appeared quite positive to the average German in 1900:

> The predominant feeling was not that they were living in a backward monarchy. [For citizens of that time] what mattered was not the question that was so often asked for the 19th century after 1945: 'Democracy – yes or no?' Rather ... [what mattered] was questions of justice and human things ... [such as] whether they had a good livelihood and a good life, what the educational opportunities were.[102]

This 'positive' reading of nineteenth-century German history is where most of the criticisms of Richter have been centred. Yet two further aspects of her argument are especially relevant to interpretations of the 1918–19 Revolution. First is her assertion that revolutions from below, as 'violent' and 'bloody' events, are necessarily an 'exception' rather than the norm on the path to democratisation – indeed, something of an interruption.[103] In particular, they are 'primarily the business of young men' and follow the largely non-empathic logic of that stratum of society.[104] As such they stand apart from what Richter argued could be the new national and international narrative of how Germany became a democracy. In this account, in the German-speaking parts of Europe, as elsewhere in the West, democracy 'began ... as a State affair, as a bureaucratic elite and reform project' around the year 1800.[105] Furthermore, as an evolutionary process, it was much more respectful of bodily autonomy than 'bloody revolutions', especially when it came to protection of women of all social classes against violence.

For Richter, the years 1871–1914 were also an important period of democratic advance. Among the many examples she gives are Bismarck's social reforms in the 1880s introducing State-backed pensions and workers' accident and sickness insurance, and further reforms introduced in the decade after 1900, including the entry of (small numbers of) women into higher education.[106] In particular,

> Berlin was [a] stronghold of women's liberation, there were excellent girls' schools there, large educational initiatives such as the renowned *Letteverein* and high school courses for women. In line with international trends, conservative women throughout Germany, such as Anna von Gierke, built female empires around social work in which they controlled and directed and changed the world – these are also sources of women's emancipation and democracy.[107]

If the Weimar period, too, was a great age of 'democratisation' and progressive legislation, then the implication from Richter's work is that this was more a continuation of the patient, bureaucratic spirit of reform developed across the years 1780–1914, which had been bloodily interrupted but fortunately not completely eradicated by war and revolution between 1914 and 1919.

Richter's critics have pointed to many flaws in her depiction of the Kaiserreich as a time when reformers at State level or with State connections and access to State funding were committed to making democracy a 'German affair'. Eckart Conze, for instance, underlines the consistent refusal of the 'bourgeois' parties to work with the SPD, even after the latter had become the largest party, with one-third of the seats in the Reichstag in 1912.[108] Heinrich August Winkler argues that, in her rush to draw attention to the 'progressive sides of the Kaiserreich', Richter has downplayed its overall 'authoritarian, nationalist and militarist lineage'. Above all, it was a system in which the Kaiser enjoyed the absolute right of personal command (*Kommandogewalt*) in matters of State appointments and military security, and thereby the power to send male bodies to war and condemn women, children and the elderly to the wasting effects of economic warfare on their bodies. To command his armies into action at home or abroad he did not even need the countersignatures of Government ministers, let alone the prior approval of the Reichstag.[109] In short, the German people were no closer to achieving sovereignty in public affairs or autonomy over their own bodies in 1914 than they had been in 1871.

Yet this debate also has important international and transnational dimensions. In other words, it is not just a matter of the nature of the Kaiserreich as an 'authoritarian national and imperial state', as Conze calls it, although it certainly was that, in spite of its modest progress on issues such as women's education.[110] Rather, it is also a question of the interdependent, nineteenth-century origins of all European revolutions in the early twentieth century – 1905 and 1917 in Russia, the 'tragic week' (*Setmana Tràgica*) in July 1909 in Barcelona, the general strike in August 1917 across Spain, 1918–19 in Germany and central Europe, 1919–20 in Italy, and even 1923 in Bulgaria. According to Stefan Berger, all of these revolutions, in spite of their many differences, had in common the goals of democratisation, national self-determination and social justice, and shared a set of narratives around what these goals entailed.[111] In the words of another writer, Amerigo Caruso, they were part of a 'democratic protest culture', emerging in the period 1904–14 in opposition to what 'from the [transnational] conservative viewpoint' was a 'necessary containment of the workers' movement' and developing during the war into something more sustained, more determined and (even) more transnational.[112]

European and global context 247

The notion of bodily and sexual autonomy – one of the key criteria used by Richter to identify democracy as a specifically German as well as global project of the nineteenth and twentieth centuries – is of no less importance in marking out 1918–19 as the culmination of and springboard for the continuation of democratic protest cultures. The Revolution coincided with the showing of the first openly gay film anywhere in the world, *Anders als die Andern* (*Different from the Rest*), put together by the Austrian-Jewish director Richard Oswald and cleared for release in Germany. Despite subsequent attempts to have it banned by homophobic groups – attempts that had succeeded by October 1920 – it enjoyed its first public screening at the Apollo Theatre on Berlin's Friedrichstraße on 28 May 1919 (see Figure 8.3).[113] As it called directly for the abolition of paragraph 175, and featured a walk-on part by Magnus Hirschfeld as a 'sympathetic' doctor, it fired the imaginations of both sexual reformers and their conservative critics.[114] The case for legal change was made in the context of respect for difference and diversity, thus opening up new ways of seeing – by dint of being 'surrounded by' – claims to equality of all human beings.[115]

The Munich-based psychiatrist Emil Kraepelin, already mentioned in Chapter 1, and two of his colleagues, wrote to various State censorship boards – set up after August 1919, when Article 118 of the Weimar Constitution permitted the appointment of such bodies to protect youth from 'smut' and 'trash' and to shield the public as a whole from the supposed dangers of obscene motion-picture productions (*Lichtspiele*) – to urge the film's withdrawal.[116] The alleged seducing of young men towards sexual perversion, they argued, had parallels with the seduction of the German people as a whole by revolutionary propaganda. Both had their roots in the 'sickness of our state of mind' ('die Krankhaftigkeit unseres Seelenzustandes') that had been exposed in the years 1918–19.[117] But it was precisely this revolutionary spirit, this new way of seeing, that fired progressive political imaginaries and laid the historical foundations – even if only nascently and inchoately – for some of the most important emancipatory movements of the 1970s and beyond. In this example – one of many that inform global visions of democracy and celebrations of cultural/sexual diversity in the late twentieth and early twenty-first century – November 1918 remains a *necessary* revolution.

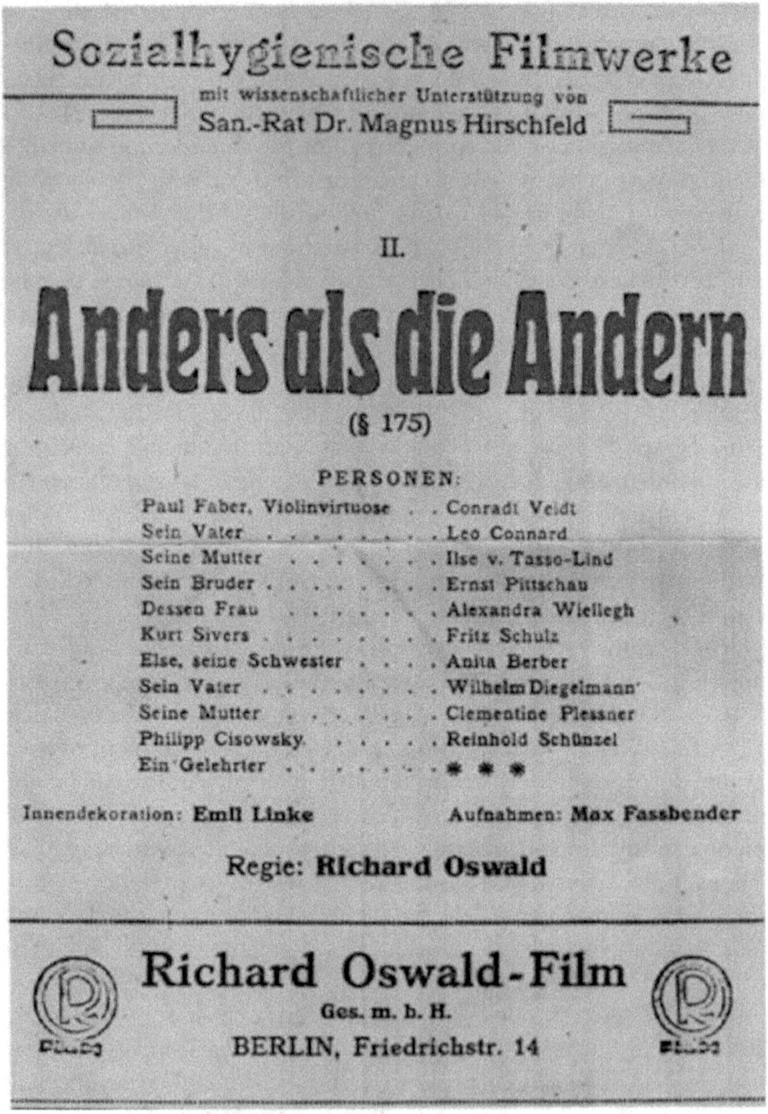

Figure 8.3 Poster for the film Anders als die Andern (*Different from the Rest*), the world's first openly gay film, directed by Richard Oswald, which premiered at the Apollo Theater on Berlin's Friedrichstraße, 28, May 1919. Alamy.

Notes

1 See Wolfgang Niess's popular centenary book *Die Revolution von 1918/19: Der wahre Beginn unserer Demokratie* (Berlin, 2018).
2 Two good examples, among many, are Olaf Matthes and Ortwin Pelc (eds), *Menschen in der Revolution: Hamburger Porträts 1918/19* (Hamburg, 2018); and Kinzler and Tillmann, *Die Stunde der Matrosen*.
3 Paul Betts, '1989 at Thirty: A Recast Legacy', *Past and Present*, 244 (2019), 271–305 (272).
4 *Ibid.*, 273. Compare also the optimism expressed in Winkler's two-volume work *Germany: The Long Road West*, with the palpable sense of unease apparent in his later study of the post-2015 era, Heinrich August Winkler, *Zerbricht der Westen? Über die gegenwärtige Krise in Europa und Amerika* (Munich, 2017).
5 Betts, '1989 at Thirty', 281–3.
6 Franka Maubach, 'Weimar (nicht) vom Ende her denken: Ein skeptischer Ausblick auf das Gründungsjubiläum 2019', *Aus Politik und Zeitgeschichte*, 68 (2018), 4–9 (4).
7 Compared to Niess this is the more sober, but still largely affirmative, interpretation offered by Gerwarth, *November 1918*.
8 See Tim B. Müller, 'Die transatlantische Diskussion um die globale und soziale Demokratie nach dem Ersten Weltkrieg', in Thomas Stamm-Kuhlmann (ed.), *November 1918: Revolution an der Ostsee und im Reich* (Cologne and Weimar, 2020), 35–65.
9 TNA, FO 425/542, Addison to Alexander Cadogan, 10 October 1923.
10 Adrian Zimmermann, 'Die Niederlande und die Schweiz im November 1918', *Schweizerische Zeitschrift für Geschichte*, 63.3 (2013), 453–78 (453).
11 Stefan Berger, 'Die deutsche Revolution 1918/19 in ihren europäischen Kontexten', in Frank Bischoff, Guido Hitze and Wilfried Reininghaus (eds), *Aufbruch in die Demokratie: Die Revolution 1918/19 im Rheinland und in Westfalen. Beiträge der Tagung am 8. und 9. November 2018 in Düsseldorf* (Münster, 2019), 17–29.
12 See, for instance, Douglas Newton, *British Policy and the Weimar Republic, 1918–1919* (Oxford, 1997).
13 Bessel, *Germany after the First World War*, 218.
14 Cox, *Hunger in War and Peace*, 207–11.
15 *Ibid.*, 207, 214–21.
16 Margaret Macmillan, *Paris 1919: Six Months that Changed the World* (New York, 2003), 480.
17 *Ibid.*, 94; McElligott, *The German Urban Experience*, 122.

18 Conan Fischer, *The Ruhr Crisis, 1923–1924* (Oxford, 2003).
19 Macmillan, *Paris 1919*, 488–92; Leonhard, *Der überforderte Frieden*, 1179–82.
20 Sebastian Conrad, *Globalisation and the Nation in Imperial Germany*, trans. Sorcha O'Hagan (Cambridge, 2010; German original, 2006), 393.
21 Ilya Dementev, 'From October to November: The Reception(s) of 1917–1918 by Russian Thinkers', in Stamm-Kuhlmann, *November 1918*, 67–86 (67).
22 Erez Manela, *The Wilsonian Moment: Self-Determination and the International Origins of Anticolonial Nationalism* (Oxford, 2007).
23 Leonard V. Smith, *Sovereignty at the Paris Peace Conference of 1919* (Oxford, 2018), esp. 47–9, 165–8, 182–8.
24 Leonhard, *Der überforderte Frieden*, 1178.
25 Robbie Aitken and Eve Rosenhaft, *Black Germany: The Making and Unmaking of a Diaspora Community, 1884–1960* (Cambridge, 2013), 197–8.
26 Andreas Eckert, 'The First Postcolonial Nation in Europe? The End of the German Empire', in Martin Thomas and Andrew Thompson (eds), *The Oxford Handbook of the Ends of Empire* (Oxford, 2018), 102–22 (116; citing Stuart Hall).
27 Brigitte Studer, *Reisende der Weltrevolution: Eine Globalgeschichte der Kommunistischen Internationale* (Berlin, 2020), 65–6, 119.
28 Prithwindra Mukherjee, *The Intellectual Roots of India's Freedom Struggle (1893–1918)* (London, 2018), 209–15, 308.
29 Sukhbir Choudhary, *Growth of Nationalism in India (1919–1929)* (New Delhi and London, 1973), 546. See also John Green, *Willi Münzenberg: Fighter against Fascism and Stalinism* (London, 2019), 189; and Studer, *Reisende*, 204.
30 Aitken and Rosenhaft, *Black Germany*, 211; Studer, *Reisende*, 292–3.
31 See James A. Miller, Susan D. Pennybacker and Eve Rosenhaft, 'Mother Ada Wright and the International Campaign to Free the Scottsboro Boys, 1931–1934', *American Historical Review*, 106.2 (2001), 387–430 (403).
32 *Ibid.*, 417.
33 Green, *Willi Münzenberg*, 187–95.
34 *Ibid.*, 188. Studer, *Reisende*, 239, 245, notes that around 500 Indian nationalists/revolutionaries and an equivalent number of Chinese, mostly students, lived in Berlin in the late 1920s. This went hand in hand with smaller numbers of Koreans, Japanese, Cameroonians, Egyptians and Persians.

35 Robbie Aitken, 'Surviving in the Metropole: The Struggle for Work and Belonging amongst African Colonial Migrants in Weimar Germany', *Immigrants and Minorities*, 28.2–3 (2010), 203–23 (205).
36 Aitken and Rosenhaft, *Black Germany*, 199–200.
37 *Ibid.*, 201.
38 Aitken, 'Surviving', 203 and *passim*; Studer, *Reisende*, 246.
39 Aitken and Rosenhaft, *Black Germany*, 107–8.
40 *Ibid.*, 226. See also Aitken, 'Surviving', 207, 217.
41 Aitken and Rosenhaft, *Black Germany*, 207.
42 *Ibid.*, 201–2.
43 C. L. R. James, *The Black Jacobins: Toussaint L'Ouverture and the San Domingo Revolution*, new edn (London, 1963 [1938]), 97–117 and esp. 98–9.
44 *Ibid.*, 300.
45 Lilli Jannasch, *Schwarze Schmach und schwarz-weiss-rote Schande* (Berlin, 1921). See also Erika Kuhlman, 'The Rhineland Horror Campaign and the Aftermath of War', in Ingrid Sharp and Matthew Stibbe (eds), *Aftermaths of War: Women's Movements and Female Activists, 1918–1923* (Leiden, 2011), 89–109 (104–6).
46 Louis Brody, 'Die deutschen Neger und die "schwarze Schmach"', *B.Z. am Mittag*, 24 May 1921, trans. Robbie Aitken, at https://blackcentraleurope.com/sources/1914–1945/louis-brody-on-black-germans-and-the-black-shame-1921/ (accessed 16 May 2022).
47 Green, *Willi Münzenberg*, 189; Studer, *Reisende*, 254–62.
48 Matt Perry, *'Red Ellen' Wilkinson: Her Ideas, Movements and World* (Manchester, 2014), 161. On the LAI's opening conference, and Wilkinson's presence, see also Studer, *Reisende*, 265–71.
49 *Reichskommissar für Überwachung der öffentlichen Ordnung und Nachrichtensammelstelle im Reichsministerium des Innern: Lageberichte 1920–1929 und Meldungen 1929–1933*, 121st situation report, 28 March 1927. Collected on behalf of the Bundesarchiv and available as a microfiche edition at the German Historical Institute London.
50 On the growing links between the West German labour movement and countries in the 'Global South' from the early 1960s onwards see Quinn Slobodian, 'West German Labour Internationalism and the Cold War', in Tobias Hochscherf, Christoph Laucht and Andrew Plowman (eds), *Divided but Not Disconnected: German Experiences of the Cold War* (New York and Oxford, 2010), 77–89. Also, more broadly, Gray, *Germany's Cold War*.
51 Berger, 'Die deutsche Revolution', 28.
52 Jones, *Founding Weimar*.
53 *Ibid.*, 5.

54 Joseph Roth, *Die Rebellion: Ein Roman*, new edn (Cologne, 1997 [1924]), 13.
55 *Ibid.*, 56.
56 *Ibid.*, 56–7.
57 Ablovatski, *Revolution and Political Violence*, esp. 79–80.
58 *Ibid.*, 193–203, 210–26.
59 *Ibid.*, 44.
60 Dillon, 'The German Revolution', 27. See also Gallus, review of Gerwarth's *November 1918*, 146–7.
61 Richard Bessel, 'The Great War in German Memory: The Soldiers of the First World War, Demobilization, and Weimar Political Culture', *German History*, 6.1 (1988), 20–34 (21).
62 Ziemann, *Contested Commemorations*, 15, 35–6.
63 Dobson, *Authority and Upheaval*, 261–3.
64 *Ibid.*, 193, 291.
65 *Ibid.*, 293.
66 Holzer, *Krieg nach dem Krieg*, 8.
67 Front cover of *Vorwärts*, 2. Extraausgabe, 9 November 1918, reproduced in Holzer, *Krieg nach dem Krieg*, 127.
68 Cited in Gerwarth, *November 1918*, 12.
69 *Was ist in Deutschland geschehen? Eine Übersicht über die Revolutions-Ereignisse*, undated pamphlet [1919], 6. Copy in Staatsarchiv Hamburg, 424–24/99: Wohlfahrtsamt Altona.
70 Ablovatski, *Revolution and Political Violence*, 227.
71 Holzer, *Krieg nach dem Krieg*, 146–7.
72 On these stories, which are sometimes attributed to Lenin, see Richie, *Faust's Metropolis*, xxxviii.
73 Andrew Donson, '*Arbeitsunlust*: No Desire to Work in the November Revolution', in Dillon and Wünschmann, *Living the German Revolution*.
74 Gerwarth, *November 1918*, 12.
75 Gerwarth, *The Vanquished*, 190–1.
76 *Ibid.*, 198.
77 Gerwarth, *November 1918*, 203.
78 See also Gerwarth and Horne, *War in Peace*.
79 See Gallus, review of Gerwarth's *November 1918*, 147.
80 Keil and Stibbe, 'Ein Laboratorium', 556–60.
81 Gerwarth, *November 1918*, 7–8, 151–2; Clayton J. Whisnant, *Queer Identities and Politics in Germany: A History, 1880–1945* (New York, 2016), 91.
82 Robert Beachy, *Gay Berlin: Birthplace of a Modern Identity* (New York, 2014), 164.

83 'Uneheliche Mütter', *Die Kämpferin*, 15 January 1921. For Article 128 of the Weimar Constitution see Huber, *Dokumente zur deutschen Verfassungsgeschichte*, Vol. III, 147.
84 Laurie Marhoefer, *Sex and the Weimar Republic: German Homosexual Emancipation and the Rise of the Nazis* (Toronto, 2015), 12.
85 *Ibid.*
86 *Ibid.*, 13.
87 *Ibid.*, 26–31.
88 Whisnant, *Queer Identities*, 167.
89 See Jens Hacke, 'Ein Land aus Stuck: Robert Michels, Freund Max Webers, früher Parteienforscher und scharfer Kritiker des Wilhelminismus, ist jetzt auch als Frauen- und Genderforscher neu zu entdecken', *Die Zeit*, 2 September 2021, 53.
90 Ella Lachmann, 'Ehe und freie Liebe', *Die Kämpferin*, 14 October 1920.
91 Margarete Behrendt, 'Mutterschaft und Schande', *Die Kämpferin*, 19 August 1920.
92 'Zur Frage der Prostitution', *Die Kommunistin*, 22 January 1921, 3–4.
93 *Reichskommissar für Überwachung*, 2nd situation report, August 1920.
94 Brenner, *Der lange Schatten*, 182–3.
95 Gerwarth, *November 1918*, 151; Marhoefer, *Sex and the Weimar Republic*, 128.
96 Robert Plant, *The Pink Triangle: The Nazi War against Homosexuals* (New York, 1986), 154.
97 Albeit on a non-murderous level, the early West German state also persecuted gay men under paragraph 175 (while refusing to recognise those who had survived Nazi persecution as victims of State violence deserving of compensation). See Clayton J. Whisnant, *Male Homosexuality in West Germany: Between Persecution and Freedom, 1945–69* (Basingstoke, 2012).
98 Richter, *Demokratie*, 105.
99 *Ibid.*, 36.
100 *Ibid.*, 107.
101 *Ibid.*, esp. 144–60, 163–4.
102 *Ibid.*, 142.
103 *Ibid.*, 34.
104 Hedwig Richter, 'Demokratiegeschichte ohne Frauen? Ein Problemaufriss', *Aus Politik und Zeitgeschichte*, 68.42 (2018), 3–9 (4).
105 Richter, *Demokratie*, 34.
106 *Ibid.*, 140–1, 158.

107 *Ibid.*, 159.
108 Eckart Conze, *Schatten des Kaiserreichs: Die Reichsgründung von 1871 und ihr schwieriges Erbe* (Munich, 2020), 127–8.
109 Heinrich August Winkler, 'War Hitler doch ein Betriebsunfall?', *Die Zeit*, 4 February 2021, 15.
110 Conze, *Schatten des Kaiserreichs*, 103–96.
111 Berger, 'Die deutsche Revolution', 18.
112 Caruso, *'Blut und Eisen'*, 39, 240.
113 Whisnant, *Queer Identities*, 175.
114 Beachy, *Gay Berlin*, 164–6.
115 Berger, *Ways of Seeing*, 7.
116 Beachy, *Gay Berlin*, 166; Whisnant, *Queer Identities*, 179–80. For Article 118 of the Weimar Constitution see also Huber, *Dokumente zur deutschen Verfassungsgeschichte*, Vol. III, 146.
117 Kraepelin, 'Psychiatrische Randbemerkungen', 171.

Conclusion

For all the fanfare around the centenary in 2018–19, the German Revolution of 1918–19 remains – as it was for Alexander Gallus in 2010 – a largely 'forgotten' or at best only faintly 'rediscovered' affair.[1] Several recent theoretical works and anthologies on revolution barely mention it. The Italian scholar Enzo Traverso, in his *Revolution: An Intellectual History* (2021), says nothing at all on November 1918, and instead moves directly to the 'Spartacist Uprising in Berlin [and] the council republics in Bavaria and Hungary', which 'possessed a very pronounced proletarian character' but nonetheless 'resulted in calamitous defeats'.[2] It was in the cities of Berlin, Munich, Budapest and Vienna, he writes, that 'the outposts of a Western socialist revolution tragically failed ... between 1919 and 1923'.[3] The events of 1918 seem irrelevant. Jack A. Goldstone's *Revolutions*, written for the Oxford University Press 'Very Short Introductions' series in 2014, says no more than that 'following [its] defeat in World War I', Germany had a 'worker's [*sic!*] revolution' that 'helped topple the last German monarch and install the Weimar Republic'.[4] The American scholars Keith Michael Baker and Dan Edelstein included a contribution by Gareth Stedman Jones on the 'German Revolution' in their influential 2015 anthology *Scripting Revolution*, but this was a piece on 1848, not 1918–19.[5]

Middle East specialist Mehran Kamrava's *Concise History of Revolution* (2020) does not even contain the word 'Germany' in its index, although it does include entries for 'Arab Spring', 'China', 'Cuba', 'Egypt', 'France', 'Iran', 'Mexico', 'Nicaragua', 'Russia', 'Syria', 'Tunisia' and 'Vietnam'.[6] 'Central Europe', including its German-speaking parts, appears only in relation to 'negotiated transitions' from Communist rule to democracy at the end of the 1980s, which, together with South Africa's largely peaceful dismantlement of Apartheid in 1990, are then contrasted with the 'spontaneous revolutions of France in 1789 and Iran in 1979'.[7] Meanwhile, the 1918–19 centenary anthology edited by Andreas Braune and Michael Dreyer, *Zusammenbruch, Aufbruch, Abbruch?* (2019), includes contributions by Wolfgang Niess on the 'unloved revolution' and by Martin Sabrow on the Revolution as an event that is simultaneously 'hated, honoured and forgotten' in German memory culture but – apart from one piece by Gleb J. Albert on 'revolutionary interactions between Germany and Russia in 1917–1919' – no sustained discussion of the transnational or international impact of the Revolution.[8]

As underlined by Franka Maubach, the manner in which the centenary of the Revolution and the founding of the Weimar Republic were marked in Germany at national and local level in 2018–19 has become part of the problem, inadvertently contributing to the countervailing trends of indifference or forgetting. The careful packaging of particular fragments from 1918–19 in museum exhibitions and accompanying artwork, photography and theatrical performances, has created an unhealthy disconnect between awareness of the past as something that constitutes a part of what seems ostensibly *present* for Germans now, in the late 2010s and the 2020s, and consciousness of the Revolution as a *real historical event* played out by real historical actors in real historical time.[9] The starkest example here would be the portrayal of the granting of female suffrage on 12 November 1918 as a de-ideologised and decontextualised moment in the development of democracy, gifted by men to women because it was the logical thing to do, or because they finally came to recognise the timeless virtue of an elite campaign for the vote waged by feminist reformers from the late eighteenth century onwards. The significance of public demands for universal suffrage made during strikes and mass street protests organised by socialist and working-class women in Germany (and elsewhere) in the decade before and during the First World War period is thereby erased. Instead, 12 November 1918 is either treated as an ahistorical given, i.e. as something that did not need to be fought for because its coming was natural and essential, or honoured for the wrong reasons – as a point when men graciously 'gave' women the vote as a 'reward' for their supposed 'natural reticence' and patient waiting.[10]

Yet beyond the short attention spans of those who in the late 2010s lived in a permanent *Jetztzeit* (now-time), uninterested in the complexities of the past and shielded from the half-forgotten realities of twentieth-century warfare and patriarchy by a tendency to cast 1918, 1945 and even 1989 as belonging to 'late antiquity',[11] there are also deeper historical reasons as to why the Revolution remains forgotten. Its failure to follow the political scripts inherited from 1789, 1830 or 1848 meant that whatever its 'objective' achievements in fields such as the eight-hour day, trade union recognition and social legislation, even its chief protagonists and beneficiaries – older male German workers in the pre-1914 social democratic tradition – dubbed it a failure in the subjective sense.[12] Benjamin Ziemann has also recently reminded us of the sheer 'diversity and plurality' of events in the twenty-two states with hereditary rulers and the three 'free' Hanseatic cities (Hamburg, Bremen and Lübeck) that made up the outgoing Kaiserreich during 1918–19. At one end of a very broad political spectrum, in Bremen, Braunschweig and Munich, attempts were made to introduce fully fledged socialist- or anarchist-led councils republics. And at the other end, in the two Mecklenburgs (Mecklenburg-Schwerin and Mecklenburg-Strelitz) the real shift was from a form of political representation that still harked back to the Middle Ages to one that more readily approximated to modern notions of parliamentary sovereignty and 'checks and balances'. Yet efforts to 'decentre' narrative accounts of the Revolution, i.e. to move away from the fixation on Kiel, Berlin and Munich, and the overdramatised political battles in the councils movement there, Ziemann argues, can only be achieved at the expense of rendering objective claims about the Revolution's success or failure in establishing democracy even more precarious.[13]

Following Hayden White, the only solution, for Ziemann, is to allow for explanation by emplotment, in this case by a narrative (re-)structuring of the Revolution centred around the meta-story of 'missing comedy'.[14] Because there was no early opportunity to stage crowd-pleasing moments in the form of paradoxical gestures of reconciliation between the revolutionaries and representatives of the old regime, symbolising their shared commitment to human values and resourcefulness beyond political rivalries, the Spartacists – a small minority without the numbers to launch their own successful revolution, but masters of rhetoric – were able to move the plot on in rapid succession from extremely short-lived revolutionary romance to (premature) revolutionary tragedy, emphasising civil war and sacrificial death as the only way to redeem the Revolution as early as 20 November 1918.[15] From this perspective, the class character of the Revolution is both too disparate to pinpoint in any objective sense, and irrelevant to its subjective denouement. Furthermore, if its final act was already visible in a rhetorical sense just three weeks after the first stirrings of naval rebellion in Kiel, then this was a play without the dramatic staying power of the French Revolutions of 1789, 1830 and 1848; the 1848–49 revolutions in central Europe; or, for that matter, the Iranian Revolution of 1979.

While it can be agreed, then, that 1918–19 remains a relatively 'forgotten' and 'unloved' revolution, it is more difficult to predict what new directions academic debates will take in the next ten-to-twenty years. Nonetheless, three broad developments seem likely, if not inevitable: a growing wariness of cultural determinism and the way it creates needless dividing lines, or what Bulgarian political scientist Ivan Krastev calls a 'cult of interior uniqueness' ('Kult der eigenen Einzigartigkeit'), in place of societal cohesion and political resilience;[16] a shift away from the history of experience to histories of the construction of revolutionary subjectivities based on 'living' sights, sounds, smells and tastes; and the return of political history in the guise of a long-overdue focus on the question of sovereignty. These three developments all touch upon the four ways of seeing the Revolution highlighted in the introduction to this book: as a movement of liberal political change from above, as a moment of mass democratic protest from below, as a spur to new political imaginaries and ideological mindsets, and as a transnational as well as national phenomenon. They also touch upon the double meaning of the word 'seeing' in the sense of John Berger's pithy commentary: 'It is seeing which establishes our place in the surrounding world; we explain that world with words, but words can never undo the fact that we are surrounded by it. The relationship between what we see and what we know is never settled.'[17]

The limits of the new cultural history

As mentioned in the introduction, as far as writing on Germany's 1918–19 Revolution is concerned, the impact of the new cultural history only really became evident in the 2010s. This somewhat belated arrival is significant. Certainly cultural history approaches have produced some important new insights, particularly at the level of political imaginaries, male and female subjectivities, and the gender politics of the Revolution.[18] Yet they have also exposed questions that cultural history cannot answer and gaps in knowledge that it cannot fill.

Early advocates of the new cultural history in the 1980s and 1990s were at pains to stress that their intention was not to replace the supposed straitjacket of structuralism with an equally rigid cultural determinism. Lynn Hunt, whose book *The Family Romance of the French Revolution* (1992) was and still is particularly influential, noted that she did not mean her work to act 'as a replacement for traditional political history', still less to 'reduce politics to fantasies, either individual or collective'. Yet she still insisted that fantasies – some of them unconscious – did have an impact on both concrete representations of the French Revolution as a story of 'family conflict and resolution' and on the way in which knowledge of political experiences of the Revolution came to be communicated. Thus, 'differences over family policy divided a broadly defined political left, which proposed sweeping changes in family laws, from a broadly defined right, which resisted those changes'.[19]

This book cannot judge whether Hunt's claims about the relationship between unconscious and conscious fantasies and the cultural framing of political experience during the French Revolution are also applicable in the context of other modern revolutions. However, when superimposed onto the German Revolution of 1918–19 they end up being misleading. This revolution was many things, but its romantic phase, if it existed at all, was compressed into days or weeks, not months or years. Does this matter? It does to those scholars whose main preoccupation is with cultural representation and communication. The latter may also take comfort in Enzo Traverso's recent observation that

> Rehabilitating revolutions as landmarks of modernity and quintessential moments of historical change does not mean romanticizing them. Their susceptibility to lyrical recollection and iconic representation does not impede a critical gaze from grasping not only their liberating features but also their hesitations, ambiguities, misleading paths and withdrawals.[20]

Hunt's metaphor of the 'family romance' works for a number of reasons in the context of the French Revolution of 1789.[21] It stays on the right side of Traverso's observations about the need for a 'critical gaze', whilst also capturing what he calls the 'ontological intensity' of political experience during revolutions.[22] It can also be linked to famous allegorical paintings such as Eugène Delacroix's *Liberty Leading the People* (1832), a work of homage to the July 1830 Revolution in Paris. Here Liberty is presented not as a subject in her own right – in other words, as a 'real woman of the people' – but as an object of popular fantasy and Romantic longing with a pure, uncorrupted femininity and the robust bodily appearance of an ancient republican goddess.[23]

As Philip Oltermann has recently reminded us, the idea that metaphor and allegory can be used to construct or (for cultural historians) to *re*construct the innermost feelings and desires of revolutionaries has its roots in the Romantic era of the 1820s and 1830s.[24] Two decades or more of cultural history approaches to the Revolution of 1918–19, however, have produced nothing to match the explanatory power of Hunt's work on the French Revolution. And, as stated above, there is an obvious, straightforward reason for this: the German Revolution does not lend itself to being narrated through lyrical melodrama or romance. For instance, *knowing* that 'consumers of lesser means' – the construction used by Belinda J. Davis in her study *Home Fires Burning* (2000) – existed in Berlin during the First World War, and *understanding* that they were the direct instigators of food riots and, indirectly, the main protagonists in a debate about the future of citizenship that also drew in the police and other guardians of order in the German capital, is a useful and credible way of writing women back into the history of the Revolution.[25] But it does not help us to see the Revolution, when it finally came in 1918–19, with the living intensity that contemporaries saw it, women included. This is because the cultural construct 'consumers of lesser means' is not an enchanting metaphor providing drama or pathos to political experience, but a literal reflection of painful material facts about rising prices, wasting bodies and growing queues in front of shops.[26] Hunger, family separation, wartime bereavement and military defeat meant straightforward sorrow and pain without any ennobling interior features or mitigating thrills.[27] The intensity of political feeling in 1918–19, if it existed, therefore has to be sought elsewhere, in the new, unscripted ways of seeing, hearing and sensing that came with the end of the war and then the Revolution, and not in the realm of (conscious or unconscious) sense-making (*Sinnstiftung*) drawn from growing popular awareness of artistic allegory or historical comparison.

Histories of experience and ways of seeing

What other ways are there, then, of seeing the Revolution in all its intensity? Some of the answers to this question are already beginning to be provided, for instance in the findings of Julian Aulke on revolutionary 'spaces';[28] Nadine Rossol on emotions and anticipatory affects;[29] Christopher Dillon on the Revolution as 'a lived and contingent event';[30] Gaard Kets and James Muldoon on 1918–19 and political theory;[31] Daniel Siemens on the 'ambivalent expectations' of German Jews;[32] Andrew Donson on the 'reluctance to work' (*Arbeitsunlust*);[33] and my own research, with Corinne Painter and Ingrid Sharp, on female subjectivities 'beyond the script'.[34] But it is worth digging a bit deeper in order to understand how these ideas and findings might also point in the direction of a future revival of political history as the more radical, incisive and illuminating counterpart to cultural history.

Benjamin Ziemann, in his *War Experiences in Rural Germany, 1914–1923* (2007), defines experience, in the way that historians use the term, as a 'communicative construction', and contrasts it with discourse, a concept that 'emphasises … the limits of what may be said and written about certain subjects within the public sphere'.[35] In terms of constructing war experiences during the First World War, the main communicative media, whether on the home front or the fighting fronts, were private letters and diaries. But these appear only when people have time and privacy to write. What if limits to publicly constructing and communicating experience are imposed not only objectively – i.e. by discourses that exist independently of the protagonist's own volition and the question of who owns/controls the means of communication – but subjectively, in other words by the very intensity of the experience itself, and the lack of time and privacy the protagonist has to pause and reflect? Does this not entail a different way of seeing and a different way of communicating, one based first of all on visual scenes remembered, and only then on words chosen to communicate that memory?

One example would be the following account given to the East German Party archive by veteran Communist Franziska Rubens, who in 1918 was a twenty-four-year-old student in Berlin:

> During the [revolutionary days of] November 1918 we [i.e. her future husband Hermann Bergmann and herself] were active but very inexperienced fighters. We made permanent contact with comrades from the ranks of the working-class youth movement, especially with Fritz Heilmann and Marthel [Martha] Globig ... This was how we experienced the November events, how we came to take part in demonstrations, in armed street fighting ... Every day brought new experiences. Together we stormed down [Unter den] Linden as one mass ... endless columns of vehicles, soldiers with bayonets, red flags fluttering ... And amid all this there is a quite personal memory, which Marthel and I still look back on even today. On one of the first days of the revolution we bumped into each other at another demonstration in the city. I squeezed Marthel's hand in excitement and said to her: 'Congratulations, Marthel! We've done it, we've won!' Whereupon she smiled indulgently [at my naivety] and replied: 'What are you saying! This is only the beginning!'.[36]

Without knowing it, this passage follows the creative writing dictum 'show, don't tell', particularly through the author's use of immersive description to bring alive immediate sensory and political experiences rather than resorting to formulaic expressions or rhetorical devices such as metaphor, allegory or allusion. Of course, all ways of seeing and remembering have an underlying ideological component, including Rubens's, which – by moving away from the older male socialist's gaze – was clearly at odds with the SED leadership's 1958 definition of 1918–19 as a 'failed bourgeois revolution'. But to paraphrase John Berger, the critical question is not between innocence and knowledge, youth and maturity, or nature and culture, but who past political experience belongs to: 'to those who can apply it to their own lives', or those who might use it for a different purpose: to situate the power claims of a particular individual, class, gender, or party in history.[37] To see, revolutionary actors have to look, to remember, they have to recall, and to show they have to move beyond the banal, the rhetorical or the formulaic when *re*constructing the past. What's more, in Karl Marx's words, they have to do so 'not under circumstances they themselves have

Figure 9.1 Soldiers join striking workers on Unter den Linden, Berlin, 9 November 1918, on their way to hear Karl Liebknecht speak at the city palace. Note the presence of women too. This is probably the demonstration remembered by Franziska Rubens. Alamy.

chosen, but under the given and inherited circumstances with which they are directly confronted'.[38] In fact, this is just another way of saying that (making) history was – and is – a political issue, not a cultural one: a matter of power and sovereignty, not of lifestyles and identity.

Sovereignty

'The German Reich is a republic. Political power emanates from the people.' So reads Article 1 of the Weimar Constitution, coming into effect on 11 August 1919.[39] If we follow Ziemann in adopting the definition of a revolution as a 'change of power within the framework of an existing state', this is the moment when the outcome of the German Revolution was formally anchored in law.[40] The twenty-two princes and three city-states were no longer sovereign; the people were. This makes it all the more astonishing that so few studies have grappled with the issue of popular sovereignty as seen by the 76 per cent of German voters who supported the 'Weimar coalition parties' in the National Assembly elections in January 1919, and who thereby gave their approval to the establishment of a democratic, parliamentary form of government that would serve the people, one and indivisible.[41]

The concept of sovereignty of course came up in other, more complex guises after January 1919, with revolutionary idealism increasingly giving way to abstract, legalistic arguments, debates about states of exception or arbitrary notions of 'struggle' (*Kampf*). Certainly the German parliamentarians of 1919–33 more often acted to empower the State and financial experts than to empower ordinary people.[42] Yet equally they were not so terrified of Communism and threats to property rights from popular expressions of sovereignty that they resorted to 'recalling the King', a phenomenon that Christopher Hill identifies as the endpoint of the English Revolution in 1660.[43] Anti-democrats and sceptics (*Vernunftrepublikaner*, or 'reluctant republicans') instead turned to the conservative legal scholar Carl Schmitt's authoritarian alternative from 1922: 'Sovereign is he who decides on the exception.'[44] From spring 1919 onwards, individual Reich Ministers, especially those in charge of State finances, the interior or the Reichswehr, were granted temporary powers to manage particular aspects of central governance and guarantee law and order during the transition from war to peace. Article 48 of the Weimar Constitution, building on the provisional law of 10 February 1919, famously re-established the sovereign power of the Reich, via the President's right to suspend parts of the constitution 'if public safety and order be seriously disturbed or threatened'.[45] It also in effect resurrected the sovereignty of individual states, which were empowered to take similar action 'for [their] own territory' should a threat to public safety reach such heights that 'there [would] be a danger in delay' if the prior consent of the Reich President had to be sought.[46]

At the national and international level, meanwhile, as Hedwig Richter has argued, the sovereignty and dignity of the body formed a key focus of German middle-class reformers' understanding of democracy from 1780 onwards, continuing through the 1918–19 Revolution and finding its way into parts of the Weimar Constitution.[47] Article 161 thus required the State to 'establish a comprehensive scheme of insurance ... for the preservation of the individual's health and capacity to work, for the protection of mothers, and for the amelioration of the economic consequences of old age, infirmity, and other life circumstances'.[48] For Leonard V. Smith, State sovereignty and national self-determination were also at the heart of discussions about the reform and improvement of international relations at the Paris Peace Conference in 1919–20. This was of central importance to German nationalists insofar as 'the Treaty of Versailles ... deprived Germany of the material attributes of a Great Power – a large army and navy, overseas colonies, even control over its own borders'.[49]

Finally, thinking about Communist alternatives, Philip Oltermann has recently reminded us that Johannes R. Becher, left-wing poet and East German Minister of Culture in the 1950s, was famous for saying that literature needed to be granted the 'standing of a great sovereign power' ('eine Grossmachtstellung') if the GDR were to hold its own against the rival claims of the capitalist Federal Republic.[50] Projected back to 1918–19, traces of this Communist belief can be found in the emplotment of the Revolution as tragedy from 20 November onwards. Indeed, given the tiny number of actual supporters the Communists had at that time – in particular followers who might be willing to sacrifice their lives for the cause in armed street fighting with Government troops – cultural allusion necessarily became the key imagined weapon in the class war between proletarians and the bourgeoisie that the Spartacists and then the KPD wished to launch.[51] The weapon is only the means, however. The end goal was power, whether understood politically or theologically or in both ways, as it was for the Communists' opponents.

For all that, sovereignty cannot just be about parties or nations, states or rulers, or even the body and the self. It is also, as Hill argues, about the people.[52] But equally it is about republican politicians who saw the legal instrument of the state of exception as a means of upholding and protecting at times of extreme threat the principle that 'power emanates from the people' as opposed to permanently overriding it. How sovereignty was 'medialised', and how it was experienced and understood both by republican parties and by ordinary Germans in the period between the overthrow of the Kaiser on 9 November 1918 and the coming into force of the new constitution on 11 August 1919, is one of the most pressing questions about this Revolution, which remains to be investigated.

Notes

1. Gallus, *Die vergessene Revolution*. See also Christopher Dillon and Kim Wünschmann, 'Historicizing the German Revolution of 1918–19', in Dillon and Wünschmann, *Living the German Revolution*.
2. Traverso, *Revolution*, 15, 91, 395.
3. *Ibid.*, 389.
4. Jack A. Goldstone, *Revolutions: A Very Short Introduction* (Oxford, 2014), 70.
5. Gareth Stedman Jones, 'Scripting the German Revolution: Marx and 1848', in Baker and Edelstein, *Scripting Revolution*, 169–80.
6. Mehran Kamrava, *A Concise History of Revolution* (Cambridge, 2020), 185–92.
7. *Ibid.*, 4.
8. See Wolfgang Niess, 'Die ungeliebte Revolution: Die verdrängte und politisierte Erinnerung an 1918/19 im geteilten Deutschland'; Martin Sabrow, 'Verhasst – verehrt – vergessen: Die Novemberrevolution in der deutschen Gedächtnisgeschichte'; and Gleb J. Albert, 'Revolutionäre Wechselwirkungen: Deutschland und Russland 1917–1919'; all in Braune and Dreyer, *Zusammenbruch, Aufbruch, Abbruch?*, 289–307, 309–24 and 33–45 respectively. Werner Bramke already noted that it was 'an unloved revolution' in 2009; see Bramke and Reisinger, *Leipzig in der Revolution von 1918/19*, 9–26.
9. Maubach, 'Weimar (nicht) vom Ende her denken'.
10. Sloane, *Uncontrollable Women*, 25. For a critique of this approach to understanding 12 November 1918 see also the various contributions to Corinne Painter, Ingrid Sharp and Matthew Stibbe (eds), *Socialist Women and the Great War: Protest, Revolution and Commemoration* (London, 2022).
11. Iris Radisch, 'Vorwärts, es geht zurück', *Die Zeit*, 2 March 2022, 58.
12. Föllmer, 'The Unscripted Revolution', 161.
13. Ziemann, 'The Missing Comedy'.
14. *Ibid.* See also Hayden White, *Metahistory: The Historical Imagination in Nineteenth-Century Europe*, 40th anniversary edn (Baltimore, MD and London, 2014 [1973]).
15. Ziemann, 'The Missing Comedy'.
16. Ivan Krastev, 'Jetzt beginnt eine neue Geschichte: Die Zeit der sanften Macht ist vorbei', *Die Zeit*, 2 March 2022, 57.
17. Berger, *Ways of Seeing*, 7.
18. See esp. Canning, 'Gender and the Imaginary of Revolution'; and Föllmer, 'The Unscripted Revolution'.
19. All quotes in this paragraph are taken from Lynn Hunt, *The Family Romance of the French Revolution* (Berkeley, CA, 1992), xv.

20 Traverso, *Revolution*, 16.
21 For its applicability to 1989, and especially to the 'Velvet Revolution' in Prague on 17 November, see James Krapfl, 'Revolution and Revolt against Revolution: Czechoslovakia, 1989', in McDermott and Stibbe, *Revolution and Resistance in Eastern Europe*, 175–94.
22 Traverso, *Revolution*, 16. See also Krapfl, 'Revolution and Revolt against Revolution', 178.
23 In this sense I would disagree with Hobsbawm that Delacroix's *Liberty* directly 'represents the people' and that her 'concreteness [as a real woman of the people] removes [her] from the usual allegorical role of females'. See Eric Hobsbawm, 'Man and Woman in Socialist Iconography', *History Workshop Journal*, 6 (1978), 121–38 (124).
24 Philip Oltermann, *The Stasi Poetry Circle: The Creative Writing Class that Tried to Win the Cold War* (London, 2022), 90.
25 Davis, *Home Fires Burning*.
26 Oltermann, *The Stasi Poetry Circle*, 57.
27 Ziemann, 'Weimar was Weimar', 549.
28 Aulke, *Räume der Revolution*.
29 Nadine Rossol, '"Die Abdankung unseres Kaisers hat mich nicht besonders getroffen ...": Emotionen, Erwartungen und Teilhabe an der deutschen Revolution 1918/19', in Braune and Dreyer, *Zusammenbruch, Aufbruch, Abbruch?*, 161–75.
30 Dillon, 'The German Revolution', 27.
31 Gaard Kets and James Muldoon (eds), *The German Revolution and Political Theory* (London, 2019).
32 Daniel Siemens, 'Ambivalent Expectations in Times of Crisis: The Revolution of 1918–19 and the German Jews', in Dillon and Wünschmann, *Living the German Revolution*.
33 Donson, '*Arbeitsunlust*'.
34 Stibbe, Painter and Sharp, 'History beyond the Script'.
35 Ziemann, *War Experiences*, 10.
36 SAPMO-BArch, SgY 30/0787, Franziska Rubens, unpublished memoirs, n.d., 4–5. See also Matthew Stibbe, Veronika Helfert and Olga Shnyrova, 'Women and Socialist Revolution, 1917–1923', in Ingrid Sharp and Matthew Stibbe (eds), *Women Activists between War and Peace: Europe, 1918–1923* (London, 2017), 123–72 (123–4).
37 Berger, *Ways of Seeing*, 32.
38 Marx, 'The Eighteenth Brumaire', 146.
39 Weimar Constitution, Article 1, in Huber, *Dokumente zur deutschen Verfassungsgeschichte*, Vol. III, 129.
40 Ziemann, 'The Missing Comedy'.
41 Two important exceptions are Peter C. Caldwell, *Popular Sovereignty and the Crisis of German Constitutional Law: The Theory and Practice*

of *Weimar Constitutionalism* (Durham, NC and London, 1997); and Daniel Siemens, 'Revolutionäre Justiz? Volkssouveränität und Recht bei Erich Kuttner und Walther Lamp'l in der frühen Weimarer Republik', in Braune and Dreyer, *Zusammenbruch, Aufbruch, Abbruch?*, 233–46. Heiko Bollmeyer discusses the separate but nonetheless related concept of 'the people' in his essay 'Das "Volk" in den Verfassungsberatungen der Weimarer Nationalversammlung 1919: Ein demokratietheoretischer Schlüsselbegriff zwischen Kaiserreich und Republik', in Gallus, *Die vergessene Revolution*, 57–83.

42 Middendorf, *Macht der Ausnahme*.
43 Christopher Hill, 'Die gesellschaftlichen und ökonomischen Folgen der Reformation', in Klein and Streisand, *Beiträge zum neuen Geschichtsbild*, 88–104 (103–4).
44 Carl Schmitt, *Political Theology: Four Chapters on the Concept of Sovereignty*, trans. George Schwab (Chicago, IL, 2005; German original, 1922), 5.
45 Weimar Constitution, Article 48, in Huber, *Dokumente zur deutschen Verfassungsgeschichte*, Vol. III, 136–7.
46 *Ibid.*, 137. See also Peter C. Caldwell, 'The Weimar Constitution', in Rossol and Ziemann, *The Oxford Handbook of the Weimar Republic*, 119–39 (127–30).
47 Richter, *Demokratie*, 98–107, 212, 260–1.
48 Weimar Constitution, Article 161, in Huber, *Dokumente der deutschen Verfassungsgeschichte*, Vol. III, 152–3.
49 Smith, *Sovereignty at the Paris Peace Conference*, 32. See also Raffael Scheck, 'Women against Versailles: Maternalism and Nationalism of Female Bourgeois Politicians in the Early Weimar Republic', *German Studies Review*, 22.1 (1999), 21–42.
50 Oltermann, *The Stasi Poetry Circle*, 25–6.
51 Ziemann, 'The Missing Comedy'.
52 Hill, *The English Revolution*, 9.

Further reading

This is a list of the most important books and articles in English. Readers who wish to delve deeper, including into German-language works, should consult the endnotes after each chapter.

Major interpretative accounts and historical overviews

Bessel, Richard, *Germany after the First World War* (Oxford, 1993).
Carsten, Francis L., *Revolution in Central Europe, 1918–19* (London, 1972).
Davis, Belinda J., *Home Fires Burning: Food, Politics, and Everyday Life in World War I Berlin* (Chapel Hill, NC and London, 2000).
Feldman, Gerald D., *The Great Disorder: Politics, Economics, and Society in the German Inflation, 1914–1924* (Oxford, 1993).
Fritzsche, Peter, *Germans into Nazis* (Cambridge, MA, 1998).
Gerwarth, Robert, *November 1918: The German Revolution* (Oxford, 2020).
Haffner, Sebastian, *Failure of a Revolution: Germany, 1918–19* (London, 1973; German original, 1969).
Jones, Mark, *Founding Weimar: Violence and the German Revolution of 1918–19* (Cambridge, 2016).
Kolb, Eberhard, *The Weimar Republic*, 2nd edn (London and New York, 2005; German original, 1988).
Peukert, Detlev J. K., *The Weimar Republic: The Crisis of Classical Modernity* (London, 1991; German original, 1987).
Smith, Jeffrey R., *A People's War: Germany's Political Revolution, 1913–1918* (Lanham, MD, 2007).
Stibbe, Matthew, *Germany 1914–1933: Politics, Society and Culture* (Harlow, 2010).
Watt, Richard M., *The Kings Depart: The Tragedy of Germany. Versailles and the German Revolution* (London, 1969).
Winkler, Heinrich August, *Germany: The Long Road to the West*, 2 vols (Oxford, 2006–7; German original, 2000).

Essay collections

Dillon, Christopher and Kim Wünschmann (eds), *Living the German Revolution 1918–19: Expectations, Experiences, Responses*, forthcoming.
Hoffrogge, Ralf and Norman Laporte (eds), *Weimar Communism as Mass Movement, 1918–1933* (London, 2017).
Kets, Gaard and James Muldoon (eds), *The German Revolution and Political Theory* (London, 2019).
Painter, Corinne, Ingrid Sharp and Matthew Stibbe (eds), *Socialist Women and the Great War: Protest, Revolution and Commemoration* (London, 2022).
Rossol, Nadine and Benjamin Ziemann (eds), *The Oxford Handbook of the Weimar Republic* (Oxford, 2022).
Rürup, Reinhard (ed.), *The Problem of Revolution in Germany, 1789–1989* (Oxford, 2000).
Weinhauer, Klaus, Anthony McElligott and Kerstin Heinsohn (eds), *Germany 1916–1923: A Revolution in Context* (Bielefeld, 2015).

Social Democrats, Communists and the German labour movement

Berger, Stefan, *Social Democracy and the Working Class in Nineteenth and Twentieth Century Germany* (Harlow, 2000).
Dorpalen, Andreas, *German History in Marxist Perspective: The East German Approach* (London, 1985).
Epstein, Catherine, *The Last Revolutionaries: German Communists and Their Century* (Cambridge, MA, 2003).
Grebing, Helga, *History of the German Labour Movement: A Survey*, rev. edn (Leamington Spa, 1985; German original, 1966).
Hoffrogge, Ralf, *Working-Class Politics in the German Revolution: Richard Müller, the Revolutionary Shop Stewards and the Origins of the Council Movement* (Leiden, 2014).
Mommsen, Wolfgang J., 'The German Revolution, 1918–1920: Political Revolution and Social Protest Movement', in Wolfgang J. Mommsen, *Imperial Germany, 1867–1918: Politics, Culture and Society in an Authoritarian State* (London, 1995; German original, 1978), 233–54.
Ostrowski, Marius S. (ed.), *Eduard Bernstein on the German Revolution: Selected Historical Writings* (London, 2019).
Rosenberg, Arthur, *A History of the German Republic, 1918–1930* (London, 1936; German original, 1935).

Rosenberg, Arthur, *Imperial Germany: The Birth of the German Republic* (Oxford, 1970 [1931]; German original, 1928).
Ryder, A. J., *The German Revolution of 1918: A Study of German Socialism in War and Revolt* (Cambridge, 1967).

Soldiers and sailors

Horn, Daniel, *The German Naval Mutinies of World War I* (New Brunswick, NJ, 1969).
Horn, Daniel (ed.), *War, Mutiny and Revolution in the German Navy: The World War I Diary of Seaman Richard Stumpf* (New Brunswick, NJ, 1967; German original, 1927).
Stephenson, Scott, *The Final Battle: Soldiers of the Western Front and the German Revolution of 1918* (Cambridge, 2009).
Ulrich, Bernd and Benjamin Ziemann (eds), *German Soldiers in the Great War: Letters and Eyewitness Accounts* (Barnsley, 2010; German original, 1997).
Ziemann, Benjamin, *Contested Commemorations: Republican War Veterans and Weimar Political Culture* (Cambridge, 2013).
Ziemann, Benjamin, *Violence and the German Soldier in the Great War: Killing, Dying, Surviving* (London, 2017; German original, 2013).
Ziemann, Benjamin, *War Experiences in Rural Germany, 1914–1923* (Oxford, 2007; German original, 1997).

Women, men and political imaginaries

Boak, Helen, *Women in the Weimar Republic* (Manchester, 2013).
Canning, Kathleen, 'Gender and the Imaginary of Revolution in Germany', in Klaus Weinhauer, Anthony McElligott and Kerstin Heinsohn (eds), *Germany 1916–23: A Revolution in Context* (Bielefeld, 2015), 103–26.
Daniel, Ute, *The War from Within: German Working-Class Women in the First World War* (Oxford, 1997; German original, 1989).
Föllmer, Moritz, 'The Unscripted Revolution: Male Subjectivities in Germany, 1918–1919', *Past and Present*, 240 (2018), 161–92.
Marhoefer, Laurie, *Sex and the Weimar Republic: German Homosexual Emancipation and the Rise of the Nazis* (Toronto, 2015).
Stibbe, Matthew, Corinne Painter and Ingrid Sharp, 'History beyond the Script: Rethinking Female Subjectivities and Socialist Women's Activism

during the German Revolution of 1918–1919 and Its Immediate Aftermath', in Christopher Dillon and Kim Wünschmann (eds), *Living the German Revolution 1918–19: Expectations, Experiences, Responses*, forthcoming.

Whisnant, Clayton J., *Queer Identities and Politics in Germany: A History, 1880–1945* (New York, 2016).

Urban spaces

Ablovatski, Eliza, *Revolution and Political Violence in Central Europe: The Deluge of 1919* (Cambridge, 2021).

Dobson, Sean, *Authority and Upheaval in Leipzig, 1910–1920: The Story of a Relationship* (New York, 2001).

Föllmer, Moritz, *Individuality and Modernity in Berlin: Self and Society from Weimar to the Wall* (Cambridge, 2013).

McElligott, Anthony, *The German Urban Experience, 1900–1945: Modernity and Crisis* (London, 2001).

Weinhauer, Klaus, 'World War I and Urban Societies: Social Movements, Fears, and Spatial Order in Hamburg and Chicago (*c.* 1916–1923)', in Stefan Rinke and Michael Wildt (eds), *Revolutions and Counter-Revolutions: 1917 and Its Aftermath from a Global Perspective* (Frankfurt am Main and New York, 2017), 287–306.

Transnational aspects of the Revolution

Aitken, Robbie and Eve Rosenhaft, *Black Germany: The Making and Unmaking of a Diaspora Community, 1884–1960* (Cambridge, 2013).

Eckert, Andreas, 'The First Postcolonial Nation in Europe? The End of the German Empire', in Martin Thomas and Andrew Thompson (eds), *The Oxford Handbook of the Ends of Empire* (Oxford, 2018), 102–22.

Emerson, Charles, *Crucible: The Long End of the Great War and the Birth of a New World, 1917–1924* (London, 2019).

Gerwarth, Robert, *The Vanquished: Why the First World War Failed to End, 1917–1923* (London, 2016).

Manela, Erez, *The Wilsonian Moment: Self-Determination and the International Origins of Anticolonial Nationalism* (Oxford, 2007).

Newton, Douglas, *British Policy and the Weimar Republic, 1918–1919* (Oxford, 1997).

Smith, Leonard V., *Sovereignty at the Paris Peace Conference of 1919* (Oxford, 2018).

Other revolutions, other times

Baker, Keith Michael and Dan Edelstein (eds), *Scripting Revolution: A Historical Approach to the Comparative Study of Revolutions* (Stanford, CA, 2015).
Bernstein, Eduard, *Cromwell and Communism: Social Democracy in the Great English Revolution*, with an introduction by Eric Heffer, MP (Nottingham, 1980; first published in English in 1930; original German edition, 1895).
Conway, Martin, *Western Europe's Democratic Age, 1945–1968* (Princeton, NJ, 2020).
Desai, Radhika and Henry Heller (eds), *Revolutions* (London and New York, 2021).
Edele, Mark, *Debates on Stalinism* (Manchester, 2020).
Eley, Geoff, *Forging Democracy: The History of the Left in Europe, 1850–2000* (Oxford, 2002).
Goldstone, Jack A., *Revolutions: A Very Short Introduction* (Oxford, 2014).
Hill, Christopher, *The English Revolution 1640: An Essay* (London, 1940).
Hobsbawm, E. J., *The Age of Revolution, 1789–1848* (London, 1962).
Hufton, Olwen H., *Women and the Limits of Citizenship in the French Revolution* (Toronto, 1992).
Hunt, Lynn, *The Family Romance of the French Revolution* (Berkeley, CA, 1992).
James, C. L. R., *The Black Jacobins: Toussaint L'Ouverture and the San Domingo Revolution* (London, 1963 [1938]).
Kamrava, Mehran, *A Concise History of Revolution* (Cambridge, 2020).
Marx, Karl, 'The Eighteenth Brumaire of Louis Bonaparte' (1852), reproduced in Karl Marx, *Surveys from Exile*, ed. David Fernbach, trans. Ben Fowkes (London, 2010 [1973]), 143–249.
Merriman, John, *History on the Margins: People and Places in the Emergence of Modern France* (Lincoln, NE and London, 2018).
Merriman, John, *Massacre: The Life and Death of the Paris Commune of 1871* (New Haven, CT and London, 2014).
Richardson, R. C., *The Debate on the English Revolution*, 3rd edn (Manchester, 1998 [1977]).
Schama, Simon, *Citizens: A Chronicle of the French Revolution* (London, 1989).

Sloane, Nan, *Uncontrollable Women: Radicals, Reformers and Revolutionaries* (London, 2022).
Traverso, Enzo, *Revolution: An Intellectual History* (London, 2021).

Index

Ablovatski, Eliza 204, 235
Abusch, Alexander 69
Academy of Sciences (GDR)
    13, 117
    Arbeitsgruppe Erster Weltkrieg
        (Research Group on the
        First World War) 126
    Institute for History 115, 116,
        119, 139
Addison, Joseph 225, 226
Adenauer, Konrad 85, 88, 90, 96
African Welfare Association (in
    Germany) 232
Aitken, Robbie 229
Akwa, Thomas Manga 229–31
Albert, Gleb J. 256
Alexsandrov, Georgy 66
Allied economic blockade of
    Germany (1914–19) 40,
    176, 226
Altona 29, 237
American Civil War (1861–65) 244
American Historical Review
    (academic journal) 137
American Revolutionary Era
    (1765–91) 244
Anders als die Andern (film, 1919)
    240, 247
Anglo-Irish War (1920–21) 239
Anti-Bolshevik League 202
antisemitism 27, 146, 199,
    200, 235

APO (Extra-Parliamentary
    Opposition 1966–68)
    96, 100
Arco auf Valley, Anton von
    (Count) 213
Arendsee, Martha 196
Arendt, Hannah 98
Arendt, Hans-Jürgen 127
Augsburg 198, 212
Augspurg, Anita 128
Aulke, Julian 7, 193, 195,
    206, 261
Austria, post-1918 republic 10,
    38, 169
Auxiliary Service Law (1916) 92

Baer, Gertrud 128
Baker, Keith Michael 4–5, 255
Barcelona
    Setmana Tràgica (1909) 246
Barnes, George 225, 226
Bartel, Walter 119, 123
Barth, Emil 214
Battle of Britain (1940) 59
Battle of Stalingrad (1942–43) 63
Bauhaus (art school) 216
Bavaria 65, 85, 113,
    181, 195, 212
    Ministry of Justice 213
    Niederschönenfeld fortress 212
    Strafanstalt Aichach 212
    Wülzburg fortress 212

Bebel, August 154
Becher, Johannes R. 265
Beethoven, Ludwig van 176
Behrendt, Margarete 242
Belgium 167, 168, 170, 206
Bellers, John 63
Berger, John 197, 200, 258, 262
Berger, Stefan 225–6, 233, 246
Bergmann, Hermann 262
Bergsträsser, Ludwig 37
Berlin 1, 7, 25, 36, 39, 40, 52, 54, 60, 66, 68, 70, 71, 89, 95, 110, 121, 122, 140, 146, 151, 170, 173, 177–8, 180, 185, 196, 197, 198, 200, 204, 205, 208, 209, 214, 215, 229, 231, 232, 233, 240, 243, 245, 255, 257, 260, 262
   Alexanderplatz 196, 212
   Friedrichsfelde cemetery 216–18
   Friedrichshain cemetery 214, 215
   Friedrichshain Park 216
   Lichtenberg 198, 211
   Maikäferkazerne (military barracks) 212
   Neukölln 52, 124, 212, 216
   Plötzensee jail 211
   Prenzlauer Berg 230
   Tempelhofer Feld 214
   Tiergarten 202, 213
   Unter den Linden 262
   Wedding 52, 212
   see also East Berlin; West Berlin
Berlin: Sinfonie der Großstadt (film, 1927) 206
Berliner Illustrirte Zeitung (newspaper) 11
Berliner Tageblatt (newspaper) 197
Berliner Vollzugsrat (executive committee of workers' and soldiers' councils in Berlin) 30
Bernstein, Eduard 27, 30–1, 35–6, 38, 42, 63–4, 109, 204
Bessel, Richard 168, 171, 178, 235
Betts, Paul 223
Bevin, Ernest 66
Beyer, Hans 113, 125
Bez, Uli 181
Bieber, Hans-Joachim 174–5
Bielefeld 207
Bilé, Joseph Ekwe 228
biological-medical interpretations of the Revolution 38–45, 194, 198, 200
Bismarck, Otto von (Count) 8, 24, 243
   social reforms of 245
Black liberation movements (German and global) 228–33
Black Lives Matter movement 224
'Black Shame' campaign in the Rhineland (1920–21) 232
'Blutmai'/'Bloody May' (Berlin, 1929) 52, 205, 212
Bohnes, Gerhard 214
Bölke, Milli 206, 214–15
Bolshevism 55, 73, 87, 90, 91, 98, 101, 102, 103, 112, 152, 154, 200, 202, 235
Bonn 38, 57, 73, 136, 141
Bösch, Frank 3
Boy-Ed, Karl (Captain) 27–8
Bramke, Werner 139, 140–1, 143–4, 147–9, 151, 154–5
Brandenburg 152
   Brandenburg jail 212
Brandt, Willy 100, 142
Braune, Andreas 256
Braunschweig 9, 180, 183, 257
Brecht, Bertolt 179
Bremen 9, 33, 257
Bremen Councils Republic (February 1919) 200
Bremerhaven 206
Brenner, Michael 7
Britain 59, 61, 66, 82, 88

Brody, Louis (Bebe Mpessa) 232
Brown, Timothy Scott 96
Budapest Councils Republic (1919) 235, 255
Bulgaria
  Agrarian Uprising (1923) 239, 246
Bundestag ((West) German Parliament) 135, 149
Bürgerräte (councils formed by middle class occupational groups and peasants) 93, 174–5
burials 213–18
  see also funerals
Buschmann, Maximilian 210
BVP (Bavarian People's Party) 23

Cameroon 228, 229–31
Canada 128
Carsten, Francis L. 56, 154, 155
Caruso, Amerigo 199, 246
Catholic Centre Party 41, 66
Catholics 54, 135, 171, 214
CDU (Christian Democratic Union) 73, 85, 86, 87, 96, 151
  Alliance for Germany (1990) 145
Chattopadhyaya, Virendranath 228
China 227
  'Hands off China' campaign (1925–27) 232–3
  Kuomintang nationalist movement 229, 232
Chinese Revolution (1949) 5, 97
Churchill, Winston (Sir) 63
citizenship 10, 11, 175, 176, 178, 179, 260
civilians 16, 170, 173, 174–80
Cold War 1, 4, 6, 11, 16, 53, 65, 70, 81, 82, 86, 109, 111, 117, 119, 134, 136, 141, 177, 180, 193, 233

Comintern (Third International) 31, 33, 122–3, 232, 242
Communist Party of Great Britain (CPGB) 61–2, 88
  historians' group 61
Communist Party of Italy 143
Communist Party of the Soviet Union (CPSU) 139, 143
  twentieth congress (1956) 113
Communist Party of Yugoslavia 73
Conrad, Sebastian 227
Constituent National Assembly 7, 8, 14, 25, 41, 57, 65, 90, 92, 93, 94, 95, 100, 102, 198, 264
  elections to (January 1919) 43, 66, 94, 99, 165, 174
Conway, Martin 65, 71, 88
Conze, Eckart 246
Council of People's Deputies 8, 10, 14, 15, 30, 31, 32, 35, 55, 57, 87, 89, 94, 99
councils movement (*Rätebewegung*) 30, 32, 88–90, 91–5, 97–100, 101, 109, 117, 127–8, 140, 149
  women's councils (*Frauenräte*) 128
Cromwell, Oliver 62
Cuban Revolution (1959) 97, 233
'cultural turn', *see* new cultural history
Cuxhaven 206
Czechoslovakia 53, 119
  Communist seizure of power in (1948) 70

Dähnhardt, Dirk 171
Dalton, Hugh 66
dance crazes 10, 44, 186
Daniel, Ute 180, 183, 184
Darmstadt 38
Däumig, Ernst 94–5, 98, 99, 102
Davis, Belinda J. 177–80, 260–1

DDP (German Democratic Party)
    28, 37, 38, 66, 243
decolonisation 227–33
Deist, Wilhelm 168, 171
Delacroix, Eugène
    Liberty Leading the People
    (1832) 260
Dementev, Ilya 227
Demeter, Karl 28
Deutsche Historiker Gesellschaft
    (DHG) 82
Deutsche Liga für Menschenrechte
    (German League for
    Human Rights) 38
Deutscher Verein für Armenpflege
    (German Association
    for the Care of the
    Poor) 181
Dibobe, Martin Quane 229–31
Diehl, Ernst 143
Dillon, Christopher 7, 195,
    235, 261
DKP (German Communist Party,
    post-1968) 96, 100
DNVP (German National People's
    Party) 23
Dobb, Maurice 61
Dobson, Sean 236
Donson, Andrew 163, 184,
    237, 261
Drechsel, Max 65
Dreyer, Michael 256
Duisberg, Carl 174
Duncker, Hermann 124
Duncker, Käte 124
Duncker, Wolfgang 124
Düsseldorf 116
Dutt, Ranjani Palme 61

East Berlin 70, 72, 115, 119, 125,
    135, 136, 142, 143, 144
    German Historical
    Museum 116
East Germany *see* German
    Democratic
    Republic (GDR)

Eberlein, Hugo 122–4
Eberlein, Werner 122–3
Ebert, Friedrich 8, 11, 14, 15,
    31, 32, 84, 91, 92, 97,
    99, 101, 109, 154, 208,
    225, 226
Edelstein, Dan 4–5, 255
Egelhofer, Rudolf 42, 199,
    211
Ehrenburg, Ilya 65, 66
eight-hour day 92, 127, 257
Einstein, Albert 237
Eisler, Gerhart 67
Eisner, Kurt 10, 27, 85, 113, 125,
    128, 213
Engelberg, Ernst 81, 125, 141
Engels, Friedrich 10, 56, 96, 138,
    151, 152
English Civil War (1641–49) 3
English Revolution (1640–60) 2, 5,
    59–63, 67, 264
Enlai, Zhou 97
Erdmann, Karl Dietrich 57,
    83–6, 90, 91, 102,
    103, 111
Erfurt 118–19
Erhard, Ludwig 96
Erpenbeck, Jenny 153
Erzberger, Matthias 41
*Es geht durch die Welt ein
    Geflüster* (film, 1989)
    181
Eschenburg, Theodor 83, 102,
    103
Essen 7, 184–6, 195, 207–8
    Krupp armament works 197
    soldiers' and workers' council in
    89–90, 91, 94

Faulhaber, Michael 214
FDP (Free Democratic Party)
    96, 100
Federal Republic of Germany
    (FRG) 1, 29, 73, 109,
    111, 112, 128, 135, 141,
    147, 154

films, see *Anders als die Andern* (1919); *Berlin: Sinfonie der Großstadt* (1927); *Es geht durch die Welt ein Geflüster* (1989); *Nerven* (1919)
Finnish Civil War (1918) 239
First World War 5, 9, 24, 29, 39, 112, 115, 119, 121, 124–7, 142, 163–87, 194, 197, 213, 228, 256, 260, 261
Fischer, Fritz 154, 155
Fischer, Joschka 147
Flieg, Leo 124
Föllmer, Moritz 7, 207
food riots 9, 127, 165, 177–80, 181–2, 260
Ford, James 228
Foucault, Michel 3, 134
France 69, 100, 167, 168, 170, 176, 206, 228, 231
Frankfurt am Main 37, 96, 98, 240, 241
Frankfurt Parliament (1848–49) 37
Frankfurter Zeitung (newspaper) 165, 204
Frauenhilfe für politische Gefangene (Women's Aid for Political Prisoners) 215
Free German League of Culture (London, 1939–46) 59
Free Socialist Youth (FSJ) 180, 185, 206, 212, 214
Freie Jugend Groß-Berlins (Free Youth of Greater Berlin) 121, 180
Freikorps 6, 55, 91, 154, 199, 211, 215, 236
French Revolution (1789) 2, 4, 5, 35, 37, 52, 59, 63, 86, 97, 103, 113, 134, 152, 171, 175–6, 179, 185, 232, 256, 257, 258, 259–60

French Revolution (1830) 257, 258, 260
French Revolution (1848) 5, 9, 36, 152, 258
Freud, Sigmund 39
Freundschaft, Die (gay newspaper) 240
Fricke, Dieter 141
Friedrich Ebert Foundation 86
Fritzsche, Peter 146
Frölich, Paul 31, 33, 34
FSJ, see Free Socialist Youth (FSJ)
Fulbrook, Mary 118
funerals 202, 213–16
   see also burials

Gallus, Alexander 7, 235, 255
Garman, Douglas 61
Gatzke, Hans W. 83
Geffke, Herta 114–15, 173
gender 5, 137–8, 146, 175–6, 179–80
   of the German Revolution of 1918–19, 16, 195, 259
General Congress of Workers' and Soldiers' Councils
   first congress (December 1918) 55, 93, 94
   second congress (April 1919) 94–5, 98
generational identities 183–7, 211
German Democratic Republic (GDR) v–129, 1, 29, 45, 81, 83, 87, 138–41, 218, 265
German empire (Kaiserreich) 8, 23, 27, 116, 125, 185, 197, 227, 243–6, 257
German reunification (1989–90) v–155, 16, 129, 223
Gerwarth, Robert 164, 167, 172, 235, 239
Geyer, Martin H. 186
Glaeser, Ernst 209
Globig, Fritz 124

Index

Globig, Martha (née Jogsch) 121–2, 123–4, 262
Goethe, Johann Wolfgang von 69, 176
Goldhagen, Daniel Jonah 146
Goldstone, Jack A. 255
Gorbachev, Mikhail 138, 139
Grebing, Helga 89, 91, 94, 142, 144, 150–1
Greek–Turkish War (1919–22) 239
Green Party 135, 153
    Bündnis 90 (Alliance 90) 145
Grieder, Peter 139
Groener, Wilhelm (General) 84
Grotewohl, Otto 31, 72–3
Gutsche, Birgitte 118
Gutsche, Willibald 117–19

Haase, Hugo 27, 31, 198, 214
Habeck, Robert 153
Habsburg empire 164, 169, 239
Haffner, Ernst 209
Haffner, Sebastian (Raimund Pretzel) 2, 56, 97, 99
Hager, Kurt 139, 143
Haitian Revolution (1791–1804) 232
Halle 31, 33
    Strafanstalt Lichtenburg 212
Haller, Karl 28
Hamburg 29, 33, 180, 183, 186, 197, 205, 257
    Fuhlsbüttel jail 212
    Senate Commission on the Administration of Justice 169
Hamburg Uprising (1923) 33
Hanover 69, 180
Harari, Yuval Noah 6
Harich, Wolfgang 114
Harvey, Elizabeth 181, 183, 184, 209
Haussmann, Georges-Eugène (Baron) 197

Heilmann, Fritz 262
Heine, Wolfgang 240
Heinsohn, Kirsten 7
Helfert, Veronika 38
Herder, Johann Gottfried 69
Herrmann, Joachim 140
Herrmann, Ursula 127, 128
Hertwig, Manfred 114
Herz, Heinz 118
Herzfelde, Wieland 210–11
Heß, Ulrich 140, 143, 144
Hesse 37
Heymann, Lida Gustava 128
Hilferding, Rudolf 35
Hill, Christopher 59–63, 264, 265
Hindenburg, Paul von (Field Marshal) 25–6, 54
Hirsch, Felix 83
Hirschfeld, Magnus 241–2, 243, 247
Historikerstreit (Historians' Quarrel, West Germany, 1986–87) 146
history from the margins 224
history of experience 124–7, 136, 261–3
history of the body 244–7
Hitler, Adolf 28, 52, 57, 58, 60, 63, 64, 67, 71, 83, 146
Ho Chi Minh 229
Hobohm, Martin 30
Hobsbawm, Eric 9, 267
Hoffmann, Johannes 240
Holocaust 65, 138, 146, 147
Holzer, Anton 197, 236–7
Honecker, Erich 101, 144
Horn, Daniel 171, 174
Horne, John 164
Hué, Otto 94
Hufton, Olwen 175
Humboldt, Alexander von 69

Hungarian Revolution (1956) 88, 97, 113
Hungary (post-1918) 236
Hunt, Lynn 259–60
Hutton, Ronald 2

identity politics 153, 263
IG-Metall ((West) German trade union) 98
Iggers, Georg 83
IKD (International Communists of Germany) 33
Illustrierte Blatt, Das (newspaper) 165–6
Indian Revolutionary Committee (Berlin) 228
Institut für Sexualwissenschaft (Institute for Sexual Research, Berlin) 241
Institut für Zeitgeschichte (Institute for Contemporary History, Munich, IfZ) 83
International Congress of Historical Sciences
  eleventh congress, Stockholm, 1960 82
  sixteenth congress, Stuttgart, 1985 128
International Congress of Negro Workers
  first congress, Hamburg, 1930 228
International Labor Defense (ILD) 228
Iranian Revolution (1979) 3, 5, 135, 256, 258
Irish Civil War (1922–23) 239
Issues in Historiography (MUP series) 13
Italy 1, 100
  Two Red Years (1919–20) 97, 233, 246

Jagow, Traugott von 177
James, C. L. R. 231–2
James, Harold 134
Janka, Walter 114
Jannasch, Lilli 232
Japan 227
Jews 23, 27, 42, 60, 65
Jones, Mark 7, 234
Just, Gustav 114

Kahn, Eugen 38–40, 42
Kämpferin, Die (USPD newspaper) 242
Kamrava, Mehran 255
Kant, Immanuel 176
Kapp–Lüttwitz Putsch (March 1920) 205, 212, 236
Karlsbad (Karlovy Vary) 54
Kautsky, Karl 27, 31, 34–5, 109, 140
Kellogg, Vernon 40
Kershaw, Ian (Sir) 3
Keßler, Mario 117
Kets, Gaard 261
Khrushchev, Nikita 113
Kiel 9, 14, 171, 172–3, 206, 257, 258
Kissinger, Henry 97
Klein, Fritz 125–7
Klemperer, Victor 192
Kleßmann, Christoph 111
Kluge, Ulrich 89, 90, 91
Köbis, Albin 164
Kocka, Jürgen 149–50
Koenen, Wilhelm 33
Kolb, Eberhard 89, 90–1, 94, 95
Kollwitz, Käthe 125
Kommunistin, Die (KPD newspaper) 242
Korean War (1950–53) 81
Korfes, Otto 25, 29
Kornilov, Lavr (General) 170
Korsch, Karl 99
Koselleck, Reinhart 137
Kosovo War (1999) 147

KPD (German Communist Party)
28, 31–4, 36, 38, 42,
52–3, 54–7, 60, 66–70,
72, 85, 86, 87, 89, 95,
98, 100, 109–10, 112,
113–15, 117, 118, 119,
120, 121–5, 128, 138–9,
142, 148, 151, 154, 202,
214, 228, 232, 233, 242,
243, 265
   Berlin headquarters
(Bülowplatz) 216
   Stalinisation of after 1925, 33
KPD-O (German Communist
Party-Opposition) 34,
52–3, 69, 89, 110, 116
Kraepelin, Emil 38–40, 42,
44, 247
Kramer, Alan 168
Kramer, Hilde 43, 199, 211–12
Krastev, Ivan 258
Kriegsernährungsamt (War Food
Office) 177
Kristallnacht (1938) 53, 138
Kronstadt Uprising (St Petersburg,
1921) 97
Kuczynski, Jürgen 59–63, 65,
67, 124
Kuczynski, Robert René 60, 124
Kuda, Rudolf 97–100
Kuhl, Hermann von 26
Kuhlbrodt, Peter 127
Kurz, Achim 14
Kyffhäuserbund 25

Labour Monthly (CPGB
journal) 61–2
Lachmann, Ella 242
Lafayette, Marquis de 176
Landauer, Gustav 211
Lansing, Robert 41
Laschi, Rodolfo 41
Law on the Provisional Authority
of the Reich (10 February
1919) 14–15, 66, 264

League against Imperialism (LAI)
229, 232–3
   first international congress,
Brussels 1927, 233
League of Nations 37, 63,
226, 227
Lefebvre, Henri 193
Legien, Carl 92
Lehnert, Detlev 186
Leibniz Association 151
Leipzig 33, 117, 124, 127, 128,
143, 148–9, 182, 205, 236
Leitner, Maria 209
Lenin, Vladimir Ilyich 31, 34, 35,
45, 62, 72, 110, 112, 113,
114, 122, 140, 151, 152
Levetzow, Magnus von (Rear
Admiral) 28, 174
Levien, Max 199
Leviné, Eugen 123, 205, 237
Lewald, Theodor 240
LGBTQ+ rights 11, 241–3, 247
Liebknecht, Karl 36, 55, 60, 72,
122, 124, 144, 165, 180,
202, 204, 205, 213, 214,
215, 216–18, 239
Linke, Die (The Left) 151,
152, 153
Lippe 207
Littlewood, Joan 164
Lloyd George, David 225
Löbe, Paul 71
Lombroso, Cesare 41
Louis Napoleon (Napoleon
III) 196
   coup d'état (2 December
1851) 5
Lübeck 206, 257
Ludendorff, Erich (General) 54,
84, 170
Lukács, György 113
Luxemburg, Rosa 35, 36, 55, 62,
72, 122, 144, 151, 165,
204, 205, 213,
216–18, 239

Index

Maderthaner, Wolfgang 169
Maercker, Georg Ludwig Rudolf 236
Magdeburg 122, 180
Mahler, Horst 96
Mann, Heinrich 125
Mann, Thomas 58, 125
March 1848 revolutions (Germany, Austria, Central Europe) 37, 38, 52, 53, 56, 65, 67, 68, 69, 70–2, 86, 103, 109, 134, 185, 257, 258
Märzgefallene (March Fallen) in Berlin 38, 214, 216
March Action (Halle-Merseburg, 1921) 33, 205, 212
'March Battles' (Berlin, 1919) 9, 198, 211, 234
Marcks, Erich 28
Marhoefer, Laurie 241
Marinearchiv 24–5
Markov, Walter 175
marriage, attitudes towards 242
martial law 198, 199
Marx, Hugo 38–42
Marx, Karl 5, 10, 56, 96, 121, 151, 180, 262
 'Eighteenth Brumaire of Louis Bonaparte, The' (1852) 5
Marxism 11, 14, 73, 83, 87, 88, 151, 174
Marxism-Leninism 3, 34, 35, 72, 73, 82, 126
Masaryk, Jan 70
masculinities 10, 24
Materna, Ingo 151
Maubach, Franka 224, 256
Maizière, Lothar de 145
McElligott, Anthony 7
Mecklenburg-Schwerin 257
Mecklenburg-Strelitz 257
Mehring, Franz 122

Meinecke, Fredrich 28
Merkel, Angela 151
Merleker, Hartmuth 172
Merriman, John 193, 196
Merseburg 33
Mertz von Quirnheim, Gudrun 25
Mertz von Quirnheim, Hermann Ritter 25
Mexico 69
Meyer, Ernst 122
Meyer-Leviné, Rosa 123
Michels, Robert 241
middle classes 28, 54, 67, 94, 116, 126, 174, 175, 184–6, 195, 196, 208, 235, 236, 264
Mies van der Rohe, Ludwig 216
Miller, Susanne 142
Mills, C. Wright 88
Mittelbayerische Zeitung (Bavarian newspaper) 65
Modrow, Hans 145
Molkenbuhr, Brutus 214
Mommsen, Hans 142
Mommsen, Wolfgang J., 101–2, 103
Mosse, George L. 213
Moyn, Samuel 3
Mühlheim an der Ruhr 206, 214
 Mühlheim-Broich cemetery, 215
Mühsam, Erich 213
Muldoon, James 261
Müller, Karl Alexander von 28
Müller, Richard 30, 94–5, 98, 99, 214
Müller-Wolf, Gustav 184–5
Münchner Neueste Nachrichten (newspaper) 186, 204
Munich 7, 28, 39, 42–3, 83, 125, 128, 186, 196, 198, 199, 215, 237, 243, 255, 257
 Munich-East cemetery 214
 Stadelheim jail 211–12

Munich Agreement (1938) 53
  renounced by Britain (1942) 63
Munich Councils Republic (April–
  May 1919) 39, 42, 113,
  198, 199, 204, 211, 213,
  234, 235, 255
Münzenberg, Willi 229, 232
Mussolini, Benito 1, 71

Nagy, Imre 113
Namibia 229, 244
National Socialism 59, 64, 83
naval mutinies 9, 14, 164, 171–4
Nazi Germany, *see* Third Reich
Nazi Party (NSDAP) 28
Nazi–Soviet Pact (1939) 58, 61
Nerven (film, 1919) 44
Netherlands, the 10, 225
Neues Deutschland (SED
  newspaper) 112, 121,
  123, 138, 139
Neumann, Heinz 123
new cultural history 2, 4, 6,
  146, 258–61
New Left 82, 88–95
Niess, Wolfgang 115, 256
Nolte, Ernst 29
Norden, Albert 67
North Atlantic Treaty
  Organization (NATO)
  29, 81, 86, 88, 101,
  113, 147
Northcliffe, Lord (Alfred
  Harmsworth) 27
Noske, Gustav 11, 15, 56, 91, 92,
  99, 173, 208
  Schießbefehle (execution orders
  1919) 198, 239
Nuremberg 198

Oberhausen 206
Oertzen, Peter von 89–90, 91
Ollenhauer, Erich 86
Oltermann, Philip 260, 265
Organisation Consul 27
Ostrowski, Marius S. 36

Oswald, Richard 247
Ottoman empire 164, 227
  genocide against the Armenians
  (1915–16) 239

Pacelli, Eugenio (Pope Pius
  XII) 199
Padmore, George 228
Painter, Corinne 261
Paris Commune (1871) 9, 41, 97,
  152, 196, 198, 213
Paris Peace Conference (1919–20)
  265
Paris Peace Settlement (1919–20)
  227–8
Parliamentary Council (West
  Germany, 1948–49) 37
Parteihochschule Karl Marx (Party
  Academy Karl Marx,
  Berlin-Kleinmachnow) 73
Paterna, Erich 72
PDS (Party of Democratic
  Socialism) 145, 147,
  149, 150–1
peace history 126–9
peasants 54, 67, 69, 115, 196
  German peasants' war
  (1524–25) 112
Petzold, Joachim 11, 13, 142, 143
Peukert, Detlev J. K., 2
Pieck, Wilhelm 66, 120
Plener, Ulla 151–2
Polak, Karl 73
Poland
  declaration of martial law in
  (1981) 101
  post-1918 republic 236
  Solidarity movement in
  (1980–81) 101, 135
police 175, 177, 178, 181, 182,
  183, 194, 196, 209, 210,
  216, 237
  political police 182
Polish minority in Germany 23
Popp, Lothar 173
postcards 10, 204

Index

posters 9, 200, 202, 203, 206
Potsdam 24, 29
Potthoff, Heinrich 142
Pravda (Soviet newspaper) 66
Pretzel, Raimund, *see* Haffner, Sebastian
prisons 210–13, 215
 hunger strikes 210, 212–13
Proll, Thorwald 96
Protestants 184–6, 207
Prussia 52, 55, 58, 109, 207, 208, 240
 Pomerania 114, 184–5
 Prussian Saxony 205
 Westphalia 207
Prussian House of Representatives 151

railways and railway stations 206–9
Rantzsch, Petra 128
Rathenau, Walther 27, 60, 66
Red Front Fighters' League (RFB) 32
referendum on the dispossession of the former princely households (1926) 38
Reich Colonial Office 229–30
Reich Commissariat for Maintaining Public Order 233, 242
Reich Justice Office 183
Reich Ministry of Finance 15
Reich Ministry of Interior 233, 240, 241, 242
Reich Naval Office 200
Reich Office of Interior 181
Reich Penal Code
 paragraph 175, 241, 243, 247
Reichpietsch, Max 164
Reichsarchiv 24–9, 37
Reichsbanner 37, 38
Reichsbund der Kriegsbeschädigten, Kriegsteilnehmer und Kriegshinterbliebenen
 (Reich Association of War Disabled, War Participants and War Dependants) 236
Reichstag 38, 54, 56, 71, 85, 163, 183
Reichstag Peace Resolution (1917) 163, 168
Reichswehr 11, 175, 199, 200, 204, 236, 264
 Truppenamt (Troop Office) 24–5
Reinert, Robert 44
Reisinger, Silvio 148
Remmele, Hermann 123
reparations 226
Reuter, Ernst 31, 70–1, 72, 73
revolutionary scripts 4–5, 255, 257
revolutionary shop stewards' movement 30, 173
Revolutionsdenkmal (*Monument to the Revolution* Berlin-Friedrichsfelde) 216
Richardson, R. C. 59
Richter, Hedwig 178, 244–7, 264
Ringer, Fritz K. 23
Ritter, Gerhard 1, 28, 29, 81, 102
Robespierre, Maximilien 35, 178
Röhl, John C. G. 119
Röhrig, Arnold 94
Römer, Willy 204
Roosevelt, Franklin D. 63
Rosa Luxemburg Foundation 151
Rosenberg, Arthur 53, 54–7, 84, 88, 89, 91, 100
Rosenhaft, Eve 229
Rossol, Nadine 7, 184–6, 195, 207, 261
Rote Fahne, Die (KPD newspaper) 35, 95, 204, 215
Rote Hilfe (Red Aid) 215
Roter Frontkämpferbund, *see* Red Front Fighters' League (RFB)
Roth, Joseph 234–5

Index

Rothfels, Hans 83
Roy, Evelyn Trent 228
Roy, Manabendra Nath 228
Rubens Franziska 262
Ruge, Wolfgang 112, 115, 116, 138, 139–40, 154, 155
Ruhr crisis (1923) 227
Ruhr Uprising (March–April 1920) 175, 205, 215
Ruhr valley 7, 9, 180, 184, 196, 206
  chemical industry 174
  mining industry 89, 91–2, 94, 95
Rupprecht, Crown Prince of Bavaria 27
Rürup, Reinhard 89, 90, 91, 93, 94, 101–2, 142
Russian Civil War (1917–20) 35, 239
Russian Federation
  invasion of Ukraine (2022) 153, 224
Russian Revolution (1905) 2, 97, 152, 246
Russian Revolutions (1917) 1, 2, 5, 9, 35, 85, 97, 112, 114, 116, 134, 140, 152, 164, 171, 246
Ruttmann, Walter 206
Ryder, A. J., 92, 215

Sabrow, Martin 256
sailors 16, 55, 112, 169, 171–4, 179
Saint-Just, Louis Antoine de 35
SAPD (Socialist Workers' Party) 34, 69
Sarasin, Philipp 3
Saville, John 88
Saxony 205
Saxony-Anhalt 152
Schäfer, Dietrich 28
Schama, Simon 4, 5, 11, 175–6, 178, 179

Scharmanski, Benno 181
Scheidemann, Philipp 8, 32, 99, 154
Schmidt, Günter 116
Schmidt, Helmut 100, 101
Schmidt, Walter 141
Schmitt, Carl 264
Schneider, Dieter 97–100
Schönhoven, Klaus 142
Schreiner, Albert 32, 64, 67, 115–17, 170
Schumacher, Kurt 69–70, 73, 86
Schutzhaft (protective custody) 210–13, 215
Scott, Joan W. 137, 180
'Scottsboro Boys' campaign (German and international) 228–9
SDS (Socialist Student League) 96
Second World War 29, 58, 83, 85, 118, 149, 216
SED (Socialist Unity Party) 33, 68, 70–3, 96, 100, 110–11, 112, 117–18, 119–22, 124, 125–6, 136, 138–9, 141–5, 147, 150, 173, 180, 214, 216, 262
  Central Committee 114, 115, 122, 139, 141, 143
  Central Party Control Commission 111, 114, 121, 122
  Institute for Marxism-Leninism (IML) 114, 115, 120, 121–2, 123, 142–3
  Politburo 72, 114, 122
Seeber, Gustav 141
Seeckt, Hans von 24
Seitz, Gustav 125
Seitz, Karl 169
Selchow, Bogislav von 200
Sender, Toni 241
Severing, Carl 240
sexualities 5, 10, 43, 183, 198, 240–3
Sharp, Ingrid 261
Siere, Martina 128

Simmel, Georg 194
Sino-Soviet split (1960s) 81, 233
sites of remembrance 213–18
slavery 231, 244
Smith, Helmut Walser 147
Smith, Leonard V. 265
Sneeringer, Julia 178
Socialist Unity Party (SED)
  Central Committee 111
  Institute for Marxism-Leninism (IML) 124
Soja, Edward W. 196–7, 210
soldiers 16, 31, 54, 94, 112, 167–71, 172, 173, 179, 197, 215
  deserters 168–71
Souchon, Wilhelm 173
sovereignty 164, 246, 258, 263–5
Soviet Union 66, 72, 120, 121, 122, 124, 126, 138, 139
  invasion of Czechoslovakia (1968) 96
  invasion of Hungary (1956) 88, 98, 113
Sozialistische Monatshefte (SPD journal) 172
Spanish flu 186
Spanish Civil War 97
Spartacist League 27, 31, 32, 55, 94, 110, 117, 119–24, 140, 168, 170, 204, 213, 214, 234, 257, 265
Spartacist Uprising (January 1919) 8, 9, 34, 202, 216, 234, 239, 255
Sparzwangserlässe (compulsory saving orders) 182–3
SPD (German Social Democratic Party) 8, 29–38, 52, 55–7, 60, 67, 68–70, 71, 84, 86–8, 89–92, 93, 94, 95, 99, 100, 101, 102–3, 109, 116–17, 136, 139, 141–4, 148, 150, 151, 154, 168, 185, 200, 204, 205, 207, 208, 210, 231, 232, 237, 243, 246

Bad Godesberg Programme (1959) 86, 100
Commission on Fundamental Values 141
Görlitz Programme (1921) 36
Heidelberg Programme (1925) 37, 86
Historical Commission 89, 141, 142–3
Sputnik (Soviet journal) 138
'stab-in-the-back' legend 1, 26–8, 29, 39, 44, 86
Stahl, Richard 208
Stahlhelm 25
Stalin, Joseph 34, 62, 66, 70, 72
  death of in 1953, 120
  History of the Communist Party of the Soviet Union (Bolsheviks): Short Course (1938) 60
Stalinist terror 69, 110, 113, 120–4
Stampfer, Friedrich 87
Stasi (East German secret police) 139
states of exception 208, 265
Stauffenberg plot (July 1944) 64, 83
Stedman Jones, Gareth 255
Steinberger, Bernhard 114
Steinmetz, Max 81, 118
Stelzner, Helenefriderike 38–40, 42–4
Stephenson, Scott 170–1
Stern, Leo 81
Stettin (Szczecin) 114, 173, 185, 206
Stinnes, Hugo 92
Stinnes–Legien agreement 92, 93
Stone, Marla 134, 136
street demonstrations 10, 173, 197–8, 205, 256
Streisand, Joachim 109

strikes 199, 225, 246, 256
    postwar strikes 9, 33, 205, 208, 236, 237
    wartime strikes 9, 30, 164, 168, 173, 204
Stumpf, Richard 171, 173–4
Stuttgart 32, 64, 116, 180
Süddeutsche Monatshefte (conservative-nationalist journal) 28, 39, 44
Sudeten German Social Democratic Party 54
Switzerland 10, 225
Syrian refugee crisis (2015) 153

Taylor, A. J. P. 65–6, 68
Taylor, Alonzo 40
Tehran Conference (1943) 63
Thälmann, Ernst 33, 34, 52, 54, 56, 123
Theweleit, Klaus 6
Third International, *see* Comintern
Third Reich 2, 16, 44, 56, 64, 65, 66, 84, 111, 117, 146
Thompson, E. P. 88
Thuringia 205
Tirpitz, Alfred von (Grand Admiral) 27
Togliatti, Palmiro 143
Toller, Ernst 164, 213
Tormin, Walter 89, 91, 94, 116
Torr, Dona 61
trade unions 10, 54, 92–5, 98, 115, 149, 257
traffic 205–9
Traverso, Enzo 255, 259–60
Treaty of Rapallo (1922) 66
Treaty of Versailles (1919) 25, 28, 64, 227, 265
Treitschke, Heinrich von 58
Trinidad 228
Trotha, Adolf von (Admiral) 28, 173
Trotsky, Leon 35
Tucholsky, Kurt 34
'turnip winter' (1916–17) 177

Ulbricht, Walter 33, 66, 110, 119, 122, 124
    theses on the November Revolution (1958) 111–19, 139, 140, 143, 262
Ulrich, Bernd 169, 171
United Nations 63, 69, 70
United States 30, 67, 82, 88, 116, 176, 227, 231
universal suffrage 94, 127, 165, 256
urban space 10, 193–218
USPD (Independent Social Democratic Party) 8, 27, 30–7, 54–7, 60, 66, 67, 72, 86, 89, 91, 93, 95, 98, 99, 109, 114, 115, 116–17, 123, 128, 140, 148–9, 168, 173, 174, 198, 214, 240, 241, 242
USSR, *see* Soviet Union

Valentin, Veit 38
Vanguard of Indian Independence (later *Masses of India*) 228
Vansittart, Lord Robert 58, 64, 68
Verband der Historiker Deutschlands (German Historians' Association, VHD) 81–2
Vierteljahrshefte für Zeitgeschichte ((West) German academic journal) 83, 111
Vietnam War 96
violence 164, 194, 199, 213, 215, 233–40, 245
Vögler, Albert 94
Volkskammer (East German Parliament) 138
Volksmarinedivision (People's Naval Division) 55, 195, 200, 206, 215

Volkswacht (SPD regional newspaper) 207
Vorwärts (SPD newspaper) 87, 237, 241
    seizure of building by Spartacists (January 1919) 204

Wachsmann, Nikolaus 210
Warsaw Pact 81, 96, 113
Washington, George 176
Watt, Richard M. 56
Weber, Hermann 142
Weimar 8, 25, 57, 65
Weimar Constitution 23, 66, 127, 240, 264, 265
    Article 1, 263
    Article 48, 14, 264
    Article 118, 247
    Article 128, 240
    Article 161, 264
Weimar National Assembly, *see* Constituent National Assembly
Weimar Republic 5, 23–45, 57, 58, 67, 84, 85, 90, 117, 140, 145, 146, 154, 193, 212, 224, 227, 229, 239, 255, 256
Weinhauer, Klaus 7, 197
Weißbecker, Manfred 141
Weitz, Eric D. 145–6
Wels, Otto 237
Wermuth, Adolph 216
Weser-Zeitung (newspaper) 27
West Berlin 70, 71, 73, 96
West Germany, *see* Federal Republic of Germany (FRG)
Westarp, Kuno von 40
Wette, Wolfram 200
White, Hayden 257
Wilhelm II, Kaiser and King of Prussia 8, 15, 27, 55, 169, 176, 265

Wilhelm II, King of Württemberg 170
Wilhelmshaven 9, 171, 172–3, 174, 206
Wilkinson, Ellen 232
Wilson, Woodrow 24, 41, 169, 227
Wimmer, Walter 141, 142–3
Winkler, Heinrich August 1–2, 101–2, 103, 143, 144, 246
Winstanley, Gerrard 60, 62
Wirth, Joseph 28
Wolf, Richard 114
Wolff, Theodor 31, 197
women 10, 43, 181, 196, 235, 241, 245, 260
    middle-class women 256
    middle-class women's movement 128, 245
    reproductive rights 5, 242
    revolutionary women 127–9, 175, 195, 199, 240–2
    women's history 128, 177–80
    women's suffrage 7, 127, 145, 256
Women's International League for Peace and Freedom (WILPF) 10
workers 30, 33, 35, 36, 54, 56, 64, 67, 87, 91, 94, 99, 100, 110, 112, 114, 140–1, 145, 152, 170, 196, 257
Wright, Ada 228
Wünschmann, Kim 7
Württemberg 23, 32
Württemberg Citizens' Party (Württembergische Bürgerpartei) 23

youth 10, 163, 178, 180–7, 195, 208–9, 211, 215
Yugoslavia 135

Zeitschrift für
 Geschichtswissenschaft
 ((East) German academic
 journal) 81, 110, 127,
 140, 143
Zentralarbeitsgemeinschaft
 (Central Working
 Association) 93

Zetkin, Clara 128
Ziemann, Benjamin 44, 167,
 168–9, 171, 195, 204,
 236, 257, 261, 263
Zietz, Luise 214
Zimmermann, Adrian 225
Zirkel, Helene 196
Zöger, Heinz 114

EU authorised representative for GPSR:
Easy Access System Europe, Mustamäe tee 50,
10621 Tallinn, Estonia
gpsr.requests@easproject.com